The Family Recovery Guide

A Map for Healthy Growth

Stephanie Brown, Ph.D., and
Virginia M. Lewis, Ph.D.,
with Andrew Liotta

New Harbinger Publications, Inc.

Publisher's Note

This publication is designed to provide accurate and authoritative information in regard to the subject matter covered. It is sold with the understanding that the publisher is not engaged in rendering psychological, financial, legal, or other professional services. If expert assistance or counseling is needed, the services of a competent professional should be sought.

Distributed in the U.S.A. by Publishers Group West; in Canada by Raincoast Books; in Great Britain by Airlift Book Company, Ltd.; in South Africa by Real Books, Ltd.; in Australia by Boobook; and in New Zealand by Tandem Press.

Copyright © 2000 by Stephanie Brown, Virginia Lewis, and Andrew Liotta
New Harbinger Publications, Inc.
5674 Shattuck Avenue
Oakland, CA 94609

Cover design by Poulson/Gluck Designs
Edited by Clancy Drake
Text design by Michele Waters

Library of Congress Catalog Card Number: 00-134873
ISBN 1-57224-218-3 Paperback

All Rights Reserved

Printed in the United States of America

New Harbinger Publications' Web site address: www.newharbinger.com

02   01   00

10   9   8   7   6   5   4   3   2   1

First printing

Contents

Part 1
Sacrificing the Self
The Drinking Stage 1

Part 2
Hitting Bottom and Beyond
The Transition Stage

Preface

What happens when a parent stops drinking? What is it like for the alcoholic individual, the partner, and the children, both young and old, when one or both parents move from active addiction into recovery?

During the decade of the 1990s, we asked recovering families to answer these questions, among many others about their experiences during active drinking and abstinence. This book describes what we learned. It tells the story of family recovery: how hard the long road can be and what experiences in recovery are "normal."

The word "normal" is an odd one. Most people want to feel that they are "normal," but what in the world does that mean? Many people living in an alcoholic family think that a drinking family is "normal," even if it's also unhealthy. Many never question the alcoholism until the family starts to deteriorate and, hopefully, finds its way to recovery. Suddenly, everything that seemed "normal" no longer does. What a shock this is!

We started our research with the idea that discovering what is "normal" in recovery would be helpful to all family members who have lived with alcoholism and are now living with the uncertainties of recovery. We knew that the end of drinking does not bring instant happiness or a simple cure for all the family's problems, but we didn't know exactly what *does* happen. How does a family experience the shift from active alcoholism to recovery? What can family members expect? How do they cope? Are there stages of change that most families experience? Can tasks be defined for each stage? Most families experiencing the tensions of early abstinence don't know the answers to these questions; they simply long for an end to the trauma of active addiction, believing that anything else would be an improvement.

Many of our families agreed: everything about recovery, good and bad, easy and hard, *is* better than drinking. But many of these families admitted there were times when they weren't so sure, or times when the awful certainties about drinking seemed easier to deal with than the massive uncertainties that came along with recovery.

In this book we will explore a curious but common situation: since the unhealthy state of alcoholism, with its unpredictability, anxiety, and danger, is often (paradoxically) normal for the family, the beginning of a committed process of change—recovery—is experienced as an unsettling disruption. Abstinence, the longed-for magical solution to the family's problems with alcoholism, actually brings its own massive turmoil, chaos, and uncertainty. This upheaval can feel far from comforting, but it allows the foundation to be built for a long-term process of family redevelopment. Family members in recovery will, over time, turn themselves upside down and inside out, rebuilding their beliefs, values, attitudes, behaviors, emotions, communication patterns, and all the roles and rules that made their alcoholic family feel "normal." In the following chapters we will describe how families make these dramatic changes and how they survive the turmoil that accompanies the changes.

We did our research, which we called the Family Recovery Project, at the Mental Research Institute in Palo Alto, California. We worked with fifty-two couples and families who identified themselves as "in recovery" from alcoholism and other addictions. Our couples had lengths of total abstinence ranging from 79 days to 18 years. They met with us for a three-hour interview during which we asked them all kinds of questions about their experiences living with active addiction, being in recovery, and being part of a "recovering family."

We reported our results from this research project first in an academic text called *The Alcoholic Family in Recovery: A Developmental Model*, which was published by Guilford Press in 1999. In that text, we outlined a theory of recovery, including the major tasks and stages in this long-term process of change. We recommend this book to all readers who are interested in a more complex theoretical perspective of recovery and want further information on the details of the research design.

The book you are reading is not a textbook. It's a nuts-and-bolts guide for the family in recovery. It describes what the experience of recovery feels like, what tasks need to be addressed, and how you endure the anxieties and obstacles that lie on the path to healthy change. You can think of this book as a survival guide. Recovery is hard work, and the normal process of healthy growth is expected to be difficult. This book gives you a map of the territories of recovery: the swamps that slow you, the dark forests that can block out the sun, and the occasional meadows and sunny vistas that inspire you along the way. It is our hope that with the help of this map, you can remain on course when you face the challenges of recovery.

We will arrive at the end of the book with a new definition of "normal" that includes being happy and healthy. The final stage of recovery is not the arrival at some magical perfection. Rather, the ongoing stage of recovery entails accepting reality and learning to live with it, being honest with yourself and others, and showing up for the complicated, uncertain experience of living life without needing to control it. Being in recovery means not knowing some things, and being able to accept that fact—sometimes even being empowered by it. Recovery means being able to ask for help, and understanding that needing support is part of being human.

All of our research families told us that the road to recovery is very hard work, but they also told us it was well worth it. As you travel your own road of recovery, we urge you to read through this guide at your own pace. Digest only as much as you can. If the going gets tough, you can always put the book down and come back to it later. Some parts of this book may be very challenging if you are still new to recovery. If you feel discouraged or overwhelmed by some of the harder facts of transition and early recovery you may want to skip forward to the final section (part 4) to see how the story turns out. This section describing ongoing recovery can give you an infusion of hope and help you keep things in perspective, reminding you that things will get better, just as they got better for the families in our research. These people may not have become perfect, and they may not have changed as fast as they would have liked, but they did change, and the life they found through the process was rewarding and satisfying. We hope you hear our voices throughout, telling it like it is and affirming, with our family examples, that it is indeed worth it.

    We would like to express our gratitude to all the individuals, couples, and families who participated in the research and to all the recovering people who have shared their stories with us over the years. Without them, this book would not exist.

Acknowledgments

I hold a lifetime of gratitude for the personal and professional "experience, strength, and hope" that have been my great gift from so many countless people—those struggling with active addiction, those brand-new on the recovery path, and those with long years who have the tender wisdom of solid recovery as a way of life. I am grateful to friends, colleagues, patients, and those people the world over who have all taken what is to me, the greatest risk: to see, feel, and know the truth about themselves, to accept it, and then to courageously build and live their lives on the foundation of that reality. I frequently tell others that I am the luckiest person alive for what I have been given—a "mission" to ask the question and to study it for years: What happens to people after they stop drinking?

This book is the story of family recovery. I thank all those who participated in this long, huge research effort: our staff, donors and friends of the project, MRI, and all our research families in recovery. I thank my codirector, Virginia Lewis, for her commitment and continuing dedication, Ben Hammett for extraordinary support, and New Harbinger for their enthusiasm and terrific skills and people. And, to our writer, Andy Liotta, I give my profound gratitude. Listening with an exquisite ear, Andy took our academic ideas and language and translated them into the images and metaphors that became this moving story.

Finally, as always, I thank my husband Bob Harris and our daughter Makenzie, for our loving family.

—Stephanie Brown

The Family Recovery Project (FRP) is in its twelfth year. It feels like only yesterday that Stephanie Brown and I had lunch and talked about a joint endeavor. At the same time, however, the Project feels like an eternity, always present in mind and work.

It is particularly gratifying to see our treatment curriculum—MAPs (Maintaining Abstinence Program)—transformed into book form. This change was possible only because of Andy Liotta's excellent writing and editing abilities. His grasp of the material was remarkable.

There are so many people who contributed directly to the Project by volunteering their time and their willingness to be under the psychological microscope. Our gratefulness to the Focus Group, a longitudinal study of couples in long-term recovery; our fifty-two research families who were studied in depth on their experiences in recovery; and lastly, the participants who went through the twelve-week MAPs curriculum. The MAPs was field tested in two San Francisco Bay Area hospitals: MPI Treatment Services at Summit Medical Center in Oakland and El Camino Hospital in Mountain View. Each group who completed the curriculum responded to questionnaires about their learning experiences and the program's usefulness. It is from all of these participants that we learned how to map out the process of recovery. My gratitude to all of the families and couples is deeply felt. What I learned went well beyond my professional life.

Again, I am indebted to both Stephanie Brown for her vision and wisdom and Ben Hammett for his dedication and never-ending efforts to help out in any manner needed. Lastly, our appreciation to the Mental Research Institute (MRI) of Palo Alto for continuing to provide us with a research home. We still have mountains of information and data to analyze and understand.

—Virginia Lewis

This was a truly rewarding experience, and I want to thank the people who made it possible. Thank you, Stephanie and Virginia, for making the project inspiring and easy; you've taught me a great deal. Thanks to the folks at New Harbinger, especially to Matt McKay for giving me this great opportunity, and to Heather Garnos for shepherding with patience and skill.

I want to thank my family for the endless support (not to mention the laptop). And mostly I want to thank my wife, Kristin Beck, and my son, Cormac, for making it a joy to be alive. I love you.

—Andrew Liotta

Introduction

> It took me thirty days in a hospital to finally dry out. It was without a doubt the hardest month of my life, and I was dead set on making sure I would never face anything so terrible again. When I got home, I just expected everything to be perfect. The folks at the hospital told me it would take some time for adjustment; but I just figured they didn't know my family. I knew how relieved my wife and kids would all be when they saw the new me. I expected my homecoming to be my prize for having survived. I was completely unprepared for how hard it would be. You may find this hard to believe, but coming home sober turned out to be the hardest thing I ever did.

Russell's experience is not unusual. In fact, his is a very common expectation for the alcoholic who gives up drinking: "Since alcohol is the source of all my problems, if I quit drinking, my problems will be solved." This, however, is rarely, if ever, the case.

The alcoholic is not the only one whose expectations can be dashed by the realities of early-stage abstinence. Russell's wife, Caroline, had been living with Russell's binge drinking for over a decade. She had spent so much of her time focused on her husband's behavior—making sure he made it home alive, trying not to let things get out of control around the kids, making sure he didn't lose his job—she logically assumed his quitting would leave them time to focus on themselves as a couple. Instead, even though he seemed truly committed to Alcoholics Anonymous, she was in even greater discomfort than ever:

> I had always thought that without the drinking, I would be free; but with sobriety, I was more focused on Russ than ever. I watched him to make sure he wouldn't drink. And even in those moments when I believed he was doing fine, I worried that the kids or I might do something to upset

things. It was hard and could get out of control while he was drinking, but it was even harder after he stopped. At least when he was drinking I could blame the trouble on something. Without the drinking, there was nothing to blame; it just seemed like there was something wrong with me. I found myself losing it over the smallest things. My kids thought I was crazy.

The children are also victims in the alcoholic home, and the trauma of recovery can be as upsetting as the drinking. Even if the kids are young enough not to understand the drinking problem, they will still be thrown off by how the family has changed. If the children are old enough to recognize there is a problem, they will be both wary of the sudden change and crushed if it seems that nothing has changed—or, if anything, that things have gotten worse. Russell Jr. was eight at the time; and now at fifteen he can look back with some clarity:

I used to pray that Dad was going to get better. He was always sick. Now I know it was the drinking; but back then, I was sure he was going to die or something. When he came back home, Mom told us he was finally going to get better. But things were still bad. My father was so scared, and my mother was so angry. I just remember thinking, this is what I was praying for?

The Way of Recovery

The story above is a common one, yet few families know this. "Recovery" is such a well-known term, but the realities and dynamics of this complicated process are a mystery to most. Alcoholics Anonymous and Al-Anon can provide support and tell you that it's going to be hard, but until you face the realities of giving up drinking, you will have no real idea what that means.

Most families mistakenly expect that:

- Stopping drinking will fix all the problems caused by drinking.

- Family recovery is the responsibility of the alcoholic alone.

Both these assumptions seem logical. Since the drinking caused the problem, stopping drinking should solve the problem. And since the alcoholic is the one drinking, the alcoholic is the only one who needs to change his or her behavior. But not only are these expectations mistaken, they actually make the process of recovery more difficult for everyone.

This book will describe the path of recovery so you will have a good idea of what to expect; or at least so you will learn what not to expect. If your sights are set too high, you will be frustrated by the slow process of healthy growth.

The mistaken expectations described above derive from two popular misconceptions about alcoholism:

- Quitting drinking is equal to recovery.

- Alcoholism is the alcoholic's problem alone.

Let's take these one at a time.

It's understandable why many people think quitting drinking is the same as recovery. There is, after all, a final glass of beer or sip of scotch. It is a tangible limit: either you are drinking or you are not.

There is, however, a difference between abstinence and recovery. You can abstain without recovering, but you can't be in recovery without abstinence. Alcoholism is a disease of thinking, as well as of behavior. Active drinking may be in remission, but if the beliefs and problems that caused it are still in place, they will lead to other problematic behaviors and interactions. This is known as being in a "dry drunk." In order to solidly maintain abstinence, you need to make core changes in your life and your sense of yourself. Recovery, the process of relinquishing the alcoholic behaviors and mind-set, is ongoing; it's a series of stages one must pass through.

The second misconception also seems to make sense on the surface. Since the alcoholic is the one with the drinking problem, it seems logical that he's the one who can solve that problem. If you live with an alcoholic (or someone who drinks too much), you might also live with the daily mantra that everything would be fine if it weren't for the drinking. But, as anyone who has survived living with an alcoholic can tell you, alcoholism does not only affect the drinker. Alcoholism is an oppressive disease that forces the surrounding world, including the alcoholic's family, to adapt.

When a family lives under an alcoholic, the trauma goes deep. Even when the drinking stops, these defenses remain in place. The family does not "go back" to being the healthy family it knows it could have been had there never been any drinking. In Caroline's case, she was even more vigilant after her husband stopped drinking; her anxiety actually got worse. Even though the drinking ends, the adaptations the family made to alcoholism remain.

Alcoholism Is a Family Disease

Although one person's alcoholism may be the main source of the family's problems, others in the family must conform to the alcoholic behavior and thinking in order for the alcoholism to continue unchecked. This conforming includes changes in the most fundamental beliefs and perceptions of the partner and children. For the alcoholic to maintain her belief that her drinking is not a problem, the family usually colludes. Any perception that goes against this belief must be denied and pushed aside. The result is the alcoholic family.

An "alcoholic family" doesn't mean that everyone drinks (though multiple drinkers and future drinkers are often the result), but that the family has organized itself around the alcoholism. There may be only one alcoholic, but the rest of the family is either in collusion with the drinker or has taken on unhealthy roles and beliefs in order to allow the drinking to continue. For a nondrinking spouse, this usually means an addiction, or unhealthy attachment, to the drinker. The partner of the alcoholic—hereafter known as the coalcoholic—obsesses about the drinking behavior, keeps everything safe for the drinker, and lies to protect the drinker. For the children, adaptation usually means forgoing their own development to attend to the needs of the unhealthy family. Instead of having the security to focus on their own lives and discover the world with a sense of inner confidence, they must constantly monitor their threatening surroundings, accepting the false sense of reality that supports the drinking. Healthy development is interrupted by this focus on the parents and the perceived need to "take care" of them.

Though an unhealthy situation has been created, the family grows used to it; the system becomes predictable in its unpredictability. So when the drinker finally hits bottom and gets sober, this change can be quite traumatic. Even though abstinence is the thing most needed, no one knows how to handle it. The rug has been pulled out from under the family; it doesn't matter that the rug was moth-eaten and smelly and everyone had to spend all their time working to keep it from falling apart.

Recovery Is a Developmental Process

The popular view of alcoholism is much like the Hollywood version. Almost every movie on the subject focuses on the battle a person has with active drinking. We see the character in Act I, flushed and happy. Sure, she likes a few belts now and again, but all things considered, she's doing fine. Then in Act II, we follow her slow but steady downfall as her drinking escalates and her life comes undone. In Act III she hits bottom and has to face her demons. She heroically puts aside the bottle, and guts out her withdrawal. As the hallucinations fade, her life comes back in all its pristine beauty: her husband takes her back, her children come running, and they all live happily ever. As with most things, the Hollywood version reflects our culture's wishes and expectations about the subject, not the realities.

Though there is truth to this path of decline for the alcoholic, as with most things Hollywood, the story ends just as it gets interesting. In the world of recovery, quitting drinking is only Act I. In Act II there is a great deal of struggle and hardship as the alcoholic and her family pull down the unhealthy structures that were set in place by the drinking. Before Act III ends, the world has been torn down and rebuilt, as each member of the family has faced her own demons about the alcoholism and herself. By then, abstinence and new family structures of recovery are well in place and are directing healthy new relationships and family function.

Like the plot of a story, recovery is a developmental process, which means there are different stages you pass through on the journey. For each stage there are a number of tasks you must complete before moving on to the next. A metaphor that will get some use in this book is that of building a house. With a house, you have to build the foundation first, and you don't move on until this foundation is solid. So it goes with each successive step. You can't put up the wallpaper if you haven't built the frame yet. It is the same with recovery.

Recovery has four distinct stages:

1. **Drinking.** This is the period of active alcoholism.

2. **Transition.** This includes the escalation of drinking or coalcoholic addicted behavior, until a critical point is reached. The alcoholic or other family members "hits bottom," stop drinking or coalcoholic addicted behavior, and turn to new abstinence, which is usually an intense time of crisis.

3. **Early recovery.** The basic foundations of abstinence are in place. Recovery structures, such as twelve-step groups and counseling, now provide the framework for healthy growth and change.

4. **Ongoing recovery.** When abstinence and recovery growth are strong, the alcoholic, coalcoholic, and family can focus on other matters, including relationships.

In the following chapters you will learn about the details and dynamics of each stage. The more you learn about the process of recovery—the ups and downs, the healing and the pain—the more trust you will have in your journey.

Family Recovery

Individuals in recovery have been studied to a certain extent. The alcoholic, the coalcoholic, the child of an alcoholic, and the adult child of an alcoholic all have been subjects of research showing how their paths are likely to go. Mostly, the focus has been on the individual. This is as it should be. The primary move for the individual in recovery, after getting support, is to focus on the self. You can't help anyone until you help yourself.

In this book we will make important distinctions between individuals and the family as a whole. Let us state unequivocally now that abstinence, for any and all individuals, is a good thing. Recovery is also a good thing. Family recovery is good too, but it is not automatic and it is not easy. Family recovery must grow on a foundation of individual recoveries. You can't have the healthy "whole"—family recovery—without the contributing "parts"—individual change and growth.

We have spent over ten years studying the alcoholic family in recovery, and we have found that there is a developmental process of recovery for the family that runs parallel to that of the individual. In this process, the alcoholic, his or her partner, and the other family members move from an unsafe environment in which the atmosphere and context of life are shaped by drinking, to an environment that fosters the healthy growth of each member. Family recovery is more than just abstinence from alcohol and the safer environment this brings. It is abstinence from other unhealthy behaviors, beliefs, emotions, interactions, and styles of communication that comprise an unhealthy family structure. In recovery, the family must allow familiar patterns to collapse. By ending this unhealthy system of interaction the family can then build a new system that promotes growth for each of its members and for the family as a whole.

There is a complicated interaction between the individual and the family during recovery. This is based on a central fact of recovery: **In order to free yourself from the addiction to alcohol or the unhealthy attachment to the alcoholic, you must focus on your own recovery.** Only when your own abstinence and recovery are in place can you safely reach out to connect with the other family members.

Because the family structure has become so unhealthy during the drinking period, each individual member must step outside it for support. The alcoholic must transfer his dependency on alcohol to a dependency on a group that supports abstinence from drinking. The coalcoholic must trade her focus on the drinker's behavior for a recovery program that forces her to focus on herself as separate from the alcoholic. The children can also benefit from help outside the family; there are twelve-step programs for even the youngest kids. These external supports may be used intensely and exclusively for several years while new healthy behavior is being learned, internalized, and stabilized. In the end, the family is rebuilt as a stronger system of healthy individuals.

Turning focus away from the family can be very traumatic, especially for members who have built their identities on monitoring the family for signs of trouble or calm. When one person steps out of the system, the entire system is changed. When the old system collapses there is a void left in its place, and the family members naturally want to fill that void with the comfort of familiar behavior. Unfortunately, what is familiar at this stage is also what is most dangerous. Anxiety runs high at this time, because the very things the family did to release anxiety—drink, argue, focus on each other instead of themselves—are all counterproductive.

The alcoholic family is like a sinking ship, and anyone who grabs on to its structures will go down with it. Each member needs to find a safe haven outside the family for support as a new ship is built. Then the family can set sail again together. This would be less difficult if family members could easily leave each other and come back together again when everything is well. But that's not how the world works. Most families must endure living together while the system is collapsed. Even if one of the adults decides to move out, they still have to take care of their kids.

One way you will be able to endure these hardships is by learning what causes them, and why they occur. Education about how families work will help you along the road to recovery. Here are a few key concepts you will become familiar with throughout this book:

- The family unit is an interconnected system. Change one member and the entire system responds; change one member and you potentially change the entire system.

- Recovery has a profound effect on the individual and on the family.

- Being in recovery means the family cannot operate the way it used to.

When one family member is in recovery, every aspect of family life, including the way the other family members interact with each other, changes. In order to support the new recovery, the old "drinking" system must change and a new, nondrinking identity and pattern of interaction must be found.

Families beginning recovery typically feel chaotic, confused, lost, and frightened. They start to wonder if abstinence is the route to a better life. Are they doing something wrong? It is natural to feel threatened by the anxiety of this traumatic change. A return to drinking may even seem logical to restore balance. But if you can understand why it is that these pressures are occurring, how these problems that seem so serious and unhealthy are natural and to be expected, you can endure the hardships instead of feeling that recovery has failed and that you have to "fix things" by flushing months of work down the drain. Feelings of discomfort, chaos, and unpredictability are normal in early family recovery.

A Map of the Journey

Imagine you're in the car with your family, and you're driving to a vacation spot you have never been to before. Your friend said it was an easy trip: you just get off the familiar freeway at such and such an exit and you keep going till you get there. You've now been driving for quite some time, and as the unfamiliar landscape flies by, you become more and more anxious that you may have made a wrong turn. "Maybe we took the wrong off-ramp," your partner suggests. The anxiety is spreading; the pressure in the car grows. Your children keep asking, "Are we there yet? Are we there yet?" The youngest has started to cry. Outside it has become pitch black. If only you had a map of the terrain, you could hazard a guess at how much longer you had to go, or you could at least say with authority, "Trust me; we're on the right path." Finally the anxiety is too great. You turn the car around and head back to the familiar freeway. There's a collective family sigh. Even though we're turning back, at least it's toward someplace familiar. The sad reality is that often you turn around just shy of your destination.

This book is a map of the family recovery process. It describes what typically happens to the family that makes these changes. How does a family shift from an unhealthy rigid organization to a more open, flexible unit with room for healthy individual development and close family ties? How do individuals grow? How do they give up their attachment to the unhealthy family and focus on their own separation and development? How do they build a solid foundation so they can establish close relationships inside and outside the family?

Many people expect that recovery will be a steady passage from bad to good. This is rarely the case. For some, the hardest part of the process is the beginning. Even if you know the move from drinking to nondrinking is a definite change for the better, and even if the family environment had grown intolerable with the drinking, the family will be thrown into a period of even greater chaos when the family's organizing principle of active alcoholism is changed. The first thing that the recovering family must understand and understand well is this: **Recovery usually gets worse in many ways before it gets better.** The months after the drinker or others hits bottom are the hardest. Everyone in the family has been set adrift. You might even find yourself wishing you were back in the drinking stage—at least then you knew where you stood. This was the case for Russ and Caroline and their family.

But even after the earliest months of sobriety, the path is uncertain. The reality is that recovery, like all healthy growth, happens in fits and starts. You may take three steps forward only to fall two steps back. Sometimes you will take the two steps back before the three steps forward. If you are not prepared for this reality when you set off on your journey, you will end up resisting the two steps back even though they are necessary for the later growth. It is natural to want to feel comfortable, but in recovery it is important to understand that discomfort and pain are normal and healthy. It is crucial to recovery that you don't identify pain as a proof that you have taken a wrong turn. Remember, when you are driving through unknown territory, anxiety is natural.

Discovering You're Normal

If you are in a family where one or more members are going through recovery, it is common to feel like you are going insane. More than anything, you will want to make your surroundings comfortable by falling back into old behaviors. In a chaotic family situation, you will try to summon control in any way possible, enduring enormous self-sacrifice in an attempt to make an uncomfortable situation comfortable.

Children in alcoholic families often become expert contortionists, bending to the chaotic behavior and thinking in any way that might make that behavior and thinking seem normal and helpful. For those whose lives have been organized around a deep instinct to smooth over the uncomfortable, discomfort seems like a dangerous and threatening thing. To them, it means something is wrong and needs to be fixed. For some, the hardest thing to learn in recovery is how to withstand discomfort.

One goal of this book is to show how the impulsive need to undo discomfort and other seemingly pathological behavior is natural and is to be expected. When you are seeing the world through the pressures of an alcoholic environment, you cannot realize that your behavior is the natural result of these pressures. As you learn about the causes and effects of this disturbed world, and what happens when it is taken apart, you will see that your behavior is natural. You will understand that anxiety, backsliding, and anger are all normal. Without this understanding, you most likely set out to "fix" these emotions, which in turn sets up serious obstacles to healthy growth. In recovery, painful and frightening feelings are not necessarily a sign that you are doing something wrong; they are often a sign that you are doing something right.

Mentors

Every family's journey is both unique and universal. Though the details vary, the path is often similar. Like the many heroes of legends, families travel through many different lands and conquer a variety of dangerous beasts, yet there is a similar structure to their journeys.

One of the clearest ways to show the natural progress of recovery is through the stories of people who have lived through it. When a person has successfully navigated the path of early recovery and reached the ongoing stage, he or she not only earns a clear view of the present reality, but also a clear view of the past.

Throughout the book you will hear stories of families who have made it through the darkness to the light. They will talk about the difficulties, the anxieties, the backsliding, and the joy they encountered with even the most minor triumphs. By framing the darkness of the unknown in the light of ongoing recovery, these stories offer a hopeful perspective that may seem elusive, even impossible, as you begin the process. But as you identify with these storytellers, you will also be identifying with their success.

When you are in the middle of a journey, it's hard to see the meaning in the crazy events you live through. But when you arrive at your destination and look back over your travels, you can see each episode as building one on top of another. This perspective can be helpful when you hit one of these harrowing spots. Think of yourself looking back from the future, when the meaning of this pain will be clear.

Much of recovery is about accepting the fact that you can't understand where you are until you have passed through. Learning to tolerate this lack of understanding is difficult and takes time. It's hard to accept that you don't know what the future brings and that you don't have control over your journey, but rather are controlled by it. This is especially hard for a person who has lived in an alcoholic home, where control and self-protection held such a premium. The ability to accept that where you are is where you need to be is one of the skills learned in recovery. When you learn to be patient and endure the unknown, you discover that understanding often arrives on the other side. The more you do this, the more comfortable you will be not knowing. Soon the unknown becomes a welcome companion, even an ally.

The people sharing their stories in this book have made the journey you are undertaking. They will be your mentors. They are no different than you; they are just further along in the process. When you witness the traumas of their lives as they now do—through the clarity that is central to ongoing recovery—it can be inspiring. You will see that your problems—the things you are ashamed of, your anxieties—are all normal. Facing them is painful, but it is a necessary step in the growth process.

How This Book Works

This book is divided into four parts, one for each stage of recovery. (These stages are drinking, transition, early recovery, and ongoing recovery.) We will take a detailed look at how each stage works, what tasks need to be completed to move on to the next stage, and how to survive the difficulties that come with this period of growth.

Each of the four parts will be divided into three chapters called, respectively, "mapping the territory," "points of view," and "survival, maintenance, and coping skills."

Mapping the Territory

These chapters will give a general explanation of how the family works at each stage, focusing on the environment created by the family and the way the family members interact with one another. In a sense, we will be drawing a map of the stage by describing what the stage looks and feels like and suggesting why things are the way they are.

The rules a family operates under can go largely unnoticed for their being so familiar. But as you start to see how these dynamics functioned during drinking, you will see how recovery has reorganized the rules by which you live. The more you understand how your family situations work, the better you will understand the tensions and obstacles that lie along the path of recovery.

These chapters will also describe the tasks of recovery—the bridges that need to be crossed and the work that needs to be done so family members can move on in the right direction.

The exercises in these sections will focus on helping you recognize the dynamics of your own family. You will learn to look at your surroundings and see what rules and rituals are in place; you will discover what behavior is left over from the drinking period, and what is new.

Points of View

The second chapter in each part focuses on finding the individual's place on the map; that is, describing how each family member experiences the stage from his or her own perspective. We will also offer moments of insight from different mentors—simple realizations that can open your eyes.

When you read these chapters, you will discover that what you are going through is not unique. Hopefully, this will lead you to a deeper understanding of why you see things the way you do. Similarly, you will learn why other family members are doing what they are doing. Hopefully, this will lead to an increase in empathy. When you start to realize that your family members aren't crazy but that they are just reacting to living under tremendous tensions and trauma, their behavior suddenly seems much more understandable and forgivable.

These chapters will look at each stage from the viewpoints of the alcoholic, the coalcoholic, and the children. The alcoholic's addiction to alcohol is well-known, but the coalcoholic's addiction to the alcoholic is more subtle. Each partner must go through a recovery process of his or her own. The children can have the hardest road of all. Not only are they in an increasingly tense situation, but their parents are both stepping out of the family roles to get help with their own recoveries. The children can feel abandoned at these times, wishing for the old "stability" of the drinking stage. One of the main issues discussed in this book is how to look after the children while the family system is collapsed during the early period of recovery. It is a delicate balancing act, but it can and must be done.

The exercises in these chapters focus on your identification with the different points of view, examining the ways your own perspectives are similar or different. It is often very helpful for the recovering individual to explore a variety of different perspectives. This process helps clarify what makes a particular family's situation both unique and universal.

Survival, Maintenance, and Coping Skills

In the coping skills chapters, we will discuss skills that can help you endure the bumps and setbacks along the difficult but healthy path of recovery. You can think of these chapters as travel tips—or at times, emergency road service.

As you have already heard (and as you will hear again and again), anxiety and pain are normal, natural parts of healthy growth. It can be a huge relief to understand that your anxiety is based in real experiences and that it often arises from sensible attempts to survive a chaotic situation. However, you still have to get through the discomfort, and that's where the survival, maintenance, and coping skills chapters come in. You will learn communication skills, hear suggestions on how to deal with rebuilding the family system, and get advice for dealing with anxiety and impatience.

The exercises in these sections will focus on making these skills more concrete, so you can rely upon them with greater and greater ease. We will also teach you some games you can play with your children. In each stage of recovery, you'll need to ensure safe methods of interaction with each other, ways to practice communication without crossing boundaries and violating the space necessary for each individual's recovery.

Although the last chapter in each part specifically offers advice and encouragement for coping with each stage, both the mapping and the points of view chapters also provide valuable information for coping. The mapping chapters help you understand the lay of the land, so you can anticipate the difficulties that lie ahead. If you're not expecting a smooth, easy ride, you won't immediately look for what you've done wrong when you hit a bad spot.

Similarly, the points of view chapters give you a better understanding of the unique perspectives of yourself and your family members. One of the biggest problems in an alcoholic family is the blurring of boundaries between the members. Because of the fact that everyone is trying their hardest to survive the traumatic circumstances, individuals often don't accurately perceive which are their problems and which are someone else's. As you make the journey to recovery, you will become more and more able to see where your responsibility ends and the next person's begins.

We suggest you purchase a nice blank book in which to record your thoughts about recovery, great sayings, quick reminders for recovery action or support, and your own personal journaling. This is also the ideal place to do the exercises found in this book. Choose any book, binder, or folder you wish. Just make sure you have a way of keeping all your writing together and in order. You will find it beneficial to be able to retrace your thoughts, see how your perceptions have changed, and see the progress you have made.

The Importance of Alcoholics Anonymous and Al-Anon

Although it may seem natural to stay inside your family for support, the alcoholic family structure is an unhealthy one that pressures you and everyone else to remain as you are. Our research has shown that the single most important factor contributing to the long-term recovery of the individual and the family is that the alcoholic and other family members reached outside the family for help.

The best, most widely known support for recovery is Alcoholics Anonymous and its related twelve-step programs such as Al-Anon (for partners of alcoholics), Ala-Teen, Ala-Kid, Ala-Tot, and so forth. For most of the families we studied, the outside help came from a twelve-step program, chiefly AA and Al-Anon. Families have also used therapy and religion. We believe this book will be most helpful if you have external support.

Alcoholics Anonymous allows a shift in dependency off of the bottle and onto the twelve-step program. The twelve steps challenge the deeply held beliefs that kept the drinking going, most of which focused on the need for control and the need to be self-sufficient. The very act of "joining" AA gives you the feeling that you are a part of something greater than yourself. The security that comes from belonging allows you to make yourself vulnerable and give up that deep-seated need for control.

The first step in the journey toward recovery is abstinence. Along the twelve-step path comes a very serious process of self-analysis, which is crucial to growth and overcoming the past behavior. But unflinching self-reflection and abstinence are difficult to keep in balance. They are both necessary to a healthy recovery, but they must be tackled in their own time. The first goal is abstinence, and the best way to get abstinence firmly in place is through a twelve-step program.

Prior to joining, many people express discomfort with AA, worrying that the program is a kind of cult that will undermine their individuality and keep them dependent. One of the hardest things to grasp about recovery if you haven't experienced it is that the road to real autonomy must pass through dependency. You must be able to give up the illusion of total self-control in order to come to a truthful understanding of your own limits. The only way to do this is in the safety of a dependent relationship. Such a relationship is very hard to establish, because members of an alcoholic family equate dependency with the unhealthy dependency that existed in their family. The idea of feeling dependent upon strangers may seem threatening, but these strangers are all people who have similarly felt that fear and taken the risk. By engaging the external support of the group, you are free to focus on yourself as you are apart from the unhealthy family system. This allows you to recognize and own up to your own responsibilities. In this way you take vital steps toward gaining a healthy understanding of your identity as an alcoholic, coalcoholic, or member of an alcoholic family.

What some see as the "religious" aspects of twelve-step programs—the discussions of "god" and a "higher power"—may make some people uncomfortable. But these concepts, at their most practical, are means to an end. One of the central goals in recovery is to overcome the alcoholic's and others' blind faith in self-sufficiency. As we will see in detail throughout the book, self-reliance and other egocentric beliefs are central to alcoholic thinking. These beliefs are based in a misguided need for control over your surroundings. Paradoxically, this need for control is directly related to the fact that you're out of control of the drinking or the drinker.

In order for you to give up your strongly held belief in self-sufficiency and control, you need to bring your ego down to its proper level. This may sound terrifying to the drinker or partner, but freedom can only come after you give up the hard-nosed self-reliance. Healthy growth is dependent on reaching out for help. God and the higher power are concepts that are individually defined by the members of AA and Al-Anon. These concepts help people remember they aren't in control and that help is available. By understanding your natural place in the world and your connection to others, you begin to find a natural and healthy sense of responsibility. Though AA and Al-Anon urge members to rely heavily on each other and the higher power, they are repeatedly confronted with the issue of responsibility. Thus the programs make it clear that they offer help, but that the real work of change must be done by the individual alone.

Although most of our research families belonged to twelve-step programs, we hope this book will help you find your way in recovery no matter what source of help you choose. By learning about the realities of the drinking family and how those realities still dominate the family even after the drinking stops, you will have gone a long way toward understanding your place on the recovery map and what it will take to travel this path.

What This Book Is Not

This book is not a substitute for a recovery program. It does not provide you with a step-by-step path to recovery; this is the purpose of recovery programs such as AA and Al-Anon. This book is meant to lend support to family members who are struggling together to make it through their recovery.

This book is not a "self-help" book for the very reason that the process of recovery cannot be "self"-contained. Although recovery requires a self-focus, a key part of the work of recovery is done by reaching out. One of the most powerful moments in recovery is sharing your story with other people—breaking the closed system. The shame that festered in the darkness rushes out into the light and is consumed. Everyone in the room has been there. This moment represents a deep connection between the individual and a supportive community. This kind of real human contact is necessary to provide the external support necessary to do the work of recovery. You need scaffolding to hold up the building while the workers break down the foundation within. This book does not provide the scaffolding, but it describes the scaffolding so you can understand why it's there and why, at times, you or other family members may have a hard time living with it.

The alcoholic family lives under the rigid belief that their closed family system is necessary for survival. Breaking out of that closed system is difficult, often traumatic. The following chapters offer internal support—understanding—that facilitates your external support—AA, Al-Anon, therapy, religion, or some combination of the three. Understanding how the system works will give you a better perspective on why you need to step outside it, and how you can make that move. The information in this book cannot shorten the process of recovery: it takes as long as it takes. The book can, however, help you avoid pitfalls that might make the labor of recovery last a lot longer than it has to.

What Is Healthy Growth?

Healthy growth is about discovering your inner spirit and finding your own individual path. This can only be done by listening to yourself. Patience is the key. You will get there in time, but you can only reconnect with others after you have taken responsibility for your own life.

We live in a bandwagon culture. We are given changing images of what the ideal human looks like and we are told to jump on board. Many books describe a "fix-it" style of change, wherein the individual is supposed to manipulate his or her personality to fit a desired end. This kind of conscious manipulation is like clipping a hedge: you change the hedge into the shape you desire, controlling its growth by cutting off the parts you deem useless. This is not the path toward healthy growth; this is control run wild.

Such attempts to live up to expectations, either your own or your culture's, can have disastrous effects. Your attempts to be who you think you should be only take you further and further away from who you actually are. This road is an anxious one indeed. Real growth occurs only after you have given up your need for control.

Healthy growth comes from inside. You cannot plan it; you let it happen to you. Often you don't recognize a move forward until it is already behind you. If you try too hard to anticipate the change, it won't come. You need to be patient, give up your control, and let the change come. Think of healthy growth like a wildflower: it blooms of its own accord, following its own natural guidelines, fulfilling its potential as a flower.

If you are shouting shoulds at yourself, you will never hear the soft voice inside that knows who you are and knows where you've been. In a way, recovery is quieting that screaming control so you can hear that tiny voice. It's like shouting down a well for a child trapped inside. "Where are you?" you scream. But your echoing voice drowns out the tiny voice that calls out the child's location. The goal is to relax, listen to yourself, and hear that tiny voice.

As we will see later in the book, there are many parallels between the stages of recovery and the stages of a child's development. As a child grows, she moves forward, trying out new skills, making her way step by step. There is a lot of crying and frustration on the way, but slowly and surely the child finds her way from crawling to walking, from babbling to talking. The alcoholic family stunts the growth of the individual, because everyone must squelch his or her own individual growth to serve the needs of the alcoholic family structure. In order to set the growth on the right track, the system must fall. The individuals must pass through the stages of development again, learning new behaviors and ways of thinking, until the way of healthy growth becomes deeply embedded in each of their lives.

Healthy growth cannot take place in an unsafe environment; too much time is spent checking if the coast is clear. In order for the first steps to be taken toward recovery, the individual must reach outside the unhealthy environment of home and into the healthy structure of AA or a similar support network. Only then can the person relax enough to try to listen for the little voice inside. When each of you regains contact with that inner voice, when you hear it guiding you, only then can you put your family back together; only then can the family as a unit enjoy healthy growth.

Recovery is a journey into the unknown. Although the word "recover" implies that you will be arriving at a place where you have already been, this is not the case. Recovery is a journey to a new place. It is a journey you only take once. It is a journey you never end. If you are constantly on the lookout for a familiar place to rest, you will be undoing a lot of good work. You will grow tired at times, you can only travel at the pace you can tolerate. But even if you can only go an inch a day, it is important to move that inch. Next day you might be able to move two and then three.

The journey does not always seem to be moving forward, but the work continues. In mountain climbing, you often have to hammer in a lot of ropes to move up to the next plateau. So the days are spent hanging ropes, while at night you return to the base camp—but not the bottom of the mountain—to sleep. One day the ropes reach the next plateau, and you pack up your camp and climb the ropes, pulling them up behind you. When you reach the plateau you set up your new camp, and the next day the climb continues from that higher plateau. So goes recovery: even the days spend apparently going nowhere are crucial parts of the journey.

Sitting Around the Fireplace

As you make your way through this book, you will probably come across insights or examples that bring up difficult memories. You may identify with a person's story, or recognize a certain subtle abuse pattern that you never saw in yourself before.

One helpful visualization may get you through some of these rough spots. Imagine you are with your family. Imagine you have spent long years on this journey and you have all gotten back together to celebrate the journey you have all taken. Imagine that you sit around the warmth of a fire as you recall this very instance of pain or anxiety. Having survived the moment (and many others like it), you'll feel it is far away, but you will also remember how important it was that you felt the emotion. The only way to pass through your feelings is to feel them. If you avoid them, or grab hold of old familiar behaviors to feel comfortable, the pain will just wait in the shadows until you venture out again. The journey you are on is long and hard, and the only way to survive it is to experience it.

Still, you may find that certain sections stir your emotions too much, and you don't feel comfortable reading further. After all, we will be discussing very painful realities. If you feel you can't go on, put the book down and come back later when you are ready. Take as much as you need and leave the rest. Remember that wherever you are, that's where you need to be. So listen to your emotions as you make your way through this book.

This book is about the relationship of individuals to the family, and the rugged, but wondrous and rewarding journey that is family recovery. We accent how hard the process is, for both the individuals and the family. Remember as you read that it's worth it and that the difficult experiences are normal. Individuals and families learn that "a good life" is something they may not have expected it to be. It's accepting the soft and the hard, the glad and the sad, the pleasure and the pain and learning how to live with all of it. Recovery is hard, it's wonderful, and it's real.

Part 1

Sacrificing the Self

The Drinking Stage

1

"Death on the Installment Plan"

Mapping the Drinking Stage

In this chapter we will map the first stage of recovery: the drinking stage. The map will chart the landscape of active alcoholism, focusing on the alcoholic environment and family system. By investigating the unstable terrain that makes up the drinking stage, you will gain a perspective on the extreme thoughts and behavior that mark this tense and unsafe living situation. Once the map is drawn, you will be able to consider the different points of view from which this territory can be viewed.

Although the drinking stage is not a step toward healthy progress, it is ground zero for recovery. As such, understanding the dynamics of active alcoholism will allow you to chart your growth by comparing where you are to where you have been, and to monitor your progress by checking for stubborn elements that remain from your unhealthy past. If you are oblivious to the details that make up your family's drinking atmosphere, they are more likely to follow you into the early stages of abstinence. Those who don't know their own history are destined to repeat it.

As recovery continues and the family members start to stabilize in their new, abstinent environment, one of the important tasks for continued growth is facing the dark period of drinking that went before abstinence. Understanding the way the family works during the drinking period will help your investigation into your own unique family dynamics. For example, it is often a powerful experience to recognize that the behaviors and thoughts that seemed so extreme and dangerous were in fact understandable and grew out of a complex system that was in place. This doesn't mean, however, that the behavior should be forgotten and the slate wiped clean. Understanding motivation does not undermine individual responsibility, but sets it in a realistic context of the unhealthy family.

One of the goals of this book is to help you see the unique features of your own family and how they affect your own and your family's recovery. Awareness of the family's dynamics can make the difference between surviving recovery and succumbing to the intense anxiety that is typical during these traumatic changes. In order to understand your family and the individuals within it, you need to become familiar with the subtle ways the alcoholic family works. By mapping the drinking stage, you will explore the complex set of relationships at work within your family.

The Stage of Active Alcoholism

Active alcoholism refers to a period when the family and every facet of its life are organized around drinking. This doesn't mean that everyone in the family drinks or that every interaction is about alcohol or that every event has alcohol as its purpose. It means that during active alcoholism, the simple fact is that the most important thing in the family is the drinking, and anything that threatens it must be pushed out. Judith, who grew up with her father and mother "drinking together constantly," recalls the unspoken tyranny of the bottle. "My brothers and I spent our childhood tiptoeing around in the mornings. We knew that Mom and Dad were real sensitive, and it was really important that we not make a sound. If you made the mistake of waking them up, it would be over for you. We just figured grown-ups needed to sleep a lot. It wasn't until we got much older that we recognized our morning vigilance was protecting their hangovers."

The drinking stage may start innocently enough with moderate drinking that does not seem unhealthy. There are no rules for the shift to alcoholism; the drinking can increase incrementally over a long period of time or it can escalate rapidly, often during a period of heightened anxiety or crisis. A key quality that distinguishes alcoholism from non-problematic drinking is that the alcoholic *needs* to drink in order to function. Once this need is felt, the prime motivation for the alcoholic becomes explaining away this need—"I drink because of the stress of the job." The partner and children are likely to fall in line and support the drinker's distorted view of reality. They believe, either consciously or unconsciously, that in order to preserve the unity of their family, they must protect the alcoholic's drinking. And in order to maintain this distorted view of reality, all members must practice the main characteristic of this stage: denial. The real problem—the drinking—is never identified, but is explained away instead.

Alcoholic Thinking

During the active alcoholism that defines the drinking stage, the family is squeezed between two contradictory elements: the reality that everyone is dominated by the alcoholism, and the need for everyone to collude with the alcoholic in denying the alcoholism. Two core beliefs dominate every aspect of family life:

- There is no alcoholism.

- There is no loss of control over drinking.

The deep dark secret that must be protected at all costs is that the drinker has lost control, which is reflected in the fact that he or she has lost the ability or the desire to stop the destructive drinking. The coalcoholic family members cannot control the alcoholic, so they adapt by trying to control the surroundings.

The denial that lies at the heart of the alcoholic family is a defense mechanism. The family feels it must defend itself from a reality that is threatening. Denial is a part of "alcoholic thinking," or rationalizations and excuses that explain the need for the drinking: "Though the drinking may look bad, it was just because I had a bad day"; or "I'd be fine if the boss wasn't such a jerk." Though the alcoholic may be the first one to use alcoholic thinking, this becomes the norm for all family members. **You don't have to be an alcoholic to suffer from alcoholic thinking.** Everyone in the family must collude with this thinking, no matter how glaring the evidence to the contrary is. This can be particularly devastating to the children's development: they have to choose between their parents and reality. They will most likely choose their parents, but in so doing they lose the real world, the ability to trust their perceptions, and their healthy development.

This unhealthy thinking operates at a very deep level and is often not noticed as being out of the ordinary. The denial can be conscious or unconscious, and the longer it lasts, the deeper it sinks into the psyche, until the perception of reality—both of the world and of the self—is completely distorted.

Through this ongoing distortion and collusion, the family organizes around the drinking. This concept—that the family system organizes itself around the active alcoholism—may seem a bit abstract, but it is actually quite concrete. As you will see throughout part 1, all elements of the family structure and the individual identities within it are shaped and molded by the pressures of active alcoholism. Though not every choice is directly related to alcohol, there is an underlying pressure to protect the alcoholism at all costs and at all times.

This kind of alcohol-first thinking is extremely destructive, especially to children, who are in a crucial period of development when they need a safe environment in which to experiment and try out their own identities. Denial of reality demands a massive effort to keep out the unwanted information, and this effort comes first, before any growth can take place. The vigilance necessary to keep an unwanted reality out means children can never really relax, and never experience the safety necessary to find their own way.

Life in the Drinking Stage

The family and its individual members contort themselves in order to preserve the unhealthy situation that is in place. They hold fast to the core belief that there is no alcoholism and no loss of control over drinking. In order to maintain the unhealthy family patterns the members will need to do the following:

- Deny the existence of any problem with alcohol.
- Invent explanations and rationalizations for the alcoholic reality.
- Cover up the family secret.

The Unstable Foundation

Though you may have an easy time spotting active alcoholism in another family, it can be harder to recognize in your own, because you live with it every day, day in and day out. Once the denial is firmly in place, causes and effects can easily get mixed up. Usually the fact that drinking exists will be recognized, but the central place it holds in the family life will often be overlooked—mistaken for being just one among many details in the chaotic household. The drinking may even be seen as a reaction to the chaotic household or to something else that is identified as the "real" problem.

Imagine a house that has been built on an unstable foundation. Inside the house everything might look normal, but every once in a while, and seemingly for no reason, some minor catastrophe occurs: a crack forms in the wall; the roof starts to sag; the floors start to buckle. When you live inside the house, you see these events as unconnected. You slap some paint on the wall, put up a support for the sagging roof, and sand down the warped floorboards. You can't figure out why these minor emergencies keep cropping up. Everyone loves the house: it's home. And yet, with every new day there is something else to fix.

After a while, the paint is the only thing holding the crumbling walls together, the rooms are choked with supports for the roof, and the floors have been sanded until they're paper-thin. The house has become a dangerous place, but since the focus is always on the individual crises and since you always view the house from the inside out, you can't see the real source of the problem.

Since you live with it every day, the drinking becomes a normal and expected part of the surroundings. So when a small crisis pops up, you don't think to look for the cause in the constant and unchanging family structure. You fix the problem and go on with your life. No one recognizes that the alcoholism has become the foundation of the family. At most, it is seen as the drinker's problem. This denial—like the paint, the supports, and the sanding—covers up all of the crises, never allowing you to step outside, so to speak, and take a real look at the situation. But the only way to gain an understanding of the danger and damage building up inside the alcoholic family is to take that difficult step outside it. This requires a crack in the family's shield of denial. It is through this crack that the first light of healthy change can shine.

The Move to Recovery

In order to shift in a direction toward recovery, the family patterns must break down. That shift occurs when denial breaks down for any family member. If you change one part of the system—if one family member moves into recovery—the entire system will respond. If the whole family moves into recovery, the structure of the system will change.

Seeing When You're Ready

Seeing the past clearly is an important part of recovery. But you can't force these insights if you are not ready to face them.

In order to see the drinking stage clearly, you need some distance from it. You can't expect to face those difficult memories in the earliest moments after hitting bottom. You will need some time before you are ready to start digging into the past. The main problem is that facing the drinking can come with feelings of great guilt and shame, and for individuals in the alcoholic family, the anxiety that comes with these emotions will often bring back unhealthy ways of coping with distress. In other words, drinking and denial can be means of escape, and if you make yourself confront the troubling memories before you're ready, you may feel a need to escape using these unhealthy means.

One of the themes you will see repeated in this book is that you shouldn't force things before you're ready. You may be anxious to start the process of recovery and the difficult work of self-examination, but you will sense right away if it's just too soon to do this work. If you find you're too uncomfortable, take a step back. This material will be here whenever you are ready to use it. You need to listen to your intuition: that little voice inside that knows how far you are comfortable going. If you are comfortable pushing your limits, by all means push them, but listen to that voice.

One of the hallmarks of alcoholic behavior is that your conscious, controlling mind leads the way with an iron hand, squeezing the little voice into silence. If you force yourself too far, you will just be falling back into the old drinking behavior: imposing rigid controls on yourself and stretching your limits too far. One of the goals of recovery is to reconnect with your intuition. So use this material if you can, or leave it for later. And always use what you need and leave what you don't

In the early period after hitting bottom, the main focus has to be on abstaining from the unhealthy behavior. If thinking about the past undermines this process, leave it till later. When the abstinence is in place and you are ready to face the darkness of the drinking years, the information in this chapter will help you organize your memories into a clear map of your family landscape.

Thumbnail Map of the Drinking Stage

- The family is dominated by an alcoholic environment, and the atmosphere and context of living is characterized by all the anxiety, tension, and trauma of active drinking.

- The family denies the drinking and its consequences as the system becomes increasingly rigid and organized around alcohol.

- New information on what drinking is doing to the family cannot be acknowledged because it poses a threat to denial.

- Instead, the family accommodates to the drinking, altering behavior and beliefs to maintain the drinking system.

- Individual growth and well-being are sacrificed to the needs of the unhealthy alcoholic system.

- In the end, the system ends up feeding on itself. The family's problems are largely systemic, but they are blamed on the individuals. Any misstep is punished by shame, anger, and denunciation. Blame is thrown around to protect the system.

- Since it's hard to stand outside the system built around active alcoholism, no one can see the weak, rigid, and perhaps crumbling foundation.

The Drinking Environment

The family environment is what you see, hear, taste, and feel around you; it's the context within which the family functions. It's like a smell in the air: If you live inside it you don't notice it. If you're away for a while and come back, you may notice the smell, but it seems familiar; for good or bad, it smells like home. The environment is both a result of the family patterns of behavior and a cause of them, in much the same way as the family is shaped by its individual members at the same time it shapes them.

The alcoholic family environment can be characterized by a number of unhealthy qualities, which can be either overt or subtle:

- Chaos

- Inconsistency

- Unpredictability

- Arbitrariness

- Changing limits

- Repetitious and illogical arguments

- Abuse

In the alcoholic home environment, the everyday experience is likely to be one of chronic tension, strain, and trauma. Even if there is no direct physical or psychological confrontation, this ongoing pressure takes its toll. Judith, who tiptoed around for fear of waking her hung-over parents, describes the constant pressure as tangible: "Nobody ever really got mad at each other, but anger was always in the air. Everyone kept a stiff upper lip, but the place was so sad. It's like nothing ever happened that you could put a finger on, but the overall result was like a beating. It was the Chinese water torture. It was death on the installment plan."

In addition to chronic trauma, you may also be the victim of or the witness to acute trauma such as marital affairs, violence, acts of humiliation, or abandonment (either emotional or physical). The acute trauma can overshadow the chronic trauma, as the tangible act pushes the more subtle pressures into the background. An act of violence can also add to the ongoing anxiety, as the alcoholic's partner and children watch out for signs of possible turmoil that might lead to further violence. This extreme sensitivity to the moods and the behaviors of others can result in anxiety problems for the family members.

Some families are better than others at hiding the depths of psychological and physical abuse that occur during active alcoholism. One of the most common ways of keeping the dark side out of sight is for the alcoholic or coalcoholic to impose elaborate and far-reaching control over the other family members. The rigid rules are laid out and the family members are told they must follow these rules to protect the family. The reality is that what is being protected is the alcoholism, which is guarded at the expense of the family. If anything happens to undermine the unhealthy situation, the person responsible will be shamed and blamed until he or she falls back in line.

These tight controls actually add another layer of psychological abuse and chronic trauma.

In order to survive under this intense pressure, an individual needs to meet the threat with equal amounts of self-protection. Often the strategy is to turn the control inward, protecting yourself by oppressively controlling your own thoughts, behaviors, and emotions. Any healthy thought that lets in the reality that is being denied comes along with intense anxiety and guilt for thinking a "bad" thought. The toxic environment is now turned inward through the ongoing pressure of shame and blame. Each individual takes the responsibility for the family's welfare on his or her own shoulders. The toxic family must be protected at all costs. In such an anxiety-filled atmosphere, it is no wonder that healthy growth is shut down.

Many individuals will describe their environment during the drinking stage as lonely, chaotic, unpredictable, and inconsistent. This was Judith's experience in her family. "I have three brothers, and I look back and think how much better it would have been if we could have talked about it. Share what was going on. But it was everyone for themselves. We worked hard to stay out of trouble, but if someone slipped up, they were going down alone. You didn't want to be around the punishment in case some of the shrapnel missed the intended victim and caught an innocent bystander. In the end, we were all so cut off from one another. It's taken years to even begin to reconnect."

Some people will describe their family life during the years of active alcoholism as just fine. Phil and Kathy, who enjoyed a relationship that included a considerable amount of time apart, saw most of their drinking years as a stable and happy time in their lives. In their case, the alcoholic drinking was split off from the family, which kept the more unhealthy by-products of the drinking from affecting the rest of the family. Now in recovery, they look back on many years of drinking when there was little or no tension in the environment: there were good feelings between them, they enjoyed one another's company, and they enjoyed the predictability and consistency of their relationship. Kathy remembers the shift: "Phil's drinking changed, and everything just fell apart. We no longer had our glorious shared reality. Phil became unpredictable, and the things I could count on would change on a whim. The relationship crumbled right along with my denial. We had had this real sense of balance, but things got thrown off, and my end of the seesaw hit the ground hard. We'd been alcoholics all along, but since we matched each other drink for drink, neither of us ever saw the other as having a problem. The second that changed, everything changed."

Family Environment—Drinking Stage

- Generally unsafe
- Chronic, acute trauma
- Tension, anxiety, chaos, inconsistency, unpredictability, hostility
- Pervasive shame, guilt, emphasis on control

(Adapted from Brown and Lewis, 1999)

The atmosphere in an unhealthy household can be a vague and intangible thing. Its power lies in its insubstantiality: since it's always there, no one notices it, and since no one notices it, the environment does its work unchallenged. Adults who have left the alcoholic environment behind can suddenly be thrown back into intense shame and anxiety when they find themselves in circumstances that are reminiscent of the environment. The trigger could be a smell, a phrase or a tone of voice, or the pressure at work: when you haven't sufficiently investigated the alcoholic environment you lived in, even these subtle cues can undermine your recovery. It is important to understand the nature of the environment you lived in so you can recognize those responses as natural, but rooted in a past that no longer has direct contact with you.

Exercise: Sensing the Environment

Take a deep breath and look at the room you are sitting in. Think for a few moments about the atmosphere of the room. Don't concentrate on the objects in it, but how the place feels as a whole. Describe the environment. You don't have to capture every detail, just write till you are satisfied.

Now think back to the atmosphere that you lived in during the drinking stage. If you have a hard time getting started, you might try to think of a particular image of yourself: sitting at the kitchen table, lying in bed at night, and so on. Just think of some words that come to you, such as "tension," "anxiety," or "darkness." You don't need to compose a poem or write a story, just capture some of the elements that make up your memory.

As you make your way through recovery, you will find that you can recall more and more about the atmosphere. In the beginning one of the hardest things is to separate your current feelings about the drinking environment from the feelings you had back when you were living in it.

If this is difficult and troubling, leave it be. You will have other chances to think back, and you may feel up to it another time.

Don't forget to date your exercise. It will be helpful when you look back over your changing perceptions to know when you felt a particular way. You can follow your own progress by revisiting exercises: rereading them and redoing them. Remember there are no right or wrong answers. And what you think today may not be what you think tomorrow. Don't write for posterity; write for the moment. That way when you look back in the future, you will see what you thought, not what you wanted to think.

The Family System in the Drinking Stage

"I think of those years as our fishbowl period," recalls Michelle, a thirty-eight-year-old nurse and mother of two teenagers. She's been in recovery for seven years and can now look back at those painful memories with an unflinching gaze. "Our house was like one big fishbowl, all of us swimming in the same water. We drank it, breathed it, relieved ourselves in it. It was really unclear where one person ended and another began; we were like one intertwined organism. We lived in the fishbowl, but the glass wasn't clear, it was cloudy, opaque. No one could see in, and nobody could see out. That was the key to keeping it all going: if you don't know what else is out there, you figure that what you've got must be all there is."

Michelle is right. A family is an extraordinarily complex living organism. There are so many sets of interactions, so many varieties of communication, and subtle groups and subgroups within it that the individual member will often have a hard time seeing the structures with any clarity or objectivity. Most people have only the vaguest awareness of how their family works. One of the difficulties you face when you try to understand the family you come from is that it's the only one you have ever really experienced; you have nothing to compare it to. The unique features of your family—whether healthy or unhealthy—are so familiar that you could easily believe these interactions to be universal. The assumption that "all families are just like mine" may result in your having an unclear concept of what makes your family different and, ultimately, how your own perception of the world is based upon these differences.

In a traumatic family environment, this lack of clarity is even more glaring. A common by-product of the traumatic family—such as the alcoholic family—is that the individuals have a very hard time separating themselves from the family. There is often so great a pressure to conform to the family beliefs—"the tragedy never happened"; "the abuse is normal"; "there is no alcoholism"; and so on—that any dissension is crushed by the group, which is threatened by the possibility of being shown that these precious beliefs are false. The irony is, of course, that revealing the falsehood of these beliefs is the first necessary step toward healing the broken family; the reality that is hidden is the very thing that must be brought to light.

Along with the blurred boundaries between yourself and your family, there will often be an overly rigid boundary in place between the family and anyone who does not share its relationship with alcohol. The family members have little access to a healthy model of the family; further, a healthy family is perceived as a threat, offering a context by which the alcoholic family can be judged unhealthy. If, on the other hand, the outsider is a drinking buddy who conforms to the rules of the traumatic environment, he or she will often share the same blurred boundaries with the rest of the family as with the alcoholic. The drinking friends make up a vital web of collaborators who allow the unhealthy behavior to continue by joining in on it. These "loyal friends" become part of the extended family, which can lead to dangerous boundary violations, such as a situation where an unsafe person who has "earned" family privileges is left to take care of the children.

How Does the Family System Work?

In order to get a better understanding of the way the family affects recovery and the way recovery affects the family, we will first need to brush up on how the family works in general, and then how the alcoholic family works in particular.

A "family" can be defined as any group of people acting together in a consistent fashion over time. Any group, large or small, will form a system in order to relate to one another in a predictable manner. For the purposes of this book we will be focusing on the traditional nuclear family, but the dynamics discussed here are applicable to any such group of people.

A family has a personality just like individuals do, and this personality is expressed through the individual's interactions with each other and the group's interactions with those outside the family. The family identity can run very deep in each of the family's members. This family personality will in large part define the normal range of thoughts and behavior: your beliefs and values, how you show emotion, the ways you interact with others. The family has a general grounding quality for any individual within it, and for a child growing up, the family is a central framework for security and self-identity.

When we talk of the **family system**, we are referring to the mechanisms by which the family keeps the household functioning. All families have a unique system that regulates daily life, including family rules, roles, and communication processes. These accepted and predictable patterns help to define the structure of the family and establish consistency.

Any change in one part of the system affects the entire family. The healthy family system is like a person; it changes and grows while it remains recognizable and consistent. These changes can be part of the normal developmental life cycle of a family, such as a child's being born, going away to college, or getting married; or they can be individual crises, such as one member's getting emotionally or physically sick or going into recovery.

Seeing the interconnectedness of the people in the family system is central to understanding the process of family recovery. Not only does the shift to abstinence in an alcoholic family constitute a change that affects all its members, but each new stage of recovery also brings changes that reverberate throughout the family system.

The structure of the family system can be very subtle indeed; many of the system's expectations and collaborations are so firmly entrenched that no one notices them. When you are doing the work of recovery, it can be helpful to become more sensitive to the nature of these structures, so that after they fall you will recognize them when they crop up again. In order to help that understanding along, we will give a brief primer in **systems psychology**. Systems psychology focuses on how people interact in a social system.

There are four aspects of a family system: **structure**, **process**, **stability**, and **change**.

Structure

The structure of a system refers to its organization: the blocks and bricks that make up the system. It includes rules, roles, rituals, boundaries, and hierarchies.

Rules are behaviors that become established and entrenched. The rules may be explicit (directly communicated) or implicit (indirectly communicated). The following are some rules that encourage healthy family functioning:

- "We listen to others without interrupting."
- "We take turns planning family vacations."
- "We allow feelings to be expressed."

Here are some rules that can limit healthy exchange and function:

- "It's okay to drink, but don't tell your mother."

- "We can't talk about sex in our family."

- "Don't praise anyone, because they'll get spoiled."

- "No one can get too close in the family."

Roles are like the parts that individuals take on in the family play. There can be different parts for different occasions, but these parts are expected and performed repeatedly, even habitually, by the individual. Roles can be healthy or unhealthy, and they can either help or hinder family function. Good role functioning for the individual involves the following:

- You know, agree to, and implement your role.

- Other family members have clear expectations of your role.

- The role works to help the family function well.

- There is flexibility to change the role when necessary.

Here are some examples of roles:

Breadwinner	Cheerleader
Caretaker	Taskmaster
Parent	Instigator
Worrier	Under-/overresponsible one
Scapegoat	Loner
Lover	Tyrant/bully/dictator
Placater/harmonizer	Victim
Martyr	Listener
Pessimist/optimist	Comic

As with other subtle aspects of the family system, roles often become unconscious: you may play a part that is demanded of you in your family, but over time, it becomes a central part of your identity. A role can bring great self-esteem or a strong sense of identity, but if it is an unhealthy role, it can also inhibit your later growth, giving you a self-concept that is based on conflict, which you carry with you always. Angela was always the pessimist in her family, gaining the title of Queen Curmudgeon. It was a comic role, which she played to the hilt. When she grew up she maintained this role, and although she was still a very funny woman, she found that she came to view everything through the negative filter of her pessimism, even though things had worked out fine for her. After some years of therapy she came to see it as a role she took on to deflect focus from her alcoholic father, whose failing business left him deeply negative. After some work she found she was able to keep the wry sense of humor, but throw away the pessimistic worldview that undermined her other successes.

This points toward a subtlety of roles: you may take on an unhealthy role in the family that builds useful skills for later in life. If you are the hypervigilant safety monitor in your home, you will have high anxiety, but in life you will have a keen awareness of the behavior of other people. It may take some time to peel away the fear and anxiety that sparked the talent, but when you recognize your role as having given you a gift, you can recognize that the role is neither all bad nor all good.

An unhealthy role, if it goes unchallenged, can be carried with the individual for life. The role becomes the template for social interaction, like a pair of eyeglasses you never take off. We will go into greater depth about the long-term effects of the alcoholic system on roles in chapter 3, when we discuss the adult child of the alcoholic.

Rituals. These are customs or family procedures that are used at certain identified times. A ritual can be any behavior carried out in a prescribed way. Here are a few examples of rituals:

- Birthday celebrations

- Martinis before dinner

- Holiday meals with the extended family

- Bedtime stories

- Beer with TV sports

- Summer vacations

- Offering alcoholic drinks to all visitors

Family rituals, healthy and unhealthy alike, are often passed down from generation to generation. They typically contain charged memories and hidden meanings, both positive and negative, that go unnoticed as the rituals stay in place. Again, as with family roles, these family rituals often remain the status quo, accepted without question. You live with them without ever challenging their usefulness or considering that better rituals may exist to suit the needs of your family.

Boundaries. The limits set by individuals, the couple, or the family are called boundaries. The family boundary is the imaginary line drawn around the family group. People's boundaries can have a variety of levels of permeability (the ease or difficulty with which they let things in or out). Michelle's fishbowl analogy is an apt description of the unhealthy boundaries that are often found in the alcoholic family: impermeable family boundary (a tight, rigid, and closed family that people cannot freely move in and out of) and nonexistent interpersonal boundaries (whereby there is no experience of autonomy and choice within the family).

Healthy boundaries tend to be semipermeable, like the walls of a cell in your body. There is fluidity of movement: some things come in and out and not others. This goes for interpersonal boundaries within the family and the family boundary itself. Healthy boundaries are usually an expression of healthy development and growth. If you have a strong sense of yourself as an individual, you will be open to new things, but also able to recognize those things that are unhealthy. Similarly healthy family identity allows family members a solid foothold in individuality and ultimately permits movement in and out of the family.

Hierarchy. This refers to the various pecking orders that are in place in the family. The hierarchy can seem simple when comparing individuals, but families also have subgroups, and the way they all relate to one another can be very complex indeed. In a healthy family context, these hierarchies are predictable, yet flexible. The standard order will have the parents at the top and the kids below. But there can be numerous subtleties. For instance, if the family was going to see the youngest daughter's favorite baseball team for her birthday, the little girl might be deferred to as the expert on the ballpark and the team. Since she is the birthday girl, she might be allowed to set the rules for what and when they eat, and who rides in the front seat. In a healthy system, everyone is allowed to take the lead at some time or another. But it is understood that if an emergency were to come up, the parents would once again be the ones in charge.

All five components of the structure are interrelated, and much overlapping occurs. For instance, it may be a rule in the family that the eldest daughter takes on the role of caretaker when the parents go out to dinner. There may be specific rituals for dinner and bedtime that go along with the new role; and the heightened authority and responsibility represent changes in hierarchy and boundaries respectively.

Process

Process refers to the way families communicate and interact.

Communication. Communication refers to the way information is exchanged. The measure of healthy communication is a mutual understanding between the person who talks and the one who listens. For people to achieve this goal, they must send messages in a clear, direct, and complete manner, and receive them in an open and receptive fashion with little distortion. Communication goes in both directions, so breakdowns can happen on the sender's end or the receiver's, or both. As anyone who has ever played the game telephone knows, the message sent is not always the message received. And in that game, people are mainly dealing with retaining the message. Add denial, defensiveness, anxiety, and guilt to the process and the result can be habitual bad communication. There are many types of communication patterns, including:

- Sending "I" messages (a self-responsible statement) rather than "you" messages (a blaming statement). For instance, "I see things this way" rather than "You always take that view."

- Sending indirect messages such as "My, it is hot outside" when you mean "I am hot and want you to open the window."

- Using assertive language like "My husband is not kind to me and I do not like it" as opposed to passive language such as "It would be nice if I had a kind husband."

- Listening through a negative filter: taking messages and hearing only the bad things. You assume that "Oh, you had a haircut" means the person doesn't like it. The listener filters out positive information or overemphasizes the negative comment.

Interaction. Every family has its own style of interaction. You might understand your own family style quite well, yet make a social blunder in another family setting because that family has a different pattern of social interaction. In your home, teasing might be a way that you show affection; but in another home teasing may be seen as mean. The following are some interaction patterns (they are not necessarily negative or positive):

- A received message makes one family member want to be closer; but when she makes a move for closeness, she is rebuffed.

- After an intimate moment, one partner uses humor to create distance because the closeness feels scary.

- To avoid potential conflict, one person walks away in a wounded manner, which signals the other to cover up anger in order to reassure.

- People fight to avoid painful discussions.

- A child acts up to take the focus off the parents' escalation of conflict, which is heading toward violence.

Stability

Stability refers to the solidity of the foundation for the family, which can be healthy or unhealthy. A stable family system means there is consistency in its structure and consistency in its relationship patterns. This consistency is necessary in order for the family to remain predictable and reliable, two crucial elements that make the healthy family a safe and secure place to develop. If you know what to expect from your family, and the system is healthy, you have the safety and security to experiment and grow.

A healthy family can maintain stability during a crisis, no matter if it comes from inside or outside the family. For example, in a family with a stable system, the routines will continue even after Dad breaks his leg and has to be home for three weeks, demanding care from busy Mom. You can have an external force (broken leg) and an internal force (Mom mad at Dad) and yet the family remains stable.

The unhealthy family may be thrown into chaos and crisis by a traumatic event. The unhealthy family may also be very stable, but the foundation is built on maintaining problems, with the system focused on defense.

Change

The healthy system has the capacity for change. Change is typically brought on by necessity, either by inner family events (a child going away to college, for instance) or by an outside event (the father getting transferred at his job). But even a healthy family will need to go through a bumpy transition as the system changes and is slowly replaced by a modified new version.

Members of the family typically resist change to the system and so the system itself seems to balk at change. The familiar routines and rituals tend to grow roots; habit and expectation are hard to budge. Even if the benefits of the changes are immediately apparent, family members and the system will take some time to adapt to the new situation. As we have already mentioned, if you change one part of the system, you change the whole system.

Four Aspects of the Family System

1. Structure
   - Rules
   - Roles
   - Rituals
   - Boundaries
   - Hierarchy
2. Process
   - Communication
   - Interaction
3. Stability
4. Change

How Does the Drinking Family System Work?

The alcoholic family is ruled—sometimes directly, sometimes indirectly—by the traumas of active alcoholism and dominated by the needs, anxieties, and tensions of the alcoholic. Explanations about the drinking, and everything else, structure the family's core beliefs, behaviors, and development. Nothing is allowed in the alcoholic house that might challenge the dominance of the alcoholic and the maintenance of drinking. The vice grips that hold behavior in place also cripple self-esteem and deep beliefs about the self and reality; they change thought patterns. The result is that, down to the core, each family member is more involved with the alcoholic than with his or her own self. This devastating self-sacrifice ultimately leads to a slowed or even halted development.

There is a great dissonance lying at the heart of the alcoholic family's self-identity: the reality that is most visible and most dominant—the alcoholism that is the central problem of the unhealthy environment and system—is also most vehemently denied. The family turns a false side to the world saying, "There is no problem here, despite what you may have seen. We can handle it." Meanwhile all the members work in an unending vigil to either rescue the alcoholic or to maintain the hazardous living conditions that were created by the inner contradictions upon which the system is built.

Perhaps the most insidious aspect of the alcoholic family system is that the alcoholism is accepted as normal. For many, it's always been there, and it seems it always will be. The drinking is such an intimate part of the family portrait that the members believe the family couldn't or wouldn't exist without it. This core identification with the drinking world makes it extremely difficult to break free of the toxic system that holds the family in place. Since every member must follow the rules to protect the alcoholic, everyone must watch each other and make sure no one slacks off. The peer pressure is devastating.

The inner family relationships are further polluted by the central defense of the alcoholic family: the denial of reality. A system that runs on denial will also tolerate deception: once reality is sacrificed, the resulting vacuum is often filled with lies. The family tends to silently condone the deceptions, as they are extensions of the necessary denial that keeps their integrity safe.

As the alcoholism gets worse, or the behavior becomes more undeniable (job loss, physical abuse, drunk driving), the denial gets even stronger. The family's few outlets are shut down, leading to a completely closed system. No one comes in; no one goes out. The shame at the heart of the alcoholism leads everyone to insist on secrecy, cutting off all possible routes of support and input. The family tries harder and harder to control a situation that at its core is out of control.

Individuals within the family are forced to develop the same disordered thinking as the alcoholic: they are controlled by alcoholism but must deny it in the same breath. Loyalty becomes the central connection of family and friends: "You're either with us or against us!" Each member is taught to believe that any lapse in the loyalty will only make the situation worse. Perceived betrayals are then viewed as the cause of the problem rather than its result. The world shrinks as the list of people who will participate in the deepening levels of denial become fewer. The more the world shrinks, the more pressure there is on the family members. The tensions and anxieties become overwhelming, and the need for an outlet acute.

In the end, the alcoholic family system is rigid and constricting. In the worst case, no one is allowed to make a move without the approval of the alcoholic. Every action must support the drinking. Denial and preservation of the system become so central that reality can no longer be perceived. Any suggestion to change is seen as a threat, any attempt at growth is seen as a hostile act. The family members end up with the deep belief that they cannot challenge the system, that change will be equivalent to death.

Of course the reality is exactly the opposite: the system is death. It is rigid, and unchanging, impedes growth, and requires global denial. The only way out is to leave the system and let it collapse, but this choice goes against everything you have been taught (which is that you don't let go and you don't give up and that the way out is to hold on tighter, exert more control).

Rules

Rules in the alcoholic family tend to be rigid, arbitrary, and organized to protect the core belief that drinking is okay and that there isn't a problem. In the "stable" alcoholic family, which can run for years, these rules become consistent, and are embedded in the system. Here are some examples of rules that allow the alcoholism to continue:

- Drinking is not to be discussed.

- The spouse will cover for the alcoholic at work or at family gatherings.

- The couple will use alcohol to foster a sense of closeness and intimacy.

- No one challenges the system. For example, the husband always gets drunk on holidays, and the family expects and even demands it.

There is often the threat hanging over the family's head that breaking these rules will lead to more drinking: "Don't upset Dad, or he'll drink." Meanwhile, all the rules are constructed to protect the drinking. Either way, the alcoholism is safe from intrusion.

As the drinking behavior escalates and the household gets more and more out of control, the rules, which are supposed to give order, are now used strictly to hide disorder. They become more arbitrary and more spontaneous to counter cracks in the denial. Soon the rules become tangled and indecipherable: what was okay yesterday is a crime today and will be demanded tomorrow. This arbitrariness creates a dangerous and unpredictable atmosphere and leads most family members to more self-protection, and avoidance of the alcoholic at this stage.

In many families, the alcoholic has the role of family dictator, setting down rigid rules and behaviors on a whim—anything to protect the gradually more visible problem. In some cases, the coalcoholic is also a rule maker. The alcoholic gives up dominion to his or her partner as an exchange for the partner's allowing the drinking behavior to remain out of control. A drop in the hierarchy is tolerable so long as the drinking is allowed to continue unhindered.

Everyone participates in making sure the rules are followed. Judith's childhood rules about no noise in the mornings were not only enforced by the parents, but by the children themselves, who didn't want the boat rocked. In a chaotic system, everyone must work to keep things orderly, so that the system can operate unchallenged.

Exercise: Drinking Rules

It's important to clarify the rules that were in place during the drinking stage, as they can be subtle and therefore easily carried into recovery. If drinking rules continue too long, they will slow down healthy growth. It is important to begin to recognize and ultimately challenge and discredit them.

- What were some of the rules that were in place when your family was in the drinking stage?

- What could be talked about? What subjects were taboo?

- Did anyone discuss these rules or were they just understood?

- Who was the rule maker?

- Who was the rule breaker?

- How were the rules enforced, and how were they punished?
- Are any of these rules still in place today?

Write your answers in your journal and date your entry. You may realize at a later date that you have overlooked some things—the past gets clearer the further you go in recovery—so if you feel the need, come back and reassess these questions.

If this exercise or the ones that follow make you feel uncomfortable, skip them and come back to them later. You may not be ready to start dealing with the realities of the drinking stage. That's perfectly natural in early recovery. Take what you need, and leave the rest. The book will be there when you are ready.

Roles

Roles, like rules, hold the alcoholic family members and the system together. These roles are often inflexible, which means family members can be locked into a deep identification with the role and its place in the system. Role challenges or trades may be perceived as a threat to stability and may be punished by all. Again, in an unstable environment, predictable and expected behavior will be clung to by all regardless of the destructive results.

Roles often start off as adaptive, and very often fit the personality of the family member. This only makes distinguishing between the person and the role that much more complicated.

Roles can be one of the most subtle aspects of the family system because they become so much a part of the person who holds the role. In any family, roles are so deeply etched and enduring that when a person leaves home, the role goes along. It's hard for anyone to see role as a function of the family system and not a core identity, but it is especially difficult for the individual in an alcoholic family. Roles have been shaped to support the drinking, so they may be very maladaptive outside, but not easy to recognize or modify.

Brigette, who is now twenty-eight, took on the role of nurturer in her family when she was thirteen. With her parents often unable to handle the duties of parenthood because of their drinking, Brigette stepped in and played the mother not only to her three younger sisters, but also to her parents. This role gave her a deep feeling of value: "Even though things were hectic, I really felt I was an important part of my family. I tried to shield my sisters from what was going on. I was my mother's confidant. I felt special. When they finally quit drinking, I had a really hard time."

When recovery begins, the roles can become outmoded. The one thing that gave Brigette self-esteem through the trauma was then taken away. She ended up feeling like she was demoted.

Exercise: Drinking Roles

This exercise is intended to help you focus on the roles that were performed by your various family members during the drinking stage.

- What role did you play during the drinking stage? You can check the list of roles from earlier in the chapter, or name another role.

- What roles did your other family members play?

It may be hard to think of a family member as playing a role; it might be simpler to ask yourself what was expected of you. What was expected of the other members of your family?

Rituals

Most rituals in the alcoholic family are in place to make room for drinking. Whether it's holidays, birthdays, or sporting events, room is usually made for the alcoholic to get his share of drinking in.

Again, it is important to recognize that in many families this drinking just seems normal. It is expected, even encouraged: "I love Pop at Christmas, when he has a few eggnogs and starts telling those old stories." Drinking as the social relaxer is often the great justification for drinking at parties: "It relaxes me!" Many of the alcoholic family's favorite memories will be centered around drinking and its aftereffects.

A family often defines itself by its rituals. They anticipated with hope and expectation. As the alcoholism becomes more and more problematic, these hopes and expectations can make the rituals the most painful casualties of all. The contrast between the beauty of Christmas and the alcoholic threatening the coalcoholic over the Christmas Eve dinner can be traumatic. The rituals begin to loom as times of dread when something terrible will happen. Slowly the family members must divest themselves of caring about the rituals, until they are hollow events where the drinking rules the entire holiday. The denial is challenged more and more and must increase or crack.

In an alcoholic family there might be one ritual that serves as the alcoholic's "proof of not being an alcoholic." This is a ritual where the alcoholic doesn't drink. In times of trouble, the alcoholic can then point at this ritual and say, "I don't drink then, so I'm not an alcoholic. I have it under control." Of course as things sink lower and lower, even the "dry" ritual will start being invaded by drinking. At that point either the "special" occasion must be justified, or the denial must shift onto another ritual.

Like the Trojan horse, many rituals have a benign package that houses devastating behavior. Since the ritual is not recognized as problematic, it more easily becomes a standard for the next generation, as rituals, like family treasures, are passed on. Alcoholism is also passed down through rituals. Charles, remembers: "We had a cocktail hour just like my parents did. We said it was our time for unwinding. Happy hour. That's a misnomer if there ever was one. But you don't even think about it. Even though my parents fought a lot when I was a kid, I wanted to be just like them. And I was."

Exercise: Drinking Rituals

This exercise is intended to help you focus on the family rituals in place during the drinking stage.

- What were some of the regular family events that were dominated by drinking? How were the holidays organized around drinking?

- What rituals were passed down from generation to generation? Did these carry the drinking with them or was this added?

Boundaries

The interpersonal boundaries in an alcoholic family tend to be overly porous, often resulting in enmeshment, a relationship structure that is too loosely connected; it lacks separateness and individuality. Since the family system must be served at all costs, each member must monitor the rest of the family for any signs of danger, any behavior that might threaten the system. The need to uphold the family loyalty and maintain the family denial leaves everyone working as a single organism to allow the alcoholism to continue unchallenged. The individual's self is sacrificed for the "greater good" of the family system. Growth is stopped. Defensiveness becomes the main style of interaction as no one has a safe boundary within which to relax.

Meanwhile, the boundary that divides the family from the rest of the world is rigid and mostly impenetrable. The only people and information allowed in or out have to be "safe"—not threatening to the status quo. The boundary can also extend to people who support the parent's drinking, often letting unsafe people inside the "trusted" family system. As was mentioned earlier, this can be a dangerous situation for children, when outsiders are treated like family, and the family has no internal boundaries.

As the alcoholism worsens, these boundaries (or lack thereof) get more and more extreme. The chaotic family has no internal divisions anymore, and externally, nothing comes in or goes out. Michelle, who thought of her family as living inside a painted fishbowl, thought at the time that this was just how things worked: "I thought we were all so close, so connected, that we were the ideal family. Sure we had our faults, but we all stood up for one another. It took me many years to realize that you can't have closeness without separation. If you are so concerned with someone else that you ignore yourself, that's not closeness, that's self-sacrifice. You can't support someone if you are leaning on them. When you're in it you just don't see it."

The alcoholic family system is normal for those who are living within it. But as the family boundary shrinks and hardens, and the interpersonal boundaries fall away to nothing, the pressures become unendurable. As children grow and come to understand the depth of their vulnerability, they may begin to consciously press at the rigid boundaries, making the family environment that much more tense. The parents end up being simultaneously intrusive and abandoning.

Exercise: Drinking Boundaries

This exercise is intended to help you focus on your family boundaries during the drinking stage.

- How would you describe the boundaries between you and your family members during the drinking stage?

■ How would you describe the boundary between your family and the world during the drinking stage?

Hierarchy

The hierarchy in the alcoholic family tends to mold to the needs of the immediate situation, and this unpredictability can become quite confusing. The single rule is that any hierarchy that protects the drinking behavior is acceptable. This automatically gives the alcoholic an indirect control, no matter who appears to be in charge. In most cases, the alcoholic is at the top of the food chain, a dictator who makes rules and regulations on a whim. The alcoholic needs to be in control of the family in order to prove that there is no lack of control. But it is also common for the coalcoholic to be the ruler of the family, as the alcoholic gives over the reins to the partner and takes on a more childlike role. The coalcoholic will often rule the house with a bitterness born of resentment. For the alcoholic, this is a small price to pay to keep the drinking going. This shift in hierarchy actually allows some of the drinker's guilt to be assuaged: after all, he or she is being deservedly punished by the hostile partner.

As was mentioned earlier, children often need to be ready to step up to a higher place in the hierarchy in order to keep the house functioning. This promotion also serves as an acceptable trade-off for the parent, and the child is led to feel more important and necessary to the system. The child, however, knows very little security, and taking care of the parents can be an anxious job. The child is not prepared to do everything, but the role makes her try. Kelly remembers having to bail her mother out of jail after a drunk driving incident. "I'm twelve years old and I'm calling bail bondsmen and trying to organize all of her friends to get some money. It was a horrible mixture of humiliation and power. After all, I was being treated as a peer among the adults. They were all real supportive—they all were big drinkers. But I also just felt ashamed, ashamed for my mom, ashamed for me."

When the alcoholic hits bottom, the ensuing shake-up can cause complex problems for the empowered coalcoholic or child. The coalcoholic may have been deriving a great deal of self-esteem from "ruling the house." Without the lowly alcoholic there to take care of, a solid source of self-esteem is gone. Often a person in this role will have a very hard time being supportive of recovery, and will resist joining Al-Anon. The coalcoholic considers him- or herself the savior, and so has a very hard time taking any responsibility for the unhealthy system that was in place.

Similarly, the promoted child will have a hard time going back to being just a kid again. Recovery means that the child eventually must return to being a child, a demotion that can really challenge the important sense of self-esteem that helped the child survive the drinking atmosphere. Also, the child's innocence is lost, so when the family finally puts a healthy hierarchy in place with the parents at the top, the child will have a hard time accepting these flawed people as the leaders. Even after her mother had gone through ten years of sobriety, Kelly had a hard time seeing her as her mother. "I just always automatically felt the need to take care of her. It's in my bones. Until I finally went to therapy and started working on those issues, I just always felt responsible for everything. It's so hard to stop."

The underlying rule of the hierarchy is based on what serves the alcoholism. If a family member holds a place of higher rank, this is easily trumped when the person oversteps the boundaries protecting the drinking. An eight-year-old will pounce on the twenty-year-old who brings up a subject at the dinner table that is known to be "upsetting." This peer-enforcement tends to add to the environment of mistrust and danger. No one is safe, and everyone is making sure it stays that way.

Exercise: Drinking Hierarchy

This exercise is intended to help you focus on how your family's hierarchy was structured during the drinking stage.

- Describe the pecking order in your family during the drinking years.
- Was the hierarchy flexible? Did it change during different situations?
- Did it change over the years? Did it become more chaotic? More rigid?
- What was your place in the hierarchy?

Communication

Whether the communication is direct or indirect, during the drinking stage the underlying context is that all communication is designed to avoid dealing with alcoholism. This is done sometimes consciously, sometimes unconsciously. As with other aspects of the family dynamics, the communication style reflects and supports the system as the system reflects and supports the style of communication.

Typically, the family will have a defensive communication style directed at keeping out any reality that might threaten the precious denial. The drinking itself will probably never be mentioned by name. This defensiveness works in opposition to any real communication. Since there is an underlying environment of fear, most of the individuals merely listen for any threatening information. Any details they will try to communicate will tend to be safe, obscure, or untrue.

For this reason, spontaneity and truth-telling are off-limits. The individuals need to monitor what they say. The central rule of the household—do not upset the system—holds, and since the truth is the most upsetting thing of all, the individuals must choose either lying or careful evasion. This can have very destructive results, as these rigid boundaries soon become internalized, and the thoughts themselves become censored. Any crack in the denial, whether inside or out, must be covered immediately for fear of threatening the system.

In the end, each individual develops the same behavioral and thinking disorders as the alcoholic: being controlled by the reality of alcoholism while simultaneously denying it. To preserve this inherent contradiction, all family members must adapt their thoughts and behavior to fit the family's "story": the explanations that have been constructed to allow the drinking behavior to be maintained and denied at the same time.

This distortion of reality becomes "reality" for the alcoholic family. This is one reason why it becomes so important to revisit the past during recovery and dig out the truth that has been hidden beneath the lies.

Exercise: Drinking Communication

This exercise is intended to help you focus on how your family communicated during the drinking stage.

- Write a list of things you couldn't talk about; then write a list of safe subjects. What did your family talk about when they talked?

- What kind of communication style did your family have? The following are some examples:

    Indirect. Rarely using "I" statements

    Defensive. Shaming and blaming

    Angry. Showing a lot of hostility, whether veiled or out in the open

    Victimized. Mostly taking a passive stance: "She did that to me."

    Closed off. Having few safe topics, and capable of no deep discussion

    Recycled. Telling the same stories and complaints over and over

    Detached. Exhibiting no give-and-take or real listening

    Judgmental. Critical listening instead of receptive and open listening

- If you have the time, try writing a dialogue from the drinking stage. It doesn't have to be perfect, just try to capture your memory of the way family members spoke to one another.

Interaction

The interactions in the drinking stage may be unpredictable or very predictable, but either way they are usually hard to negotiate. Since the rules are built to support the system and not the individual, there is no way a person can trust intuition. Instead, you have to look around for clues to the right way of behaving. Since the rules are always changing and are outside your control, interaction can become stilted, unspontaneous, and generally unhealthy.

One family might be overly tentative, another overly confrontational; one emotional, another emotionless. Either way, there is underlying tension and anxiety at each family's heart. The unspoken truth is expressed in the family's poor communication and interaction, as is the pressure the family feels living under the rigid alcoholic system.

The system does not allow connection, and it does not allow separation. Between the lack of interpersonal boundaries and the lack of open communication, during the drinking stage the family members each become isolated and enmeshed at the same time. This is a confusing situation, especially for the children who are trying to learn the proper skills for negotiating relationships. The end result is that each member feels simultaneously abandoned and intruded upon, and lonely without ever having any time alone.

This choice of extremes means the family members have a hard time finding a comfortable balance of togetherness and separation. Usually, they opt for one or the other. Michelle remembers the impossible blur of extremes: "Whenever I connected with my mom or my brothers, it made me anxious, I was afraid of being comfortable and letting my guard down, so I'd have to pull back. But then when I was alone with my thoughts, I would have this desperate need for company. I was damned if I did and damned if I didn't." Over time this becomes a fine-tuned dance, seeking a tolerable balance between closeness and distance that is based on the heightened need for safety and attachment.

Every relationship is mediated on some level by the alcoholism, even one's relationship to oneself. Family members feel unsafe together and unsafe apart. This leads to a very difficult and stilted interaction between family members who feel completely bonded, but that bond is one of not being able to connect. They are bonded by a system that demands they not get too close, reveal any secrets, or tell the truth that needs to be told.

Exercise: Drinking Interaction

This exercise is intended to help you focus on how your family interacted during the drinking stage.

- ■ Describe your family's style of interaction. What type of dance was there? Was everyone overly friendly and distracted? Was everyone distant and caustic?

Stability

An unhealthy family system tends to be unstable and inflexible and therefore more easily thrown off balance by unexpected or traumatic events. If you grow up inside an unhealthy family system, instead of focusing on your own individual growth, you need to spend your time focused on the surroundings, making sure things remain safe. If there is no safety, you need to be permanently vigilant, protecting yourself; this can result in stunted development.

Joanne, who joined AA seven years ago, recalls the environment in her house when she was drinking constantly: "I could not deal with anything at the height of it. Nothing. All that mattered was keeping things the way they were. It didn't matter what events took place—car accidents, fights, hospitalizations—I just needed things to be the way they were. It was all craziness, but I was locked into it holding on with all my might, afraid of what would happen if I let go."

Change

In the alcoholic family, the lack of healthy stability makes the individuals hold on even tighter to what is familiar. Change is resisted at all costs. There are inner checks and balances that protect the status quo, so any change will be met with heightened anxiety. One of these checks is the shame and self-blame of the family members. The family believes that if the dirty secret got out, they would not survive. This pressure keeps the individuals toeing the line, keeping the system in place at all costs.

The system in the alcoholic family will have to "hit bottom" before significant change can occur. The deepest denial can only be broken down by the stark realization that there is no more air left in the tanks, and you must either swim to the surface or die.

After hitting bottom, the dark period continues. Recovery gets worse before it gets better. Any move toward healthy growth must endure these initial setbacks. The real threat occurs when a family isn't prepared for the difficult reality of early abstinence, they look at the increased chaos and turmoil and suspect that they have done something wrong. The family might be tempted to think that the problem wasn't the alcohol after all. This is partly correct: alcohol is the center of the problem, but it's not the sole focus of recovery. Family recovery entails letting the old family system collapse and living with chaos for a time until a new, healthy system grows into place.

The individuals in an unhealthy system often don't notice that they're participating in keeping the past alive, since much of the system is so familiar. As one former drinker put it, "It's all we knew." This is why it's so important to investigate your family's specific dynamics as you work through recovery. The more you understand why things were the way they were, the more you can keep them from falling back into place.

The Family System in the Drinking Stage

1. The system is unhealthy.

2. Alcohol is the central organizing principle for the family dynamics:

   - **Rules** are in place, often at the whim of the alcoholic/dictator, in order to protect the drinking behavior.

   - **Roles** are performed in order to make the drinking behavior seem normal.

   - **Rituals** all include alcohol in one way or the other, or an alcohol-free ritual is taken as "proof" that there is no drinking problem.

   - **Boundaries** are overly porous within the family and overly rigid outside the family.

   - **Hierarchies** are all in place and rigid, and are defined by the ultimate hierarchy: that anyone who challenges the drinking behavior is ultimately treated as lower than anyone who works to keep the system in place.

3. The family accommodates the unhealthy system by adapting in a defensive way.

4. The defensive adaptations make the system more unhealthy:

   - Because there is little safety, there is often little real **communication**. A clear, open dialogue may not be possible about anything.

   - The **interactions** tend to be black-and-white, polarized.

   - Because there is a rigid battle to uphold a false view of reality, there is little flexibility. **Stability** is maintained by this rigidity and characterized by a short-term crisis focus. Events and behavior are often predictable in that they are unpredictable.

   - There is little or no **change**, except for the possibility of a slow descent for the family. With the unhealthy stability, there is no foundation for healthy change. Everyone resists change anyway; support goes to the system, which demands stasis.

5. The normal process of development, for the individual and the family, is slowed or totally halted.

(Adapted from Brown and Lewis, 1999)

2

"Controlling the Chaos"

Points of View in the Drinking Stage

Now that you have an overview of the way the alcoholic family works during the drinking stage, you can build a clearer view from within by exploring the individual perspectives of each of the family members. If you have lived in an alcoholic family for any length of time, you are probably an expert on the way that world looks and feels: full of tension and anxiety, chaos and inconsistency. But these memories may seem disconnected and confusing. By placing your individual point of view in the context of others' perspectives, you will be able to see the complexity of this disorganized world much more clearly.

A family is made up of individuals. Each individual both defines and is defined by the family. In a healthy family, the system is built to encourage the growth of its members and their freedom to experiment and discover life for themselves. In the alcoholic family, the individuals must sacrifice their growth in order to participate in the group lie: the denial that there is a problem with alcohol in the family. Instead of the whole being greater than the sum of its parts, the parts make themselves lesser to fit into the constricting whole.

Once individuals form a relationship that includes alcoholic drinking, the needs of the alcoholic system will dominate and take precedence over the needs of the individuals, who will be geared increasingly toward the protection and maintenance of the alcoholic system. The alcoholic may have the most direct connection to the disease of alcoholism, but the distorted defensive thinking affects everyone. This is true even in families that do not deny the drinking, and the problems with the drinking. They may experience more overt hostility directly related to alcohol and drug use. Still everyone makes accommodations to a reality that isn't changing.

Within the rigid architecture of the alcoholic family system, the individuals are glued in place. Each member sees—whether consciously or unconsciously—that the situation is out of control. Each looks for a means of protection by either exerting control or retreating to hide. Ultimately these defenses, which are meant to maintain the family relationships, end up squelching development, as the person loses touch with his or her own thoughts and feelings. The individual is thus hollowed out by the unending attention on the family, and ultimately the unsafe system is internalized. The rigidity, the denial, and the defensiveness all become central parts of the identity of each person, forming a false identity that is second nature to the person.

These false self-perceptions are defensive adaptations to trauma, but they eventually become the basis for a lot of unhealthy behavior. Since they are experienced as essential parts of the self, they are very hard to reshape. There is a deeply held belief, even much later in life, that if these defenses are lifted, the person will be threatened by great catastrophe. The potential catastrophe may be many years in the past, but the threat feels immediate.

The Individual in the Drinking Stage

- Maintains unhealthy beliefs, behavior, and emotions to support system
- Sacrifices own development to keep the system in place

Exploring Points of View

Seeing things from another's point of view is tricky, and most family members cannot do so until they have spent some time in recovery. Early on, there is too much threat still in the air for people to listen to one another without defensiveness. Just as the blurred boundaries of the drinking stage make it difficult for the family members to see the alcoholic system at work, the enmeshment or isolation that results from these blurred boundaries makes it hard for one family member to see things from another's point of view. Add poor communication habits and a defensive atmosphere, and no one has a clue about what the others are thinking. It's not uncommon for a family in recovery to be describing a memory of the drinking stage, and one member will say, "I was just sure it was all my fault." The next member will look surprised: "You thought it was *your* fault? I thought it was *my* fault!" and so on down the line. Guilt and shame are emotions that fester in darkness, and as long as the family can't talk openly, the family members each carry unique and distorted views of their own parts in the system.

Seeing reality from another person's point of view can be a very powerful experience, especially when you have had to deny the ability to connect. You might discover that a certain feeling you felt ashamed of was actually shared; or you might discover that an insight you assumed everyone had was actually yours alone. In a healthy family, individuals understand themselves as a fluid mixture of unique qualities and shared ones, resulting in a more or less comfortable balance of separation and connection. But in the alcoholic family, self-assessment can be a choice between extremes: either you felt you were just like everyone and therefore not special at all, or else you considered yourself a freak who was totally set apart from the world.

By understanding the different points of view in the alcoholic family you can begin to explore how each person functioned. It's not unusual to assume someone is crazy when you don't ever get to hear the explanation for that person's erratic behavior. And it is also common to think something is wrong with you when your own behavior seems out of your control. These assumptions and judgments are actually normal consequences of living in an unhealthy family system; one that demands denial of reality and has so much tension that every moment can feel like an emergency. Gaining insight into others' thoughts and behaviors is a valuable step toward becoming comfortable with your family's shared experiences. When the behavior can be explained it becomes much less scary, and instead of only anger and shame, you might find sympathy and understanding.

This is not to say that understanding erases responsibility. In fact, you must understand just how an action came to be to truly take responsibility for it. Understanding also goes a long way toward taking away shame.

By learning about the points of view of others, you will improve your understanding of yourself. Often in the blurry landscape of the alcoholic family, you automatically feel responsible for people's reactions to you. And in this defensive setting, people become extremely sensitive about what is okay to say and do. They readily assume that they are to blame for everything. In recovery, family members start moving away from these instant reactions. They begin to recognize what is "their stuff" and what is "someone else's stuff," a distinction that is central to surviving the early stages of recovery.

Once again, we must remind you that the recollections in this chapter may be challenging, especially if you have not yet shaped a strong support for recovery. Self-exploration is not something that comes easily. Don't push yourself. One of the goals of healthy growth is to trust your own capabilities. Wherever you are is where you need to be. At the same time, you don't have to pull back on the reins the entire time either. Think of the baby who is transitioning from crawling to walking. She pushes up against the limits, crying from frustration and trying again. She is not ashamed of her lack of mastery; she is following her natural urge to grow and develop.

"I Am an Alcoholic"—Bill Remembers the Drinking Stage

"For me, it crept up slowly," says Bill, who drank from the time he was fifteen years old until he finally went into recovery at the age of forty. "It was something I liked to do. All my friends did it. I drank in college. I drank after work. Drinking was just a part of my life. I probably had a problem with alcohol for most of my adult life: I needed the drinks, but I never would have said that at the time. It's what I did. It's what my dad did."

Alcoholism can start subtly, with nonproblematic drinking. But once you start to need the alcohol in order to function, then it is alcoholism. "Somewhere along the line, the drinking really got out of hand. I had a job that was causing me grief, my marriage was in trouble, the kids were always screaming. To me, it made sense that I needed a few drinks now and again. It never dawned on me that maybe all of these things that made me drink were actually caused by my drinking."

Denial

The denial deepens as the drinking gets more and more out of control. When the distortion of reality is firmly in place, the alcoholic's entire world is framed by the drinking. "When I look back, I can see that there just came a time when everything shifted, and my whole life became about when and how I could drink: how I was going to hide it, how I would explain it if I got caught. It was like a secret agent movie, only the secret agent was a complete jackass. You think you're so cunning from the inside of a drunk. I still get a chill every now and again when I see someone at a party or a ballgame who thinks he's 'having the time of his life' and he's really just acting all pathetic and sad. I think, 'That was me so many times: the smeared face, the glassy red eyes, the threatening behavior even when you're happy.' But back then I just figured I knew how to have a good time. I was a drinker; I wasn't a drunk. Drunks have to drink. I just liked it a lot."

Bill was clinging to two false beliefs: "I am not an alcoholic" and "I have control over my drinking." Any doubts were pushed out of consciousness, and the "false self" took over. He truly came to believe his perceptions of himself. He "knew" there was no problem. Any complaints that were coming from the world around him were seen as the problem of the complainer. "My wife would start asking me to come home earlier from work. She said she was worried, but I told her there was nothing to worry about. I needed to unwind. When she pushed it, I'd lose it. How dare she tell me how to live, when she spends my money at the grocery store, when I have never caused her any trouble, never hit her, never did anything real bad. I would say anything to get her off my back. It was like poking around until I found the sore spot. And the second she caved in and the coast was clear, I'd give in, too. 'We need to spend more time together,' I'd say. I'd be real cuddly. Anything to keep the focus off my drinking." The need for alcohol may be outside of the alcoholic's awareness, but his behavior betrays it. Bill ended up manipulating every situation to keep the drinking out of sight of his family. He saw his actions as sensitive to his family's needs. Indeed, he needed to be sensitive in order to protect his drinking.

> The alcoholic believes that there is no alcoholism and that the drinking is under control. In order to keep this false belief intact, he seeks to control the surroundings, dismissing them if they don't join him. The rest of the family has to bend their beliefs to make the behavior at home seem normal.

Control

What started out as subtle manipulation slowly turned into total control of the household. At first, Bill needed to shape the family rules to operate in the way he needed them to operate. But gradually, the family shaped itself around Bill's drinking. He held dominion without having to say anything. Bill's wife tried her best to keep things under control by watching Bill and trying to keep things safe for the kids. But soon her vigilance spread to the kids. Bill is sympathetic now, but was totally oblivious then. "Basically I was trying to control everything, while at the same time being totally out of control. My wife was trying to control me, to protect the kids and herself and me. But she wasn't going to control me any more than I was going to control my drinking. And my kids? My kids didn't know what the hell was going on."

Bill and his wife came to enjoy the illusion of control. "It'd be like a guy standing by Old Faithful and every hour saying 'Alakazam!' and up pops the geyser. But the guy isn't controlling anything; he just knows how the geyser works so it seems like he's making the geyser spout. You can go a long time living under the belief that you are in control if you can anticipate your needs."

Bill did fine for a while—as long as he could keep up the veneer that his needs were his desires. If anything cropped up to get in the way, he would meet it with an excuse or a defensive stance. "When the stuff got more out of control, or when I did something inexcusable like cracking up the car or screaming at the neighbors, I would become the penitent around the house. I'd help out more. Show I was sorry. Partly I'd be thinking, 'Look, if I can be sorry, it proves I'm not a drunk.' I'd try to be the good dad, stepping in to help the kids get to sleep. Then I'd say, 'See? I don't have a problem.' I really believed that if I could be attentive to my kids, it meant I wasn't an alcoholic. The stuff I told my wife, the lines I drew in the sand, saying, 'This far and no farther'—I believed it all. I needed to have rules to prove I wasn't drinking. But when I look back honestly now, I can look at every little thing I did as somehow being attached to the drinking, trying to prove I wasn't a drunk, or trying to cover up the evidence that I was. I would rationalize all my evasions by telling myself that my wife was just overly worried. I knew I wasn't a drunk, but I needed to hide the drinking so my wife wouldn't get upset. When she gave me a hard time, I'd sometimes nod a lot and point out how things were not as bad as she thought. But the second I thought she was getting too close, I would go off. I was one pure ball of defense."

The vicious circle is joined as control is sought through the bottle, the very source of the loss of control. "My life was spinning out of control, and the only place I felt comfortable, like I had it all together, was inside a good drunk. The more things fell apart, the more I needed to drink to feel better; and the more I drank, the more things fell apart."

Alcoholism is a disease that is centered on control. The central truth that the alcoholic can't face is that he or she has lost control over the drinking and is ruled by the need to drink. Without drinking, the alcoholic cannot function. This loss of control, as you have seen already and will see throughout this book, is the deep, dark secret of the alcoholic family, and it must be hidden from the world. On a conscious level, the alcoholic has hidden this truth from him- or herself. Doubts may occasionally creep in, but by simply relying on the rational mind the alcoholic can always find a way out. There were a few times after bad episodes when Bill would wonder if it was possible that he was an alcoholic. But he had a foolproof rationalization: "If I am wondering whether I'm an alcoholic, then I'm not one, because a real alcoholic is so out of control, he never questions his drinking." Again, the illusion of control protects the drinking.

Deflecting the Problem

A significant way the alcoholic compensates for losing control over the drinking is by exerting as much external control as possible. As you saw in chapter 1, the alcoholic family is made up of rigid and constricting rules that keep the family in place, protecting the alcoholic from any intrusion of spontaneity or truth. Bill could not control himself, so he compensated by trying to control his family.

The irony of course is that the only person over whom you can really exert any level of control is yourself, but when you're an alcoholic, this is precisely the person who is out of control. In order to hide this, the alcoholic will use any number of deflecting behaviors to make others overlook the real problem and take on responsibility for the situation, including blame, aggression, and self-pity.

Blame

Bill would always point to others as the cause of any problems with drinking. "I thought, 'If I did overdo it last night, it's because the kids were driving me crazy.' Or my wife was giving me a hard time. I was desperate not to show where the real reason lay. In recovery, I realized that blaming others is just a diversionary technique. It's a defense that you instinctively throw up when you're afraid you're going to be found out."

Aggression

Bill would attack in order to defend. This is a particularly confusing action for children, who look to themselves as the cause of the anger. "I remember exploding at my youngest daughter for cracking a dish. She was in there trying to help with the kitchen stuff and the dish fell and I went nuts, screaming, 'Why do you do this to me? Don't you respect me?' In my mind I just thought no one knew how hard I had it. If they did, they would be taking better care of me. Of course, they all were doing more than they should to take care of me. But it was never enough for me.

Self-Pity

Another way Bill tried to divert any responsibility for the family situation was by using what he calls the "poor me" plea for sympathy. "My trump card was always the stance that no one understood me. My life was so hard. No one understood the pressures I was under. I was so alone. Once this sunk in and I got the sympathy I needed, I could calm down."

These different styles of behavior are not necessarily conscious. Most of the reactions of the alcoholic are impulsive, defensive reflexes, like covering a wound. The self-protection gets put into place and any threat must immediately be dealt with and solved by whatever means necessary. This is part of the reason that the behavior is so erratic and unpredictable: the alcoholic will do anything to protect the drinking and has no eye toward anyone but him- or herself.

Bill recollects a sense of helplessness that he was unaware of at the time. "When something happened to me, I would just immediately have to act. It was necessary. I see now that it felt out of my control. But when it was happening, it just felt like conviction; a certainty that I was right and that I had something important to protect. Those instinctual defenses become the core of you. You believe you are protecting the most precious thing on earth, when, in reality, you are protecting this demon that is slowly ruining everything that is truly precious."

Ruled by Impulse

During the drinking stage, the alcoholic is a creature of pure impulse. (Often the partner and children are, too.) The alcoholic's need for alcohol is primary and the rest of his life is ruled by a system that seeks to allow for this need. Most of the behavior that protects the drinking becomes instinctual: the moment a threat is identified, the alcoholic reacts. There is no conscious mediation between perception and action. This style of interaction makes for a very unstable and dangerous environment. Since there is no conscious deliberation for the alcoholic, the person who steps out of line and "causes" the alcoholic's bad behavior is automatically blamed. At least this was Bill's logic. He remembers a phrase he used all the time: "You know how that upsets me!" He'd blame the results of his own lack of control on the person he believed triggered his outrage.

His impulsive behavior also led to his need to be right in even the tiniest discussion. "I needed to have an opinion about everything. I look back now and see myself as having to nail down every loose thought into a rigid worldview, and everyone had to agree with me. We would go on and on, fighting over the slightest thing, and as far as I was concerned, anything went. If you didn't agree, you would be belittled." If you are arguing only to win, there is no communication. The family would stick up for what they thought, but after a while, it was easier to let Bill have his way. What appeared to be a discussion of ideas was really a battle for control. Bill's impulsive need to protect his ideas made it impossible for him to see that he had ulterior motives in these "discussions." "It's so hard to see when you are doing it. I was just certain I was right. That was my experience of these arguments. Looking back, it seems more like I wouldn't allow myself to be wrong. No argument ended until you either agreed with me or I ridiculed you into unimportance." Bill, like many alcoholics, used the skills he'd learned to protect his alcoholism to become an expert arguer, twisting and turning logic and rationalizing any point of view that he had taken for his own. But underneath the faulty logic lay an unbridled impulse for self-protection.

One of the problems with acting on impulse is that only one person is allowed to do it at a time. Unless someone gives in, the impulses will clash with one another. In the alcoholic family, the other family members learn to protect the alcoholic's impulses. Soon this protection itself becomes impulsive. The entire household ends up being hardwired, with everyone ready to leap into action to protect the family system. No one has any control. The alcoholic's behavior is based on his impulse to hold on to the bottle, and the family's behavior is based on their impulse to hold on to the alcoholic.

The Developmental Model of Recovery— The Drinking Stage

One way of looking at the ongoing growth of recovery is to think of it in relation to the development of an infant. At the stage of active alcoholism, the alcoholic acts purely on impulse. This is very similar to the way a newborn experiences things. When a newborn experiences an impulse, he acts upon it; there is no consciousness to mediate between impulse and action.

The process of recovery is modeled after the healthy growth of a child. As a child grows, he slowly learns to mediate his impulses. Language acts as a wedge between impulse and action, giving consciousness a tool to help the toddler choose whether to act or not to act. As a child grows, the instincts don't change so much as they are mediated by conscious thought.

In recovery, it is much the same. You don't seek to destroy the impulse to drink; instead, you put a wedge between the impulse and the action. At first, the wedge is paper thin and extremely fragile, but over time and with hard work, you build up the mediation between the impulse and the action until you can choose your life for yourself. You don't control your instincts, you choose your reaction to them. In the end you can experience your instincts without needing to act upon them. This is what occurs in the maturation of a child.

The Alcoholic in the Drinking Stage

The alcoholic's primary focus is alcohol.

Behavior

- Loss of control

- Repeated efforts to gain control

- Dominated by impulsive behavior

Thinking

- Ruled by defenses (including denial, rationalization, projection, grandiosity, and a sense of omnipotence), which become a "false self" that hides the loss of control

- Organized around the maintenance of core beliefs: "I am not an alcoholic" and "I can control my drinking"

Emotional Expression

- Unemotional or overemotional

- Seeks to control or express emotion through alcohol

- Experiences emotional disturbances that may be a cause or a consequence of the drinking, or may exist separately

(Adapted from Brown and Lewis, 1999)

Loyalty and the Alcoholic Funnel

Though the alcoholic may seem to place great importance on the support of friends and family, the major trait that has real value to him is loyalty. This loyalty is not built on respect or love (though the alcoholic will use these terms to pressure loyal behavior out of the family member); it is based on the family members' unhealthy willingness to participate in the bad behavior or support it by looking the other way. In essence, the alcoholic needs people who will collaborate or whom he can control. As the alcoholism gets worse, the pool of loyalists shrinks. "I used to divide the world into 'us' and 'them,'" recalls Bill. "And the 'usses' were dying out quickly. I'd have to rally my team every once in a while, like a captain on a sinking ship: 'Everyone has turned against us, but we don't care,' I'd say. 'We're a family. We stick together.' The truth of it was more like, 'You're my family, so you have to support me.' People were getting crossed off my list left and right. No one was good enough to be let in. The defenses were just getting tighter and tighter."

Outside the family, the world is too big to control. "You try to stay on top of the perceptions of others. But if they start to suspect, or look at you strangely, they are no longer loyal and can't be trusted. The world starts to shrink away, or rather, the alcoholic shrinks the world to a size that can be controlled—which gets smaller and smaller. The more out of control the inner world is, the more the outer world must be controlled, and therefore the smaller the outside world becomes. You start cutting out friends, activities, anything that might threaten the drinking." It's like a funnel: the wide mouth accommodated the healthy life from long ago, and the alcoholic life slowly squeezes the family into the cone, which tapers inward to a tiny spout. Soon the alcoholic has only the family, and the pressure of this closed system creates even greater tension. The family is called upon to renounce the outside world altogether; anything short of this would be a betrayal of the alcoholic. "Everything at the end was loyalty or betrayal," says Bill. "I was desperate to hold on to what I had. The world was falling away, and as far as I could tell it was the world's fault. Inside I was desperate and scared out of my mind, but on the outside I was angry, and crazy, and I just started drinking like there was no tomorrow. And there wasn't one."

The Clenched Fist

The alcoholic's core beliefs alter all psychological processes. The self is reduced to smaller and smaller confines. Think of trying to protect something in the palm of your hand by closing your fingers. The more you perceive danger, the more you clench the hand, until it becomes a fist. But two strange things have happened here. First, the hand is now fist, which is for hitting. Though the intention is protective, the protection has become aggressive. The second thing that has happened is that whatever was being protected is now being crushed at the center of the fist. As the perceived threat gets greater and greater, the defenses get greater and greater until the defenses are all that is left. The thing being protected is forgotten. The self is reduced to a defensive posture—the false self.

The alcoholic's false self becomes more and more difficult for the family to live with. Bill would fluctuate between making intolerable rules for the family (to prove his control and further protect himself from suspicion) and seeking to befriend the family by letting them get away with anything and finding other ways to invite them into the "wonderful" shell he had created.

Tyranny and Vulnerability

If the alcoholic appears from the outside to be a fist of aggression, it's easy to overlook the fact that he is being crushed by his own grip. The alcoholic, who is out of control, sees the world as out to get him. Bill remembers it. "I was just a ball of defenses. I always thought I was being attacked. I took everything personally. I felt I had to; I never knew when the threat was coming, so I expected it everywhere." Instead of hearing the words of a harmless statement as they were meant, Bill analyzed them for any signs of judgment. The family became more and more careful about what they said to him. Soon he was even more isolated from them.

The drinker, who seems omnipotent and unflinchingly convinced of his righteousness is actually covering up vulnerability and pain.

It's hard to recognize that aggression is a defensive posture when you live in a system built on defense. The alcoholic attacks to keep from being attacked using exaggeration, justification, guilt, and blame as weapons. Emotions and actions are so closely linked in the alcoholic system that one person's aggressive behavior triggers another's reaction in a flash, and soon the situation is out of control. You never have the time to step back and see that the person attacking is terribly worried about not having control. The tyrant beats you down so you won't threaten him. The aggressor never gets the sympathy he is craving, and so knocks you back as if to say he doesn't need it. The aggressor doesn't even know your defense is operating, he just feels attacked and hurt.

Everyone's defenses become so impenetrable, and the alcoholic so seemingly powerful, that it is impossible for anyone to recognize that he is fighting a losing battle. The alcoholic can't see it because he is so convinced he is right. The family can't see it because they are too resentful or beaten down. The denial goes on. Each family member thinks the problem is his or hers alone, and the alcoholic encourages them in this thinking.

When the alcoholic goes into recovery, the slate is not instantly wiped clean. In fact, the family commonly reacts by letting all its pent-up resentment come spilling out. The tyrannized family members feel like they've been duped. The dictator is shown to be powerless, even pathetic; the years of pressure and anxiety seem even more grievous.

As we pointed out earlier, in order to view the drinking stage with any objectivity, you need to have some distance and a lot of work in recovery. Whether you're a recovering alcoholic or a family member of one, if you are still looking for someone to blame, you have a ways to go.

Exercise: "I am an Alcoholic
in the Drinking Stage . . ."

The purpose of this exercise is to gain some insight into the alcoholic's perspective when he or she was still drinking. If you are the alcoholic, the purpose is to explore the thoughts and feelings you had about yourself back then.

■ In your journal, describe the alcoholic's behavior. How did the alcoholic rationalize the behavior? How did the alcoholic put off blame on others? You can write as much or as little as you like. If you feel like it, you can write a story about an event you remember. If you are the alcoholic, imagine what someone else might have thought about you.

If you have a hard time getting started, think about some of the themes in this section: control, denial, loyalty, manipulation, and vulnerability. Don't worry about capturing the absolute truth as it happened. Just write it as you recollect it. Historical accuracy is not the goal; writing down your perceptions is.

■ Now describe how you felt when the behavior you just recalled was performed. Did you feel scared, angry, sad, or a combination of these emotions? Did you rationalize the alcoholic's behavior? Again, if you are the alcoholic, think back on how you felt about yourself during this period.

■ Now, instead of recalling the emotions you felt in the past, describe how you presently feel about the drinking stage. Do things make more sense when viewed from a distance?

Remember to date these entries. As you work through recovery, you may want to come back to this exercise and see how your perceptions have changed. As you gain perspective on the recovery process, you will see the past more and more clearly, and with these changes in perception you might discover changes in your attitudes toward the past.

If it is too early to focus on these issues, you can come back later and try out this exercise. Throughout this book, feel free to read what you want, do what you feel you can, and come back for the rest later.

"I Am a Coalcoholic"—Joan Remembers the Drinking Stage

Joan liked to drink with Bill in the early days. He was always so animated, so cheerful when he'd had a few. He had a tendency toward dark moods, and she always worried about his anxiety, so she believed it when he claimed that he needed a few beers to relax. She was not aware how deep that need went. "It was complicated for me, because I was pretty much his drinking cheerleader for a good many years. When it got worse, I never felt I could confront him, because I had held his hand right into the trouble. I felt guilty. I mean I bought everything he said. I had his beer waiting for him when he got home. It was our routine; it worked fine. I figured if he was relaxed, then I was relaxed."

Codependency

Joan is describing the central element of the coalcoholic relationship, which is also called the codependent relationship. She had founded her thoughts and feelings on Bill's thoughts and feelings. In order for her to feel happy, she needed him to feel happy. It is very easy to fall into this trap; after all, most of the problematic behavior looks altruistic and thoughtful. "I grew up in a family where I was the oldest kid and I have always just naturally taken care of people. I've always thought it's what I did best. So I slid into the role of caretaker with no problem. I think on some level I enjoyed being needed."

Coalcoholism is alcoholism in relationship. Because your actions are organized around the alcoholic's actions, you begin to internalize the same unhealthy thinking as the alcoholic. You want to believe that you have control over the drinker and that there is no alcoholism and no alcoholic relationship. "I just looked at it as my lot to take care of my husband. I never saw it as an addiction in itself. But that's what it was. The center of my life was a man who was out of control, and I did everything I could to fix him."

Denial

Whereas Bill's denial was focused on the drinking, Joan's denial lay in her perception of Bill. "Even though life got bad, I woudn't admit it was out of control. Maybe Bill was losing it, but there was always something more I could do: I didn't talk to him enough, I didn't keep the kids quiet, I didn't compliment him enough. Of course I know now that no amount was enough. A huge realization that almost knocked me to my knees a few months into recovery was that by working to fix Bill's bad behavior, I was rewarding it. I was as addicted to Bill as he was to the alcohol."

Joan had become "addicted" to the alcoholic. This means that, just as Bill's central focus in life was the drinking, Joan's central focus became Bill, to the exclusion of all else. She had no awareness of the depth of her dependence. She always saw her actions as necessary: she was taking care of the kids; she was protecting the family. There was always another excuse that had nothing to do with her attachment to Bill and his drinking. "But in the back of my mind, I was constantly monitoring how what I did would affect Bill: 'What would he do if he heard this?' or 'How could I deliver the bad news without upsetting him?' Without ever trying to, I ended up being his collaborator. It was my job to make life easy for him. It was my job to make the alcoholism work."

Joan began to work with Bill to make the household safe for his drinking. This was a subtle process, but slowly the house rules became focused around insuring a drinking space for Bill. "I looked at it as self-protection. I guess on some level I knew Bill's drinking had gotten out of hand, so I figured that it was my duty to keep it from harming the kids. So I tried to create a buffer between Bill and them so no one would get hurt. I was scared because everything was out of control. I thought if I could take over, then everything would be all right. But that's not how things worked out. Things just got worse, and in many ways I became as bad as Bill."

False Motives

Joan tried to hide the situation from the children. "I told myself I was protecting them, but I was protecting me. I didn't want them to know what was happening; I thought it would be best for them. But I was really trying to hide the shameful situation from them. What would they think if they knew? I focused on how painful it would be for them, but the pain I feared was my own." So the secret goes underground and no one dares speak its name. Even though Joan saw that she had different motivations than her husband, and even though she thought she was protecting the children, in the end Joan was colluding with Bill. She had internalized the same alcoholic thinking that Bill used. She believed that she could control her husband, and that she was not overly focused on him. But it was clear that her every move worked to help Bill make his world safe for drinking.

One way denial is kept in place is through false motives. Joan believed that she was hiding things to protect her children, when in fact she hid them to protect herself. "When denial has sunk in, you even hide the truth from yourself." Motives can seem clear and pure and yet the behavior can still be working toward a negative end. In actuality, the motive is really a rationalization. You need to act in a certain way, so you tie the action to a positive motive. But in fact, the motive doesn't lead to the action, the underlying need does, and the false motive hides the need.

Impulses

In the same way that Bill's behavior was impulsively based on his need to protect his drinking, Joan's behavior was based on her need to rescue Bill. This is the centerpiece of the alcoholic relationship: shaping yourself to the needs of the others until your instincts are centered on theirs. A chain of impulse-driven action is set up between the two individuals: Bill acts on the impulse to drink; Joan acts on the impulse to protect Bill. There is no room for the mediation of choice or self-assessment; the impulses are joined together in one fluid act that binds the partners to one another. The chain of command starts at the bottle and the alcoholic's urge to drink, which then triggers an instinctual reaction in the coalcoholic to cover up the drinking. Both Joan and Bill became strangers to their own inner thoughts and feelings, being entirely tied to these rigid connections to external objects. "We were glued together; he moved, then I moved, then he moved. There was no break. You started to believe everything you did had a certain inevitability, because that's how it felt; but it wasn't that everything was inevitable, it was that it was controlled by something outside yourself. That's no way to live."

This "impulse chain" creates an extremely tense environment for the family. The defenses are constantly on and everyone is extremely sensitive. Attack leads to defense and defense leads to attack without so much a thought. The same arguments are hashed out again and again. "I remember a key thought was, 'I just can't let him get away with that one.' But that was precisely what I had to do. I had to realize that it was not my job to let him or not let him. The second I saw that I could let him get away with something was the second that things started to change for me. I always needed him to understand the way I saw things. But he had to disagree, which locked me into trying to convince him. I was rewarding bad behavior. The second I realized I didn't need him to agree, that was huge. It finally struck me that he wasn't listening to me; he was protecting himself. All that time I had just been yelling at the wall."

A Shift in Power

The relationship between the coalcoholic and the alcoholic is like a dance, with the alcoholic taking the lead. As the coalcoholic senses that the alcoholic is stumbling, he or she tries to keep the dance going. Oftentimes the alcoholic will get so bad that the coalcoholic will have to take over the lead. This can be a satisfying move for the coalcoholic, who finally gets recognition for keeping the dance going. "There was a moment when Bill was really getting bad. He finally said he couldn't handle it anymore and that I would have to be in charge. At the time I thought things would change. The king was dead—long live the queen."

But the change in power dynamics can open the floodgates of resentment as the coalcoholic finally lets the anger fly. "It was horrible. I just laid into him in front of the kids, and he just let it go. It felt so good to be freed; it was like I had no guilt because I could finally talk. But things didn't really get better; the tyrant just changed names." Expressing the resentment may make the partner feel better about the years of accepting the bad behavior. However, it does not change the relationship itself, but just its outward appearance. Joan was still completely focused on Bill, and Bill on his drinking. Bill traded his place atop the family hierarchy to buy some more time.

The Coalcoholic in the Drinking Stage

The coalcoholic's primary focus is the alcoholic.

Behavior

- Doomed efforts to control the alcoholic and others in the family
- Impulsiveness that may dominate actions

Thinking

- Dominated by defenses (including denial, rationalization, and projection), which become a "false self" that hides the loss of control
- Organized by the maintenance of core beliefs: "I am not a coalcoholic" and "I can control the alcoholic"

Emotional Expression

- May be unemotional or overemotional
- Denies, displaces, or projects emotions
- Feels depression, anxiety, fear, and rage

(Adapted from Brown and Lewis, 1999)

Resistance to Recovery

The coalcoholic can have as much difficulty with recovery as the alcoholic does. In fact, the need to take care of the alcoholic can continue into the alcoholic's recovery. The coalcoholic doesn't recognize that by focusing on the alcoholic's abstinence, the coalcoholic is still carrying over the alcoholic thinking that was the foundation of the unhealthy family system.

Joan's view of herself as the dutiful, long-suffering, overlooked hero made it very difficult for her to face the ways in which she participated in the system. She had gained a lot of self-esteem from taking care of Bill, protecting her family, and running the household. The possibility that this behavior was as problematic as the drinking—that by trying to fix things she was actually making them worse—was impossible for her to imagine. Joan had strong ambivalence: "The reality of my own part in the matter was really hard to face. I'm still trying to put that in place."

As Bill got better, Joan felt a great deal of resistance to his recovery. The end of alcoholism can actually be a threat to the coalcoholic, for as the alcoholic gets better, the coalcoholic is left stranded. Bill's powerlessness had become a source of power for Joan. When Bill quit drinking, the balance of the relationship changed. Joan suddenly felt adrift. Though the drinking had stopped, her need for the drinking behavior continued. Suddenly she was faced with her own problems, including her need for a weak partner. She became especially cruel and blaming to Bill, yelling about how her life had been ruined by his drinking. His improving health was actually a threat to her; without the external focus, the hole at the core of her identity was exposed to view. At first, Joan dismissed outright the thought that she needed help.

But then, "I finally lost it one day: breaking things, screaming. He was just standing there. The kids were crying, and I realized who was carrying on the problem. That was so hard to see. Suddenly everything I had done up until then seemed like a lie. I went to Al-Anon that day."

Exercise: "I Am a Coalcoholic in the Drinking Stage . . ."

This exercise will focus on the perspective of the coalcoholic during active alcoholism. If you are the coalcoholic, you will be exploring the thoughts and feelings you had about yourself during the drinking stage.

- Describe the coalcoholic's behavior. How did the coalcoholic rationalize the behavior? How did the coalcoholic help justify the alcoholic's behavior? If you are the coalcoholic, imagine what someone else might have thought about you.

If you have a hard time getting started, think about some of the themes in this section: codependency, denial, false motives, impulse, and resistance. Don't worry about capturing the absolute truth as it happened. Just write it as you recollect it.

- Now describe how you felt about the coalcoholic when the behavior you've just recalled occurred. Did you feel scared, angry, sad, or a combination of these emotions? Did you rationalize the coalcoholic's behavior? Again, if you are the coalcoholic, think back on how you felt about yourself during this period.

■ Now, instead of recalling the emotions you felt in the past, describe how you presently feel about the coalcoholic's experience of the drinking stage. Do things make more sense when seen from a distance?

Remember to date these entries. As you work through recovery and gain more insight into the past, your perceptions will change.

If it is too early to focus on these issues, come back later and try out the exercise. Don't force yourself if you're not ready.

"I Am a Child of an Alcoholic"—Holly, Julie, and Bill Jr. Remember the Drinking Stage

Holly, Julie, and Bill Jr. (who are now twenty-eight, twenty-five, and twenty, respectively) all grew up being shaped by the pressures of their father's drinking and their mother's coalcoholism. When Holly and Julie were very young, Bill's drinking still seemed to be under control, and Joan successfully collaborated to keep any problems from flowing down to the children. Everything changed with the birth of Bill Jr.

Holly is the only child who has a vivid memory of the good old days. "No matter what happened to Mom and Dad, no matter how crazy everything got, I thought of them as the happy couple when I was little. To me, something changed, and if something changed, you could change it back. I longed to go back to the time before, when everything was good. I think this was my primary drive as a kid: to make things all right so we could go back to the way things were."

Julie was too young to have a clear view of the "time before the drinking," but she and Holly were bonded together from the start. "I had a sense very early that I just needed to be good. If I was good enough, then maybe things would get better. Holly really took care of me back then. It could get scary, so we'd just try really hard to make things better. She was the little mommy, and I was the little star. Billy was never included very much."

Bill Jr. never knew any other way for the family to be, since his father's drinking took a turn for the worse around the time he was born. In fact, Bill Jr.'s birth was the upset in the "stable" alcoholic system that threw things out of balance. Try as she might, Joan couldn't be as vigilant with Bill now that she had an infant to care for. Holly saw the connection: "Billy had it really hard. We were brutal to him. In our eyes, everything was fine until he came along. Mom suddenly didn't have any time for us, and Dad just got more out of control. Dad never said as much but we could see that he was under so much pressure and we just wanted to help him. It was never really a conscious thing, but we froze Billy out, punishing him for ruining the family."

Adaptation and Attachment

In Bill Jr. the two girls had a problem to focus on that distracted them from the real problem. In this way they joined in the family's distorted view of reality:

drinking is not a problem, so the issues must lie elsewhere. In their eyes, their parents had been upset by the new child and so the new child was the problem. Children will go a long way to maintain a view that their parents are good and that their dangerous world can be saved.

All children adapt to their environment, and their development is shaped by the particular environment to which they belong. The environment of blame and self-protection was natural for Holly and Julie, so it was natural to blame the new problems on their younger brother. Their parents' denial, which had already been a subtle but deeply formative influence on the girls' perceptions, became more pronounced after Bill Jr.'s arrival.

Even Bill Jr. came to believe that he was the source of the problems. As Bill Jr. was growing up inside the tightening alcoholic world, he acted out. "For as long as I could remember, I was 'the little handful.' I was out of control. Whatever happened, I was somehow in the middle of it. I was beating kids up at school, breaking stuff at home. I was told that I was destined for big trouble when I was old enough to find it, and I didn't disappoint. It wasn't until I went into recovery for my own drinking that I could look back and see that I was fulfilling expectations way back then. The family needed a distraction and I needed attention. That's a brutal mixture." The family members expected him to behave badly—and the system needed him to—so he did. The blame, which was unspoken by his parents and occasionally shouted out by his sisters, became Bill Jr.'s way of seeing himself. "When you think you're bad, then you're bad. It's a lot easier to see yourself as the problem than to see your world as the problem. You can't control the world."

All children need a close human bond—what is called a "primary attachment"—in order to survive. The preservation of this bond is of utmost importance to the development of the child. Any threat or disruption in the parent-child bond will cause tremendous fear and anxiety in a child. In a healthy family system, the parent-child bond is structured to meet the needs of the child; but in the alcoholic family system, the parent-child bond is set up to support the parent. Holly, Julie, and Bill Jr., each in their own way, were supporting the parents by acting in ways that took the pressure off the real problem: the drinking. Alcohol was the family's central organizing principle; everything else—including the children—was secondary. The parents would pay lip service to the children's security, but only after Joan felt Bill was protected, and only after Bill felt his drinking was protected.

Children's Roles

As you saw in chapter 1, in order to preserve the attachment in an alcoholic family, the individual members of the family often adapt by taking on various roles that are necessary and adaptive, but also unhealthy. Children are master contortionists, bending themselves and their view of reality to maintain the belief that their parents are good. When the members of the family have fixed roles, then behavior is predictable, and rarely spontaneous. The controlling alcoholic family system encourages predictability, because it perceives anything unknown as a threat. Also, because the family is often so chaotic, these roles provide some much-needed stability.

Holly had the role of the hypervigilant caretaker. "I was my mom's confidant. It was understood between us that I was in charge of taking care of 'the kids.' This started when I was ten years old. I thought it was pretty cool, like I was one of the adults. My mom and I were like buddies. But it was always on her terms. When she needed me I was there. But if I needed her she was always under too much pressure. Anything I needed, she always made it seem like it would be the last straw. After a while I stopped asking. I just made sure the kids behaved. I was on guard. I didn't want the camel's back to break."

Julie retreated into the distracted world of the perfectionist. She was so focused on her schoolwork that the rest of the family fell from her sight. "My success at school was a source of pride for my father. Looking back, I think he thought of it as proof that things weren't that bad in our house if I was doing so well in school. He would hold me up as proof of the family genes. School was my escape." Julie was not only Bill's favorite, she was also Joan and Holly's protégé. They tended to live through her, and she provided the victories for everyone. She never noticed the pressure at the time. "It's how I got my recognition at home; it's how I got a safe environment at school. But I never saw that. I did it because it made me feel good. It wasn't until later I discovered that, for me, anything less than perfect was failure."

With the other roles taken, and his older sister's shadow of perfection to contend with, Bill Jr.'s only means for getting attention was acting out. "For a long time I thought I was the cause of my father's drinking. And that made me miserable. But after a while I just felt like, to hell with them, I don't care what they do. I just wanted to cause trouble. I disowned myself and pretty much did the opposite of what anyone told me to do. I wanted to escape so badly. But in reality I was doing my duty as the fuck-up, giving Dad an ulcer and a reason to drink." A child sees rebellion as a means to break away from the influence of the family, but this role is as closely linked to the parents as the role of the caretaker or nurturer. Whether you do as your parents say or rebel against them, the parents are still the central reference for your decision. The alcoholic system is actually sustained by rebellion, insofar as the rebel takes the focus off the real problems. The rebel also gives the alcoholic a great rationalization for the drinking.

Escape Is Impossible

The child in the alcoholic system consciously or unconsciously understands the importance of his or her role and feels very uncomfortable even considering a change in it. But kids grow up and need to grow out of the family, too. They may feel constricted by their role at home. The family system will exert a great deal of pressure to keep the child in place. When Holly started high school, she felt she wanted more freedom, and this meant having less responsibility around the house. "In high school I discovered the outside world, and I wanted to be part of it. I was tired of controlling the chaos at home. But I had so much guilt; I felt like I was betraying my family. I just couldn't leave them." Her father's drinking was getting worse. Holly tried harder and harder to keep everything together at home while slowly stepping out into the world of her friends. Holly was aware on some level that if she left her place in the system, everything would fall down.

In a healthy system, her role would be flexible and experimentation would be acceptable. But in the alcoholic family there is a premium placed on keeping things rigid and unchanging, and her natural feeling of having grown out of her duties left her with deep feelings of shame and guilt. She began drinking with her high school friends. After years of therapy she has come to understand her reactions to that traumatic time: "The drinking took away the guilt. Not only was I numbing the pain I felt about betraying my family, but I was punishing myself. Drinking was like taking my family along with me. I worked so hard to keep the family together that the only way I could let myself go was as a drinker." Many children who try to break free of their alcoholic roles do so in self-destructive ways, punishing themselves for trying to leave the system.

Another form of escape, which Julie chose, was finding a healthy system and defining herself within it. For her it was school. Julie excelled at everything. Her hard work and success at school buffered her from her home life. In many ways the family problem created her need to succeed, but this success came with great pressures. Though she didn't feel it at the time, she carried her family on her shoulders in the outside world. At home, Holly and Bill Jr. carried her. To a great degree, she succeeded on the backs of her sister who protected her, and her brother who absorbed most of the family abuse. These pressures ended up tainting much of the success that she had.

A child's role can have positive and negative components to it. Holly, though anxiously vigilant, became very sensitive to the needs of others, a skill that could be used to great advantage in the world. Similarly, Julie's intelligence and Bill Jr.'s independence were the upsides of their perfectionism and anger, respectively. The problem comes when the child lives these roles instinctually rather than consiously. The benefits are then not experienced as tools at the child's disposal, but as defenses that spring to life in any situation that seems uncomfortable. The growth that comes from recovery results in the individual having the power to choose when and how to use the vast resources at his or her disposal. Instead of being used by your role, you use your role. Instead of reacting, you act in a manner that fits your own wants and desires.

Without the growth recovery brings, the roles may end up as a painful kind of jail. Although these roles may start out as a buffer for the child against the pain and discomfort of family life, after a while they become a central part of the child's identity. As the children grow up, these roles grow with them. As long as the roles remain unchallenged, they end up being the glasses through which the adult child views the world. These roles can be the seeds of a new alcoholic family, and the adult child of the alcoholic becomes a carrier. You'll see more about this in chapter 3.

Sacrificing Growth for Safety

In some situations, the coalcoholic is actually able to rescue the children from the pressures of the drinking stage. Joan was able to keep her two, then three, children out of the way of the alcoholism for a while. This was partly because Bill drank elsewhere, and the direct consequences of his drinking did not loom over the home. But as the drinking escalated, the pressures on the children became more and more substantial.

Children in the Drinking Stage

The children's primary focus is the alcoholic or coalcoholic parents and the alcoholic environment and system.

Behavior

- May be overly compulsive, rigid, or passive

- Includes problems such as acting out, drinking, or use of other drugs

Thinking

- Is dominated by the family defenses

- Shares the same distortions as the parents' thinking

- Shows disturbances because of denial of reality (such as difficulty concentrating, hyperactivity, and dissociation)

- Allows them to accept trauma as the normal state of things

Emotional Expression

- Developmentally skewed by adaptation to the unhealthy situation of their parents, environment, and system

- Behavioral or emotional disorders (depression, anxiety, sleep disturbance)

- Needs safety, structure, and reassurance

- Highly vulnerabile to stress

(Adapted from Brown and Lewis, 1999)

When children grow up in traumatic circumstances, they will push aside their own sense of self in order to maintain the belief that their parents and the world around them are safe and good. In holding fast to this view, children must reshape their perceptions of the world to fit. Children, on an unconscious level, often take responsibility for the way the world is, both as an attempt to have some control and as an attempt to take the blame for the suffering off the parents. We saw each of the three children do this in his or her own way—vigilance, perfectionism, and rebellion.

In order to maintain their false beliefs and perceptions, the children must continually monitor the outside world, anticipating the chaos in an attempt to keep themselves safe. If the parent is not acting appropriately, a child will create a scenario that forgives the parent. If a child does not have safety, he or she will create it. Not only will the child acquire the denial of the family, he or she will take the further painful and self-destructive step of saying, "I am the bad one for experiencing pain." The goal then becomes avoiding pain, for to experience it is an unallowable criticism of the family situation. The rigid boundaries around conversations and behavior become internalized, and the child's thoughts themselves become tightly controlled. Constant thought and speech monitoring go together. Moments of accurate perception that make it through these censors produce a great deal of shame and anxiety. Any crack in the denial must be fixed immediately for fear of threatening the system and therefore all relationships.

In the end, instead of having the freedom to grow and try out their wings, the nestlings must constantly attend to the nest. The independence of flight becomes impossible as everyone must protect the family system that their parents need for safety. Gradually the entire family system becomes set in stone, and everyone works only to serve the system. By this time, the system escapes notice. It is part of everyday experience, coloring everything the family sees, hears, and thinks. This kind of core organization is so dangerous because it is so subtle. Since no one in the family can see the mutually created system, everyone focuses on individual rights and wrongs, creating an atmosphere that mixes their own guilt and shame with a need to blame others for their bad behavior. Everything becomes personal.

The Last Links in the Impulse Chain

The alcoholic system thus claims its final members in the children. Bill fashioned his life to protect his drinking, while Joan fashioned hers to protect Bill. The children then created their worlds with the goal of protecting their parents. Everyone is taking care of the family (or the bottle), and no one is taking care of themselves. In this way, the self is sacrificed and growth is halted. For children, whose development is most crucial at this time, the self-sacrifice is the most destructive. Denial becomes the core of their identity and a foundation for their development for the rest of their lives.

To grow up healthy, children must be able to act on their own initiative and intuition. For young people to be able to try things out, they must be in a safe environment where they know that coming up short will not be punished. Growth happens in fits and starts, and is smothered if a mistake is treated as a failure. In the alcoholic family, there is so much pressure to keep things in line that the children have no margin for error. A mistake can throw the system and the people in it off balance, bringing harsh punishment to the child instead of understanding. When the pressure gets intense enough, every action comes to feel like a matter of life and death for the child.

For Bill and Joan's kids the pressure was overwhelming. They ended up divided and blaming each other as a way to distract everyone's attention from the real problem. Their fighting was the perfect excuse for Bill's drinking. The system took good care of itself.

Eight years ago, Bill hit bottom and joined AA. The family was turned upside down. Joan felt a lot of resistance to AA, thinking that the family secrets would get out. At age eleven, Bill Jr. promptly began his own career of substance abuse, which lasted well into high school: his rebellion continued. Although the alcoholic had sought help, the alcoholic system was still very much in place. In the end, Joan started going to Al-Anon meetings and the children all started on their own paths to recovery. The pain is still there and the wounds run deep, but each family member has set out on the lifetime journey of real growth. They broke the chain of alcoholism.

In a family where the chain is not broken, the long-term effects on the children can be much more destructive. In the end, the children of an alcoholic family can live out their entire lives simultaneously running from their childhood and recreating it in their own alcoholic family. This will be the main focus of chapter 3.

Exercise: "I Am a Child of an Alcoholic in the Drinking Stage . . ."

This exercise will focus on the perspective of a child during active alcoholism. If you are a child or an adult child of an alcoholic, you will be exploring the feelings you and any siblings had during the drinking stage.

■ In your journal, describe the child's behavior in the drinking stage. How did the child react to the alcoholic behavior? How did the child try to make things work? If there is more than one child you can repeat the exercise for each. If you are a child or adult child, do the exercise once for yourself and repeat it for any siblings.

If you have a hard time getting started, think about some of the themes in this section: adaptation, roles, escape, and self-sacrifice. Just write it as you recollect it. Historical accuracy is not the goal.

■ Now describe how the parents felt about the children's reaction to the drinking stage. Were the parents concerned about the children's welfare? Were they confident that the children were doing fine? Did they have problems with guilt?

■ Now describe how the parents presently feel about the children's experience of active alcoholism. Have their feelings changed over time? Do they see their past anxiety or confidence as well-founded now that they have a more objective point of view?

The important thing is to explore your own perceptions of the children's experiences, and the parents' experiences in relation to the children. These perceptions will change over time as your perspective changes.

Remember to date the entries. You might want to come back later and try it again so you can compare your changing points of view as a measure of your progress.

If the exercise makes you too uncomfortable, come back to it when you feel up to it.

3

"You Carry the Danger with You"

Surviving the Drinking Stage

Survival is a key focus for everyone in the drinking stage. In order for the unhealthy family system to remain in place, all of the family members must collude with the alcoholic and deny the existence of the central problem in all of their lives. For the child, the clash between what is allowed and what is real can be very painful. In order to withstand this acute discomfort, the child must erect a complex system of defenses. These defenses assure survival in the alcoholic system.

But the instinct for survival at any cost loses usefulness once you're past the drinking stage. For healthy growth to begin, the denial that supports the system must be challenged and the system—defenses, survival tactics, and all—must fall. This is the road to recovery, which will be the focus of the rest of this book.

In this chapter, however, we will look at what happens if there is no change in the unhealthy family structures. What happens to a child in an alcoholic family when the systems are never challenged? What are the long-term psychological effects of growing up in an alcoholic family? Children heroically endure the hardships and tensions of the alcoholic family, but this endurance takes a toll. Unless the system is challenged and changed, as the children grow, they will have ongoing trouble with their perceptions of themselves and the world. These distorted perceptions can ultimately lead to their seeking out further unhealthy relationships.

Many alcoholics and coalcoholics grew up in homes where active alcoholism was never challenged. If the alcoholic system is never challenged, the survival skills that allowed you to endure chaos and danger can become the foundation for the rest of your life. Adult children of alcoholics have a host of problems that come from growing up in an environment where mother and father could not be trusted and the children's needs went largely unmet. It's a brutal paradox that the very skills that saved you from the dangers in your childhood can become the greatest hurdles for you to overcome as an adult. This chapter will focus on what happens when the defenses that were erected to protect you become your jail.

Defense and Coping

"I think the hardest thing for me to face when I finally put the bottle down was that I had done to my children exactly what had been done to me when I was growing up. I swore I would never be my mother, and here I was, just like her. And when I looked into my daughter's eyes, I knew that she was swearing that she would never grow up to be like me."

Madelaine is an adult child of an alcoholic, or ACOA. Her mother was also an ACOA. Alcoholism is passed down from generation to generation in a number of ways. In chapter 1 we saw how alcoholic rituals and rules can be passed down without the family members' being aware that these traditions are the backbone of an unhealthy system. Some studies have suggested that certain people may be genetically predisposed to become alcoholics. But perhaps the most dangerous carriers of the alcoholic system can be, ironically, the defenses with which a child survived the traumatic childhood.

As we saw in chapters 1 and 2, during the active alcoholism that defines the drinking stage, the family is squeezed between two contradictory elements: the reality that everyone is dominated by the alcoholism, and the need for everyone to collude with the alcoholic in denying the alcoholism. In order to withstand the psychological pressures that they experience in the tight space between these two opposites, children set up defenses to shield themselves from scary thoughts, feelings, emotions, and behavior. These defenses are also attempts at seizing some control in an atmosphere where the child feels powerless. The following are some common examples of children's defenses in the alcoholic family:

Perfectionism. In order to protect himself and his family, a child goes to extremes to ensure he makes no mistakes. The focus on minute details also serves as a distraction.

- Remoteness. The child detaches from the conflict and hides in her own world.

- Talkativeness. The child detaches by talking all the time. As long as his mind is filled with his words, he has no room for other, more uncomfortable feelings and perceptions.

- Clowning. By making everything into a joke, the child can create distance between herself and the painful reality she experiences.

- Rebellion. The child goes against the family grain and causes trouble, which gets him attention and distracts attention from the real problem.

Defenses are neither good nor bad; they are merely a means of coping in a difficult situation. Their relative usefulness depends on the long-term results. A defensive role that has obvious positive attributes can also bring negatives. Remember Bill's daughter Julie? Her perfectionism made her an ideal student. She excelled in her studies and maintained a solid sense of connection to her school throughout the trauma of her childhood. But as she grew older, she came to realize that the perfectionism also had a downside. "It got to where I put the most extreme amount of pressure on myself to do even the tiniest things. Mailing a letter or mopping the floor, I did them with the same level of concentration and drive as I used in my studies."

Meanwhile, Bill Jr. was acting out and raising hell in his hometown. Though his actions were dangerous and out of control, there were positive aspects to his rebellion. "Once I worked through my own drinking problems, I came to find I had a real fearlessness. I don't smile back at that behavior, but there was real independence there. I didn't take any shit. And I still don't. I used to do it out of anger, but I'm not angry anymore. I just have no problem sticking up for myself."

A Lion in the House

In his book *Why Zebras Don't Get Ulcers* (1998) Robert Sapolsky describes how stress works. In the wild, the zebra sees a lion on the veldt. The zebra's body chemistry changes at every level, maximizing oxygen intake, releasing adrenaline, stopping digestion—the entire work of the body focuses on preparing for a life or death struggle. This surge of energy is called the fight-or-flight mechanism, and it's built to be used for a few minutes at a time. Either the zebra escapes, and can relax and replenish its reserves, or it's caught, and any further survival instincts are made unnecessary.

Consider what would happen if the zebra grew up in a house with a lion. The fight-or-flight stress response would be turned on almost twenty-four hours a day. Of course, this would take a tremendous toll. Maybe the lion would attack, maybe he wouldn't. But the home would be a tremendously stressful environment for the zebra.

Now consider what happens to a little girl living in an alcoholic family where the mother and father scream at each other all the time. The screaming triggers the child's fight-or-flight mechanism, but the child can do neither. And to make matters worse, humans not only react to real stressful situations, they also anticipate potential stressful situations. And for humans, stressful thoughts actually bring about the same physical reactions as stressful actions.

So for the child in an alcoholic family, the anticipation of trauma creates an anxious vigilant child, who is ready at all times to either run to the rescue, escape, or just suffer with an inability to do either. The child tends to build an alert system whereby she can prepare in an instant to deflect stress. In the eyes of a small child, the fighting of the mother and father can seem like a life or death situation, especially if the fights get physical. So not only does the child try her best to control the situation and ready herself for any stressful situation, but she also associates these responses with the utmost level of danger.

If the family system stays in place, then chances are that later in life these defenses will still be in place. The child grows into an adult who believes the world is an unsafe place and that no one can be trusted. The only way to ensure safety is to rely on these defenses; and because of the life or death stress that the defenses were forged under, the adult clings to the defenses as though they must be upheld at all times and at all costs. These beliefs are woven deeply into the fabric of the ACOA's belief system, so the adult is rarely aware of them on a conscious level. When a child builds her identity around defense, then defense becomes a central component of herself.

Suppose, for instance, that the little girl believes that the problems of the mother and father are her own fault. This is a common defense for children in an alcoholic home: if you live in a chaotic and dangerous environment, it can feel safer to believe that you are at fault than that your parents are out of control. If it's your own fault, at least you have some control. But of course, the little girl who points the blame inward will come to believe that she is bad, and that if she were good, the problems would go away. She may have some success viewing the world this way. Instead of trembling because everything is dangerous and out of control, she can make her life understandable and focus on trying to be better. Although the level of stress is still high, it is less than it would have been if she couldn't trust her parents and she saw that she was a helpless victim of her circumstances.

This coping strategy may have been useful in the alcoholic home, but when it remains in place decades later, it can become a major obstruction for the woman trying to navigate reality. The defense is so tightly woven into her personality that she instinctively takes responsibility for every situation. But this is a huge burden to carry. She might recognize that she takes everyone's problems onto herself, she might work to try not to be so giving, but unless she challenges the core beliefs about herself that were born of her childhood experiences living with alcoholism, these defenses will remain in place.

For the grown woman, the defenses represent the core of her personality. She identifies her "faults" as central to her identity and may believe, "If I were to change those, I wouldn't be the same person." This is actually adding a second level of protection: she needs a further layer of defense to protect her from the anxiety of changing. Her basic security is tied to these deep defenses.

In essence, the adult still perceives the threat she experienced as a child; it's as if the little girl has been frozen inside her. As a child, she grew up with the lion clawing at her door, so she locked it, nailed boards to it, and pushed all her furniture up against it to make sure the lion couldn't get in. Years later, the door is still locked. The locked door becomes a symbol of safety, and as the child grows up, the one thing she can be sure of is that the threat is not coming through the door. Of course, the lion left years ago, and the only memory of it is the locked door. The biggest threat the woman will have to face by tearing down those boards and unlocking the door is the reality that that scared little girl has been running the show for all these years.

It's a paradox: in order for ACOAs to let go of their defenses, they must feel safe; but they define safety as a reliance on these defenses, since that's how it was in childhood. The ACOA who grows up without ever challenging his or her deep-seated defenses can have a hard time as an adult. An attitude that you take as a central part of your identity may only be a defensive stance that has outgrown its use and now works against you.

Packing the Family Defenses

Defensive behavior can be a vital source of healthy coping. A child with a cautious disposition will test the water with a toe before diving in; and this is a good way to ensure safety. The problem comes when a child's defense hardens into armor. If the child always finds the water to be too cold to swim in, he or she may stop using the toe to check it. This is where caution shifts from being a coping skill to being a rigid defense.

In the alcoholic family, the child must learn the acceptable story and the particular defenses that successfully maintain it. This limits the child's boundaries of thought, feeling, perception, and action. Because the active alcoholism stays in place, the child's defenses become habit, and habit eventually hardens into a set style of interaction. Ultimately this character style becomes character armor as the individual adopts the family's shield against anxieties produced by the threatening world.

What children learn about how to perceive themselves and others in their family, they naturally transfer to how they perceive the outside world. The chaotic and unsafe alcoholic family system shapes the way the ACOA perceives the world in general. The ACOA holds a deep belief that the world is a dangerous place and develops defenses against fear and humiliation. This is how it worked for Henry.

"I had an excellent system for dealing with the world. I just assumed every stranger I met was a serial killer, so I did my best not to be noticed. If someone got me mad, I swallowed it, because I figured if I shot my mouth off, this could be the guy, this guy might pull a gun." Henry had carried his unsafe childhood into his adult life. He is a thirty-five-year-old father of three and has been in recovery for four years. "The problem with the stuff you bring from your childhood is that you have no idea it's troublesome. I just figured everybody saw the world like I did."

Henry had brought a fundamental lack of trust into his adult life. He considered his vigilance to be common sense: "Why take chances? You never know who you're dealing with." When things got out of control at home with his drinking, he always rationalized it by drawing upon his distorted view of reality. "I would always say that I had to burn off steam. I spent my entire day being so careful, being so hyper-aware of everything around me, I needed to unwind and not think about anything. That's what home was for. My wife tended to drink with me; I think it was safer to be on my side than on the outside. But soon I was outpacing her by a mile."

Henry's father had also had a drinking problem; his mother also kept her husband company during the drinking. Henry always thought of his childhood as normal. "Until I did a lot of work in recovery and it was finally safe to look at the past honestly, I assumed everyone's family was like ours: there were ups, and there were downs. There was a lot of screaming and yelling, but nothing really terrible. I figured it was all just normal."

In the traumatic environment of Henry's childhood, his preferred style of defense was being the family clown. Everything was a joke and nothing was sacred. His sense of humor defused many potential family arguments, allowing the combatants to step back with a laugh rather than having to escalate. Laughter is a wonderful way for two reluctant fighters to save face and step away.

Henry loved the attention that he got from being funny. He was also doing a vital service for his family: he was distracting them from the tensions of the unhealthy system and taking the focus off of the problem in the house—namely, alcohol. The drinking was the one topic that was off-limits for the humor. "I don't remember consciously choosing not to joke about the drinking, but I just didn't. I guess I instinctively knew it wouldn't get a laugh."

Henry went off to college at eighteen and celebrated his newly found independence by starting to drink. "I never knew how much I wanted to be free until I was free. Then it was time to celebrate. College and drinking for me were just the same thing: fun and freedom."

When he went home for family visits he discovered the tension in the house for the first time. "When you live in it, you don't really notice it; but once I got outside, it all seemed so clear. I came home on one visit and I saw it—bang!—my father was an alcoholic. I felt like, 'Oh, that makes sense.' It actually struck me as kind of funny. It's like ugly wallpaper. You live with it for your whole life and never even notice it. Then you go away, get a girlfriend with some taste, start to get an idea about what's pretty and what isn't, and when you come home you realize, 'Holy mackerel, I grew up with ugly wallpaper.'"

And what does the child of an alcoholic do when he realizes his home is an ugly place? One avenue is to keep wearing the family blinders. "I drank a lot at home. I drank a lot at college too, but it never struck me as anything but fun. At home it was work. It made everything a lot easier. I had no awareness of drinking as self-protection; I just did it. I found I got along a lot better with everyone if I was a little hammered. Basically, it was the tension reliever.

"After a while I had no desire to go home from college and visit. This of course made me feel extremely guilty. I felt like I was abandoning my family, so I never missed a holiday. I guess you have to like going home to be able to choose not to. Anyway, those family dinners became tougher and tougher. It was pure pressure. Once you see it, you can't go back to being oblivious. Those dinners were awful. So I would drink. And soon, instead of just being the clown, I was the drunken clown. Nobody noticed a difference."

After graduation, Henry got a job, married his college girlfriend and started a family. When he opened his eyes ten years later, the same system he had grown up under was in place in his adult home. "When the drinking started getting bad, I always had a foolproof test that proved I wasn't an alcoholic. I knew what alcoholics were like. I'd say to myself, 'My father is an alcoholic, and I am nothing like him. He never thought about his drinking. He never cared about how it affected his family. He did what he wanted.' Just because you know what something looks like from the outside, doesn't mean you know what it looks like from the inside."

When Henry finally hit bottom, it was after a moment of insight that cracked through his foolproof test. "My son picked up his apple juice and asked, 'When can I drink daddy juice?' It floored me. I suddenly realized that he was me when I was his age, and I was my father. And I suddenly saw that though my father was this tough guy on the outside, he was probably just like me inside. We were the same. I started shaking. That was it. I was in AA the next day."

In the same way it is hard to have insight into your family system when you are living inside it, it is very hard to have a clear perception of your own behavior when you are living it. Even if you are fortunate enough to step outside the family system and walk away, the work is not done. When you grow up inside an unhealthy system, you internalize the system and carry it with you. Unless the system is challenged, the defensiveness and self-protection can end up being the foundation for the rest of your development. And since it is the only way you have ever seen your life, you have no objectivity with which to make changes.

In future chapters we will discuss why it is so important that you reach outside your system for external support to allow the system to change. By using external support, such as AA, Al-Anon, a therapist, or religion, you can gain some objectivity about your own perspective and behavior that is unavailable when you are relying only on your own perceptions. The very denial that allowed you to survive your unsafe childhood can keep you from perceiving reality as it actually is.

Even if you were asked about your defenses, you probably wouldn't see that they were there. This is because they are part of your normal assumptions about the world and your place in it. Henry points out that starting a family is similar to boarding an airplane. "You know when you get to the ticket counter and the agents ask you, 'Have you had your baggage in your possession at all times?' You say yeah, as though that means that the contents of the baggage are safe. But if you grew up in a family where time bombs were sitting all around, you might pack that bag and think, 'No problem, these time bombs are great to have around.' And on you go to your airplane, headed toward your new destination, feeling safe and hopeful and excited, and all along you are carrying this bomb that is going to go off. Unless you take the time to question what the bombs are for and are they really good things, that's how you are going to travel. You are going to carry your danger with you."

The Defensive Arsenal

There are a number of different defense mechanisms that are commonly in place for the ACOA. They are hard to pull down, because they are so central to the person's sense of self.

Denial

If you are the adult child of an alcoholic family, you probably had to become an expert at denial. Denial can take many forms, some direct and some indirect, including a bad memory, obliviousness, or a pervasive sense of confusion. All of these behaviors are often seen by the ACOA as an organic part of his personality. This belief represents a second level of denial: denying that the denial exists. The web of diversions can grow very complex.

In relationships, the ACOA will tend to shut out or redefine anything that would threaten the bond with the loved one. An ACOA might protect the relationship by building a version of reality that plays to the needs and wants of the partner, even if it means excluding his own needs. One way of doing this is to take all the responsibility for any problems and maintain the image of the partner as flawless. Instead of dealing with conflicts as they come up, the ACOA assumes the blame and immediately sweeps the conflict under the table, so the resentment can fester out of sight.

Since denial is the central reality of the alcoholic home, the adult will have a particularly hard time breaking free from it. To push aside the denial and see things as they really are would be a betrayal of the family. To see the past clearly would be to expose the family shame. Of course, challenging denial is a key aspect of recovery. One of the reasons recovery is so traumatic is that the family members must challenge their deepest beliefs about safety and identity. When you expose your core defenses, you make yourself vulnerable, and with vulnerability comes a great deal of anxiety.

Control

A natural response to an out of control situation is for the child to try to take as much control as she can. So even if the boat is getting torn apart on the jagged rocks, her private compartment can be made to seem safe to her. One way she expresses this control as an adult is through a reliance on personal autonomy: if she doesn't need anyone, then she controls her own destiny.

Often an ACOA will equate personal survival with control of herself or others. This is similar to the belief that most alcoholics operate under. The ACOA may also demand perfection from herself and others. This control doesn't apply only to present experiences, but also to future and past experiences. If the ACOA anticipates a situation will be out of her control, she will experience anxiety and perhaps avoid the situation. Likewise, a past situation that didn't turn out the way she wanted will be treated as a mistake that will not be repeated.

Even though the ACOA may not drink, the alcoholic system is still deeply in place. The world must be shrunk to a controllable size, and even anticipated events must fall inside controllable limits.

These beliefs must be challenged in order for recovery to go forward. Autonomy forms a powerful defense against feeling vulnerable or dependent, two keys to can be. In order for the ACOA to embrace the truth that he or she can't control everything, these defenses must be challenged to their core.

All-or-Nothing Thinking

The ACOA has a hard time holding on to conflicting thoughts and feelings at the same time. In the alcoholic family, seeing things as they were, in all their shades of gray, was a threat to the system. So, polarized thinking was put in place: "This is bad, this is good, end of story." The rigidity of this way of seeing can be quite comforting, and can bring with it the illusion of control. If ideas are simple concrete entities, they can be nailed down and put away. In the alcoholic family, there is a premium put on simplicity. Any idea that takes too much thinking will distract from the need for self-protection, so the children learn to grab the simple answer and move on. There is no need to dwell on the complexities: you just sort parts of the world into one of two piles, and you are ready to continue your vigilance. These hard and fast opinions seem to set in place a solid foundation to offset the chaos that swirls around you.

One of the results of this kind of thinking is that people are seen as either allies or enemies, with no one in between. The very concept of in-betweenness brings a deep sense of anxiety, and anxiety is to be avoided at all costs. The defenses were put there to help you avoid anxiety. With polarized thinking, the perception of even the most minor flaw can lead to an all-consuming criticism of the person. The ACOA also thinks that others judge the world the same way, and that therefore the ACOA's own thoughts and actions will be subject to the same rules. This leads her to try to keep everything perfect, since any flaw that escapes her notice will mean a fall from grace. You can see how this ties in neatly with her need for control.

In relationships, these extreme thoughts can lead to the mistaken view that connection results in the loss of self. If things are black and white, there cannot simultaneously be a "we" at the same time there is a "you" and a "me." In most alcoholic families, there is ample evidence that connection only comes with the loss of the self.

Interestingly, this form of thinking is age-appropriate for a child who is first growing aware of his family system. In the alcoholic family, this childlike point of view is frozen and later becomes the point of view for the adult. This rigid thinking gets in the way of recovery, because the ACOA wants to make total, all-or-nothing changes, relying on willpower to push forward. This belief makes it hard to take the small incremental steps that are necessary in recovery.

Overresponsibility

As mentioned earlier, if the child in an alcoholic family recognizes that there is something wrong with the family, he is likely to hold himself responsible. Although carrying the burden of personal responsibility might seem like adding pain to punishment, this belief can actually provide the child with a sense of being needed. He feels central to the family, rather than being on the periphery where he risks feeling abandoned. Polarized thinking helps keep this defense in place, as the child's sense of responsibility is an either/or proposition rather than a dynamic interaction between the child and his circumstances. Overresponsibility also supports denial, allowing the adult child to maintain an idealized version of the parents.

The focus of overresponsibility is usually on what goes wrong, not what goes right. In this ultimately self-defeating situation, the ACOA takes care of everyone but himself. For instance, one of the results of overresponsibility is that the ACOA believes his success causes everyone else misery by making them feel less successful in comparison. You can't enjoy the game when winning makes the other person feel bad. This is related to survivor guilt: how can you feel good and be successful when others are hurting so much—especially if you feel you caused it?

Overresponsibility can also make the ACOA feel omnipotent and in control, feelings that arise from his belief that he is the center of his universe and is therefore responsible for everything in it. The illusion of autonomy that comes with this defense provides a feeling of power, but also gets in the way of making a connection with others. Since the ACOA spends so much time trying to make everything perfect for the other person, he never lets his partner perceive him as he actually is. This is a lonely way to live.

A major result of overresponsibility is hypervigilance. Since the ACOA believes everything is his fault, he must constantly guard against doing anything to hurt anyone. If you believe you are at fault for the chaos of the family, you will tend to be in emergency mode at all times, ready to save the day or avert disaster. This emergency thinking carries over into adulthood, operating as the default position for dealing with the minor anxieties that pop up in life. This constant, exhausting vigilance also contributes to anxiety and depressive disorders.

Much of the ACOA's focus becomes taking care of others while downplaying his needs. This behavior is at the heart of codependency and is very common among coalcoholics. The ACOA becomes so good at fixing everything before there is a problem that the alcoholic never notices what's happening. The central focus of the ACOA's life, his vigilance, goes unnoticed. This self-sacrificing character style is forged in the chaos of family alcoholism.

As we saw in chapter 2, overresponsibility stands in the way of recovery because the vigilant and responsible person usually gets an important sense of strength from taking care of others. The idea that the one thing the person takes pride in is actually a central aspect of the unhealthy system is hard for a person who has endured years of self-sacrifice to swallow.

Pessimism

Often ACOAs have a negative outlook on the world. These expectations are a natural result of growing up in a dangerous and out-of-control environment. The normal world, as they grew to understand it, was a painful place where self-protection was necessary for survival.

As adults, ACOAs anticipate the future with a focus on the worst-case scenario. An unfortunate result of this focus is that the ACOA comes to rely on such preparation, and to believe that the unknown carries nothing but pain and heartache. Instead of seeing a new experience as having the potential to inspire growth and learning, the ACOA will focus on her own vulnerability and fear whatever the unknown offers. She will avoid the unknown at all costs.

When the ACOA is forced to go out into the world, the pessimistic view can have a poisonous effect. This defensive posture says that it's best to be pessimistic, because if things go badly, you're prepared, and if they go even marginally well, you'll be happy because reality exceeded your expectations. The problem is that the negativity can become a self-fulfilling prophecy, as the person brings a bad attitude to the situation and makes no effort to enjoy it.

The ACOA's need for control makes her focus on how she wants things to turn out, leaving no room for her to cope with how things actually go. The world doesn't often go as planned, and a pessimistic attitude can make a minor shortfall into a vast disappointment, a small mistake into a complete failure.

A pessimistic attitude is a giant obstacle to recovery in that it sees every shortfall as a failure and every bump as a "wrong way" sign. One major purpose of this book is to point out that the natural course of recovery will have downturns and bumps, anxiety and discomfort. To let go of the pessimism is to let yourself be vulnerable to the unknown. It is scary and anxiety-provoking to relinquish the negative expectations, but ultimately they will give way or soften.

Lack of Trust

Another way the ACOA protects himself from being vulnerable is by not trusting others. This defensive stance is a natural outcome of growing up in a home where you couldn't trust anyone to be stable and constant. The ACOA might believe he trusts others, and point to evidence of friendships where there is a mutual respect. But trust is essentially the same as making yourself vulnerable to others. Conversely, a lack of trust is essentially the inability to turn off your defenses with respect to another person; to do so would mean letting down your vigilance. This is almost impossible for the ACOA, who views his defenses as vital to survival.

This attitude is another huge obstacle in the way of recovery. In order to make the step outside of the family system, ACOAs must reach out and connect with an external source of support. They must find a trusting place where they will allow themselves to feel safe in order to examine and challenge their own defenses.

The Trouble with Relationships

Since the ACOA grew up amidst a system of unstable relationships, it is natural that he will bring discomfort with him into his adult relationships. Relationships are seen as either dangerous and harmful or as the source of a miraculous rescue from the pain of childhood. It's no surprise that ACOAs often feel confused, anxious, defensive, and out of control in close relationships. A serious relationship activates the painful problems that ACOAs grew up with, such as difficulty feeling separate from family members, social isolation, difficulty coping with feelings, attempts to control others, and chronic stress.

The ACOA's early experiences in relationships with her parents will shape and limit her future relationships and family systems. For example, the ACOA may have anxiety over separation and abandonment because of parental inconsistencies during childhood. She will often deal with this anxiety by alternately moving too close too fast and distancing herself too abruptly in personal relationships. Some ACOAs need constant drama in relationships in order to feel "connected and alive." The inability to create and manage a comfortable amount of intimacy with a partner is a central codependence problem.

An intimate relationship can rekindle deeper issues of vulnerability that may have been hidden for many years. A sudden experience of vulnerability can result in a fear of involvement with others. Coming from an unsafe environment, the ACOA has never learned the trust that comes with firm boundaries. The ACOA worries that he will be hurt, but also that he will hurt another; he worries that he will need too much and that he will be needed too much. The unclear boundaries of the alcoholic family forced the child to become his own security guard, and now that vigilance makes real connection difficult.

If an ACOA can allow herself to form a bond, whether with another ACOA or with a non-ACOA, she often gets stuck in the early stages of the relationship. In these stages, the couple's focus is on feelings of merger, avoidance of conflict, and minimization of obvious differences, according to Ellyn Bader and Peter T. Pearson, who in *In Quest of the Mythical Mate*, outline stages of couple development (1988). Or, the relationship may come to be dominated by anger and conflict as a way of keeping any change, particularly independence, in check. There is often chronic mistrust between the partners. If both partners are ACOAs, they may both fear abandonment and loss, and therefore vacillate between clinging and fleeing.

As the relationship continues, each partner tends to become more independent and emotionally separate from the other while continuing to be in the relationship.

This is an uncomfortable process for both partners, since each often has opposing needs: one wants more space while the other wants to be close. The process of differentiation is frequently misunderstood by ACOAs, who tend to perceive their partners as abandoning or betraying them. In fact, unless the couple can accept the natural separation, this is the time when relationships either break up or when one or both partners start to use unhealthy ways to cope, such as numbing out feelings by drinking excessively.

The Freedom to Dance

Linda went into recovery at age thirty-nine. Though she had been apart from her alcoholic parents for over twenty years, she never realized she was still carrying the family baggage around inside her. When anything went wrong in her life, she immediately assumed she had made a mistake. She felt she deserved whatever happened to her, especially if it was bad. After her umpteenth failed relationship, she finally went to talk to a therapist. The therapist suggested Al-Anon, and after a lot of hard work using both sources of support, she has come to see her life with some clarity. "The mind is built to serve the soul, the spirit, whatever you want to call the thing that is the essence of a human being. In Al-Anon they call it the higher power; I think of it as intuition, the wisdom of the inner music. Your mind is there to be a problem-solving machine to help you fulfill the urgings of your intuition. It's a tool, like a cookbook or an automobile. But when you grow up with alcoholics, you don't have the luxury to listen to the inner music. You have to rely on your mind to keep watch and make sure everything stays in place. After a while at center stage, your mind becomes the central aspect of you, and your spirit is buried under the fear."

Her self-consciousness made it difficult for her to feel comfortable in public. "As an adult, I could never relax around other people. The only way I knew how to relax was to vegetate in front of the TV. Otherwise I was on the go. I would work so hard at my job, and yet I was never that productive. I would look around and see everyone else doing the same amount of work and yet no one else was breaking a sweat. I think I had such a hard time because my mind was always doing double duty. I never just worked; I was always monitoring myself at the same time, wondering if I was making the grade, making sure I wasn't sticking out.

"You can't dance if you are relying on your mind to guide you. The only way to dance gracefully is to feel the music. When you grow up with drunks, you learn to dance to their music. It's usually not safe enough to hear your own. So, you watch the other person's moves and try to keep rhythm with them. You may figure out the steps, but you never know what you're dancing to. It was really hard for me to stop the impulse to focus on everyone else and just listen to myself. I've still got a lot of work to do, but my dancing has improved a thousand percent."

Taking off the Defensive Glasses

In order for Linda to find her music, she had to quiet down the defenses that were drowning it out. Letting down the defenses means letting yourself become vulnerable, and this takes a lot of courage and a lot of work. But it's not something that happens all at once; it's something you work on a little bit every day. It takes practice. Like they say in AA, "One step at a time."

Building a healthy identity requires challenging the past and all the deep faulty premises upon which a person has based his self-view. The first step is to notice that these defenses are there. Only when the ACOA steps into an external structure that allows a real feeling of safety can he or she try out a few steps without these defenses. Recovery is a long slow process.

If you are an ACOA and you are going through recovery with your family, you may have the urge to do some work on healing the unhealthy system you came from. It's natural to want to reach out to your family of origin, especially when you are feeling the positive effects of recovery. Healing can make you feel omnipotent at times. Though the urge to reach out is natural, it's important to approach your family with care.

ACOA issues run very deep, so your first focus must be yourself. After you have built a strong individual foundation, you can focus on your own present family, building a healthy system and healthy relationships. Although you are always working on your own issues internally and with your immediate family, it's hard to know when, if ever, you can directly approach your parents. If your parents have never dealt with their alcoholism, you may be in for a horrible ride.

As an ACOA, you may feel yourself caught in a terrible bind: either everyone in your family of origin gets sober, or you need to cut yourself off from them. It doesn't have to be so all-or-nothing, but it is important to be able to step back and maintain a strong foundation in your own recovery. It is difficult to hold your own within the traumatic system that you have worked so hard to detach yourself from. The pressures are huge, and often even when you have reached ongoing recovery, being in a situation that resembles your family of origin can cause you to backslide in your healthy thinking. Being with your actual family of origin—who may challenge your ideas of sobriety and will feel defensive about their own drinking—can be a painful challenge with little or no satisfaction.

If you are an ACOA in transition, or if you feel the need to confront your family but have not yet put recovery on track, you must set firm boundaries. You may want to write a letter and describe your situation, making it clear that you need to separate yourself for the good of your recovery. Even if you feel strong in your recovery, the old family system can have a tidal pull that is very difficult to resist.

The Heroism of Recovery

Many ACOAs have a double problem in hitting bottom: not only do they have to face their own alcoholism, but they also have to face the realization that they did to their own families what their parents did to them. They know all too well what their children are going through. Even if the details are different, the story is the same.

If you grew up in an alcoholic family, then you know what it means when alcoholism is passed on. But if you are taking the step into recovery, then you also know what is at stake. You are breaking a chain that may go back generations. By stopping the flow here and changing its course, you give your children and your children's children a chance to grow up in a healthy environment.

The purpose of this chapter was to show the long-term effects of growing up in an alcoholic home. Now you know what is at stake for your children if the unhealthy system is left in place. And if you are an ACOA, you probably recognized some of the defensive ways in which you view the world, defenses shaped by the experiences of your childhood. These defenses are the normal outcome of growing up in a traumatic household. So as you walk down the difficult path of recovery, remember that it is painful to challenge these deep beliefs. It's scary to look at the things you have been hiding from. It can be terrifying to feel vulnerable if you have spent your life covering up.

It is so important for the family in recovery to understand the depth of the identity problems that have to be challenged. In this sense, the trauma of recovery is not only normal but also natural. It's hard work, and the path of recovery is not an easy one, but the rewards are rich indeed. Step by step, you can learn to dance with a freedom and grace that you have never known before.

Part 2

Hitting Bottom and Beyond

The Transition Stage

4

"The Trauma of Recovery"

Mapping the Transition Stage

The second stage of recovery is the transition stage. Transition begins with the downward spiral at the end of the drinking stage, includes the acute trauma of "hitting bottom," and continues into the earliest steps of abstinence and recovery. In the transition stage, family dynamics are changing almost constantly, which can make it the most traumatic stage in recovery.

Although active alcoholism is unstable and dangerous, there is at least the illusion of structure. The family members have had time to grow used to the unhealthy family system. The alcoholic family is cushioned from much of their pain by denial, which allows them to endure recurring hardships. During transition, however, denial starts to crack, and the reality that was kept at bay now begins to intrude into the family's perceptions. What was accepted as normal is revealed to be unhealthy, and the small comforts that the family members created for themselves are shown to be illusions. Each member is torn between the painful light of reality and the "comforting" darkness of denial.

In the transition stage of recovery, the alcoholic system collapses while the family desperately tries to keep it in place. The family members naturally want to save this crumbling structure: after all, throughout the drinking stage each individual's entire focus has been on keeping the system in place at the cost of their own wants and needs. But in order to survive the chaos of transition, each member must go against these instincts and let the system fall. Each must reach outside the family for help and support; this is also painful, since each individual has to overcome the deep belief that reaching out is a betrayal of the family.

Martin, who has been in Al-Anon for four years, remembers his crazy feelings when his wife moved into abstinence. "It was a horrible situation. She was the savior for going to get help, and at the same time she was the devil for having destroyed our family. I was so angry. The kids were scared to death. I swear there were entire weeks when no one said a word in our house. In the past, we had always been the fun-loving family; my wife was what you would call a happy drunk. But now she was terrified. It's so hard to be optimistic when the very moment you catch a glimmer of hope is the same moment you recognize how bad everything has been; how bad everything is. I never want to go through anything like that again."

Because of the heightened and ongoing state of crisis that characterizes the transition stage, a map of its treacherous landscape can be a vital tool for surviving the journey. Recovery is a slow process that demands a lot of faith and patience, two things in very short supply during the earliest traumas after abstinence. In recovery, things often get worse before they get better, and it's crucial that you are able to make it through this time. If you believe pain and discomfort mean you are doing things wrong, you will be tempted to fix "problems" that are actually healthy but difficult steps along the path to recovery. This chapter will help you understand why, even though you just made a change for the better, life suddenly got a whole lot worse.

Since recovery is a developmental process, each stage has a number of tasks that must be fulfilled before you can move on to the next stage. The following are the tasks of the transition stage:

- Break denial.

- Begin to challenge core beliefs.

- Realize that family life is out of control.

- Hit bottom and surrender.

- Accept the reality of alcoholism and the loss of control.

- Enlist supports outside the family (twelve-step program, treatment center, therapy).

- Shift focus from the system to the individuals, who begin detachment and individual recovery.

- Allow the alcoholic system to collapse.

- Learn new abstinent behaviors and thinking.

(Adapted from Brown and Lewis, 1999)

The Downward Spiral of Active Alcoholism

Active alcoholism demands that family members maintain a subtle balance between denial and reality. As long as the behavior stays within its acceptable limits, or grows slowly enough that the denial can grow with it, this balance can remain in place for a long time. But when there is a break in the normal course of events—whether from an external cause, like a DUI, or from an internal cause, like a family member moving out—the balance is lost and cracks start to form in the denial. This is how it was for Jeff.

"I remember it so clearly. I got home late from work. I had hit the bar like usual, had a few, stayed a little too long. You know how it is; when you're having a good time it never feels like it's time to go. Anyway, I walked in and the house was quiet.

For the past few days my wife had been waiting up for me, laying into me as I walked through the door. It just made me stay later at the bar. So I figured I'd finally outlasted her. I went into the kitchen, fixed myself a bologna sandwich, grabbed a pair of beers, and went to the living room to watch the tube. It was just one of those perfect moments. I had everything I wanted right here. That's the image I hold on to when I think about where drinking got me. 'Cause when I went up to the bedroom about an hour later, my wife wasn't there. I checked the kids' rooms. Empty. No note, no nothing. It kind of summed up my whole drinking life: I was so happy, I had everything I wanted, and I had no idea my family was gone."

Jeff has been sober for four years, but that night still stays with him. For him, everything changed after that. Suddenly the negative aspects of Jeff's drinking were staring him in the face and he reacted as many have before him: he got angry and upped his intake of alcohol. This led to a vicious circle: he drank to fill the cracks in the denial, but the increase in his drinking caused him to be more out of control, which caused more cracks, which led to more drinking.

Transition task: Break denial.

Transition begins with a crack in the shield of denial. Jeff's wife couldn't take it anymore. What seemed like a benign power struggle to Jeff was actually his wife's final attempt to keep her denial in place in the face of his bad behavior. But as he pushed further and further, the negative aspects of the drinking outweighed the positive benefits for her of having a system that worked.

Typically, the downward spiral at the end of active alcoholism plays out as a variation on this theme. Evidence of the alcoholism gets more and more obvious, the alcoholic drinks more and clings to denial, and the evidence escalates further. The family, believing their survival is dependent on the system's survival, is desperate with fear as the system seems to be coming apart.

Amy could see the signs, but that didn't stop her and her husband's drinking. "Every social occasion would end with a horrible fight between us and our friends. I remember these pow-wows my husband and I would have afterward. 'What is wrong with everybody?' we used to ask. We had an unbreakable support system: each other. As long as we were fine together there was no threat. We were always so busy pointing the finger at everything else as the cause of our misery that we never looked in the mirror."

As we discussed in part 1, as the alcoholic behavior increases, the alcoholic tightens his grip on control. The family gets squeezed inside the fist of the leader, who is trying to prove he has control. As his central loss of control grows, he responds by being more controlling. This is an extremely anxious atmosphere for a family to live in.

The family members respond to the increased anxiety as always, by clinging to the defenses that protect them. But though everyone tries to keep the system in place, the system has to fall. The family's impulse to hold on is natural: when a tornado blows through, the instinct is to hold on to something strong. But in the alcoholic system, holding on keeps the tornado blowing harder and harder. Letting go is terrifying, but it has to be done.

Transition task: Begin to challenge core beliefs.

In order to hold on to their false beliefs, the alcoholic family has to exclude more and more reality from the picture. The family turns in on itself, the pressure and anxiety move to a higher level, and the family system starts to implode. Amy and her husband's last desperate resort was to include their fifteen-year-old son in their drinking. The message was clear: he could be an adult as long as he could keep the adults' secret. "We let our son do what he wanted. It was very lax. We figured if we were drinking, it wasn't fair to make our son abstain. We thought we were such open-minded parents, but really we were just conning ourselves. We were bribing him to keep him quiet. He got to feel cool; it was like the consolation prize for having unsafe parents."

In the end, Amy's son ended up a victim of the system and the source of its destruction. "Over time, our son started drinking more and more, doing crazy things. We all just laughed about it. He was flirting with disaster and we weren't seeing it. We came home one night and he was passed out on the floor. He had drunk most of a bottle of vodka. This is a sixteen-year-old kid. We thought he was dead. My husband was dialing 911, but I wanted to try to sober him up ourselves. I couldn't bear the thought of going to the emergency room where everyone would see me drunk with my drunk kid. The ambulance showed up, and so did the cops. They took our son away; they actually had to resuscitate him on the way to the hospital. The cops took us in on reckless endangerment. It was the worst night ever. We both made a pact to go into AA."

The alcoholic clings to three false beliefs:

- I have control of my drinking
- I am not an alcoholic.
- I do not need help.

As the spiral sinks lower and lower toward hitting bottom, the alcoholic clings to these beliefs. Meanwhile the family holds on desperately to their own denial, but reality is stretching the denial to the breaking point.

The House Is Sinking

During the drinking stage, there was a measure of stability, and all the small crises could be covered up as they came along. Thus, the family could go on living in their increasingly unsafe home. As the family enters transition, the crises become more dangerous, the behavior more crazy, and the situation more difficult to ignore. The house on the unstable foundation has actually started to sink, and the family's powers of denial are not up to the task of blocking out this fact.

For Beth and John, who had been drinking together since they were high school sweethearts, the sinking family showed itself in their worsening arguments. They argued about everything: the children, the bills, their jobs, politics—everything but the drinking itself. As the drinking got worse, the arguments became physical. First, there were threats, and soon there was grabbing and shaking and throwing of dishes. It became harder and harder for their two daughters to plug their ears in front of the TV. Soon friends weren't coming over anymore, and every dinner ended with an argument.

> **Transition task: Realize that family life is out of control.**

The alcoholic is struggling for her drinking life while the family stands around trying to rescue her. But as their own lives start to be threatened, their instinct for self-preservation, which has been so long denied, may finally kick in. The family members are torn between the need to rescue the alcoholic (and the alcoholic family system) and the need to flee. Many families stick together until the end, and for young children, there is no other choice. But for older children, or the coalcoholic who can no longer deny the negative effects on the children, escape may be the only choice.

Meanwhile, the alcoholic scolds the deserters as if they were rats fleeing a sinking ship. She still clings desperately to the illusion of control, which is all that stands between her and the devastating reality.

Hitting Bottom

When the pressure is great enough, the alcoholic or coalcoholic can no longer hold up the shield of denial, and it comes crashing down. The alcoholic's false beliefs are shaken to the core as the reality of alcoholism is faced for the first time. People in Alcoholics Anonymous call this experience "hitting bottom," and it's been likened to suffocating, being torn apart, having a heart attack, or dying. Alcoholics commonly describe it as the most extreme experience of their lives.

Painful as it is, hitting bottom is the catalyst of recovery. The central elements of recovery all grow out of the surrender that comes when the alcoholic or coalcoholic hits bottom. When desperation overwhelms you and denial falls away, you see the crippling helplessness at the bottom of your soul. This crack in your armor allows you to take the necessary steps to begin healing:

- Realizing the extent of your loss of control

- Identifying yourself as an alcoholic or coalcoholic

- Reaching outside the alcoholic system for support

There are as many ways to hit bottom as there are people who have landed there. One man crossed the final line when he was in a drunken fit and struck his five-year-old daughter. One woman finally got it when she forgot to pick up her daughter at school; when the principal dropped the seven-year-old girl off, he found the woman passed out in the front doorway of the house, the car keys in her hand.

Waking up in jail after a DUI, losing a job, being deserted by your spouse—every person has a breaking point. This line can be drawn at quite an extreme place. One man had always held to the belief that as long as he was never institutionalized, he wasn't an alcoholic. It took waking up in the psychiatric ward after two days of violent delirium to open his eyes.

It may seem hard to understand why people usually need such a disastrous event to finally see clearly. But alcohol is a complicated drug. The alcoholic's normal routine is to escape shameful behavior by drinking more. Being drunk makes denial so much easier. It often takes a real catastrophe to get an alcoholic to the point where the cycle is broken. So many lives have been lost to alcohol through bad judgment, auto accidents, violence, and suicide: many times hitting bottom leaves no opportunity for salvation.

Transition task: Hit bottom and surrender.

Self-destruction just doesn't get through to some alcoholics and coalcoholics, and it takes a family catastrophe to wake them up. Too often, the pressures of the home lead the children to push their limits with dangerous behavior. Many times the victim of the catastrophe is a teenager who acts out in a desperate cry for help. It took Amy's son almost drinking himself to death to finally open her and her husband's eyes to their problem.

When you hit bottom, the vulnerability you experience is devastating. Every denial you held on to so tightly is exposed. Because this is so painful, you need to reach out and get help before the denial can reassert itself. The moment the desperation is lost, you can tell yourself it was just a scare and go back to the drinking, saying, "I'll just be more careful this time."

Surrender

When you hit bottom, you face the fact that the drinking is out of control. The very focus of all your energy—your attempts to control your environment, your family, and yourself—is shown to be fruitless. The first and most important moment in recovery is in surrendering to this loss of control. Since control has been central to the alcoholic's sense of security, giving up on it can be a very anxious experience.

Transition task: Accept the reality of alcoholism and the loss of control.

Surrender is summed up in an AA slogan: "Let go; let god." This phrase can make the nonreligious a bit wary, but "god" does not have to be seen in a literal way. It simply means that, while you may pretend to be in control, something other than you runs your life. For some, this "something else" is god; others think of nature or the unconscious. Many in AA like to use the term "higher power." By accepting that there is something in control beyond your own self-reliance, you become able to challenge the grandiosity that comes with your illusion of control.

Surrender is not something you can rationally choose; you have to experience it. Left to his own devices, the alcoholic will keep fighting for control until he is knocked down. Beth's husband John remembers: "To stay in control, you have to meet pressure with pressure. If you get pushed, you push back. You don't want to stop fighting, because it feels like quitting. In reality, quitting the fight is the first step toward letting yourself off the hook. You're too close to your opponent to see who it is you're fighting, so you just keep slamming away and hope for the best. But when you take a step back, you see that your opponent is yourself."

The alcoholic believes he is in control, but his urge to drink is actually controlling everything. The coalcoholic believes she is in control, but her urge to save the alcoholic is steering the way. By letting go and surrendering, both accept that control comes from outside. In recovery, each transfers the outside dependency from an unhealthy object—alcohol or the alcoholic—to a healthy one—a recovery program.

Hitting Bottom

- Desperation or crisis cracks your defenses, exposing your vulnerability and loss of control.

- When the defenses come down, you can see that you are an alcoholic or coalcoholic and that you need help.

- Surrendering to these realizations forces you to reach outside the family for support.

- It is vital that you keep focused on your lack of control, keeping the window of vulnerability open and acting on it. If your desperation is allowed to wane, denial will return. You will explain away the crisis as a momentary lapse—a warning—and go on with the unhealthy behavior.

Reaching Out

When your defenses fall and you realize your inner supports are shattered, you need a solid external support system that will hold you together while your insides can heal—like putting a broken leg in a cast. Reaching outside the family for external support (joining Alcoholics Anonymous, starting an addiction treatment program or therapy, or seeking help through a religious group) gives you a place to find the solid foundation and sense of security you need to heal. Continuing to depend on the unhealthy family system not only keeps you from real healing, but also keeps that system alive when it should be allowed to crumble.

In the earliest period of recovery, the alcoholic or coalcoholic has only one focus. For the alcoholic it's not drinking; for the coalcoholic, it's not trying to save the alcoholic. In order to allow themselves this focus—and to keep from being swallowed by the anxiety caused by the newly exposed vulnerability—each needs support.

> **Transition task: Enlist supports outside the family.**

Dependency Is the Path to Autonomy

Throughout the drinking stage, the alcoholic and coalcoholic often live under the false belief that they are self-reliant and strong. This illusion is shattered when one of them hits bottom, and it becomes clear that they were slaves to their impulses either to drink or to rescue the drinker. Their first step in freeing themselves from these impulses is to transfer their dependency from the unhealthy object to a healthy one.

It may seem like a paradox, but a healthy autonomy grows out of dependency—not an unhealthy dependence on alcohol or the alcoholic, but a healthy dependence on a healthy support system. Autonomy is not the same thing as self-sufficiency. An autonomous individual is free to act on his or her own desires rather than being ruled by the demands of others. Self-sufficiency is a defensive goal common to those who grow up in a dangerous world, where needing help opens you up to pain. Conversely, a child living in a healthy family environment can safely ask for help, and doesn't need to protect herself by becoming staunchly self-sufficient.

She grows up in an atmosphere of safety and healthy dependency, where she is allowed to experiment and make mistakes. Eventually, she is able to leave the nest with a strong internalized sense of self-esteem, confidence, and healthy autonomy.

In the alcoholic family, there is no safety, so there can be no healthy dependency. Since the parents are unreliable and the boundaries are unclear, the children cannot relax their impulse toward self-sufficiency and find their own way to genuine autonomy. Similarly, the parents are not independently strong, but dependent upon each other in an unhealthy way. Amy described her relationship with her husband as enmeshed. "We were like two boards leaning against one another, holding each other up. If you moved one, the other would fall. To us that was stability. We thought of it as intimacy. What it was was codependency. I think when you are afraid to trust, enmeshment is the only way you can feel safe." Amy and her husband's fear of falling to the ground kept them in place until the night they found their son unconscious. Then her husband moved, and down they both fell. Only when they let the system collapse could they reach outside and get the help they needed.

> **Transition task: Shift focus from the system to the individuals,**
> **who begin detachment and individual recovery.**

As long as you are caught up in the indistinct boundaries of the alcoholic family system, you will deflect your issues onto others, or take other members' issues onto yourself. Stepping out of the system and into a supportive environment where you can let your defenses down allows you to begin taking personal responsibility for making changes in your life. This involves seeing how you played a part in the system's function. This focus on the self jump-starts the process of healthy individuation, which may have stalled during an unsafe childhood or relationship. Self-focus is one of the keys to recovery.

The shift into recovery is like a mirror of the final drinking phase. The beliefs that are held on to most strongly at the end are inverted, and become the foundation of the work in recovery:

I am in control → I am out of control

I need to control others → I cannot control others

I don't need help → I need help

I am not an alcoholic/coalcoholic → I am an alcoholic/coalcoholic

I need to be defensive → I need to remain vulnerable

Earliest Abstinence

As we have mentioned before, it is natural for the family to assume that after the storm of active alcoholism, abstinence will bring back the sunshine. In earliest recovery, however, all the unhealthy structures are still in place; the only change is that the drinking has stopped. For the alcoholic, this is a major crisis. For the family, the experience of one or both parents hitting bottom is devastating. The desperate parents, who once kept the family structure together, are now vulnerable and helpless. The system is left without its staunchest supporters, and the children are stranded without the structure they have come to expect.

During this period, family members experience conflicting urges to keep things the same and to let everything go. Both urges are normal. But the emergency thinking that comes with the crisis won't allow the family to accept this ambivalence. In an emergency, everything needs to be fixed immediately; any hesitation leaves you open to pain and disaster. When family members are accustomed to seeing things as all black or all white, ambivalence becomes a threat and causes further anxiety.

> **Transition task: Allow the alcoholic system to collapse.**

Even though the family may understand that the move toward abstinence is the only course to salvation, everyone is thrown into crisis as the denied reality is finally let in and everyone suddenly has to deal with the shame of admitting they live in an alcoholic family. They may feel abandoned by the alcoholic, who is focused intently on recovery. They can become angry and discouraged when it only feels like things are getting worse. Because of the heightened tension, new crises are often sparked among the family members. Other addictions fill the vacuum. Children may act out. Marriages may be tested by an affair or a separation.

Children who have grown up in an unsafe environment have built defenses that suit it. With the environment changing, the children will be desperate to seek out safety but will not know how to find it. Younger children will be terrified to see that their parents are frightened and are having a hard time keeping it together. The parents' vulnerability upon hitting bottom is a strain on the child, who wants to believe in the strength of the parents. The chaos of alcoholism may look preferable to that of recovery, and the children may want to step backwards. They may act out or become disturbed by the situation. They may also have a hard time trusting that any change is real or positive. And the parents won't be able to watch over their kids as well as they might like, because they must mind their own individual recoveries.

Support for the Children

"My mom was completely self-centered when she drank," remembers Claire, whose mother quit drinking five years ago. "She would just talk about herself. And when I would talk about me, she would agree by talking about herself. It drove me nuts. I was so excited when she quit drinking. I thought I might get a friend out of the bargain. But in recovery she was even worse than before. Now, not only did she talk about herself, she talked about her recovery. All that AA stuff just sounded so corny. I found myself wishing for my old mom: at least she was cool and talked about drinking."

Often children who have felt abandoned by the parents during the drinking stage have longed for the closer contact they thought would come with abstinence. But the alcoholic and coalcoholic must focus on surviving early recovery. This consuming task leaves them little time for closeness to and support of their children, whose world has been turned upside down by the ordeals of both drinking and the end of the drinking.

Though the parents often cannot provide all the attention the children need, they can see to it that the children are getting that support. After-school programs, Boys and Girls Clubs, family friends: all these can provide much-needed connection and stability for children who are going through this time of major crisis. There are also twelve-step programs for kids: AlaTeen, AlaKid, and AlaTot. Some treatment programs and schools now have specialized support groups for children of alcoholics.

It is crucial for your children to have a safe place to discuss their thoughts and feelings about the alcoholism they have endured. As much as parents may want to be the sole support for their children at this time, the kids need a safe, neutral place to share what they have experienced. In chapter 6, we will discuss ways of making sure your children are safe throughout early recovery, while still maintaining the self-focus necessary to start your individual healing.

A Wedge Between Impulse and Action

During the drinking stage, the alcoholic individual confuses his identity with a false self. Among other things, this false self held on to the defensive belief that drinking was not a problem and that it caused no loss of control. During transition, the earliest foundation of a new self is put in place—a self based on the alcoholic's acceptance of his loss of control. The alcoholic has to learn to live with the raging impulses that have enslaved him without acting on them. The way to do this is to put a wedge between the impulse and the action: new behaviors must be substituted for the drinking behavior. An action language provides concrete direction: "If you have a craving make a call." At the beginning, these substitutions may feel superficial, but over time they will become more internalized and feel more natural. The coalcoholic faces a similar process in recovery.

Bob remembers how his connection to his sponsor started shakily, and ended up being quite deep. "At first I had to carry around an index card with my sponsor's telephone number. I was so frazzled in the beginning, it took me over a month to memorize it, and I looked at it about a hundred times a day. I wore that thing out. I think I knew the number, but I never trusted myself to get it right, so I would check. Then one day, I had the urge to drink and I just started dialing. It was like that all along. I would be frustrated with myself, and then when I wasn't looking, I'd have moved forward. After a while I would be on the phone with him before I'd even thought about the drink. One day, I just knew what Curt would have said. I didn't even consciously decide not to call. I just knew it. It's like I could be dependent on myself; I had my sponsor inside me. Of course, I called him to tell him. Nowadays the index card hangs in my den. I got a frame for it. It's one of my favorite possessions."

> **Transition task: Learn new abstinent behaviors and thinking.**

For the coalcoholic, the dependency that needs replacing is the rescuing behavior. This can be extremely difficult to contemplate after the alcoholic hits bottom, because the alcoholic will seem so much worse and the coalcoholic will still want to look out for his or her partner. Mary remembers those early weeks. "I was going nuts. I was all over Bob, checking in with how the meetings were going. I remember when he said I should go to Al-Anon. 'But there's nothing wrong with me,' I said. I was trying to take care of the kids, but I was coming apart. Finally I went. At first I was sure I didn't belong. Everyone sounded so selfish to me. To me, if you took care of yourself that was selfish. But as I listened to people speak, I kept hearing pieces of my own life. It was spooky. It took me a while, but when it started sinking in, I was floored."

In chapter 6, we will look at some methods to help maintain these substitute behaviors in the beginning, when they feel strange and new.

Thumbnail Map of the Transition Stage

- In transition, the family remains dominated by an alcoholic environment.

- The environment is often more anxious, frightening, and traumatic than during the stable drinking period.

- The growing pressure in the alcoholic system can lead one or more members to hit bottom.

- The alcoholic family system may collapse, partially or fully.

- A full collapse allows the family focus to shift radically: moving away from preserving the unhealthy alcoholic system toward fostering individual recovery.

- Healthy personal growth is characterized by the individual's detachment and disengagement from family dynamics in order to turn the focus on the self.

- This process can be facilitated and directed by involvement in a twelve-step program, therapy, or another external support system that focuses on recovery and healthy growth.

(Adapted from Brown and Lewis, 1999)

The Environment in Transition

The environment surrounding a family in transition is highly unstable and tense in both the last period of drinking and the first period of recovery.

As we've seen, hitting bottom is a devastating psychological event for an individual, and the repercussions are felt throughout the home. The move into recovery tends to be equally devastating. The family that was once trapped within the tight space between alcoholism and its denial is now lost between an alcoholic system that no longer functions and no system at all. There will be arguments as the members are pulled in different directions. One person will cling to the sinking ship, another will break free, and each will blame the other for not doing the right thing.

"For us, the only difference between the end of the drinking and the beginning of recovery was the absence of booze. It was a madhouse before, it was a madhouse after." So says Rachel, who has been sober for eleven years. She puts her story together from her own memories and from the conversations she has had with her husband and children. At the time, she was too out of it to remember much. She takes her lack of memory as proof that it was intensely traumatic. "My daughter went to bed every night thinking I was going to die. Whenever I was late coming home from anywhere, my husband would panic. And when I finally got sober I was just a zombie. My memory is actually worse about the period after quitting. For the first few weeks I could do nothing but sleep and go to meetings. I was completely crazy. I really don't know how I got through it. My family was terrified. All they could think was 'What happened to Mommy?'"

Whereas Martin's family, whom we heard about at the beginning of the chapter, lived in silence for some time, Rachel's family screamed. "We had the cops come to our house twice in that period. I had been drinking heavily for eight years and the police never knocked once; then I started recovery, and suddenly I was disturbing the peace." No matter how traumatic the environment was before quitting, it was an environment that everyone had grown used to and that was shaped by the family's anxious need for consistency (even if that consistency was illusory). In a sense, the family makes peace with the alcoholism, and quitting drinking disturbs this peace in a very real way.

The Family Environment in the Transition Stage

The drinking phase is characterized by:

- Intense chronic and acute trauma
- Danger

The abstinent phase is:

- Still unhealthy, but usually less unsafe
- Characterized by chronic and acute trauma
- Dominated by chaos and crisis
- The beginning of the "trauma of recovery"

(Adapted from Brown and Lewis, 1999)

Exercise: Environment in Transition

To get the most out of this discussion and the ones that follow, try to recall the atmosphere of your family during the transition between drinking and abstinence. Recalling these traumatic times can be painful, and if you feel you aren't ready, by all means let it go and come back later. There is no rush; this book will be here when you are ready.

- Sit in a chair and relax. Take a few deep breaths, and think of a memory from the period when the drinking was getting out of control. If you are having a hard time picking a moment, it might be helpful to consult your journal entry for the "Sensing the Environment" exercise in chapter 1.

- When you have a memory in mind, relax and let it come to you. Instead of focusing on the event, focus on the surroundings: the feelings, sights, sounds, and smells. Write your feelings about the atmosphere in your journal. Only write as much as you feel is necessary. You may want only a few descriptive words; you may want to write a few pages.

- When you are done, repeat the exercise, but this time choose a memory from the period after the shift to abstinence. Again, this may be painful, so don't push it. If you're able to recall this environment, write down your impressions of it in your journal.

Don't forget to date both entries for future reference. You may want to try this again someday.

The Family System in Transition

Although many families are grateful for abstinence, despair and ambivalence are common early on. Families who are not aware of this reality may wonder what they are doing wrong. As we have seen, the alcoholic system often leads to over-responsibility in its members, and here is the perfect situation for overresponsibility. Something that was longed for as the answer to painful problems seems to have made everything worse than ever. The overresponsible family thinks, "It must be someone's fault. We must be doing something wrong. Our family is bad." There are so many ways of expressing these feelings.

It bears saying again: It is perfectly normal to have a hard time in this early period. In fact, a smooth and easy transition may be a sign that the family is still holding on to old beliefs and to denial. High anxiety, tension and a host of painful emotions are never comfortable, but they are unavoidable if you and your family are going to do some difficult and courageous work: challenging the core beliefs that have kept you afloat for so many years.

Resistance from the System

As we saw in chapter 1, resistance to recovery is common among family members. When one partner hits bottom and seeks help outside the family, the family is changed. The family, threatened by the change, will often challenge and discourage the person who is leaving. After all, this person is abandoning his or her assigned role, and upsetting the system.

Often the coalcoholic will be outwardly supportive of the alcoholic's move into recovery while avoiding all responsibility for his or her own part in the alcoholic system. This is how it was for Martin, whom we met earlier. He blamed his wife for all the problems of the family. While she tried to focus on herself in the present and work on abstinence, Martin harangued her constantly about past indiscretions he had "let her get away with."

The coalcoholic in recovery can also meet with family resistance if her partner is still drinking. Paul, whose coalcoholic mother, Kay, hit bottom before his alcoholic father, remembers feeling angry at his mother for making his father upset. Kay was in Al-Anon and Barry was still drinking, and the dinner table became the center of the tension. "I can see who had the problem now. But back then, I just wanted peace at the dinner table. So when my mom would make a comment, I would get upset at her. I hated her for rocking the boat. Now I look back and I think it was just safer for me to attack my mom than for my father to get disturbed. I was doing his dirty work."

Alcoholism is a family disease, and for the family to be healed, it's best if everyone takes part in the treatment. This means each member must take responsibility for changing behaviors that support the unhealthy system. If the parents are divided on recovery and one person works to keep the old system alive, the family can be torn. This is a particularly confusing situation for the children, who are getting mixed signals from the two parents.

The family may also resent the fact that the alcoholic is getting all the attention and being branded a hero for doing the right thing and getting help—when, after all, the drinking was the cause of the problems. All the anger that has been boiling undercover over the years will bubble to the surface. This was the case for Chuck, who took over two years to follow his wife into recovery. In the beginning, his resentment bubbled away, and he couldn't help railing against his wife. "My kids could sense the vibe in the air. My wife was so repentant and I was so angry. It was an ugly situation for all involved. I blamed her for everything. I just could not see my part in any of it. All the time I was screaming about how blind she was, I was the blind one. I would scream; then my kids would scream, and Rachel would call her sponsor and off she'd go. So the kids and I would scream at each other. I kept punishing her for a long time, but the funny thing was that she was getting better anyway. One day I realized who it was that had the problem; who it was that I was mad at. I needed help."

Barry and Kay's house went in the opposite direction. When Barry finally quit, everyone walked on eggshells, afraid that any disturbance would propel Barry back to drinking. This was difficult for everyone, especially Kay. "I was the first to hit bottom, but I was still under the spell. I needed for him to be better so I made sure everything was smooth for him. It wasn't until a few months had gone by, and the messages of my Al-Anon meetings started sinking in, that I realized I could not keep him sober or save him from drunkenness. That's when my recovery really started."

Another source of resistance to recovery is the family's sense that the alcoholic isn't doing enough to make up for the years of bad behavior. During very early recovery, the alcoholic can only focus on her new recognition that she's out of control. The painful realities of the past are often too anxiety-provoking for her to face right away; first she must work at shifting her behavior from drinking to abstinence. Although it may seem to other family members that the alcoholic's surrender has allowed her to slough off responsibility for the actions committed while she was drunk, it is just not yet time for her to dwell on these experiences. The family, on the other hand, craves immediate satisfaction. This need is a natural result of the emergency thinking that kept the system alive for so long; that is, every problem must be solved immediately because an unsolved problem leaves you vulnerable.

Through the work of recovery, the family learns patience. As their panic subsides, the members realize there is time and that they don't have to confront things immediately. Unfortunately, this knowledge isn't really available when it's needed most: in the beginning. Patience doesn't really appear until the family is deeper in recovery and has started to trust in the security of their new support systems. As the alcoholic stays on the path of recovery, she will become able to address the past. It just takes time.

Rules

During the downward spiral, tensions press in on the family rules. The alcoholic is desperate to keep her surroundings in order and therefore makes the rules more rigid. But as the alcoholic behavior spirals increasingly out of control, it becomes more difficult for the family to follow the rules. If the alcoholic is missing too much work, it may be impossible for the coalcoholic to continue lying for her; and as tensions get greater at home, it may be difficult for the children to keep quiet.

In the past, the rules were more stable: frequently, everyone knew what to expect and punishments for breaking the rules tended to be consistent even if not truly understood. But the rules start to change as the alcoholic or coalcoholic responds to the extreme pressures of the worsening problem. One day the alcoholic will demand silence at the dinner table; the next night, she will complain that everyone is giving her the silent treatment. This kind of inconsistency is crazy-making to the people who have spent their lives trying to smooth out family tensions. In the past you knew how to make things all right, but now, with the anxiety going through the roof, no move is safe.

Adolescents who are trying out their own individuality will be particularly sensitive to the growing pressures to conform to their parents' out-of-control rules. One family enacted a strict curfew for their teenage children. The alcoholic claimed the change was motivated by concern over the children's schoolwork, but in reality the parents couldn't bear the thought of their teenagers being outside the locus of their control. When the oldest girl got home late one evening, the mother, who had been "drinking over her worry" about the daughter, went into a rage, hurling abuse and threats about following the guidelines. Didn't the daughter know how their "nerves were fraying"? The daughter couldn't help but see that the rule existed not for her protection, but to keep her parents happy. At sixteen, she didn't feel comfortable sacrificing her own autonomy any longer, especially when all her years of loyalty were thrown aside over one instance of lateness. Next time she was out and the curfew came around, she decided not to go home at all.

After one or more members hit bottom there is an uneasy give-and-take in the rules. As denial is shattered, some of the rules are immediately exposed as unhealthy, while others are more difficult to spot. Since these less-obvious rules have been a source of security for the unstable family, members will hold on to as many as they can in the crisis. The connection to drinking may never be made. "Don't disturb Mommy in the morning" may still be the acceptable rule even though hangovers are no longer a problem. There will be fights as different members stick to and resist different rules. Personal interpretation will take the place of group accord.

In order to let go of the old rules, each individual must attach to a new support structure. You must make a commitment to a new set of healthy rules that let you work toward healing yourself. You need to discover your own individual rules, before you are able to work with your family and put new family rules in place. This is a long slow process, and at first the individuals will feel off balance.

Exercise: Rules in Transition

The purpose of this and the following exercises is to help you understand the changes that occurred in the alcoholic system as your family moved from the downward spiral at the end of the drinking phase into the abstinent phase.

- Look back at the journal entry from the "Drinking Rules" exercise in chapter 1.

- Go down the list of rules and describe how a particular rule changed as the family spiraled out of control. Were there new rules put in place? Did the old rules become more rigid? Less rigid?

- Now describe what happened to the rule as the family entered the abstinent phase. Did different family members hold on to different rules? Did the rules fall all at once or a little at a time? Were new rules put in their place?

Remember to date the exercise in your journal so you can refer back to your answers after you have made more progress in recovery.

Roles

The roles are also pulled in two directions during the sinking of the alcoholic system. With behavior and environment getting more extreme, there is greater pressure on everyone to hold on to their roles in an effort to keep things afloat. But at the same time, the roles are exposed as inappropriate and, often, as part of the problem. In extreme situations, a family member may be forced from the role she is accustomed to fill in order to protect herself from a more acute trauma.

For instance, one young woman is a coalcoholic and had always been able to win the confidence of her alcoholic husband by agreeing with him. But when he was sinking low, he began to include her in his attacks. She would stand by as he lashed out at everyone else, but now that she was the object of his derision, she was devastated: "All those years of taking care of him, and all I did was keep things the same." The coalcoholic realized she wasn't helping the alcoholic get better: she was allowing him to get worse. This realization was a crucial step for her in reaching out for help.

Still, as the system careens into the abyss, many people will cling to their roles as if they were life preservers. As we've seen, a role can provide vital armor for a family member. So the perfectionist, who is usually distracted from danger by the details of homework or cooking, will dive deeper into these tasks to push out the increasingly crazy environment that whirls around him. But the life-saving function of this extreme focus eventually gives way, leaving the individual acutely vulnerable. The tighter the role is clutched, the more likely something will knock it free altogether.

As a family member hits bottom, roles are challenged still further. Often the first person to break from the system is seen as a threat: if one person rejects his role in the system, his action threatens to expose everyone else's roles as similarly unhealthy. This threat to denial can be intolerable, especially during the violent last gasps of the drinking system, when every vestige of stability is hoarded like water on a life raft. The person who has broken with the system often becomes a scapegoat, ganged up on by the rest of the family. This attack is the system's way to bring back the status quo, which is familiar and comfortable. The deserter may even join in the attack on himself. He may believe deeply that his shift of focus off the family and onto himself was a betrayal, albeit a necessary one. When you have lived for so long under the doctrine that self-sacrifice is the only acceptable path to family service, it's common to experience a deep sense of guilt for leaving the family behind to help yourself. Until everyone steps out of the system and starts on the path of recovery, each member will be battling to keep the others as collaborators.

In an unsafe environment, the loss of a familiar role can be a threat to an individual's identity. This role is like a protective cloak; you know, take comfort in, and derive a sense of identity from it. When you shed the protective role, difficult feelings can suddenly arise: "Who am I?"; "I feel lost, naked, and vulnerable"; "I simply don't know how to function in the world." You may feel there is something wrong with you; your family members will feel the same. In reality, you have each been living in a kind of straitjacket without knowing it. When you take off the roles you wore for protection, you give yourselves a chance to become yourselves and, over time, adopt new roles that you can put on and take off when needed.

Once important coping behaviors, the roles dictated by the alcoholic family become outmoded as the family members disengage from one another. As denial is peeled back and the catastrophe is revealed, individuals may also have profound feelings of failure and self-criticism; they feel they have "let the family down" in some way. A "failed" role can end up being despised by the person who played it. For example, the caretaker who sees the poor outcome of his caretaking can want to rid himself of the nurturing side of his personality.

In recognizing how your role helped keep the system going, you may feel shame at first. It's painful to see that a part of you is keeping an ugly situation from getting better. As you grow stronger in recovery, you will be able to see the skills you developed in a more objective way. A role that became a problem will also have some benefits. You can then reclaim these skills and use them to your benefit, rather than living as a slave to them.

As the parents start to make recovery work for themselves, some roles that gave the children esteem will be taken away. A child may have been flattered to be her father's confidant, but this was not an appropriate role. After abstinence, it can be hard for a child to switch back to being (or learn to be) "a normal kid." When the child has been privy to the parent's secrets, it will take some time and effort before the child is able to look upon the adult as an authority figure.

Exercise: Roles in Transition

This exercise will help you understand the changes that occurred to the roles your family members played when the family went through transition.

- Consult your journal entry for the "Drinking Roles" exercise in chapter 1.

- How did your role change as the family experienced the downward spiral? Were you more diligent about your place in the family? Less diligent?

- How did your role change after abstinence? Did you challenge your role, or use it for support?

- How did the other family members' roles change during the downward spiral?

- How did their roles change after abstinence?

  Remember to date this exercise in your journal.

Often people experience attitude and role changes without realizing that the changes were connected to the traumas around them. Hopefully, you will come to see that your family's changes were natural, even unavoidable. This realization can go a long way toward understanding that during extreme times, people often behave in extreme ways.

Rituals

Rituals, like rules and roles, may be challenged by the heightened tensions of the period before hitting bottom. With the alcoholic behavior becoming more extreme, a ritual that once seemed like a healthy way for the family to connect becomes a painful routine. A perfect example of the precarious nature of family rituals during this period is the family dinner, often the only time when the entire family is together. Even in an unhealthy environment, these group meals can be a vital source of bonding for everyone in the family.

During the downward spiral, the dinner table can become the central focus of tension. With the rules and roles being challenged and the alcoholic behavior spiraling out of control, dinner can become a chore for everyone in the family. Alone, the individual members can keep up the curtain of denial; but when they're together at a table, they find it harder to ignore the anxiety, disconnection, desperation, and dangerous behavior.

Meanwhile, the alcoholic or coalcoholic may need to see these dinners as proof that everything is fine—and will exert a rigid control to maintain this illusion. Other family members come to dread the moments when they witness the unhealthy interactions that they have tried to deny for so long. As things get worse, and these rituals become more pressured, every family member comes to want to avoid the others as much as possible.

Ritual gatherings can also be where the family gangs up on members who are pushing at the rules or who have challenged the system in some noticeable way. For instance, the person who has sought outside help can expect to be roasted every night—the sacrificial lamb offered up to the failing family system.

After hitting bottom, the family rituals often fall away with the collapsed system. This can leave a great deal of unstructured time for the alcoholic and coalcoholic, who used to pass time through routine. The individual who reaches out for support can establish new rituals to replace the old drinking or coalcoholic routines. Going to meetings, taking walks, calling a sponsor—these things can break up the day in new ways. These substitutions are vitally important in the early days of recovery: they help keep you from falling back into old habits, giving you room to change your behavior. Gradually, as abstinence is put in place, new alcohol-free rituals can be designed, rituals that celebrate the courage and hard work of family members in recovery.

As we saw in chapter 1, many rituals are subtle, and can survive into the abstinent phase without the family's noticing. It is important to question all the routines of life, because they often bring with them hidden connections to drinking behavior or other aspects of the unhealthy system. People often find themselves wondering what ever happened to the old routines. Spending some time investigating them helps you see how these rituals played into the drinking and how, in some cases, they prolonged the life of the alcoholic system.

Exercise: Rituals in Transition

This exercise is designed to help you look at how your family rituals were affected by the transition stage.

- Consult your journal entry from the "Drinking Rituals" exercise in chapter 1.

- How did these rituals change during the downward spiral? Was there more pressure put on them? Were there rituals that were always voluntary that suddenly became mandatory? How did the increased drinking affect the rituals?

- After hitting bottom, how were your family rituals altered? Did the family hold on to them for a while or were they let go quickly?

- How did the family adapt to having more free time? Did your family members find individual activities that were substitutes? Did recovery offer new rituals?

Be sure to date this entry in your journal.

Boundaries

The internal family boundaries become even more blurred as the family system starts to collapse. The heightened anxieties cause everyone to become more careful and more vigilant about their surroundings. Each individual's main focus is the other members of the family. In contrast, the external boundaries are solidifying, possibly even to the point of sealing the family off altogether from the outside world. As the alcoholic tries to control his environment, he must keep putting tighter and tighter limits on it. The family becomes like a black hole: the world shrinks and the gravitational pull of the alcoholic system grows. The alcoholic's desperation begs the family members' loyalty and help, at the same time as his single-minded grab for control denies that any help is needed.

When the alcoholic hits bottom and reaches outside for support, the rest of the family often holds to the familiar pattern of trying not to upset the alcoholic. Even though the family is trying to support a healthy change, by protecting the alcoholic, they are still keeping the blurred boundaries intact. In a similar way, the family may fear that reaching out for help for themselves might somehow threaten the alcoholic's recovery by bringing undue attention to it. Though the motivations for it have changed, the external boundary is kept in place. Only the alcoholic is freed; the rest of the family continues the familiar pattern of self-sacrifice.

When all the members step into programs or support systems of their own, the crushing black hole is inverted, and all the boundaries change. By shifting the focus off the family and onto the self, the once-blurred boundaries between family members become much less permeable. At the same time, by reaching out, the family members break through the once-impenetrable external boundary. The process of recovery is based on this new set of boundaries, which supports the health and growth of the individual, and which must be the starting point for still another set of boundaries—the healthy, semipermeable boundaries within the family. As we will see in later chapters, a healthy family is built of healthy individuals. The boundaries that were built up to serve the family at the expense of the individual are thrown off for boundaries that serve the individual. Only after individual recovery has been thoroughly set in place will the family connections be plugged in again.

In the earliest period of recovery, trust will be at an all-time low. Everyone will be protecting themselves from everyone else. The only safety will come from the external support system. It will be some time before family members feel comfortable being vulnerable to one another. This will also be a difficult time-in-transition with friends. Old drinking friends may eventually be left behind while new friends who share the attitudes and beliefs of the new abstinence will be brought into the family's life.

Exercise: Boundaries in Transition

Consult your journal entry from the "Drinking Boundaries" exercise in chapter 1.

- What happened to the interpersonal boundaries in your family during the downward spiral? Did the family become more enmeshed or less?

- What happened to the boundary between the family and the outside world when the alcoholism spun out of control? Was less and less connection allowed? Was the change gradual or sudden?

- After the shift to abstinence, how did these two boundaries change? Did the family members put greater amounts of space between each other? Did individuals reach outside the family and connect with external support?

Hierarchies

As with the other elements of the system's structure, the family's hierarchies become a source of increased tension as the alcoholism spins out of control. The alcoholic's need for control makes the hierarchies rigid, while at the same time causing the alcoholic to shift the balance of power on a whim. On one hand, the alcoholic needs the hierarchy in place in order to delegate responsibility, which is easiest if there is an orderly chain of command. Sometimes alcoholics will forfeit their place at the top of the hierarchy to gain a truce that enables them to keep drinking. So a family may have the father and eldest daughter at the top with the alcoholic mother off to the side. When the oldest child is made a caretaker of the rest of the children in this manner, this role comes with a lot of power, but also a lot of pressure. This pressure, when combined with the tension in the house, can challenge the child's ability to maintain denial.

On the other hand, the alcoholic will manipulate the hierarchy as a way of punishing those who step out of line. This makes the hierarchy highly unstable. For instance, if the coalcoholic steps out of the system for help, the alcoholic may enlist the rest of the family to challenge the traitor. The coalcoholic, who may have once occupied the top of the food chain, is demoted to the bottom. Or, if an alcoholic mother in recovery reasserts her position at the top, the coalcoholic father and caretaking eldest daughter may resist, especially if the alcoholic system has not fully collapsed. Thus in the alcoholic system, anyone who conforms to the denial is placed higher than anyone who lets in the dangerous reality. This results in a dog-eat-dog system that rewards the collaborators and punishes anyone who challenges the denial. After a few of these shifts, the hierarchy begins to lose its importance, and no one trusts their place anymore. Power is only useful if you can wield it, and the alcoholic hoards all the power, assigning only the illusion of power to others.

As the alcoholic hits bottom, the hierarchy is thrown into turmoil, with a vacuum left at the top. The tyrant is shown to be a frightened and powerless mortal, which often leads to resentment from the rest of the family, who are bitter for having been manipulated by an imposter. For children, seeing one of their parents so undone can be a traumatic experience that leaves them very angry at the parent's weakness.

As the individuals in the family all make the move into recovery programs, they step outside the unhealthy hierarchies, and into a hierarchy that is based on strengths like practical skills and length of time in recovery. In AA, a new member will get a sponsor, who helps the individual through the process. The focus is now on individual growth and healing the damage of the drinking period.

At home, some hierarchy may need to be put in place for practical purposes during early abstinence. We will discuss this more in chapter 6.

Exercise: Hierarchies in Transition

Consult your journal entry for the "Drinking Hierarchy" exercise in chapter 1.

- How did the pecking order change during the downward spiral in your family? Was the system of power unstable? Were there a lot of shifts in people's places? What behavior would cause someone to be demoted in the family ranking? Was there one person who meted out these punishments or did the whole family work together?

- During the time after the shift to abstinence, what happened to the power structure? Was there a vacuum formed at the top? Did the family members reach out for new healthy hierarchies?

- How did the family react to the changes?

Communication

While the family system is collapsing, communication will be awkward. The increased danger may lead family members to seek refuge by connecting with each other; but at the same time, the tension will make everyone even more defensive than usual. These contradictory motivations will result in arguments and confrontations as members waver between vulnerability and distance. The style of communication will vary from family to family: some will experience a quiet environment bristling with tension, while others will live with nonstop yelling. No matter which way your family leans, the pressure will lead to awkward communication and therefore greater distance between the stressed-out family members.

When the alcoholic hits bottom and the system collapses, communication will also hit bottom. The anger, confusion, and despair of the crisis will make communication more difficult than ever. To make matters worse, the family also may worry about disturbing the abstinence, so family members will choose their words with even greater care. This in turn leads to still greater tensions and awkwardness.

George remembers the earliest time after his quitting drinking as a communications nightmare. "It's like we all spoke different languages. It wouldn't have been so bad if we could have had even a little silence. But everyone was so nervous that we all just talked at the same time. It was like that for months: everyone talking and no one listening. If I wasn't crazy already, this would have pushed me to it."

When the family members each enter individual recovery programs, they will be on parallel paths, learning a new vocabulary that will allow them to speak about the things they are experiencing. They will have the opportunity to discuss their thoughts and feelings with their support groups. At home, things will still be awkward, so family members will need to construct temporary guidelines for communication that respects each other's boundaries. We will discuss some of these skills in chapter 6.

Exercise: Communication in Transition

Consult the journal entry for the "Drinking Communication" exercise in chapter 1.

- How did family communication change during the downward spiral? Did the number of topics that were off-limits rise? Did conversation become more or less common?

- How was family communication affected by the shift to abstinence? Was everyone walking on eggshells? Was there a lot of arguing? A lot of silence?

- Was there a new recovery vocabulary being put in place? If there was, did the family resist it or take part?

Interaction

During the downward spiral, family relationships are strained to the breaking point. Extreme demands cause everyone to become extremely defensive. Alliances are made and broken on the spur of the moment. Since everyone is relying on emergency thinking, they will instinctively grab for safety at every turn. If that means ganging up on a scapegoated member, so be it; if it means neglecting the children, then that's what happens. Often in recovery, individuals have to face a lot of guilt over how they acted in those final dark days before hitting bottom. Most people think they will respond in a dignified way in a crisis, and cannot understand how people do the things they do when under extreme pressure. But when you are on a sinking ship in the middle of the ocean, all bets are off. People will do horrible things to one another to protect themselves.

When the bottom is hit, the family can be in collective shock. Surprised to have survived the ordeal, individuals may be afraid to exhale for fear of disturbing the peace. As life goes on and abstinence has not proved the magical cure it was hoped to be, despair can settle over the house. Meanwhile, the family may either walk on eggshells to protect the alcoholic or attack the weakened tyrant.

It is crucial that the individuals move into recovery programs, so they can begin to heal and practice new and healthy interaction. At home the tension will remain painful as everyone waits for the next tragedy. But in their recovery programs, the individuals are taking their first steps toward sharing their thoughts and feelings and allowing themselves to be vulnerable. These are key steps on the road to recovery.

Exercise: Interaction in Transition

Consult the journal entry for the "Drinking Interaction" exercise in chapter 1.

- How did the family interaction style change when the drinking behavior became more extreme and dangerous? Were family members drawn together or pushed apart?

- How did interaction change after the shift to abstinence? Were family members more distant? Did family members have places outside the family where they could go to feel safe?

Stability

As the family system disintegrates, the alcoholic and coalcoholic will cling to any shred of control and stability they can find. For a long time there has been the illusion of control and the appearance of stability, but now the limits of this illusory control have shrunk. The only control left is to try to hold the family in place. The rigidity of the structures and the precariousness of the interactions make the family increasingly unstable. Paradoxically, the more the alcoholic and coalcoholic try to impose stability, the more unstable the family becomes.

When the alcoholic or coalcoholic hits bottom, it is often with a stark realization that the system is out of their control. As the system collapses before their eyes, all the family members need to surrender to the loss of control that was at the heart of the unstable system. This need for surrender leads them to step outside of the family for the external support of a recovery program. It is only after they face the truth of the family's instability that healthy stability can grow. The first step is in individual recovery.

As the family members move into recovery programs and settle into supportive structures, the family system is allowed to remain collapsed. Meanwhile, each member works within the framework of his or her healthy and supportive external structure. This stability affords the individuals the security to face the inner loss of control that has so long been denied. After much hard work, the individuals will internalize this stability and can rejoin their family in creating a healthy family system: one made up of healthy and stable individuals.

Change

As the family spirals downward, everyone works together to resist the perceived enemy: change. But the more it is resisted, the more unavoidable it becomes. The system is crashing, the end is resisted with great urgency, and the tension and pressure build. Something's got to give.

When the alcoholic or coalcoholic hits bottom, it unleashes an explosion of stored-up energy, essentially remaking the alcoholic family's world. As we saw earlier, for the alcoholic, the moment of hitting bottom brings powerful inversions: control becomes loss of control, defensiveness becomes vulnerability. For the family, who has fought reality on the alcoholic's behalf, the change brings tremendous anxiety. The system that once provided stability, even if it was only the illusion of stability, has collapsed, and now they have to face reality. In the face of all this critical change it is no surprise that many families hold tight to the fallen system, even as the alcoholic is stepping out of the system and into the external structure.

As the individuals all step out of the system and into individual recovery programs, they are each taking responsibility for changing their own lives instead of living within a system that calls the shots. Eventually, they will work toward having a family made up of people who are committed to their own change and healthy growth and who bring their own intuition and capacity for change into the mix. We will watch this path unfold in parts 3 and 4.

A Summary of the Family System in the Transition Stage

Drinking Phase

1. The system is becoming more unhealthy.

2. As cracks form in the denial, it becomes harder to overlook the oppressive nature of the system.

3. Most of the familiar structures are nearing a state of collapse.

4. Individuals move toward hitting bottom.

5. As the home gets more out of control, individuals tighten their defenses. The family may pull together in an attempt to keep out the knowledge of the impending downfall.

6. There is both growing rigidity and the beginnings of collapse in the structure and process of the family system:

   ■ **Rules** are tightening in an effort to keep things in place. But as denial slips, the rules become less binding.

   ■ **Roles** are also tightening. But as the individuals feel the rising pressure, the restrictive quality of the roles becomes more obvious.

   ■ **Rituals** are becoming more strained and dangerous as the family can no longer deny the role of alcohol in them.

   ■ **Boundaries** are blurring even more as the state of emergency makes all the members sacrifice themselves to help the others. Meanwhile the family boundary is solidifying, as the outside world is slowly being blocked out entirely.

   ■ **Hierarchies** are switching between rigidity and chaos depending on the whims of the alcoholic and coalcoholic. Anyone breaking the denial is punished by a demotion in the family's esteem.

   ■ **Communication** may waver between awkward and confrontational, as the tensions of the house make healthy communication all but impossible. With the defenses up, very little connection can be made among family members; most of their discussions are attempts to reconnect with the crumbling denial.

   ■ **Interaction** may waver between awkward and confrontational. Alliances are made and broken on a whim in order for individuals to protect themselves from the dangers of the environment.

   ■ **Stability** erodes as the system implodes, and the family dynamics become severely unstable. The more the family clings to the crumbling structure, the greater the tension becomes.

   ■ **Change** is the only consistency, but it is mainly traumatic and painful. The family is eaten up by anxiety and despair. Although the change will result in improvement, it is felt as a steady decline.

Abstinent Phase

1. Although a healthy move to abstinence has been made, the system as a whole still remains unhealthy.

2. The family experiences the "trauma of recovery."

3. The individuals shift their focus off of the family system and onto external systems of support.

4. With the collapse of the system, the family is torn between their old, unhealthy structure and processes, and the vacuum that has been left in their place. Healthy, outside support systems begin to take the place of the old system and fill the vacuum left by its collapse:

   - **Rules** are exposed as problematic. There is ongoing tension as the family wavers between the chaos of no rules and the "stability" of the outmoded rules.

   - **Roles** are no longer working to smooth out problems, because the system that supported them has collapsed. Still, the family members hold on to the roles, often identifying deeply with their coping behavior. Or, they may reject their roles completely, since the roles didn't save the family after all.

   - **Rituals** are let go. This leaves a lot of unstructured time that the alcoholic and coalcoholic must fill with healthy substitutions for unhealthy habits.

   - **Boundaries** are still blurred between family members and impermeable between the family and the outside world. In order to commit to individual recovery, each member must break through the family boundary to reach out for help; and each person must also create an individual boundary within the family that allows the self-focus necessary for recovery.

   - **Hierarchies** are dismantled. As the parents hit bottom, there is a vacuum created at the top of the food chain. In recovery, family members find a new healthy hierarchy based on time and work in recovery. Each individual starts as an apprentice and learns the trade from a veteran outside the family system.

   - **Communication** tends to be awkward, as the family may fear upsetting the new abstinence. Trust has not yet been built among the family members. In recovery, the individuals are learning a new vocabulary and a way to talk that will help them discuss the alcoholism and recovery in a useful way.

   - **Interaction** may range from walking on eggshells around each other to attacking the weakened tyrant. As the family members step into recovery, there will be distance between them as they try to sort out the proper boundaries to assure the self-focus needed for healthy recovery. This can take some time.

   - **Stability** is uncertain because the system has collapsed. Individuals become very dependent on external supports to provide stability while they heal.

   - **Change** affects everything. Again, the individuals are getting support from their recovery programs, which tend to offer a systematic process by which healthy growth can be fostered. This framework gives the recovering person a much-needed anchor.

(Adapted from Brown and Lewis, 1999)

5

"Dancing on Thin Ice"

Points of View in the Transition Stage

Now that you have an overview of the transition stage and its effects on the alcoholic family system, you can explore each family member's points of view: how each experiences the trauma and dramatic changes that are taking place at this time. The pressure in the household can make it seem that every situation is an emergency. This means you never have the security to step back and consider how you and your family members fit into the larger system. With emergency thinking comes a sense of panic, which is a key challenge to transition. The best way to fight this panic is through understanding as much as you can about your situation and those of your family members.

Seeing yourself as part of your surroundings can shed new light upon your thoughts and behavior. A family system shapes the individuals within it just as the individuals create the system. With the blurred boundaries and unsafe environment of the transition stage, you may feel completely isolated and at the same time like you have no space to call your own. Though these feelings may seem contradictory, they aren't. They are the natural result of the unhealthy alcoholic system, which demands that you sacrifice your individuality to protect the group (giving you no space of your own), while at the same time giving you no real security or connection (leaving you feeling isolated).

In order for the system to go on working, this alienation needs to be denied. Much of the first part of this book discussed the many ways people learn to ignore their pain and discomfort by focusing on their need to protect the system. Now that the system is falling apart, it becomes harder to ignore the hole at the center of your self. What you thought was a solid foundation was only the illusion of a foundation, which may now be disintegrating beneath your feet. Panic may be setting in as everyone tries to hold the illusion together. Reality, which is painful to face, is pushed aside again and again, but as things get worse it gets harder to hide from it.

In chapter 4 we looked at family dynamics at play during transition. Now it is time to explore the individual perspectives of the family members. The objectivity afforded by stepping back to see how you fit into the world can be very comforting, but the step back can also feel dangerous. In some ways, this knowledge is precisely what the members of the alcoholic family are afraid of: a mirror that shows them to themselves, warts and all. Though this can be scary and undermining, it is an important step on the path to healthy recovery.

The Individual in the Transition Stage

In the drinking phase, the individual:

- Sacrifices her own development to preserve the endangered system
- Is dominated by trauma
- Defends against surrender
- Experiences cracks forming in her denial
- Experiences despair
- Feels defeated

In the abstinent phase, the individual:

- Shifts from family focus to individual focus
- Shifts to external help
- Forms an attachment to recovery and the new recovery identity
- Goes through a time of intense dependency
- Experiences feelings of depression, anxiety, abandonment, confusion, fear, dominance of impulse

(Adapted from Brown and Lewis, 1999)

"I Am an Alcoholic"—Peggy Remembers The Transition Stage

"The first time I really let my problem out of the bag was when we hosted a party for Stan's coworkers. I had been to a few small gatherings, but I had always been able to hide in the corners. Now I was going to be the center of attention: they were coming into my world. I was nervous and wanted to make a good impression. I felt like this was my chance to make some friends; people would like me once they saw how wonderful a party we could throw. I was so anxious, I had a couple of drinks to calm my nerves. A couple of drinks quickly turned into five. Then the guests arrived. To make a long story short, I got very drunk. Afterwards, I couldn't remember anything. The story Stan told me was worse than anything I could have made up: I was insulting people, I got sick, and at one point I was trying to take my clothes off. It was very ugly. The funny thing was that afterwards, we never discussed the drinking. Instead,

Stan just wanted to know why I was punishing him. Like I had plotted the whole thing as my revenge for his never being home."

Peggy and Stan grew up in a small town in western Minnesota. "I remember it as a drinking town," recalls Peggy. "I mean, there were people there who didn't drink; we just didn't know any of them." At forty-five, she's been sober seven years. "My family drank, his family drank: everyone drank. It's what you did. When you spend your time with drinkers, drinking is normal. You can't see that things are extreme unless you've got something to compare it to."

When Stan was transferred from his office in Minnesota to the San Fernando Valley, north of Los Angeles, Peggy packed up the house and her kids and moved west with a smile on her face. "I was excited. This was a great opportunity for Stan. I was pretty naïve thinking it'd be easy. I knew we'd miss our families, but they were getting vacation time in California out of the deal: not a bad trade."

With the promotion came more responsibilities for Stan, so his time at the office grew. With her daughter in junior high and her son in high school, Peggy was left alone much of the time. Back in Minnesota, Stan and Peggy matched each other drink for drink, but now Peggy was beginning to drink alone. "I think we both had a drinking problem in Minnesota, but the move to California changed that. It pushed Stan's problem into the background and shoved mine to center stage."

At first no one noticed, since everything seemed to function well around the house. Stan was not home much, and Peggy didn't share her complaints. But she was suffering: "I was miserable, but Stan was thriving; so I didn't want to be a burden. Drinking seemed to ease the pain. I had a laundry list of excuses: I was so homesick; I didn't have any friends; I had too much extra time. My mom was always a phone call away, so we'd talk for hours, drinking and smoking; it was the one time I felt connected. I ran up the phone bill and poured down the bourbon. I'd be pretty wobbly when Stan would finally come home, but we'd have a couple of drinks together. He called this our 'bonding' time. He would tell me how hard things were for him at work and how great he thought I was doing. I knew he felt guilty about never being home, so I would just smile and tell him things were fine. I was also secretly relieved that he didn't seem to notice my drinking. If I had a problem, my husband would notice."

Denial

Peggy went to a few office parties with Stan. But she quickly realized that these parties were different than the ones they had back home. "I was used to loud talking, laughter, music. But these parties were so sedate. There'd be wine but no booze. I felt like a fish out of water." She'd have a few drinks and keep to herself, feeling out of place and hoping to leave as soon she could. "It was like trying to play a game where you didn't know the rules. I was certain that even the tiniest gesture I made was somehow awkward. It was horrible. I just wanted to feel comfortable."

For Peggy, comfort had been defined by the alcoholic community she and Stan had left behind in Minnesota. Stan had replaced this sense of community with an office community that didn't include the drinking he had done before he moved. Peggy had no replacement for her lost social system and had only its key component—the drinking—left to keep her company. At least that's how she saw it:

"During the period that my drinking was really getting heavy, I remember feeling like it brought my home back to me. You know when a smell brings back your childhood? That's what drinking was; it was this familiar sensation. Warmth and belonging were only a couple of drinks away. That's what I told myself. But soon the explanation was just an afterthought to the need to drink."

When Peggy found evidence of her own problem, she'd quickly adapt her behavior to hide it. "We had a recycling service for our neighborhood. And I remember one week I was putting out the recycling and there were four vodka bottles in there. I just had a panic attack. I actually asked myself, 'Whose bottles are these?' Like maybe Stan had been dropping them off. Well, from that day on, I began to recycle one bottle a week, and the others I would dispose of in the garbage or at the supermarket recycling bin. That way it was always one bottle at a time. One bottle was never too much."

Her new environment also threatened to expose her problem. "In Minnesota, we used to blame the seasons when we were drinking. It's so hot outside in the summer, so we need to cool off. It's freezing outside, so we need to warm up. It's amazing, alcohol can be made to be the cure for everything. People need to drink so they invent reasons for it. Well, in L.A. it was perfect every day, so I was just drinking to drink."

Even with the edges of her problem exposed to her, she maintained her denial. She wasn't the one who was abnormal: everyone else was weird. "I would talk to my mother for hours at a time complaining about the Californians. Everyone was so uptight; no one trusted each other. I took no responsibility for my isolation."

Growing Isolation

Things were deteriorating, but Peggy didn't notice it. Then she hosted that fateful office party. "That was the first real crack in the armor. Before then, I had inklings of a problem, but I was sure that no one had any idea. But after that humiliation, I had to do something to let everyone know I had things under control. For another person, the humiliation of that party might have been enough to send them looking for help. But I needed to take care of my family. I was strong; I felt I could handle it. In reality, I was using my family as an excuse not to face the music about my drinking. As long as I felt I was crucial to our family, I was convinced that I couldn't afford the luxury of getting help. So I just quit cold turkey. I did it partly out of shame and partly to prove that I didn't have a problem."

Drinking had been Peggy's antidote for loneliness, and suddenly she was without it. And after the debacle at her party, she felt more isolated than ever. It became difficult for her to go back to another party. She was suddenly cut off from a source of friends. "Before the meltdown at the party I could hold on to the fantasy of hanging out with the other wives, but now I knew that wasn't going to happen."

Without the alcohol, Peggy was left to face her unhappiness without the numbing effects of intoxication. "I felt pretty good for the first couple of weeks; I thought I had licked it. But soon the novelty wore off, and I got so tense. I would sit in the living room thumbing through magazines over and over. That's when my son, Craig, stopped spending time at home, and Melissa disappeared into her room. I would go back and forth between feeling relieved to be alone and feeling abandoned. Stan would get home, and I'd be irritable, and we would fight. You can only go so long balanced on willpower alone. I started taking sleeping pills for my anxiety, but nothing really helped. In the end, I think Stan actually brought home a bottle of wine one night, sort of saying, 'Time for you to be normal again.' I was more than happy to oblige."

The Tension Between Drinking and Abstinence

An alcoholic can waver between drinking and abstinence for a long time without any real change happening. That's why in most cases the alcoholic needs to hit bottom before the seeds of deeper change can finally be planted. "I went back and forth between drinking and quitting for a couple of years. But when I'd be 'on the wagon' I was always sneaking drinks. That was the major change after the office party, I didn't change the drinking so much as I changed how I drank. Earlier on I was hiding it from the outside world, but now I was hiding it from my family. I started buying breath mints. You think you're being sly and fooling everyone, but I wonder. I don't believe you can fool anyone who doesn't want to be fooled. My husband was happy with his job and he needed everything to be all right with me, so as long as I made it look like everything was better, he was fine."

The family system was organized around Peggy's drinking. Stan and the children had a tacit agreement that time spent in their home was spent making sure she was not bothered. "The house became my realm. I was queen. I needed everything to be where it needed to be. I was spinning out of control, and I needed something to hang on to. This doesn't mean that the house was clean or orderly, just that it was arranged as I wished it, when I wished it. Stan was guilty, and my kids were scared, so I just took up all the space in the middle. In my mind I was keeping everything together. But I was really just protecting myself. I was in so much pain, I felt I needed to hold on to my small piece of turf."

Things were getting out of control, but no one was there to see it. Craig was never home and Melissa kept to herself. Stan's work day got longer and longer. "I started to notice how I was slipping and I couldn't handle that. By then I had quit drinking five times, each time I swore it would last. Each time it lasted less than the time before. And I wasn't even really quitting. I would pretend to quit, but I couldn't even keep up the illusion of quitting. I started using more and more sleeping pills. I was a mess. I don't know how I got anything done. I was like a zombie."

Hitting Bottom

Although it was impossible for Peggy to see any benefit from her suffering while she was experiencing it, pain and discomfort are an important part of the recovery process. Despair, isolation, and anxiety are all catalysts for change, pushing the alcoholic toward the critical moment of hitting bottom. As long as Peggy clung to the false belief that she was in control of her drinking, she had to fight off painful thoughts and emotions; and her chief tool to keep the pain away was the drinking, which ultimately brings only more pain.

Once Peggy started the decline, she gained momentum all the way down. Peggy needed to accept her loss of control. Her core beliefs needed to change from "I am not an alcoholic and I can control my drinking" to the opposite: "I am an alcoholic and I cannot control my drinking."

But no matter how much she personally suffered, Peggy couldn't let go and reach out for help. "My last line of defense was my belief that the family needed me. I was the mother. I couldn't afford to lose control because everything would fall apart. I convinced myself that this was the selfless thing to do; I believed I was taking care of everyone else. Of course the truth was that I was a slave to the bottle, and I wasn't paying attention to the family at all."

Peggy had drawn a line in the sand: as long as her family seemed all right, she was all right. But her family was far from all right. Her husband and son were never home and her daughter was sinking into a deep depression. "I didn't see any of it. I wasn't looking. It took reality punching me square in the face to finally make me open up my eyes." The blow was struck when her daughter, Melissa, tried to commit suicide by overdosing on her mother's sleeping pills.

"There was nowhere left for me to hide. The one thing I had been holding on to, my being a good mother, was shattered. I had painted this lie. Suddenly the curtain was drawn up and here was the awful truth behind it. Seeing Melissa strapped to all those tubes and hoses, teetering between life and death, I just lost it. I felt it was my fault. I prayed and prayed, asking for one more chance. My life had just shrunk down to this tiny place, my daughter dying in the hospital. That was all there was. I called information from the waiting room and got a number for Alcoholics Anonymous. I made a deal with myself: if my daughter died, I would die; but if she lived . . ."

Melissa came out of the coma after two days. On the drive home from the hospital that day with Stan and her son Craig, Peggy announced she was quitting drinking. "No one believed me. If anything, Stan was angry, like I was trying to upstage my daughter's crisis. I was trying to convince them that this time it would be different. But no one budged. They'd heard it all before. One of the early motives for my recovery was to prove to them that I could do it. The recovery didn't really begin until I realized that the person I needed to prove it to was myself. It took a catastrophe for me to get help, but it was only that huge hurdle that allowed the person I had become to die."

Death and Rebirth

"Hitting bottom is like dying. It's like I had a terminal disease, and I had been fighting for my alcoholic life. Since that was the only life I knew, since the bottle was so much a part of my identity, letting go seemed impossible. But in the end, you can't fight anymore; you have to give in."

Even though Peggy had decided to get help, she hadn't surrendered yet. For her, reaching out was a decision; surrender was an experience. "I was still in shock from what had happened to my daughter. Somewhere inside I was hooked on the thought that if I made a change, it would help everyone in my family. I was still holding on to my warped rationalizations, but in this case they got me to my first meeting. Once I got there, the reality of where I was just floored me. Suddenly it wasn't about anyone but myself. There were about thirty people there, thirty alcoholics, and I was there, too. I just froze—a deer in the headlights. I don't think I heard a single word. I think the shock was wearing off and the weight of what I was doing was starting to sink in for the first time.

"I found myself in my car after the meeting. I felt like I was going to vomit, like there was this uncontrollable force in me that I was terrified to let out; if I let it out it would kill me. And suddenly out it came. But it wasn't vomit, and it wasn't death; it was tears. I was giving up the fight with the disease. The disease had won. In AA we call this 'surrender,' and there is no better word for it. I had lost the battle. And with the tears came a sort of relief, letting out something I had been holding on to for so long. And on the heels of that relief came desperation: I realized I needed to get to another meeting as soon as possible."

The powers of denial are so strong in an alcoholic, that giving them up feels like giving up life itself. And unless the alcoholic takes advantage of the helplessness and desperation of surrender, denial can creep back in. Once she gets back on her feet again, she can explain away the crisis as just another setback. Peggy's desperate realization that she needed to get to another meeting was caused by an intimate experience of her own helplessness. For the first time she saw her enslavement to alcohol: "I had thought I was the captain of my ship, but I suddenly realized I was a cork floating in an ocean. I had no control. The control had been a fantasy." After a lifetime spent clinging to this control, her realization of her helplessness brought with it crushing anxiety. She needed to get to a meeting; she needed help.

If hitting bottom is like dying, surrendering is like being born all over again. Letting go of the core belief that you have control over the drinking leaves you helpless and vulnerable, like a baby fresh from the womb. You are a creature of impulse. Your impulses are not new, they've been enslaving you for the entire period of active alcoholism. Then, you saw them as choices; you saw your needs as desires. Now, the curtain of denial has been pulled back, revealing the naked impulses underneath. At this moment it is critical to grab hold of the security of an external support structure so you can let yourself experience the chaos that has been so long denied.

"When you're an alcoholic, you feel like you're walking on the moon. You're certain there is no oxygen in the atmosphere, so you have to wear a space suit called denial or you'll suffocate. The suit seems to keep you alive, but the longer you live inside it the more the outside world disappears. Your sole focus becomes that 'life support,' and after a while all that's left is the suit. And then the suit starts running out of oxygen. As it gets harder and harder to breathe, you have to choose between staying in the suit where you are sure to suffocate, or pulling off the suit to take a breath of the air you are convinced is poisonous. Taking off the spacesuit is a terrifying moment, but you suddenly realize you weren't walking on the moon, you were on earth all along. And there is actually oxygen. You don't need the suit." The problem for the alcoholic who has surrendered and let go of the spacesuit is that her mind has lived so long with the belief that there is no oxygen, that even though every breath brings proof to the contrary, she still has a deep need for the suit. Peggy needed something to replace the suit.

"I called AA and found another meeting across town. When I finally said the words aloud, 'I am an alcoholic,' it was like god took his knee off of my throat. The spacesuit just kind of fell off. And even though there was oxygen in the room, I was sucking for air like there were just two breaths left in the world."

The Power in Powerlessness

"In those first few weeks I just felt so small, so worthless. For a while, I felt like without my meetings I would disappear altogether. At home, I was clueless. Every corner of that house seemed to lead to the bottle. It was as though drinking was my whole life, and now that I was without it, I had no life. I fell into old routines, trying to keep everything in the house in its place—like if everything looked all right on the outside, I would feel better on the inside. I would end up distracting myself, which is dangerous in the early period of recovery. When you are distracted you fall into habits, and habits are the enemy. When I wasn't distracted I just stared at my own helplessness. I don't know how I got through those days."

Painful as it is, insecurity is necessary to the early work of recovery. You need to be focused on your powerlessness in order to rebuild your individual foundation. This powerlessness makes you feel dependent on the healthy structure and willing to hold on tight to it. In an alcoholic system, the alcoholic clings to an unhealthy dependence on alcohol. Shifting your dependency onto recovery structures can feel like a step backwards—like you are becoming a child again: helpless, vulnerable, trusting, and confused. In order to build a solid individual foundation, you must surrender entirely to your loss of control. You must give up your false perceptions of power in order to build on the reality of your powerlessness.

At first, you don't experience surrender as a hopeful change for the better. Hitting bottom and surrendering involve experiencing the complete hopelessness of your way of perceiving the world. You can't be "reborn" if you are trying to control, and therefore avoid, your "death." You may believe in the possibility of rebirth—even hope and pray for it—but you can't expect it. If you do, you are still working within the framework of alcoholic logic: trying to control a moment that, in its essence, is about loss of control.

"Before AA, I had a hole in my life and I filled it with alcohol. That's like filling one hole with another. And the second hole is even more dangerous; it imprisons you and then closes in on you. With AA, I finally had something positive to fill the void: a program of recovery and a community of people who knew what I was going through. I didn't want to leave those meetings when they were over. I felt such a strong sense of belonging when I was there."

The addiction to alcohol is often replaced by an addiction to abstaining from alcohol. The impulses are still out of control, but they are pointed in a positive direction. The solid structure of the twelve-step program gave Peggy the security to let herself be vulnerable. "It's terrifying to feel that you have no control. And more than feel it, you have to focus on it. You have to experience your loss of control without hiding from it, allowing your impulses to wash over you. It's not about willpower, and pushing your needs down. It's about feeling those needs and doing something healthy instead. You can't control your impulses, but you can choose how you act on them."

The Developmental Model of Recovery: Transition

During active alcoholism, the alcoholic experiences life much like a newborn. She is a creature of unbridled impulse. If she has the urge to grab, she grabs; if she has the urge to drink, she drinks. In an infant there is little consciousness to mediate these urges.

But soon an infant grows into a toddler, who is learning a lot about the world. She is still ruled by impulses, but she is learning that there is an outside world upon which these impulses are directed. She begins to learn new ways of expressing these impulses. The acquisition of language gives the child an important tool by which she mediates impulse and action. At the beginning of abstinence, the alcoholic is like an infant—all impulse, sensation, and need. Her focus is on behavior change with simple substitutions. Soon, the alcoholic is comparable to a toddler. The impulses are still raging inside, but new language and behaviors are being acquired to redirect these impulses toward healthy ends. In Alcoholics Anonymous, people talk in concrete language: "Put the plug in the jug" and "One day at a time" are familiar slogans. This is language a toddler can understand, and it helps form a wedge between impulse and action.

The Alcoholic in the Transition Stage

In the drinking phase, the alcoholic's primary focus is alcohol.

Behavior

- Sense of loss of control intensifies
- Out-of-control behavior increases

Thinking

- Cracks form in denial and beliefs
- Growing awareness of loss of control

Emotional Expression

- An increase in impulsive outbursts against others and self
- An increase in feelings of guilt, depression, desperation, despair, and defeat

In the early abstinent phase, the alcoholic's primary focus shifts onto an external support structure such as AA, a recovery program, or therapy.

Behavior

- Solid, concrete focus on new abstinent behaviors and new substitutes for drinking, such as going to a meeting or picking up the phone instead of drinking
- Impulses still dominant

Thinking

- Confirmation of surrender and new belief in loss of control
- Concrete focus on new beliefs, new identity, and a new language of recovery
- Old beliefs are challenged
- Reconstruction of perceptions of the past; building of the narrative of what really happened
- Construction of a new perception of the present

Emotional Expression

- May be contained or denied through a focus on thinking and behavior
- Emotions may be expressed through substitute behaviors, especially focusing on action
- Depression is common; some alcoholics experience elation (flying on a "pink cloud")

(Adapted from Brown and Lewis, 1999)

Guilt as a Distraction from Self-Focus

"When Melissa came home, everything was very tense. I wanted so badly to be there for her, but I was so shaky. There were days when I'd go to three and four meetings and be on the phone with my sponsor for hours more. I was a basket case. And when I looked at my daughter I felt so much remorse. Stan was very angry about everything. He had to take over most of the household work and he was not happy about it. He made it pretty clear that he was ashamed of me. My son, Craig, was also very resistant to what I was going through. To him, I had gotten off the hook. I had ruined his life and then just cleaned the slate by going into recovery. My family back in Minnesota totally could not face it. My getting help was so threatening for them.

"This was the hardest time for me. Sometimes I just wanted to run away and start all over again. But I knew this wasn't the time for rash decisions. I took responsibility by gutting it out while I worked at recovery. I felt guilty, but at the same time I had no choice. I apologized all the time when I was at home, but deep down I knew that if I didn't stick to my program, I wouldn't survive at all."

It's a huge challenge for the alcoholic in early abstinence to deal with the feelings of guilt that may come along with quitting drinking. For the first time, reality is being let in, and it is often hard to look at it after all the problems the drinking has caused. It is not uncommon for recovery to be derailed in early abstinence because the drinker doesn't feel entitled to the self-focus necessary to move forward. Wanting to make everyone feel better, the alcoholic may feel compelled to try to make up for the bad behavior. This impulse is natural and has its roots in the long-standing alcoholic system: where there is no security, problems feel unendurable, and must be solved immediately. But these short-term fixes ignore long-term health and growth.

When you experience anxiety and pain, it's natural to want to comfort yourself as quickly as possible. But in order to work toward long-term health, you need to endure short-term anxieties. The way to do this is to rely on your external support, which will allow you to experience anxiety without jumping in to fix it. This strategy is at the heart of AA: instead of drinking to quell your impulse to drink (the short-term solution) you substitute healthy behavior, and you endure the anxiety of this substitution by going to meetings or talking to a sponsor.

It is critical that the alcoholic keep a focus on alcohol and recovery. If you're distracted from your self-focus, you may fall back into old routines that threaten the foundation of your recovery. This focus can be very difficult to keep. It won't be perfect; at times you'll be torn. But when push comes to shove, you must treat the alcoholism first and the family problems second. This was very difficult for Peggy, who was at a critical point of early abstinence when her daughter Melissa came home from the hospital. "I wanted so desperately to be able to stand there and be strong for my daughter. But I couldn't do it. I wanted a drink so bad."

Contrary to what many people hope, surrender does not clean the slate; old behaviors are deeply etched into the alcoholic system. The gravitational pull of the past can be overwhelming, so you must allow your unhealthy system to collapse. You can't do this for every member of the family, only for yourself. But when you step outside the system, you deal it a devastating blow. By reaching outside the old system for external support, you begin to create the foundation for a new. healthy system. Hitting bottom and surrendering are important experiences, but building a new life takes patience, discipline, and hard work. Like birth, surrender is both an event and the beginning of a lifelong process of growth.

Strong and Vulnerable

"After a while I realized I couldn't save my family. I could only save myself. I had to focus on the changes I could make. The only way I could help my family was by being a model of recovery. So I set out to do it right, to be strong and vulnerable. All my life I thought strength meant being invulnerable. But invulnerability is a shield to protect weakness. True strength is built on vulnerability, being open to the pain and discomfort that life has to offer. So I try to stay strong; it's something I have to work on every day."

In order to build this inner strength, you must start with a firm foundation. The foundation of recovery is your focus on your identity as an alcoholic and your deep loss of control. You can't move on to the next step until the first one is strongly rooted. This solid foundation gives you the confidence to live without fear and hypervigilance. You may have moments of doubt, but the strength built upon patience and self-focus will enable you to take the time to decide whether the bump in the road is a hazard that needs smoothing or an anxiety that can be endured.

This is how a developmental process works: one step at a time. For the alcoholic, self-focus is difficult because it has been denied so strongly for so long. Facing your lack of control can make you feel helpless, anxious, and scared. Every instinct that was honed in the alcoholic system tells you to ignore your own life and focus on the lives of others, ignoring the problems you can change to focus on the ones you can't. But Peggy has held to her self-focus through thick and thin, allowing the process of growth to evolve naturally, without her trying to take the controls. "Once I knew I was heading in the right direction, I could relax and enjoy the trip . . . at least some of the time."

Exercise: "I Am an Alcoholic in the Transition Stage . . ."

The purpose of this exercise is to gain some perspective on the alcoholic when he or she was in the transition stage. If you are the alcoholic, then its purpose is to allow you to explore the thoughts and feelings you had about yourself back then.

■ In your journal, describe how the alcoholic hit bottom. How did the alcoholic's behavior change during the descent toward the bottom. How did the alcoholic make excuses for the increasingly out of control behavior? What happened when the alcoholic surrendered? How did the alcoholic's behavior change when recovery began? Was there more trauma or less? If you are the alcoholic, imagine how someone else might have described your behavior during the fall, when you hit bottom, and when you started the road to healing.

Write as much or as little as you like. If you feel like it, you can write it as a story. Don't worry about capturing the absolute truth as it happened. Just write it as you recollect it. Historical accuracy is not the goal; writing down your perceptions is.

■ Now describe how you felt about the alcoholic when the above behavior occurred. Did you feel tense, angry, sad, or a combination of these emotions? Did you rationalize the alcoholic's behavior? How did you feel when the alcoholic hit bottom? What were your emotions when recovery began? Did you feel relief? Were you disappointed by the slow progress? Again, if you are the alcoholic, think back on how you felt about yourself and your behavior during the transition stage.

■ Now, instead of recalling the emotions you felt in the past, describe how you presently feel about the alcoholic's experience of transition. Do things make more sense when viewed from afar?

Remember to date the entries. As you work through recovery, you may want to come back to this exercise and see how your perceptions have changed. As you gain perspective on the recovery process, you will see the past more and more clearly, and with these changes in perception you might discover changes in your attitudes about the past. If it is too early to focus on these issues, you can come back later and try out the exercise. You can read what you want, do what you feel you can, and come back for the rest later.

One of the gifts of recovery is that you come to understand that those extreme hardships you had to endure in order to survive are often the most important turning points in your growth. As this truth sinks in, you may slowly begin to recognize your present pain and anxiety as the toll you need to pay to cross an important bridge. The objectivity of your perception can be a very helpful ally as you navigate the pitfalls and obstacles on the road to recovery. We'll talk more about this concept in the next chapter.

"I Am a Coalcoholic"—Stan Remembers the Transition Stage

"When we came to L.A., the future was burning like the sun. We didn't get much sun in Minnesota, and I felt like I was escaping. So when my wife started to be homesick, she became, for me, part of what I was escaping. I was a major-league drinker growing up, but I never had a problem calling it a night. Peggy was different; once she got started, she would drink till the cupboards were bare. I'd kid her about it, but it never seemed all that serious." As long as both partners were engaged in the problem drinking, they had no contrast by which to judge excess.

"When her drinking started to get out of control, I just threw myself more deeply into my work. I rationalized it by saying to myself that if the move was causing this much trouble, I had better make it count. I became a workaholic. As much as I tried to explain it otherwise, my job was an escape from the increasing pressures at home. I left the three of them to fend for themselves, telling myself the kids were old enough to take care of themselves and Peggy was just going through a transition."

There but for the Grace of God . . .

"I'd come home and have a few drinks with Peggy after work. I told myself I was helping her, but this ritual was for me. It made me feel less guilty. When things are tense, you don't feel safe pointing out other people's problems. I wasn't perfect either; it could have been me with the problem if the circumstances were different. I didn't think it was fair being holier than thou, when I was just as flawed. This was how I was thinking. Now I have to laugh at these 'selfless' motives I thought I had. It was all just a smokescreen to allow me to do nothing. I was a drinker born of drinkers, so I didn't think drinking could be a serious problem. I thought that alcoholism was something that happened to other people; people who never learned how to drink."

When Peggy got embarrassingly drunk at the office party they were hosting, Stan became angry. "I saw her behavior as a reaction to me, like she was punishing me for being busy. This was my guilt talking again: I felt bad about abandoning her and letting her sink, so I saw the sinking as my punishment. Denial is a complicated thing. I basically focused on my own guilt to ignore her growing alcoholism. I guess on some level I figured that if her drinking was directed at me, then I had some kind of power over it."

From that point on, Stan was wary about any socializing. Unaware of how isolated his wife had become, he isolated her further by turning down any social opportunity that arose at work. "I told myself I was protecting her, but I was protecting myself. As I have learned in recovery about how the alcoholic family works, I can see how my wife and I were acting as a team to tighten the control over our lives. We were both shutting down the outside world. I had only my office and my home, in that order. At home I felt constant pressure to make things better for her, letting the kids know that their mom's 'nerves were frazzled,' or whatever my current euphemism was."

The more they tried to fix their family without confronting the drinking, the worse things got. Even when there was a momentary focus on alcohol, it was not taken seriously. "Peggy's attempts to quit drinking were halfhearted at best. Abstinence always seemed to make things worse, so we'd go back to the way things were and gut out a few more months. It got to the point where I couldn't stand being at home."

Dancing on Thin Ice

"This was all taking an incredible toll on my kids. My son followed in his father's footsteps and stayed away, and my daughter just got sucked under in that horrible tension. I was aware that things were bad, but I had no idea how bad. I felt I was doing everything I could, that I couldn't do more. When things are really bad, you'll hold on to the bad for fear of things getting worse."

Stan describes the downward spiral as dancing on thin ice. "Skating is too graceful an activity to describe what we were doing. We were all out there trying to dance and falling on our behinds and wondering what was going on. At first you think it's kind of fun. Then you think it's a bit frustrating, but no one is going to get hurt. Somewhere along the line you notice the sign on the shore saying 'Thin Ice!' but you quickly look away; after all, you've been dancing all this time and nothing has happened so far. If either of the kids so much as looked at the sign too long we'd have to distract them. So everyone ignores the danger, and you keep dancing. You come up with wide-ranging explanations for falling, none of which mention the ice: 'This is how I learned to dance' or 'I'm just not a very good dancer.' The ice is beginning to crack, but no one's ever fallen through, so what's the big deal? That's how we lived for almost two years. And then someone fell through the ice."

Stan was at work when he got the hysterical call from his wife. "Peggy woke up late, as usual, and when she got downstairs she discovered a message on the phone from school saying Melissa had cut class. Peggy checked Melissa's bedroom, and there she was on the floor. I met Peggy down at the hospital. Melissa was in a coma. They told us if they had gotten to her earlier it would not have been nearly as critical. I blamed Peggy: Melissa had taken her sleeping pills, and she would have been fine if Peggy were awake to answer the phone instead of sleeping off a drunk. I was just furious. I didn't even think about the fact my daughter had tried to kill herself and how desperate our home life had become; my sole focus was that it was all my wife's fault."

It was easier for Stan to blame Peggy than it was to take responsibility for his part in the tragedy. "My immediate defensive reaction came from the shame that the ugly secret had gotten out of the bag." Stan was ashamed that the world would find out he had "allowed" Peggy to become an alcoholic. "My wife's being an alcoholic made me look like a failure. At the same time I was denying my part in my wife's drinking, I was trying desperately to keep the old rules of silence and hiding in place. I just wanted to put that genie back in the bottle. Peggy was facing her alcoholism, and I was holding on to denial for all I was worth.

"As horrible as it is to admit, one of the things I felt was inconvenienced. I felt like I had held up my end, and my wife had let me down. This was pretty much the attitude I stuck to for the first year of my wife's recovery. I regret the way I treated her during the beginning of her abstinence even more than my collaboration during her drinking. I understand why I felt like I did, and I know I can't change what happened, but I still get flashes of remorse about how cruel I was to her."

Building Resentment

The biggest change that occurred when Peggy joined AA was that Stan had to cut back on work and start pitching in at home. "I just resented the hell out of that. She was holding me back from my job. That's how I felt. Looking back, I think the thing that scared me the most, the main reason I was angry, was the discovery that I *could* pitch in at home. All that time at the office hiding, telling myself work wouldn't get done without me—all that time I could have been helping the family, facing the problems I had turned away from. There was no way I wanted to face that. That was too scary."

The object of Peggy's addictive attachment was clear and tangible: it came in a bottle and when consumed it caused drunkenness. For Stan, things were not so cut-and-dry. The object of his attachment was his wife, the alcoholic. And she was going through a terrifying ordeal in surrendering to her addiction. This only inspired Stan to be more focused on her. The fact that Stan was angry at his wife does not mean his attachment to her was any less strong. On the contrary, anger can be an expression of a very strong attachment. Like a child rebelling against parents, the coalcoholic's resentment of the partner can be evidence of deep enmeshment.

"With Melissa and Peggy both in trouble, I had to prove to myself that I was a good father. I tried to be selfless and take care of everything. I was protecting my image of myself as the perfect husband and father. I tried to make up for my earlier selfishness, figuring I would be the savior who would take care of everyone. But try as I might, I couldn't let go of the anger at my wife; I was seething the whole time."

Stan's attempts to control his family left him feeling frustrated and disappointed. He needed to see immediate positive effects of his sacrifice, but the healing process does not work on a time line. "I was so impatient. I would think to myself that she was wallowing in this 'I am an alcoholic' thing. I wanted everything over in a flash, and anything less than that meant Peggy was not trying hard enough. She became so unattractive to me. I felt like she was married to AA. I was doing all this work and she wasn't appreciating any of it. All the time I was resenting her, I was the one wallowing. I was threatened by her recovery. I wasn't there when she needed me, and now that she didn't need me, I was all over her: criticizing her one moment and looking for praise the next."

Stan started thinking of walking out. "I even had a talk with my son about it. He was very angry at Peggy, too. Craig became my confidant during the recovery. I felt bad about complaining about her to her son, but I had to talk to someone. If I had it to do over again, I would talk to a therapist, but back then I was so invested in denial that I couldn't let my 'shameful' thoughts into the real world. Instead, I burdened my son with them. And he was more than willing to accept the promotion."

Another Bottom

"When my wife joined AA, I quit drinking, too. I said it was to show solidarity, but I think I wanted to show her how easy it was for me. Then a funny thing happened. As she started to get better and grow strong in her abstinence, I started drinking again. Since we had moved to California, I had really cut down, but I started creeping back up to my Minnesota level. It was like I could mend my wounds and express my resentment at the same time. I never did it at home; I went out to a bar.

"During this period, Peggy would come back from a meeting feeling good and I felt compelled to burst that bubble. It was never about anything specific, I just wanted her to know who was sacrificing so she could go to these meetings. I felt like I was being left behind and I was mad about that."

It was around the sixth month of Peggy's abstinence when Stan finally went too far. Stan brought home a six-pack of beer and put it in the refrigerator. It was the brand they drank back in Minnesota. "I remember thinking, 'This is my house, too. Just because my wife is a drunk doesn't mean I have to become a monk.' I don't know what I expected would happen when she saw it. When she opened the refrigerator door she froze there. I asked her what the problem was. She turned to me and stared, with tears running down her face. Something shifted inside me then. It's like I had been in shock for all those months, and suddenly our situation sank in.

"Later that night I asked Peggy for the first time how I could help with her recovery. She said I couldn't help, but I could stop getting in the way. She told me about Al-Anon and how she wanted the kids to get in a program. I could see her start to get this hopeful look in her eye; I could immediately feel myself getting angry again. It suddenly dawned on me that I was only happy if she was sad, and if she was enthusiastic I resented it. It was like a power struggle. As she got better, I needed to knock her down more, like I was afraid I was going to lose my strength if she lost her weakness. It was ugly. That was no way to live. I realized I needed help."

Stan went to Al-Anon and found the support of men and women who had been where he was. "The whole time I was angry with Peggy, I was ashamed of my anger. I thought there was something wrong with me. It seemed sick to be so resentful of someone who was trying to put her life back together. In Al-Anon I found other people who had stood in my shoes. It took a huge load off me to find out I wasn't some deviant. I came to understand how I was tied to Peggy. Our codependence was a relationship issue we had carried with us from Minnesota. It was nothing new, but it got a lot worse when the tensions of the move to California hit us. My focus on Peggy's drinking was a great way to hide what was wrong with me. I was suddenly the savior, and I could help out and she'd be grateful. The second she quit, I was afraid of being exposed as someone with problems. By focusing on her, I could avoid my own responsibility for the way things had turned out. I thought I knew everything back then, but my certainty often came from my need for control. Recovery for me has been about learning to accept uncertainty; and that's harder than it sounds."

The Coalcoholic in the Transition Stage

During the drinking phase, the coalcoholic's primary focus is the alcoholic.

Behavior

- Loss of control intensifies

Thinking

- Cracks are forming in denial
- Becoming aware of loss of control

Emotional Expression

- May experience an increase in impulsive outbursts against others and self
- May feel increased guilt, depression, desperation, despair, and defeat

During the abstinent phase, the coalcoholic's primary focus shifts to an "external authority," such as Al-Anon, a treatment center, a therapist, or a religious support group.

Behavior

- Concrete focus on substitutions for the attachment to the alcoholic, such as going to meetings and calling a sponsor
- Lessening of unhealthy attachment to the alcoholic and the alcoholic system

Thinking

- Confirmation of surrender and new belief in loss of control
- Concrete focus on new beliefs, new identity, and a new language of recovery
- Old beliefs are challenged
- Reconstruction of the perceptions of the past; building of the narrative of what really happened.
- Construction of a new perception of the present

Emotional Expression

- May be contained or denied through a focus on thinking and behavior
- Emotions may be expressed through substitute behaviors especially focusing on action
- Depression and anxiety are common; some coalcoholics experience elation

(Adapted from Brown and Lewis, 1999)

Excommunication

The family back in Minnesota had always been concerned with Peggy's sudden "dose of morality," as her father described it. As long as Stan resisted the change, there was a feeling of stasis, as though Peggy might return to the fold when she was done with her "little experiment," as her mother put it. But when Stan joined Peggy in recovery, his parents let their dissatisfaction be heard in a more severe way. "My family pretty much cut me off. They laid down the law: until we got over our 'nervousness'—that was another one of their condescending descriptions—we were not welcome. We were no longer allowed to come for the holidays. They said it wouldn't be festive with us there judging them." The family's reaction gave Stan a stark realization of what Peggy had gone through during his resistance. "Their own shame about drinking reduced my relationship with them to being about drinking. They were angry because we were a threat to their denial. It's sad. Both of my parents died never believing they had a drinking problem. They would talk about it's being a different generation, that they didn't try to fix everything like us youngsters did. I don't know. As much as I was hurt by their attitude, I recognized it. It's pretty much how I had behaved when my wife went into recovery."

Now that Peggy and Stan have years of recovery between them—after four years of Al-Anon, Stan started AA two years ago to focus on his own drinking—things are much clearer to them. "It's so hard to get an objective view of the harms of alcohol when you come from an alcoholic family that never faced its addictions. When I was struggling through recovery, there were times that I thought about my own family. They seemed fine. Was I just weaker than they were? Was there some toughness that I lacked having grown up in the relative comfort of the late twentieth century? But as I grew stronger, I was able to really look at my upbringing and see all the pain and trauma that had never been talked about. Peggy had much the same experience. Our families' resistance to our recoveries was not based on their perception of our flaws, but their denial about their own."

Exercise: "I Am a Coalcholic in the Transition Stage . . ."

This exercise will focus on the perspective of the coalcoholic during transition. If you are the coalcoholic, you will be exploring the thoughts and feelings you had about yourself during the shift from drinking to abstinence.

- In your journal, describe how the coalcoholic hit bottom. How did the coalcoholic's behavior change during the descent toward the bottom? How did the coalcoholic make excuses for bad behavior? What happened when the coalcoholic surrendered? How did the coalcoholic's behavior change when recovery began? If you are the coalcoholic, imagine how someone else might have described your behavior during the fall, when you hit bottom, and when you started the road to healing.

  If you feel like it, you can write it as a story. Don't worry about capturing the absolute truth as it happened. Just write it as you recollect it.

- Now describe how you felt about the coalcoholic when the above behavior occurred. Did you feel tense, angry, sad, or a combination of these emotions? Did you rationalize the coalcoholic's behavior? How did you feel when the coalcoholic hit bottom? What were your emotions when recovery began? Did you feel relief? Disappointment? Again, if you are the coalcoholic, think back on how you felt about yourself and your behavior during the transition stage.

- Now, instead of recalling the emotions you felt in the past, describe how you presently feel about the coalcoholic's experience of transition. Do things make more sense when viewed from afar?

Remember to date the entries. As you work through recovery and gain more insight into the past, your perceptions will change. If it is too early to focus on these issues, come back later and try the exercise then. Don't force it.

"I am a Child of an Alcoholic"—Craig and Melissa Remember the Transition Stage

In Minnesota, Peggy and Stan and their two children seemed to be a happy, well-functioning family. Stan and Craig spent long hours on the weekends practicing sports and going to Craig's games. Peggy and Melissa were also best friends, sharing favorite books with one another and going to the movies once a week with Peggy's mom, after which they would spend hours reviewing the pluses and minuses of that week's offering. Underneath this comfortable exterior, both Stan and Peggy were drinking quite a bit, and the occasional ugly scene would remind everyone in the family that all was not completely safe.

The move to California shook up the family and interfered with the parents' relationships with their kids. Stan's work made it hard for him to spend time with Craig, who now played high school ball and spent his time with the team. Melissa and Peggy tried to keep up their Thursday movie day, but with Peggy's growing anxiety and the difficulties that Melissa had assimilating into her new school, neither felt much like going out. They let go of the ritual, telling each other it wouldn't be the same without Grandma.

The relationship between Melissa and Craig also took a hit. "Back in Minnesota, we were really good friends," recalls Craig. "We basically shared the same social scene. It was a tight community and everybody knew everybody else. But when we moved to California, we got separated. I hooked up with a group of friends pretty quickly because I played football. Melissa had a harder time."

Melissa's shyness and quiet demeanor made it hard for her to fit in. "I was never very good at making friends. I was an introvert, so I just didn't connect easily. The kids called me 'the nun' because I wore dark clothes and didn't say much. It was horrible. You go through life thinking you're normal, and suddenly you realize you don't fit in. It was a really hard move for me."

Escape and Enmeshment

For a teenager who is preparing to leave the nest, the crisis situation of transition can be an unsteady launching board. With Peggy's drinking getting worse and Stan spending less and less time around the house, their two children were left to fend for themselves during the downward spiral. Craig, who was a senior in high school when his mother hit bottom, followed his father's cue and stayed away as much as possible. "I just remember being really alone in the family. When we were still trying to have family dinners, everyone was so distant, not talking about anything, it just seemed so phony. I can't say that I knew my mom was an alcoholic, but I knew that I did not want to be there. Part of me felt sorry for my sister; I could see she was sad. But another part felt that there was no room for taking care of anyone else; if you try to save a drowning man, he'll pull you under. My family was a drowning man, and I was desperate not to be pulled under." There is a paradox in the fact that Craig was distancing himself from the family while at the same time participating completely in its unhealthy structure. The denial and escape that were the hallmarks of his parents' lives became his central focus as well. By running away from his family, he was following in their footsteps.

Meanwhile, Melissa's isolation became more and more pronounced. "I started thinking there was something wrong with me. In order not to feel like a victim, I started to live the part. I made weirdness my decision. If I was going to be isolated, it would be my choice. There was some feeling that I had some control over my place in the world, but the end result was that my efforts at weirdness only made me more isolated. I spent my entire eighth-grade year in my room with my headphones on." Like Craig, Melissa also yearned for escape from the tensions of her home, but because of her age she couldn't do it physically, so she retreated psychologically. In this way she was following her mother's lead.

At the same time Craig and Melissa were distancing themselves as a means of self-protection, they were tying themselves more tightly to the family system. If escape is your primary goal, then the situation you are trying to escape becomes the defining core of your life. Craig stayed away with his anger and Melissa tried her best to hide while sinking into her depression, but in the hearts of these teenagers was the unhealthy family system, which wins if you collude and wins if you resist. The only solution is to let go, and each child felt far too vulnerable and far too enmeshed in the family to realize that this option even existed. And, for children, letting go is only an option if there is a protective person or place to turn to for help. Children are often amazed at their ability to find positive people, such as neighbors, teachers, an aunt, or a sibling. Yet, because of the family denial, they still may not be able to openly acknowledge reality.

Decline and Desperation

Things got worse when Melissa started high school and discovered that her big brother was no longer her protector. "In Minnesota, Craig had always been my connection to friends. High school was sixth to twelfth grade back there, but in California

I was by myself in eighth grade. Things were going downhill with Mom and Dad, and Craig did not like to be home. When I started high school in ninth grade, my life got way worse."

By the time Melissa started high school, Craig spent most of his time away from home. His social scene at school became a life preserver to him, so when his "freaky" sister showed up, he couldn't let her threaten his popularity. "I was pretty terrible to her. I hated being home, so my friends at school and on the football team were my life. Melissa was like a sacrifice I had to make to keep my social circuit. She had become really spaced out in junior high, and I had really hung with the in crowd. When she showed up in high school, I was merciless. I think she was a stand-in for my mom. I just murdered her with insults. I was a senior in high school when she started and I let her have it. My favorite name for her was 'fatso.' It was short and simple, and it hit the spot. She wasn't even overweight, but it didn't matter. Nothing like starting a new school with your big brother ready to label you for everyone else."

Melissa and Craig were no longer close. With school life being almost intolerable for Melissa, she spent all her time at home. Melissa sometimes thought of her isolation as necessitated by her mother's ill health. "I would come home and my mom would be passed out on the couch with all the drapes closed. I would clean up a little and try to take care of things around the house. I would tell myself I had to take care of her, but if I heard her start to wake up, I would get to my room before I'd have to talk to her."

After a semester of suffering in high school, Melissa couldn't take it any longer. "I hated school; I hated my father, because he was never around; I was so unhappy. I started 'borrowing' my mom's sleeping pills. I was stealing them for months, once or twice a week. She never noticed; or if she did, she didn't care. I would take them at school. It was my way of saying, 'You're not shutting me out, I'm shutting you out.' It was a hollow victory. I was so lonely; I felt empty, and I had no one to talk to about it. One day I started stealing my mom's sleeping pills and not taking them. I stole one a day; my plan was that if I could steal a sleeping pill a day for a month and not get caught, I would take them all at once. I think I wanted to get caught, like it was a test to see if my mom would notice. Thirty pills in thirty days, but she never noticed."

When a child's cries for help are not heard, the cries will get more and more desperate. Melissa's isolation went unnoticed by her parents, and so did her drug use. The more she was ignored, the greater the crisis became. "I don't know which came first, the feeling of complete hopelessness or the feeling that nobody cared about me. Maybe they're the same thing." In the end, Melissa's cry for help went unheeded, and she chose a path that too many children take. "I just couldn't take it anymore. I felt completely invisible. When I took the pills, it actually felt like someone else was taking them, like I was standing outside and watching myself. Then I put my headphones on and listened to some music. That's the last thing I remember."

News of Melissa's suicide attempt sent shock waves through the family. Craig was torn between feelings of guilt for his "betrayal" of his sister, and anger at his mother for "ruining" his life. "I couldn't deal with my guilt, so I was angry instead. I think I was scared to death, and my fear came out as anger. I thought I had driven Melissa to do it, and I was angry at my mom for making things so that I abandoned my sister. It's still not one hundred percent clear to me. I was full of fear, guilt, anger, and confusing feelings. I just focused all of it at my mom, and then all of a sudden my mom is in recovery. I hated her for that. It felt like she was getting away with murder. I thought all our family problems were her fault. She had done all this damage, and now she was getting off scott-free. At the time, I had no idea what it meant to be in recovery or what she was going through. I thought she was running away from her responsibility. I realize now that she was doing the complete opposite, but from my point of view she had run out on us."

Tension and Release in Early Abstinence

Craig's perception of his mother's recovery was further tainted by the fact that his father confided his own anger to him. "Suddenly, my father and I were pals again. I was actually pretty excited about it. He'd tell me how mad he was, and I couldn't blame him. To me, he was as much a victim as Melissa and I were. You feel so important when your father shares his thoughts about things. But I wasn't getting the whole picture. It wasn't till years later that I discovered he was avoiding his own responsibilities about the family and his part in letting things get so out of control. Looking back, I realize that I was not the person my father should have been talking to. He wanted someone to complain about Mom to. It was inappropriate, but I got a sense of value from it. Hearing him vent his resentment helped me avoid my own guilt. If my father was angry, too, then I wasn't so bad."

Although Peggy had reached outside the family for help, Craig and Stan maintained their allegiance to the unhealthy system. By relying on one another to vent their anger, they tied themselves together in their resistance to the change that was occurring. Like two men drifting on the high seas, they linked their fates and decided to sink or swim together. But this solution prevented them from doing either effectively. Instead of making change in a positive or negative way (the equivalent of swimming or sinking), they stayed in a limbo of denial and resentment.

Talking to his father didn't make Craig feel any better in the long run. "Though I had this privileged position with respect to my father, I still wanted to get away. I had lost respect for everyone, including myself. When I left for college I was the happiest person on earth: I was leaving it all behind; I felt like I was getting a chance to start over. But even at college, I carried my family problems around inside me. I didn't talk to Mom for six months at one point. I never answered my phone; I always thought it would be her calling. I had gotten away, but I was still totally tied into that drama. I was still trying to escape."

When Melissa came home from the hospital, she was very anxious. "I was so scared. I thought of my home as a place that had tried to kill me. It was irrational, but it was like this living entity. I could see that my father was angry. He was trying to fill in around the house, but to me it was too little too late. And the way he treated my mom drove me crazy. He was just riding her."

The tensions at home remained high. But Melissa and her mother began to create a new bond, a mutual understanding based on each person's commitment to individual recovery and growth. "In a weird way, I felt totally connected to my mom when I came home. Not like I needed her, but more like we going through the same thing. She couldn't really talk to me; she was scared of what had happened. But I could sense her conviction that she was going to get better. We never talked about deep stuff back then. We each had a place to discuss things outside the house, so when we spent time together we would check in with each other. If my father was there, he would be out of the loop. He would be protecting me from Mom, and I didn't need protection. My mom and I developed a mutual understanding that we couldn't fix each other and that we were both trying to get better, and a mutual respect. It was a great reassurance that someone else was making changes."

Still, the family was dominated by anxiety and despair. Melissa and Peggy were both battling depression as they each worked at healing. Melissa recalls that it was important to know someone understood. "That's the most powerful bond in a crisis. If you feel like you are understood, it makes all the difference. We could see each other struggle, and we recognized each other's struggle as similar to our own. I think her reaching out for help through AA made it easier for me to reach out in my therapy. I don't know how I could have held it together if I had tried to get better in that family the way it was before Mom went into recovery. There was so much pressure to avoid reality and hide. Healthy support is not about holding someone up, it's about standing beside her and letting her know that you understand, that you care."

The Ongoing Path

When Craig found out that his father had entered recovery, he felt like it was the final betrayal. "Suddenly, I was no longer my father's pal, and I was supposed to have respect for Mom, who he had bad-mouthed to me for six straight months. I thought they were total hypocrites. I was living in the dorms, and I tried to figure out some way to get a place of my own so I didn't have to go home for summer vacation. I coped with my alienation the same way my mother had: I started drinking heavily. I was punishing my family and myself at the same time. I had all this guilt and felt completely alone in the world. It wasn't until I was flunking out of school that I admitted I had a problem. It was such a crushing blow to my pride to discover I was like the family I hated."

Craig was the last one to reach out for help. Five years later, things aren't perfect, but the family can talk openly about the realities of the alcoholism and the family's subtle way of supporting it. Craig is an assistant football coach at his old high school and he is studying to get his teaching credential. Melissa is in college studying psychology. She wants to be a high school counselor.

It's a troubling irony that a child's desperate act can be the catalyst for change in the home. "When I was getting better after the suicide attempt, one of the really hard things for me to process was that something positive had come out of something so negative. I have since realized that in troubled homes, the kids are often desperately trying to fix things, but their attempts go unnoticed. The way most schools work, teachers are so overworked and underpaid you only have time to deal with the kids who are causing real trouble. No one is looking for the kids who are quietly self-destructing. That's why I want to be a counselor. A depressed kid is not going to look for help; hopelessness is the biggest symptom of depression. The help has to come looking for the kid."

Children in the Transition Stage

During the drinking phase, the children's primary focus is still the alcoholic or coalcoholic parents and the alcoholic environment and system.

Behavior

- Problems may begin or, if problems already existed, they may intensify

Thinking

- The mind-set that was in place during the drinking stage continues: it tends to be dominated by the family defenses, denial, distortion, and acceptance of trauma as normal
- Thought disturbances that were occurring during the drinking stage may increase

Emotional Expression

- The child may be feeling a sense of impending doom, or disaster
- The child may be feeling unsafe both emotionally and physically
- Emotional disorders may intensify, including depression, anxiety, or sleep disorders

During the abstinent phase, the children's primary focus remains the parents, but the children may feel abandoned by their parents' focus on recovery.

Behavior

- Problems continue or may begin in response to the "trauma of recovery"

Thinking

- Often confused and frightened
- Children's thinking largely depends on their parents' being involved in recovery and sharing clear explanations of the process
- Both parents' agreeing about what is happening to the family can begin the process of repair for the children; the absence of this agreement may make the problems worse

Emotional Expression

- Children need support, structure, and reassurance to offset their growing fears
- Disturbances may be expressed through emotional disorders, such as depression, anxiety, or sleep disorders
- Chronic trauma remains the "normal" state of things

(Adapted from Brown and Lewis, 1999)

Exercise: "I Am a Child in the Transition Stage . . ."

This exercise will focus on the perspective of a child during the transition stage.

■ In your journal, describe the children's behavior during transition. How did they react to the alcoholic behavior? How did they try to make things work? How did they experience their parents' hitting bottom? If there was more than one child, you can repeat the exercise for each.

Just write it as you recollect it. Historical accuracy is not the goal.

■ If you are a parent in recovery, describe how you felt about your children's reaction to the transition stage. Did you have problems with guilt? Were you hopeful for your child's future? Did you experience anxiety when your recovery clashed with your past focus on your children? If you are the child, describe what you think your parent's feelings were.

■ If you are a parent in recovery, how do you presently feel about your children's experience of the transition stage? Have your feelings changed over time? Do you see your past anxieties as accurate or exaggerated now that you can see the events from a more objective perspective? If you are the child, what are your present feelings about your and your siblings' experiences of the transition stage?

The important thing is to explore your own perceptions of the children's experiences. These perceptions will change as your perspective changes over time. Remember to date the entries. You might want to come back later and try it again so you can compare your evolving points of view and measure your progress. If the exercise makes you too uncomfortable, come back to it when you feel up to it.

6

"One Step at a Time"

Surviving the Transition Stage

Now that we have drawn a map of the transition stage and considered the different points of view from which the landscape can be perceived, it's time to focus on your own journey and how to navigate your road to recovery. Every path is unique, so we can't offer directions nor can we predict where and when the obstacles will occur. The one prediction we can safely make is that there will be bumps in the road. These obstacles may be small or big, and some can even threaten the foundation you are putting in place.

The earliest days of abstinence can feel like one perpetual crisis. Remember that the pain and discomfort you are feeling during these trying times are totally normal. The depth of change you are undergoing is huge. Everything you have known and come to rely upon is shifting beneath your feet. The system by which you lived your life has collapsed, and for the most part you will be operating in a vacuum. Even with outside support, this is a scary situation.

This chapter discusses coping strategies and survival techniques that can help you survive the upheaval of the transition stage and the anxieties that usually surround the earliest period of abstinence. These are not solutions. In fact, you may discover that your problems don't need to be solved, but rather set aside.

In the second half of this chapter we will discuss a particularly hard part of the road to navigate: taking care of your children during the trauma of recovery. One of the greatest challenges of early abstinence is making sure your children are safe and supported while you maintain healthy boundaries and a solid self-focus. Although you may not be able to give your children the amount of attention they want, you can see to it that they have a secure place that allows them to process these difficult changes for themselves.

During this period of crisis and upheaval, your external support system will be crucial to you. This book is not meant as a substitute for meetings or therapy. This is a time of great dependency, and you need to rely upon the help your recovery program offers. Toughing it out or going it alone are not ideal options. Not only is this self-reliant thinking one of the cornerstones of the alcoholic mind-set, it can also lead back to drinking. This book should augment your recovery program, not replace it.

This chapter will describe how the challenging experiences you encounter in recovery are understandable and expectable. You'll also learn how to better navigate an unknown landscape without trying to control your surroundings. Recovery evolves naturally; you cannot wrestle it to do your will. By coping with your anxiety, you will be coping with your resistance to the unknown, and thus allowing healthy growth to begin.

You will find further tools for recovery described in chapters 9 and 12. What we will focus on here are the earliest problems you can expect to meet, and some strategies that can make these issues more understandable and endurable. Think of this as a travel guide: you won't discover your particular path in these pages, but you will find out how to survive the journey you choose.

Understanding What You're Going Through

More than any other part of the recovery process, the transition stage is the period of greatest change and anxiety. This doesn't mean that you won't experience crises in later stages; most people do. But in transition, you are shifting from the terrors at the end of alcoholism to the trauma of early abstinence. As you saw in chapter 4, the cognitive changes taking place are almost complete reversals of old modes of thinking. Accepting loss of control and identifying yourself as an alcoholic or coalcoholic is not something that comes naturally or overnight; it takes time and patience to internalize these perceptions into deeply felt beliefs. And in the meantime, your old impulses and habits may be challenging your new abstinence at every turn. It's no wonder that many people suffer from anxiety and depression during these traumatic times.

The experience of transition and early abstinence has been described as being like a stroke for some people: the brain literally doesn't work. You don't know what's up or down. Some people can't read or even communicate. These problems can go on for months. You may feel helpless and extremely dependent. You may need to rely entirely on your external support system to keep you functioning. So if you have a family that depends on you, you may have even greater stresses as you try to balance your responsibilities to your family with your responsibility to your recovery.

If you think you shouldn't be having such a high level of pain and discomfort in your early abstinence, the first thing you have to tell yourself is that **recovery is a very serious thing**. People treat a broken leg as something serious, ooh-ing and ahh-ing over the pain of the accident and the trauma of having the leg set and a cast put on. Alcoholism is as real as a broken leg; your very sense of identity, your mind, and your impulses are broken. This is serious business. And unlike a broken leg, which can heal in just a couple of months, recovery goes on for a lifetime. If you are an alcoholic, you never stop being one. This is the central foundation of recovery: the identification as an alcoholic. So these first few days when you finally make the shift from unhealthy to healthy dependency are a time of great upheaval.

It's natural to have problems. Anytime you make a change in the way you live your life there will be setbacks as you practice your new routine. If you spent years parking in the garage and now park in the street, occasionally you'll find yourself in the garage looking for the car. The same is true for abstinence, but to a much more serious degree. You are changing your very perception of yourself; you are changing your thought and behavior on every level. You are probably changing your morality and deeper beliefs. It's natural to have troubles. It's natural to trip and fall.

During transition, the skills to face these challenges have not yet been put in place, so the problems you encounter can be much more of a threat. **In the earliest period of abstinence, everything is new.** This is the first time you will encounter many of the anxieties that will become familiar during your journey, and you will be tempted to look to yourself for explanations for and solutions to the discomfort you are enduring. The road to recovery is an uneven and badly paved path. Stumbling is to be expected. But as you gain experience in recovery, you will come to recognize obstacles and anxieties you have dealt with before. After you have tripped for the twentieth time, you will start looking to the uneven pavement that makes up this path and stop thinking you're stumbling because there is something wrong with you.

Once you understand that what you are going through is traumatic and that it is natural to feel bad, the question arises of what you can do about it. One person saw her options in a very dim light: "During my darkest times I felt I had two choices: lying down and suffering or drinking." Drinking is not an option. Suffering will occur at some times, but you don't have to wallow in it. Many folks in early abstinence feel they should be punishing themselves for their alcoholic sins, and suffering seems as good a way as any to do it. But guilt and self-punishment are not only unhealthy, they are dangerous. The focus on alcohol is threatened if, for instance, you try to make your past actions right in the eyes of your family. Another common form of self-punishment is to go back to drinking out of a belief that you don't deserve to get well.

There is a third option for living through recovery that avoids relapse while steering clear of needless suffering. This option involves learning healthy and effective methods of coping with the impulses and anxieties that are to be expected on the path of recovery.

What Is Healthy Coping?

Coping strategies are behaviors that help you deal with uncomfortable situations and painful thoughts and feelings in your everyday life. Coping strategies are neither healthy nor unhealthy unto themselves, but are rather neutral. The results of these strategies, however, can be helpful or harmful. For instance, denial can be an important and healthy defense at the onset of a crisis: a trauma may be too overwhelming, and must be pushed out of the mind in order for you to take care of other essential parts of your life. But long-term denial, like that we have seen at work in the alcoholic family, is an unhealthy strategy. It denies reality and forces the family members to retreat deeper and deeper into a false reality to maintain an unhealthy system.

One way to distinguish between healthy and unhealthy coping strategies is to consider whether the gain from performing the behavior is a short-term or long-term one. One of the key things you learn in recovery is how to have the patience to choose the long-term strategy over the immediate gratification of the short-term solution. Recovery is a long-term process, and on this path you will encounter a lot of anxiety that screams for immediate action. The need for immediate solutions to life's daily stress is what we have been calling "emergency thinking": you perceive the impulse or anxiety as a problem that must be solved immediately, as though it were a matter of life or death. In the alcoholic family, as in any family where an ongoing trauma makes the household an unsafe place, emergency thinking is often the norm.

For the alcoholic, the impulse to drink often demands immediate gratification, and any hesitation in fulfilling this need brings intense anxiety. Recognizing the impulse and making it conscious can awaken feelings of secrecy and shame. It's difficult not to deny or nullify the impulse immediately as a way of quieting these painful feelings. Much of the early work of recovery is aimed at freeing yourself from the pressure of emergency thinking in relation to your impulse to drink or, if you are a coalcoholic, to protect the drinker. As you become stronger in recovery, you begin to feel more secure with your support system; and as you feel more secure, you will have less of a tendency to react to impulses and anxieties as emergencies that demand immediate attention. By using substitutions for the unhealthy dependency and using the kind of concrete action language found in twelve-step programs, the alcoholic and coalcoholic push a wedge between the impulse and the action. After much diligent and patient substitution (for instance, going to a meeting instead of drinking), the impulse loses its ability to command. By enduring short-term discomfort you slowly but surely secure long-term health.

Healthy coping means enduring the bumps without sacrificing the growth. In order to move over the long term toward recovery and healthy growth, you will have to endure some short-term setbacks. You may experience pain; you may lose sleep; you may lose contact with friends and family members. These are not reasons to forfeit the changes you have made. A close friend may not understand why you are giving up drinking, and you may feel guilty that you are hurting her by "leaving her behind." When you have lived in an alcoholic system for a long time, you learn to sacrifice what is beneficial to you in order to "make someone else feel better." Recovery is about letting go of the need to make others feel better and grabbing on to the focus of healing yourself.

Coping is not always an active strategy; it often entails *not* confronting a problem. This may feel like cowardly behavior, or like an unhealthy defense strategy. But it may be necessary, healthy coping, which can involve correctly assessing that this is not the time for you to solve that problem, or that it is not a problem you can solve. It can be difficult to realize, for example, that your old friends may never understand how and why you have changed. But the urge to convince them may come at the expense of your own health, so it is a short-term comfort. By focusing instead on the long-term health of recovery, you can remain firm in your commitment to lifelong health and growth. If a friend is worth having, he or she will be around when you have built the foundation of your sobriety. Sometimes the most courageous choice is to do nothing, and endure the anxiety that screams for you to fix the problem. For the survivor of an alcoholic family, *not* trying to solve a problem can be a success, not a failure.

Coping Takes Time

At first, coping strategies may feel a bit unnatural and superficial. That's to be expected. New behavior and thinking don't happen in a flash, and it takes patience and practice to put new coping styles in place. **Coping means approximating healthy attitudes until you can internalize them.** Coping behaviors start as conscious choices and become automatic. The process goes one step at a time. Remember Bob from chapter 4? At first he was so anxious and overwhelmed by his impulse to drink that he couldn't remember his sponsor's phone number. Every time he had an urge to drink he'd have to fish that index card out of his pocket and phone the number. Over time, he slowly grew more secure in his abstinence. Instead of raging anxiety, he began to have a clearer head, which allowed him to remember the phone number and call it without consulting the card. In the end, he found himself on the phone before he even recognized that he needed to call. His improvement went one step at a time.

You cannot force change, you can only let change happen. Accepting loss of control allows change to come. More often than not you will discover you have changed while you were not looking. Backsliding will occur; you may slip occasionally and find yourself focusing on controlling the world around you rather than taking responsibility for your place in it. Backsliding is a natural part of recovery. Progress often takes two steps forward and one step back; sometimes it even feels like one step forward and two steps back. Recovery is not about becoming perfect, it is about becoming more open to your imperfections. The more you accept your shortcomings and imperfections, the more you accept your loss of control.

Recovery is a sequence of baby steps. Perhaps the most familiar twelve-step slogan, "one day at a time," refers to this fact. These words counsel you to take things one day at a time, one step at a time, focusing on the present. Don't try to anticipate the road ahead. If you feel you need to do something all at once, you are putting too much pressure on yourself. All you are responsible for is a little bit of progress every day. Sometimes progress means holding your ground; sometimes it even means backsliding a bit, but not as much as you have in the past. Break the task of recovery down to its smaller steps and follow through on each step slowly and patiently. The more patiently you build it, the more sturdy the foundation of recovery.

If you find yourself getting frustrated with the slow progress of your recovery, remember that the hardest thing to change is thinking. People often assume that since thinking is so intrinsic to who we are, it is easy to change, and that the change can be brought about through self-control or willpower. Not so. Accepting the fact that your thinking is outside your control is a fundamental part of accepting your overall loss of control. Trying to control thinking is like trying to change the course of a stream by reasoning with the water.

The way to bring about change in the course of the stream is to alter the path along which the stream flows. The way we do this in life is to change behavior, which then influences thought to follow its lead. This is precisely what is happening when you focus on behavioral substitutions for your impulses. You can't hope to control the impulse, but you can redirect it. In other words, in order to change what you think, change what you do.

The mind internalizes a new way of thinking only through a patient, step-by-step practice of implementing new behavior. Even then, your thoughts will only be influenced, never controlled. The impulses and anxieties will always accompany you, but the loudness with which they communicate and the urgency with which you obey slowly decrease. Soon those enslaving impulses become background noise in an otherwise peaceful world. We will return to the stepwise progress of recovery at the end of the chapter.

Strategies for Redirecting Impulses

Impulses cannot be controlled, only redirected.

The central stress of everyday life for the newly abstinent alcoholic or coalcoholic involves dealing with the overwhelming flood of impulses and feelings that wash over you. Impulses pass quickly if you express them in some way, but they build the more they are denied. During active alcoholism, impulses are expressed through the unhealthy dependency on drinking or focus on the alcoholic. In early abstinence, they need to be expressed through healthy action. If you keep the impulses inside your head and try to substitute thoughts alone, you may find you can't withstand their steady onslaught. So the trick is to allow them to be expressed—just not in the way you are accustomed to expressing them. By substituting healthy action, you release the pressure of the impulse out into the real world, taking away some of its more undermining secrecy.

In this early period of abstinence, the anxiety you experience when an impulse comes up can make it hard for you to remember an appropriate action to substitute. This is entirely normal. It takes time for your substitutions to become automatic. But in the meantime you can become a victim of your emergency thinking, which demands that the impulse be gratified immediately.

The following are a list of concrete actions that you can substitute for the focus on the alcohol or the alcoholic. You may choose any number of these coping strategies or any combination. It is important, however, that you keep a consistent pattern of substitution in order to build a strong structure. The more consistent you are with your coping skills, the sooner they will become routine, replacing the unhealthy dependent thoughts and behavior demanded by your impulses.

Index Cards

Write a list of actions that you can use when you are hit by an impulse or overwhelming emotion. You can get help developing your list from your sponsor, your therapist, or an old-timer at a twelve-step program. Write each strategy on an index card and keep the cards with you at all times. When you feel an impulse to drink or to focus on the alcoholic, take out the cards and read one. Substitute that action for the impulse.

This strategy is particularly helpful in the earliest weeks of abstinence, when the anxiety that accompanies impulse can be so great that your memory seems to shut down. The cards act as a stand-in for your memory. Here are some suggestions for action strategies that can be written on the cards:

- "Call your sponsor." You can write his or her name and phone number on the card so you don't have to memorize it.

- "Call your therapist." If you are in therapy, you may want to have your therapist's name and number on one of the cards. Sometimes even leaving a message can help the impulse pass.

- "Call a safe friend." When you are starting recovery it is important to have a list of "safe friends" on whom you can depend in a crisis. Write their names and numbers on the card. Sometimes the simple act of reminding yourself that there is someone out there who offers support can get you through a tough moment.

- "This will pass." Write down this or another mantra that will help you over the rough moments. Pick something that has meaning to you. Here are some possible choices: "Turn it over"; "Hold on until the meeting"; "It's like labor pain and I made it through that"; "See the sunset"; "Hear the ocean."

- "Go to a meeting." Keep a list of all the possible AA or Al-Anon meetings in your vicinity. In most cities there is a meeting happening somewhere at any hour of the day. Even small towns have twelve-step meetings. Having a list of them handy can allow you to get to a meeting as quickly as possible. Again, sometimes just knowing there is a meeting available is enough to let the impulse pass. Hope is a powerful tool in recovery.

- "Listen to a soothing tape." You can have someone who has a soothing effect on you make a tape telling you that you can make it through the urge to drink. Perhaps they can remind you of some helpful slogans, or repeat your mantra. Hearing a supportive voice can be as good as seeing the person.

- "Hold your comfort object." Keep a small object that has special meaning to you available, and hold it in your hand. The object can be an effective anchor when you are facing your impulses out in the world.

- "Write it down and let it go." Sometimes writing your feelings down takes the pressure off of you. Write your feelings down and put the paper away. You may want to burn the paper later as a way of symbolically letting go of the impulse; or you may want to put the paper away in a private place.

These different action strategies for expressing your impulses may seem superficial at first, but they will slowly become more internalized. As you move further through recovery, you will find that the actions on your index cards will naturally be triggered by your impulses, and that the healthy substitution will become more deeply rooted.

Breathe

Stress is experienced as an emotion that takes over the body, with the heartbeat rising and the body getting ready to fight or flee. The experience of emotional stress inspires a physical stress reaction, such as quickened breathing, and the quickened breathing in turn magnifies the emotional reaction. The result is an out-of-control experience that can feel like a full-fledged anxiety attack. Breathing is a link in this stress cycle that is, in some sense, controllable. Focusing on your breathing is one of the most effective ways of controlling your stress.

When an impulse sets your emergency thinking in gear, your breathing will start to quicken. This in turn increases the feeling of emergency and makes the impulse seem more demanding. By concentrating on your breathing and taking some long, deep breaths, you can interrupt the cycle of stress. This allows you a moment of calm to choose a healthy substitution for the impulse.

It can be difficult to remember to focus on your breathing, however. Stress shrinks your world. Healthy options tend to fall away as your mind focuses on the object of the stress and tries to figure out a way to escape the onlaught of anxiety. The shallow breathing does not allow enough oxygen to get into your lungs, so you start to get light-headed. This is no time to make big decisions. Pull out an index card, read the instructions to breathe, and do so.

The focus on the breathing can also take your mind off the object of your stress. This two-fold stress deflector is crucial to taming your impulses.

Coping with Fear Lessens Its Future Impact

It's important to realize that the more you learn to cope with fear, the less terrifying it becomes. Part of what is threatening about anxiety is the feeling of being out of control, being faced with the unknown. By enduring anxiety without succumbing to it, you learn that it can be endured. As you learn to recognize anxiety as something manageable, rather than a fearsome threat to your sanity, it will threaten you less when it attacks.

Visualization

Think of a soothing place to visit. Maybe it's the ocean, or a friend's house, or somewhere you visited as a child. When your impulse hits, close your eyes and visit the soothing place in your mind: smell the flowers, feel the dirt under your heels.

Focusing on your breathing can be an excellent way to access this soothing place. Breathe deeply and fully as you seek out your safe place.

You may want to write your soothing places on one or all of your index cards, so when you turn to a card you will be reminded of one of your safe places.

Exercise

Physical exercise is an excellent way to redirect the energy that is created by stress and break the anxiety cycle: not only do you give your mind something to focus on other than the object of your impulse, but you also give your body an outlet for the energy that has just built up. Early abstinence can be an excellent time to take up a new physical activity. Make sure it's easily accessible, like jogging, power walking, push-ups, yoga, shooting baskets, or walking. Any exercise that is too complicated or demands some central location can just add to your stress as you try to get to the exercise facility. For this reason, ice skating or rock climbing may not be the best activities to take up as a means of redirecting your impulses.

Favorite Reading

Find a favorite piece of writing and keep it with you to read at times of great anxiety. Words are powerful and can take your mind to a peaceful place. Hopeful and inspiring words can bring optimism that is sorely lacking in the pessimistic, shrinking world created by impulse and emergency thinking.

This could be a favorite poem, a few lines of the Bible or other scripture, or a favorite passage from a book or story. Even a comic strip from the Sunday papers can cheer you and break you out of that moment. Of course, reading recovery literature is also important and helpful.

Count to Ten

It may sound silly, but this simple coping skill can be a lifesaver in a moment of extreme anxiety. The simple act of counting to ten can interrupt the cycle of anxiety. Much of the power of anxiety and impulse comes from the feeling that they are unquenchable and devastating. Counting to ten allows you to step outside the maelstrom of stress and take a moment before acting. This may give you the opportunity to think of another strategy to put in place.

You can combine counting to ten with your breathing. A good way to derail the stress that comes with the impulse to drink is to realize that the stress is not you, it is something that is happening to you. Because stress seems to take over your mind, you can feel like its slave—like the stress is the core of your identity. It isn't; it's just a natural physiological reaction to trauma. By stepping outside your stress to count from one to ten, you can remind yourself that you can endure the discomfort. Instead of caving in to the demand for a short-term solution to your impulse, you can choose an alternative action that will let you stay focused on the long-term health that comes from maintaining your recovery.

Break Old Habits

One way to cope with your impulses is to avoid the situations that trigger them. To do this, go through your life and look at the habits and routines you have developed that often went along with or led to drinking. You may even want to write them down in a notebook. A good example may be the route you take to work, or to the kids' practice or the grocery store. Does it take you past a bar you frequented? Search out new ways to get from one place to the other. Avoiding one habit will help you avoid other, connected habits.

Habits and routines in your life can be so subtle that you don't recognize them. But the more subtle they are, the more dangerous they can be, so stay vigilant. As we've discussed before, some family rituals may seem benign when in fact they are closely tied to drinking behavior. You may have to give up Sunday football for a time, or movie night with your friends if it was regularly accompanied by drinking. Even if you and your friends agree to make it a dry ritual, the circumstances may still trigger the impulses. By keeping track of where your impulses occur, you may discover that what seemed like a random pattern of events has a logical basis.

There may come a time, when you are stronger in your abstinence, when you may want to sample some rituals that were pleasant and see if they are salvageable. But this is not the time. The goal for now is to create a safe environment for yourself. You need to rely on your support system and try to reshape your life in order to avoid unnecessary temptations.

Carry Your History with You

Your impulses don't care about the past; they live in the present and they demand immediate action. When you feel yourself being overwhelmed by the immediacy of your impulses, you may want to have a history lesson ready to intervene on behalf of recovery and long-term health. Emergency thinking often carries with it the lie that there is no past and no future, only an insatiable hunger in the present that must be served. But if you are in recovery, you have lived through many such moments in the past that have proven to be destructive.

When you feel strong and able, make a list of the ways alcohol has affected your life. Start the list with the simple phrase "I am an alcoholic because . . ." and then list as many experiences as you can come up with that demonstrate your loss of control and how it threatened to destroy your life. When the impulse to drink starts to break down your conviction, it's important to have your evidence at your disposal. It will remind you what you have been through and why you must stay the course of recovery. When denial starts to push at you in service of your urges and you find yourself asking "Am I really an alcoholic?" you can read from the list. Here is an example:

I am an alcoholic because . . .

- I drove during blackouts.
- I had fights with my spouse and didn't remember them afterwards.
- I lost three jobs.
- I had two DUIs and a car wreck due to drinking.
- My spouse said he would leave me if I drank again.
- I lost the respect of my children.
- I watched my son begin to have his own drinking problem.

If you are a coalcoholic, you can prepare a similar list describing the ways your focus on the alcoholic has affected your life. For example:

I am a coalcoholic because . . .

- My drinking spouse became my entire life.
- I made continuous excuses for my spouse's behavior.
- I tiptoed around my spouse to keep her from becoming abusive.
- I told the children not to rock the boat.
- I woke up one day too depressed to go on this way.
- I had to take on an extra job to bail out the family's financial crisis.

- I lost myself along the way.
- I felt like I was going crazy.

As you grow stronger in your recovery, you will learn to experience your impulses without having to act on them, feel your emotions without having to vent them, and recognize problems without compulsively having to solve them. This gives you the calm perspective from which to make informed choices about whether or not these issues really need immediate attention, or whether they can be put aside to focus on something more important.

Remember, *not* acting can also be a healthy coping strategy. After a while, your decision-making abilities will become more thoughtful, and not based solely on the knee-jerk reaction demanded by your emergency thinking. When you begin to lose your reactive haste—the emergency thinking that demanded prompt and poorly thought-out responses—you can be patient and thoughtful in your choices.

For the Coalcoholic

The urges alcoholics feel have a very concrete focus: alcohol. The coalcoholic's urges are not as singularly focused. There are many subtle ways in which a coalcoholic learns to make the alcoholic the center of his or her life. Therefore, if you are a coalcoholic, you may want to make a list of the different ways you have impulses to take care of the alcoholic. Write down as many as you're aware of, and keep adding to the list as you think of new ones. You can then use this list to come up with coping strategies to deal with your various impulses.

One excellent way to reinforce your coping strategies is to have a specific substitution for each particular impulse. To organize your strategies, you can use your trusty index cards. Write each impulse on one side of a card. Then on the other side of the card, write a substitute behavior that will take the place of the impulse. Here are some examples:

Impulse	Substitution
Checking on your partner at work	Call your sponsor or therapist. (You may only need to leave a message on the answering machine.)
Worrying your partner is drinking	Write your worry down and burn it. Repeat the mantra: "I cannot control another; only myself."
Staying awake at night until your partner comes home	Listen to soothing music; sleep in another room; do something you enjoy, like reading, painting, or playing the piano.

The Uses of Anxiety

Anxiety is often a clue that you are challenging a core defense. These defenses were put in place to protect you from the dangerous environment that existed at home during the drinking stage and that probably still exists during transition. In order to walk the path of recovery, you need to embrace your vulnerability and help-lessness, and reach out to others for help. These changes in your mind-set often challenge your defenses. Vulnerability is too risky in the alcoholic family, so feelings of vulnerability will trigger your defenses. These defenses will scream that you need to be on guard and not let your armor down for even a moment.

In short, the defenses that once protected you within your family now stand in the way of your recovery. Letting go of these deep defenses is a scary process, because it means letting in the dangerous and threatening reality they protected you from. The core defenses in an alcoholic family can be so closely identified with the self that you may believe that letting go of these defenses will result in your no longer being you. You might even believe, consciously or unconsciously, that to let go would mean you will risk death.

Recovery means letting go of these defenses; and this detachment is a slow and unsteady process. You can't do it all at once. The anxiety you feel during early absti-nence is often tied to the core belief that letting yourself be vulnerable and needy will result in your suffering some terrible harm. If you act on this belief and fold yourself back up too tightly inside your defenses, you may slow or undo the precious work that you have been building upon. Everyone uses defenses, but you don't want to be stuck in them. The way to make the darkness and desperation of hitting bottom have meaning is to build a solid recovery upon the vulnerability and helplessness that resulted from this experience. You will be slowly challenging your defenses; in order to survive the challenge, you need to learn how to cope with the anxiety it brings.

By practicing coping strategies for anxiety, you can ultimately use this once-threatening emotion in a productive way. Anxiety can serve as a messenger, inform-ing you that your defenses are being challenged. As you grow more comfortable with your recovery, you will be able to hear the alarm without reacting to it, as you will now more readily recognize the source. Instead of a fire alarm, the anxiety becomes something more akin to a doorbell: there may still be some anxiety about the unknown (just as there can be some anxiety as to who rang the doorbell), but you don't immediately anticipate a threat or an imminent life-or-death situation. By learn-ing to understand your anxiety and facing it instead of running from it, you can learn to live with it and to make it serve your recovery.

Impulse and Anxiety

Here is a helpful way of understanding impulse and anxiety. The following are not all-encompassing definitions, merely simple descriptions of the connection between impulse and anxiety during early abstinence. The clearer your under-standing of why you feel the way you do, and why that feeling is a natural result of your circumstances, the less frightening these feelings will seem.

- The **impulse** is the urge to drink (or to protect the drinker). In early absti-nence, the need to drink or, for the coalcoholic, to focus on the drinker demands immediate gratification. The first step in breaking your enslave-ment to these impulses is to substitute concrete actions for them

■ The **anxiety** is the discomfort you feel when you put off gratifying an impulse. It can be acute when you are fending off a strong impulse, or chronic while you are living through the daily reality of fending off multiple impulses. In early abstinence, this discomfort may feel at times like a nervous breakdown, overwhelming you to the point of paralysis. The first step in breaking your enslavement to the anxiety is to learn how to cope with it

Reframing Anxiety

A good way to make progress in coping with your anxiety is to simply recognize what it is and what it does. When you understand that anxiety is a natural physiological response to your psychological perception of danger, you can see it as something separate from your identity.

Sometimes, anxiety is triggered by something unrelated to your unhealthy impulses. For example, the symptoms of fear can be physiologically identical to drinking a couple of cups of coffee. If you drink the two cups of coffee when you don't feel you're in danger, your body will start to behave as though you *are* scared. In this circumstance, you may try to identify the physiological reaction as fear and start to search for a reason you are experiencing it. The truth of the matter is that the coffee has caused the reaction; the mind is mistakenly searching for a psychological reason for the stress.

One man in recovery remembers just such an event on a trip to Paris during early abstinence. "I was visiting my brother, and I was pretty shaky at the time, but I was really glad to be in France. The change of locale was doing me wonders. The first morning I went for a walk and climbed up to Sacre Coeur [a beautiful cathedral overlooking Paris from the north]. I was so happy to be there. I was feeling excellent, when suddenly I got this sinking feeling. It was like I was having a nervous breakdown. My heart started beating so fast. I thought I had really gotten a head start on my recovery, yet here I was having an anxiety attack. And in the most soothing place I could think of. And out of the blue it struck me: my brother and I had each drunk two espressos with breakfast. I wasn't breaking down, I was flipping out on caffeine. Just the recognition that the coffee was at the heart of the emotion was like a break in the cycle of fear. Nothing changed in my body—my heart was still going a mile a minute—but I stopped panicking. That was really a life-altering experience."

The same sort of thing can happen with food or sleep. The upheaval of early abstinence can affect your diet and sleeping habits, which can make you very anxious all of a sudden. You may start to think you are coming apart when all you really need is a bite to eat or a short nap. This is why it is important to stay mindful of your eating and sleeping. When you are experiencing a traumatic experience, it is common to assume that every bump is the result of the trauma. But often, seeming setbacks can be traced to an unrelated source with a simple solution.

Another way to look at anxiety is to think of your body as becoming alert to danger. A former boxer, who just passed his twenty-year sobriety birthday, was asked if he was afraid when he got in the ring. His answer was instructive: "It's only fear if you call it fear. For me, I depend on adrenaline, the blood pumping, the senses getting sharp. These are tools in a fight. My body is getting ready to go into battle. Other people may think of that feeling as fear, but when you get used to it, you can use it to your advantage."

Sharpened senses and increased aggression can be alarming in early abstinence. But these are natural effects of your body's reaction to stress: the fight-or-flight mechanism. You will be working to learn to relax, but when the anxiety does start to rise, it can be helpful to consider it as your body's way of preparing itself for danger. This will allow you to see the anxiety as something happening to you, rather than something controlling you.

"The tough thing about anxiety is that it makes you dumb." So said a survivor of transition. "When you get stressed, it's like your brain turns off. I got to where I had to write 'calm down' on my hand just so I'd remember to do it when I would get riled up." You may want to make a checklist for dealing with anxiety:

- Am I hungry?

- Did I drink too much coffee?

- Have I had enough sleep?

- Have my defenses turned on for some reason?

If one of these turns out to be a possible source of your distress, they can all be remedied. Even if the stress cannot be reduced immediately, the simple recognition that it has a physical source can help you relax. And finally, even if you have no luck discovering the source of the stress, stepping outside it to look for its cause can have the valuable effect of breaking the cycle of anxiety.

If all else fails, remember to breathe deeply and let the stress pass. Stress feeds off your resistance to it. The more you fight it, the more energy it has to fight back. The most basic strategy for coping with stress is to let it flow over you.

Writing Out Your Anxiety

Another good way of dealing with anxiety is to write it out. If you don't know what you want to write, ask yourself why you are feeling anxious, and then start writing. You don't have to know what is causing the anxiety when you begin writing; just write and see what comes. There is no guarantee that you will pinpoint the source of your anxiety this way, but the exercise can help you bring your thoughts and feelings to the surface. Furthermore, the act of writing, of rhythmically putting one word after the other, can calm you down.

Often when stress kicks in, confusion follows close behind, making it difficult to organize your thoughts, which leads to frustration and further confusion. Cause and effect can easily get switched in times of stress. Instead of being the cause of the anxiety, your confusion is more likely its result. Writing can help you sort through your thoughts one word at a time, which can also have a soothing effect.

Try not to be critical, just let the writing spill forth. Often there will be an initial deluge of confusion and nonsense, and you may feel some frustration. But as you settle into the rhythmic flow of putting pen to paper, you might find yourself writing about feelings you didn't even know you had. You may even find a place of peace where you can untangle thoughts, feelings, and ideas that have been baffling you. This is an excellent way to make use of your journal between doing the exercises in this book.

Minding the Children

As we have seen in chapters 4 and 5, the transition from drinking to abstinence can be a highly traumatic experience for the children of alcoholics and coalcoholics. Whether they're six or sixteen or even twenty-six, the massive upheavals that can take place during recovery can make your children feel frightened and needy. These feelings are only intensified by the fact that their parents are probably less accessible, having to devote a great deal of time to meetings and other recovery work. Children may have felt abandoned during the drinking, and they may feel even more abandoned during the early part of recovery.

When you're taking those difficult first steps into recovery, almost all your attention must be focused on surviving the earliest part of the journey. Recovery must be built on the foundation of self-focus, which is difficult enough to maintain when the impulses to drink or rescue the alcoholic are relentlessly pulling at you. When you add the needs of your children to the equation, the demands on you can seem impossible to live up to.

This difficult situation is further complicated by the fact that, as denial starts to lift during early abstinence, you may experience guilt about the effects the alcoholism has had on your family, and on your children in particular. You may have a deep desire to take care of your children at the expense of your own recovery, reasoning that, after all the neglect, it's time to put the kids first.

But you must stay focused on the needs of your own recovery. You must accept the fact that you may not be able to pay as much attention to your children as you or they may want. But this doesn't mean they will be neglected. If you can understand your own limits and work within them to make sure your children are taken care of, you can take responsibility for your children without having to be their sole source of support. You need to find the tricky balance of taking care of yourself without abandoning your children at the same time. It means being willing to ask for help.

Often one of the rules in the alcoholic family, either spoken or unspoken, is that asking for help outside the family is forbidden. This rule keeps the denial in place and keeps the family isolated, so the alcoholism can be kept a secret. As you step into recovery and break that taboo, you may not notice that you are keeping this habit in place with respect to your children. People in early abstinence often want to reclaim some sense of pride to compensate for the huge vulnerability they are facing. One of the ways they do this is to try to show they can take care of their children without outside help. But this is precisely the kind of alcoholic thinking that kept the alcoholic system in place. Just as you have realized that reaching out for help with recovery is not only acceptable, but necessary, you need to understand that reaching out for help with your children is also an important step toward family healing. It doesn't make you a bad parent if you can't do it alone.

If you are having a hard time working through your guilt over how the drinking affected your children, try to focus on the improvements that recovery will bring. If you fall back into the old rules and sacrifice yourself and your recovery to take care of your child, you won't undo the damage that has been done. You will only be prolonging the difficult transition that happens after the alcoholic system has collapsed. If you are driven by the need for your children to forgive you, then no matter how much you do for them, you are ultimately asking them to support you, rather than providing support for them.

The best thing you can do for your child is to get yourself healthy. Of all the things you can do or say, nothing will have as big an impact as showing them your courage by staying the course of recovery and getting well. You will be teaching your children by example that it's okay to focus on themselves: something that was forbidden during active alcoholism. Of course there will be challenging times, and there will be days when your child is suffering right along side you. But you need to trust that, in the long run, a solid recovery will benefit the child more deeply than all of the superficial repairs that short-term solutions offer.

During early abstinence, it's important that you:

- Let your children know what is going on in the changing world around them

- Make sure they have access to the support and structure they will need to recover from the harm suffered from growing up in an alcoholic family

- Let them know that you love and care for them.

Education

The most important thing you can do for your children during the crisis period of early abstinence is to keep them informed. Few adults understand the complexities of how alcoholism affects the family, so it's no wonder that most children find the move to recovery confusing and even frightening. Children need to understand that alcoholism affects the whole family, and they need to be informed why it is that a "change for the better" may have made things worse.

Ignorance can be more than just a lack of knowledge: it can also take the form of mistaken beliefs and misapprehensions that fill the hole in understanding. If they don't know differently, children may believe, for instance, that they are the cause of the problems, and that it's up to them to rescue the family. This is a lot of pressure for, say, an eight-year-old to shoulder. The more your children learn (in age-appropriate ways) about the realities of recovery and alcoholism, the less fearful they'll be.

Children tend to respond to recovery in some fairly predictable ways:

- **They don't know what to expect from their parents.** If your children knew how to read the signs and cope during the drinking stage, then recovery may have disturbed their much-needed sense of predictability. Or, if things were unpredictable before, there is a good chance they are even more unpredictable after. Either way, your children's confidence that they understand their surroundings may be threatened.

- **They don't know what is okay to talk about.** Your children may be afraid that if they say the wrong thing, it will cause the alcoholic to drink again. They may not understand how to interact now that the rules of relating have changed.

- **They don't understand the new rules.** Your children may be following familiar rules that served them well during the drinking stage, and may feel confused when the rules no longer work.

- **They don't know their new roles.** Is your child still the caretaker? The cook? The baby-sitter? Roles can be important supports for your children's identities, and with the alcoholic system collapsed, these identities are threatened.

- **They may feel abandoned and left out.** Your children may not understand the reason the grown-ups go off to twelve-step meetings, and they may not feel needed or valued when their parents leave them behind in order to attend meetings.

- **They may not understand the new system.** Your children may be confused by the absence of old routines and the lack of new ones. The rules and the rituals have changed, so your children may be left without supports that they depended on.

- **They may not understand the new tensions.** Your children may pick up on the fact that a new and different relationship exists between you and your partner. This can be very scary, since the child has no idea what this change means.

- **They may feel responsible.** If your children have developed a coping style whereby they take responsibility for the world around them, there is a good chance they will think this new anxiety is also their fault. They will be looking for clues to what they did wrong and what they can do to fix it.

- **They may feel alienated from the family.** Your children may not understand the family's emerging identity as an alcoholic family. For example, they may have a hard time seeing how they fit into the picture since they never had a drinking problem.

- **They may feel disappointed.** Your children may have a hard time when the reality of recovery doesn't fit with their fantasy of what they think it should be. "I thought Daddy would take me to the movies a lot and be interested in my ball games when he got better; but he's around even less than he was before."

Children may attempt to control recovery in ways similar to the ways they tried to control the drinking. The following are a few common ways children cope with recovery when they have not been informed about (and therefore do not understand) the recovery process:

- **Hypervigilance.** They keep a watchful eye out on what's happening in the family and are afraid to relax.

- **Over-responsibility.** They attempt to take on tasks and responsibilities that are not age-appropriate. They may sacrifice their own well-being in an attempt to rescue the family.

- **Acting out.** They misbehave, which takes the attention away from the family tension.

- **Distancing.** They leave the family, emotionally and physically, and spend most of their time with friends, other families, or alone.

What You Can Do

There are several things you can do to help your children in early recovery.

Include Them

Include your children in the recovery process as much as they are willing. Education about what's going on helps your child feel less isolated by the strange new world that is shaped by recovery.

- Explain what alcoholism is in age-appropriate language.

- Explain what recovery means to you.

- Explain the importance of twelve-step programs and what they do. Tell them if they choose, they can be involved in a program of their own (there are twelve-step programs set up for children of all ages, such as AlaTot, AlaKid, and AlaTeen). Many treatment centers also have children's programs.

It is important for your children to be informed about your recovery, but how, when, and where they receive this information will vary depending upon each child's particular needs. Some children want to be involved in treatment, while some fight against it. Just as there is no one way for the process of recovery to go, there is no one way for children to experience recovery. If your children don't want to participate, don't force them. Respect their choice and know that you will be sharing your recovery with them just by living it around them. By keeping your children informed you will keep them in touch with recovery, leaving open the option that they may want to pursue a program when they are ready.

Keep Them Informed

Share information with the children even if they are reluctant to ask for help. You may feel your teenagers are too old to need help, or that your five-year-old is too young, but everyone needs to be kept informed about the changes that are taking place. Recovery needs to be a family matter. You need to respect the degree to which each of your children wishes to participate in actual programs and rituals centered on recovery, but they always should be kept up to date about the ongoing progress of recovery and the tensions that may accompany it. Just as denial and secrecy were the hallmark of family life during active alcoholism, truth and openness must be the foundation of the new family dynamic.

Reassure Them

Let your children know that what is happening to them is normal. Just as mapping the recovery landscape can provide vital stability and understanding to the alcoholic and coalcoholic, explaining to your children their place in the alcoholic landscape can help them understand what they are going through. They will gain perspective on what they have experienced and feel more prepared for what the future may hold. An understanding of the principles of recovery will give your children a strong framework to understand the changes taking place, and can help minimize the gap between the fantasy of what they think abstinence should be and the reality of what it is. By sharing your knowledge, you will be sharing the security that comes with understanding.

What to Say to Your Child

There is no one way to talk to your child about alcoholism. Every child is unique and has a unique set of needs. If you have two children, each one may require different amounts of information about what is occurring. Age will be an important factor in how much a child wants and needs to know. It may be best to talk to your children both separately and together as a group. This way they can ask private questions when alone but also connect with their siblings in the group meetings.

You may want to start by giving your children a general idea of what is happening. Let them know that the reason things may seem weird is because there are changes taking place. Let them know that the parents have a problem with alcohol and that they are getting help for it. Then you can ask your children what they want to know, and respond to their cues. They may be reluctant at first: it takes time to build up trust after living in an unsafe alcoholic environment. Your children may also not yet be ready to confront a frightening new reality where their parents have problems and need help. As we have said earlier, denial can be useful during trauma, and if your children need to keep their distance from the information at first, don't force them to confront it. Just letting them know that you are open to sharing the facts is an important step in helping them feel safe around the changes that are occurring at home. As you build trust with them, your children will feel more comfortable asking for information about what is happening to their parents.

Communication can be difficult at this early time because of both the tensions of the household and the rawness of your vulnerability during early recovery. Still, you need to make yourself available to the children. We will discuss communication in some detail shortly, but just be aware that it is important for your children to feel they are heard. It may be hard to listen, but your children need to know it is okay to voice their problems

Jerry Moe, an advocate for children of alcoholics, suggests a terrific compromise. Set aside a container where your child can leave questions. You can call it the "Ask-It basket." This will allow your children the safety to ask the questions that they are afraid to say aloud or in front of the rest of the family. They may feel scared to bring up an issue if they feel you will be mad, but if there is a place they can leave a question and have it answered later, they will be more likely to share their problems and questions.

The Ask-It basket also gives you or your partner some time to compose your response. You don't want your answers making things more confusing. You can even bring your sponsor or your therapist in on a difficult question, or one for which the answer is difficult to phrase for a younger child. Most important, the basket creates separation between your hearing the question and your having to respond, so your emotions won't intimidate your children. If their questions trigger your guilt and pain about life during the drinking, your children may be afraid to speak up, and may once again retreat into that anxious world where thoughts and feelings are suppressed in order to ensure self-protection. So separating the questioning from the answering can provide much-needed security for both the one who asks the question and the one who responds.

Things Your Children Need to Hear

1. **"The drinking is not your fault."** Explain to your children that they are *not* responsible for their parents' drinking or recovery. Explain that no matter what they do, they do not cause someone to drink.

2. **"You are not alone."** The children should learn that their experience is not unique and that others have been through the ordeal. It's important that they know that they are not alone. Tell them something like this: "There are other families like ours, and there are other children like you. If you ever want to meet any of them or talk to someone about these things, just let us know."

3. **"It's okay to ask for help."** Let your children know that it's good to reach out for help, and it's good to talk about their problems. Your children will need to learn new skills for solving their problems, and one of them is figuring out who is available to ask for help. This will lead to your child's feeling more empowered and less isolated.

4. **"Your feelings are okay."** Kids need to feel. They need to understand that all of their feelings are all right, even the scary ones. They also need to learn to trust their feelings to help them know what's best. Since they have learned to suppress their feelings to protect others, accepting their feelings can be difficult.

5. **"Your defenses are natural."** Your children need to know that the defenses that helped them cope with the drinking are normal, and that feeling defensive is a natural response to living with the tensions of an alcoholic home. Tell them something like this: "Defenses protect us from scary and difficult feelings. And if you see that you are defensive, you can find out what feelings are hidden underneath."

6. **"You are important."** Your children need to learn that it's okay to feel good about themselves. The self-esteem that was damaged by the self-sacrifice necessary to uphold the alcoholic system must be healed. Children need to learn that it is okay to focus on themselves. They need to learn they are important.

(These suggestions are based on discussions in *Kids' Power: Healing Games for Children of Alcoholics* by Jerry Moe and Don Pohlman, Tucson, Arizona: ImaginWorks, 1989.)

Communication

As we mentioned above, parents need to learn a new way to communicate with their children during early abstinence. In the unsafe alcoholic family, communication typically meant mixed messages. Often what seemed to be a conversation was a battle for control, and what was called a discussion was really an argument, with each person caring more about winning than about gaining a clear understanding of the other's point of view.

The first step in repairing an unhealthy style of communication is to disengage from this old behavior and learn to respect your children's individual boundaries. This means learning to communicate without needing to control the conversation, whether by trying to immediately solve your children's problems or by giving excuses to explain away their complaints.

The best way you can offer support to your children is by listening to them. For your children to begin to heal, they must be allowed to talk about their problems. This can be difficult when such discussions make you feel guilty. During recovery, it is important to respect boundaries, and in this context, this means dealing with your guilt yourself. If your children feel responsible for your guilt now, they will stop talking about their problems and push their feelings underground. You can still be honest, but be realistic about what you can do. You can't fix the things that happened in the past, and you may not be able to solve your children's current problems. You can, however, help them find a place where they can deal with those problems, and you can listen to what they have to say. Your listening will validate your children's experience, offering them an important feeling of support and security.

As you start building healthy communication with your child, it is important that you understand what you can fix about your communication style and what you can't. The following are some things you can't fix:

- **You can't fix the way another person communicates with you.** In the old alcoholic thinking, you may have focused on trying to change the way other people did things. But now you must respect the fact that the only place you can carry out changes is within yourself. If your children are having a hard time communicating, you can't fix that for them. You can only show them what good communication looks like.

- **You can't fix your relationships right now.** You can build up trust by sticking with your program, but the time to rebuild is later. It's usually wise to resist the urge to deal with deep issues. For most, this is not the time. It's understandable if you want to try to make things better, but just know that if it doesn't work out, it's completely normal. At first, it's most important to stick to your recovery. You need to build your own individual foundation before you can start connecting the family. There will be anxious times with your children, with so much change and so little stability. You can be there to listen, but you can't heal anyone but yourself. Your kids will begin to trust you more as you progress with your recovery.

Here are some things you can do to make sure you are giving your children the support they need when they want to talk to you:

- **Practice active listening.** Listening is not a passive activity. In good communication, you keep checking in with your child while you listen. Ask questions and make sure you understand. Restate the information to see if you've got it. If you don't understand something, don't pretend you do. Ask for more information. If you are distracted and can't listen effectively, say so, and schedule another time for the conversation. Discussions may start off a bit more slowly and take a bit more time, but soon you will be communicating more clearly, and your children will feel like what they are saying and feeling is being heard and understood.

- **Listen without feeling judged.** It can be painful, but you need to learn to hear what your children have to say without telling them how bad this makes you feel. It is important that the child doesn't feel the need to distort and deny; the truth must be allowed, and, painful as it is, you need to listen. If you find you are just too vulnerable to be able to listen in person, then set up a system like the Ask-It basket mentioned previously. This way you can still maintain healthy conversations with your children by giving yourself a chance to feel your emotion without sharing it.

- **Respect your child's boundaries.** Don't press your own opinions or observations. Respect your children's right to their own ideas. Pressuring your child to see things as you do will either push her away or make her succumb to your control. Neither outcome is a positive step. If you catch yourself pushing for agreement, step back, stop, and breathe. You've crossed a boundary.

- **Model good communication.** Your children may be too young to work on their own communication skills. Their defensive behavior may be deeply rooted and difficult for you to endure, but you need to stay patient. The way to teach your children to listen is by listening to them. Listen actively, resist the urge to feel judged, and make it clear if you can't help them or if you can't fulfill a request.

- **Use a time-out signal.** You need to have an escape hatch in case you feel your buttons are being pushed. This signal will let others know you can't cope and that you either need help or need to be left alone. The signal may simply be saying, "I need a time-out." This can be difficult at first. Your children may not respect your needing space, and may feel abandoned if you have to excuse yourself just as the conversation "gets interesting." It's important that you come back later for closure. You may still not want to discuss the topic that came up, but it is important that you let your children know this. If you leave the unanswered question dangling, your children may sense your evasion and worry about upsetting you. As trust builds over time, they will come to realize that you are not hiding, and that they will have an opportunity to come back to the subject another time or in another way.

- **Set up neutral topics for conversation.** Idle chatter is not useless. Communication is built on trust, and trust can be built on small things, like successful conversations about neutral subjects. If you talk about sports or music or movies, a successful communication of ideas makes the next conversation a tiny bit easier.

Just as recovery progresses in incremental steps, communication skills are learned one small piece at a time. Small changes that take place in earliest abstinence can later provide the foundation for a healthy family dynamic, as each of the family members learns to listen to the other's points of view and respect the others' boundaries. By respecting each others' individual focus, the family members will be traveling on parallel journeys, toward individual strength and individual health. Later, these healthy individuals will form a healthy family.

Structure

Living in the vacuum created by the collapse of the alcoholic system can be very difficult for your children. With the choice apparently being between the outdated alcoholic system and no system at all, your children may yearn for the old familiar system: at least back then they felt they understood what was happening around them. Although the toxic environment that was in place resulted in self-sacrifice and anxiety, it also provided a structure that they knew and understood.

Transition is not the time to begin building a new, healthy structure. During the transition and early recovery stages, the main focus must be on the individual. A healthy family system can only be put in place when each individual has built up a healthy individual foundation. The time for a closer focus on the family will come when you have put abstinence in place and regained the individual strength needed to support the system without sacrificing the self to serve it.

Nonetheless, it is important that some kind of interim system be put in place so that the family members, and especially the children, know what to expect. This interim system will help the children by providing structure and guidance in organizing their lives. It will also help the parents in recovery by clarifying their tasks and responsibilities, making their home life more manageable and thus helping them maintain a self-focus.

A great way to provide some structure and decrease the tension during early abstinence is to make a weekly schedule. A schedule lets everyone know what is expected of them. The schedule can keep track of when parents have meetings and when kids have soccer games and talent shows. The household chores can be spelled out, naming who is responsible for what. By organizing this information ahead of time, potential conflicts can be minimized. One of the great bonuses of having a schedule during the anxious months of early abstinence is that it can reduce anxious last-minute negotiating.

Although some work needs to go into making the weekly schedule, once it is there it lets everyone know what is happening so no one needs to wonder. Put the schedule on paper and post it where everyone can see it. This can make the children feel safe and secure.

The schedule may become an important family ritual in time, but it is important to recognize that during these weeks, it is merely a practical tool to help you, your partner, and your children survive the upheaval of early abstinence. Don't put too much pressure on yourself to make it perfect from day one.

The schedule also helps by giving you a good first step in family care: managing time. In these first few months, the goal is not to be the most helpful team mother, it is to get to the game on time. Instead of worrying about how to fix your son's bad grades, focus on getting him to school on time. Start small and take it one step at a time. Focus on what you can do today, set a schedule, and stick to it. As the family's time gets more organized, you will fall into a new routine that supports your recovery, while your children will feel that their home life is becoming more predictable and therefore more secure.

The following are some suggestions for ways to keep the family running more smoothly after the alcoholic system has collapsed:

- **Roles and rules.** Assign and clarify tasks in the family instead of letting your children guess what is expected of them. Make sure all the children's tasks are age-appropriate. Be aware that some changes may seem to your child to be a change for the worse. If your child had been responsible for all of the family meals and now is assigned the garbage, this new, age-appropriate role may seem like a demotion. You need to make it clear that the change is not a punishment, but an attempt to get things straightened out and properly balanced.

- **Rituals.** You may want to schedule a weekly meeting. Getting together once a week can be a good way to keep the family members in touch. The meeting could be a time when the Ask-It basket questions are answered or when the schedule for the coming week is organized. Your family could play a game together. However the time is structured, this time can keep your children in touch with the family while the rest of the week is dedicated to recovery.

- **Hierarchy.** It's important to clarify that the parents are responsible for the family. If the parents gave up their responsibilities during active alcoholism to focus on the drinking, it may take you a while to reclaim your position at the top. Let your children know that you will still need help, but that you will ask for it, not just expect it. In essence, you must tell your children that you are lifting the burden of taking care of the family off of their shoulders. They need to hear this. It may take time for them to trust that you will keep them safe, but building that trust begins with your telling them that you will take care of them—and then doing so.

Resources

It's important that your children learn to take care of themselves both physically and emotionally. At the physical level, you can teach them how to fix a meal or call the fire department, or what to do if they are locked out. You can develop a list of people to call for emergencies. Try to make learning good survival skills fun.

Many children from alcoholic homes already know how to take care of such needs as cooking and cleaning, since they have had to take care of themselves when their parents were unable to. The main skills such children must learn is the ability to ask for help. One of the most powerful ways to teach behavior to your child is to model that behavior. The fact that you ask for help from AA and Al-Anon is in itself a strong example to your children of how to meet their own needs in a healthy manner. Seeing you vulnerable gives them permission to be vulnerable as well.

The amount of external help your children need will vary. If they insist they don't need help, don't force the issue. You can check in every so often with support and an invitation to talk. Children can be very worried that talking will violate the old rules and somehow hurt or endanger the abstinence. If they need to talk, it may be helpful for them to have access to someone outside the family. This can let them open up and express their feelings about drinking and recovery.

At the emotional level, you can teach your children how to ask for what they need and listen to them when they need to talk. If you can't listen, let the child know that and see that they have someone else to talk with, whether a counselor, a relative, or the other parent. You can also teach your children ways to cope with difficult feelings. A child can be consumed by these feelings just as an adult can. Talking to a friend, writing, doing physical exercise, reading, and drawing—are all positive ways a child can express his troubling feelings and relieve some of the pressure he feels. As you work on coping with your own thoughts and feelings, you can share your growing wisdom about what works and what doesn't.

Many children have a hard time describing what feeling they are experiencing. If this is the case with your child, you can teach her words that illustrate different emotions and different degrees of these emotions. If "sad" is the one word your child has for feeling down, for example, other options like "feeling blue," "disappointed," "down," or "all choked up" may offer a more satisfying range of expression.

Lastly, try to give your children a lot of positive feedback. In the beginning of recovery, children often experience a drop in self-esteem because their world has changed and they feel scared and out of control. Reassurance and support will add to their budding sense of security and ultimately bolster their feelings of well-being.

Support

Your children will need to look behind the defenses that allowed them to tolerate the unsafe environment. In order to feel vulnerable, they must first feel safe; they need a secure environment and secure relationships that they can rely upon. Make sure your children have access to a safe and supportive place to share their feelings.

You can help your children find safe people for support. A "safe person" is someone who respects and listens to children, someone who validates their feelings and thoughts, and someone who will not use them to meet his or her own needs.

Healthy relationships with healthy people will help your child develop a solid support system. These outside supports for your children will also take some of the pressure off of you. Children need other adults in their lives, as well as trustworthy friends. Get to know your children's friends and offer them a welcome. You can also talk to your children about how to make the house feel safe for them while you are out.

Humor, Fun, and Play

Humor and playfulness can make almost any family situation more bearable, so give permission to yourself and your family to express joy and have fun. Games allow the family to take a vacation from the tensions of the household, and also to practice interactions by sharing in a neutral task. If the interaction at game time feels superficial, that's okay. Again, change is incremental, and any small moments of good interaction and communication will pay dividends in the future.

Try to give your kids access to healthy fun and entertainment. Make sure your kids have rides to their games and school programs and special events. If you have a conflict help them find a ride. Even though your focus remains on your recovery, you need to be certain that your children can lead a full and active life.

Take time to celebrate important events: the six-year anniversary for family recovery; one year for your child in AlaTeen; your son's making the honor roll; or your daughter's being chosen for the all-star team in her soccer league. These celebrations can be fun, and self-affirming, and can help foster a sense of positive family identity.

Love

The last piece of advice may be the simplest, but it is also perhaps the most important single way to smooth your child's experience of early abstinence. Let your children know you love them. In many alcoholic families, the children are isolated and live without parental warmth, attention, and loving words. Often when love is discussed it is because the parents feel guilty and need to know that the child still loves them.

Show your children you love them no matter what they do. Be careful not to subtly demand that they reciprocate or pressure them to support you. They may have problems with you during recovery: problems about the drinking, or problems about the recovery itself. It's important that they have support for themselves. If they feel resistant to your recovery, let it be. You teach love by giving it, wholly and selflessly.

Patience and Trust

People in recovery often feel they need to tackle all of their problems at once. They are afraid that if they're not working on change and self-improvement all the time, they must be doing something wrong. As their eyes open and denial begins to fall away, they see new problems and immediately jump to the task of solving them.

Edward, a twelve-year veteran of AA, remembers those first weeks of absti-nence like they were yesterday: "I was a whirlwind. My wife was very worried about me, but I just told her I'd never felt better. It was like I had spent my whole life driv-ing with the emergency brake on, and I had finally taken it off. I wanted to dive in and do everything at once. Recovery could not move fast enough." Although he experienced a kind of manic high from his early abstinence, much of the energy came from anxiety. "When I think back upon it, I was completely over the top. I felt like if I kept running around, the anxiety couldn't catch up to me. Truth was, the anxiety was fueling my running."

You can't "do" recovery all at once. A person in early abstinence needs to weigh which defenses can be challenged and which will be better faced later. **At the begin-ning of abstinence, the central focus must be your dependency on alcohol or, if you are a coalcoholic, your dependency on the alcoholic.** If you try to challenge all your defenses before you have set your abstinence firmly in place, you may jeopardize your recovery. Although you may be filled with energy during the transition stage, you need to respect the fact that you are still very fragile. The main task of early abstinence is to learn to be vulnerable and rely on your external support while work-ing on substituting healthy actions for your impulses.

It makes sense that the alcoholic and coalcoholic would be impatient to make progress: this is emergency thinking in action. During active alcoholism, you lived with the belief that the alcoholic system must be maintained at all times and all costs. You had to rely upon instant remedies and compulsive problem solving. If you were ever to hesitate, the unhealthy core of the system might be exposed.

Patience is built upon a foundation of trust: trust that your parents will do what they say; that your spouse will be there in times of need; that you can withstand a cri-sis; that you are safe; that things will work out in the future. Impatience is a natural result of living in an insecure environment. So it makes sense that you might be frus-trated with yourself if you seem to be going too slowly. It's important that you recog-nize this impatience as another defense, born of emergency thinking: "If I don't get it done now, I may never get another chance."

In the beginning of recovery, nothing goes smoothly; everything will be an effort. It's like learning to play the saxophone: the earliest work is unsatisfying—mainly just squeaks and squawks. Try to avoid the trap that is so common with alco-holic thinking: needing to get it right the first time. Ally said that in her earliest days of recovery she began to develop a sense of humor about herself that she had never had before: "I suddenly felt like everything I did was so funny. I would start to get frustrated at myself and I would think, 'Look at Ally, it's like she's nine years old and learning to ride a bicycle all over again.' And I'd have to laugh."

In the same way as your coping skills start superficial and become internalized, patience also starts small and builds slowly. You begin building up your patience when you put a wedge between impulse and action. Slowly you add to the wedge until the impulse and the action are far enough apart to allow calm reflection and choice between them.

Changing the way you perceive the world is a slow process that begins with changing the way you behave in the world. This is the purpose of the coping strate-gies you have learned about in this chapter. You learn to be patient by acting patient. Patience is the food that feeds recovery and the flower that grows from it.

Building patience means building trust in the future. A person who has never been able to trust that the future will bring a better result will grab for the immediate gratification of the present. But when the trust takes hold, you will find it easier to decline the short-term repair in favor of long-term health and growth.

One Step at a Time

When the defenses that were built to protect you end up demanding that you protect them, the first step in freeing yourself from the defenses is recognizing that they are there. It's natural to want to do more: after years living under the reign of alcoholism, it makes sense that you don't want to "waste any more time." But while it may seem a small thing to recognize that these defenses exist, it is the first step toward dealing with them. It is by way of these incremental steps that recovery progresses.

When we are faced with the expanse of the rest of our lives, it can seem like an impossible task to take it all in in a single moment. But recovery is about a lifetime, not about a single moment. The best way to secure a rounded perspective of life is to live it, one moment at a time. To spend your time planning for the one great moment means you miss the multitude of smaller ones that add up to a life.

The same holds true for any task: in order to tackle a big problem, you need to break it down into smaller parts. In order to endure the years of recovery, you need to break it down into a series of days. **Every small step forward is an experience you will draw upon in the future.** What seems impossible now will become a simple matter in the future. Remember the old proverb: "A journey of a thousand miles starts with a single step." This first step is often the hardest. Often we are so overwhelmed by our perception of the length of the journey that we can't get started; so we do nothing. Likewise, it's easy to feel lost and overwhelmed after we've begun the journey.

One of the purposes of this book is to show you how the long journey is made up of smaller ones. By seeing the larger map, you can find your place in the landscape and discover that you weren't ever lost; you just didn't know where you were.

Part 3

The Power of Not Knowing

The Early Recovery Stage

7

"Laying the Foundation"

Mapping Early Recovery

The seeds of healthy growth are sown in the transition stage; in early recovery, they begin to take root. Here, the foundation for the individual identity is set in place, bringing newfound stability. Early recovery can be a time of unparalleled personal change, hope, and excitement; it can also be a time of trauma, especially at home, where the family members are still functioning without a strong, healthy family system. Even as growth begins, tensions and setbacks are to be expected.

During early recovery, the alcoholic and coalcoholic are still extremely dependent on their relationships with their recovery programs. Their main focus at this time is education about alcoholism and the process of recovery in general, and on the specific ways in which each particular individual has experienced these realities. To facilitate this education, they learn recovery language, which helps them organize their past experiences and understand their ongoing thoughts and feelings. By internalizing this new language and the abstinent behaviors that were set in place during transition, they begin to solidify their new alcoholic or coalcoholic identities. The healthy behavior they practiced in transition starts to become less conscious and more automatic as their impulses to drink or take care of the drinker finally begin to decrease.

As their abstinence stabilizes, the alcoholic and coalcoholic start reconstructing the drinking past. Facing this long-denied reality can be an extremely challenging task. "I think the scariest part for me was when the crisis period after quitting ended," remembers Sheila, who recently celebrated her eighth year of sobriety. "In the first few months, I was so single-minded about not drinking that the rest of the world barely existed. Dealing with the screaming urges was painful and difficult, but it had a kind of simplicity to it, like I was in an emergency and there was no time to second-guess myself. But as the urges got less and less, the rest of my life suddenly came into focus, and I saw the devastation the drinking had done. Facing those issues was the hardest part of the whole journey for me."

An important task of early recovery is the construction of the "drunkalogue"—the story of the drinking. Organizing this narrative is an effective method of facing the difficult memories. The more you understand what happened and why, and what you were and were not responsible for, the more you will be able to let go of the guilt and shame that ruled the drinking stage. When abstinence stabilizes further, you can begin to explore yourself in deeper ways—who are you now without the active addiction?

The changes that take place in early recovery are more subtle than transition. People often feel they have fallen off the path when they no longer see concrete progress being made. Uncertain as to where they are headed, they may reassert control, which can interfere with the normal, opening-up growth process. Or, as the cravings start to diminish and they begin to see healthy growth, they risk becoming complacent. They need to maintain their ongoing surrender to avoid falling back into old habits.

To tolerate the anxiety of the unknown and stay on the path of recovery, many people focus on developing a relationship with a higher power, which is the heart of twelve-step programs. People learn to give up control to a higher power, which helps them live with and even appreciate the unknowns that characterize life in recovery. Relinquishing control helps them distinguish the things they have influence over from those they don't. This is a crucial distinction in recovery.

Early recovery is a complicated and uncertain time: trust is slow in coming; backsliding and crisis are a normal part of the process. You make progress through the fear and pain only by experiencing them; it gets a little less hard each time you do it. This chapter seeks to give you an overview of this part of the journey and, hopefully, the confidence to endure the unknown and allow your healthy growth to evolve naturally.

Developmental Tasks of Early Recovery

- Continue detachment and a reduced focus on the family.
- Learn and practice recovery language.
- Maintain close contact with external supports.
- Continue to learn abstinent behaviors and thinking.
- Begin to break denial over the past.
- Maintain a focus on individual recovery.
- Stabilize individual identities: "I am an alcoholic and I cannot control my drinking" or "I am a coalcoholic and I cannot control the drinker."
- Maintain parenting responsibilities.

(Adapted from Brown and Lewis, 1999)

Detachment and Parallel Growth

As we have said before, a healthy family is built of healthy individuals, so before the family can be considered, each member needs to heal. During early recovery, each member of your family needs to focus on his or her own recovery and assume responsibility for his or her life. To do this vital work, you each need to set firm boundaries and continue to detach from the old family system. You need to rely on your external supports for help, feedback, and many of the other personal needs that you once depended on your family for.

Your detachment does not mean that your children's needs should go unmet or that you should stop going to work; you need to keep your life working as best you can. Your relationships with your children and your coworkers will probably be a bit clumsy at first, but you can't attend to the repair of these relationships until you work on yourself.

Early recovery task: Continue detachment and a reduced family focus.

Stan and Peggy, whose story was told in chapter 5, found the process of detachment to be quite awkward at first. There was a time of some emotional distance while the two focused on their own recoveries. "It was hard to have distance between us," remembers Stan. "We had been having troubles for years before entering recovery. When I finally went into recovery, part of me felt like it would bring us closer together. In the long run it did, but it was hard at first. There were times when the treatment felt worse than the sickness."

With the help of their recovery programs as an external source of support, both Peggy and Stan were able to focus on the things they actually had some control over—not each other. This detachment would allow them to grow into healthy individuals who could build a healthy relationship.

"To me, it was so important to know that we were on the same road," says Peggy. "I knew what it was like when he was resistant. Stan's entry into recovery gave me hope. It's like we were driving on parallel highways, and it was comforting to see each other there, even if we couldn't get close. We trusted that if we kept driving—if we kept working on our recoveries—the highways would converge somewhere down the line."

There were hard times, and they discussed splitting up. Both are glad that they didn't act then. Peggy says, "You don't heal a cut finger by removing the arm; but lord knows we were tempted to do the surgery on more than one occasion. Though you may feel like it at the time, early recovery is not the time to make those decisions." The recovery program allows the partners to have time alone to work on themselves and postpone important choices until the options are clear. "In the end we put our relationship on hold. It took a long time for us to come out the other end with our identities intact, ready to focus on the relationship. But now we had the individual health, which gave us a new foundation, and a kind of mutual trust and respect for having gone through the recovery process. Sticking with the recovery was the best thing we did."

The work Peggy and Stan were doing on an individual basis ultimately allowed them to achieve a more satisfying couple relationship in the long run. Again we hit upon a key concept of recovery: instead of working for short-term comfort, you are working toward long-term health. This sometimes means enduring short-term hardship. Letting these hardships block your way means bowing to the pressures of the unhealthy system.

Language

For people who belong to twelve-step support groups, learning new, recovery language is a central focus of early recovery. Recovery language is simple and concrete, and it helps people resist seeing the world through the "filters" of guilt, blame, and denial that are common to the drinking stage.

Language is fundamental to the way we see things, yet we are seldom aware that it's there. The words you use to describe a situation often shape your perception of it. "I need a drink" and "I am experiencing an impulse to drink" are two ways of describing the same craving, but they imply two quite different views of that feeling. "I need a drink" has the force of a command: I *must* have a drink. These words also suggest that this state will go on indefinitely: need will exist until it's met. "I am experiencing an impulse to drink," however, suggests that the impulse is separate from the person, and that the person has some power over whether or not to act on the impulse. The second description also implies that the impulse will pass. These descriptions express beliefs about your situation, and if you believe you have a choice, you are more likely to be able to withstand the urge than if you believe you are a slave to it. The second construction may seem awkward, and it may not be terribly concise, but it is a more accurate description of the situation. By ceasing to describe the impulse as a need, you change the way you perceive that impulse, and thus empower yourself to make choices.

Early recovery task: Learn and practice recovery language.

As we saw in part 2, the best way to change how you think is to change how you behave. Language is a central part of this process. By practicing and slowly internalizing recovery language, you will be better able to make positive changes in the way you perceive the alcoholism, the world, and yourself. The following are two ways that recovery language brings about change:

- **Recovery language focuses on "I" rather than "you."** Recovery involves assuming personal responsibility for yourself; language is an important way of expressing this responsibility. Instead of using blaming language, like "you made me feel bad," you can use the less provocative and more accurate construction: "I felt bad when you did that." Using language that focuses on yourself both shows respect for the firm boundaries necessary in early recovery and reduces your listener's need for a defensive reaction, thereby improving communication.

- **Recovery language is a concrete, action language**. Solid terms that provide direction, such as "Put the plug in the jug"; "One day at a time"; and "Construct a drunkalogue," connect concepts to the real world. Abstract thoughts can spiral out of control without anything solid to attach them to, allowing you to fall prey to the power of the impulses. You need to keep your mind tied to the world during this stage of recovery.

You learn your new recovery language from your external support system, whether it is AA, Al-Anon, or a therapist. The external support is both the source of and reinforcement for your new language. Healthy language and communication are modeled at meetings, and slowly you start to internalize these new ways of describing the world. When you hear an old-timer describe her memories using "I" language, with no blame or shame, you are being taught to do the same. If you go to the meetings and continue to rely on and make use of your external support system, you will be learning at all times.

Early recovery task: Maintain close contact with external supports.

There are great benefits to practicing recovery language:

- A new language breaks the old mental habits that supported the alcoholic system.

- A shared language gives everyone in the family a new tool for communication, and helps the family identify as a recovering family, insofar as they are using recovery language.

- The new language also aids detachment. Often, specific words and phrases trigger defensive responses; if the words are expressed differently, the defenses may be avoided.

- It redefines your experience, allowing you to face otherwise difficult situations and memories.

- It can be a necessary buffer between the alcoholic or coalcoholic and the past. Since it supports responsibility, not guilt or blame, its objective, concrete terms can be used to describe memories that might otherwise be too painful to face.

- In a similar way, it can help you in your present situation. A new vocabulary helps you work through denial, face difficult realities, and clarify your feelings and perceptions.

New language, like any new behavior, can feel sterile and awkward at first. It takes time and practice for it to feel natural and automatic. The practice is a terrific way to divert your attention from cravings and anxieties, and by the time the cravings lighten up, you will have a new language working for you.

Increasing the Space Between Impulse and Action

In the drinking stage, the alcoholic or coalcoholic's impulse is so closely tied to the action that they appear to be the same thing. As we saw in chapter 4, the first step in disarming the impulse to drink is to redirect that impulse and express it in a new and healthy way. This entails learning new behaviors that you substitute for the drinking. Though awkward at first, over time these behaviors become more automatic.

By redirecting the impulse toward a new action, you disconnect it from its original action. Not only does this separation help you avoid drinking, it also demonstrates that the impulse and the action are two different things. As you continue to practice new behavior and language, the gap between the urge and the action increases. As the impulse becomes less connected to the action, you can mediate the two using your new recovery language.

Early recovery task: Continue to learn abstinent behaviors and thinking.

"I think of it like practicing martial arts," says Andrea, who has been sober for eight years and has been studying aikido for five. "Before you learn a martial art, if someone were to attack you, your only response would be instinctual. You have no training, no vocabulary of moves you can draw upon to help you recognize what the attacker is doing and what your options are. When you practice a martial art, you become familiar with combat: you begin to recognize the different kinds of attacks and you learn different ways of responding. You practice your skills until they become automatic. Ultimately, when you are attacked, it is no longer an emergency situation ruled by untrained instincts; you can react in a prepared way drawing on your practice and experience. You're able to recognize what the attacker is doing, and you have time to choose from your vocabulary of responses. Or, if you see that the attack is a weak one and is not going to connect, you may recognize that no response is necessary." By internalizing the new behavior and language, Andrea was able to recognize both her urges and her options. As this process became automatic, she shifted from a stance of frightened vigilance to a much more comfortable one of careful attention.

The Drunkalogue

Another major focus in early recovery is constructing a "drunkalogue" or "story"—the AA and Al-Anon terms for the history of active alcoholism. In order to compose your drunkalogue, you have to do the hard work of facing your past. Healthy growth is just beginning in early recovery, and you're starting to feel some confidence; so you may feel anxious about revisiting the old attitudes and behavior that you have been working hard to change. But your progress forward depends upon your looking back.

Early recovery task: Begin to break denial over the past.

As you start work on your drunkalogue, rely on your external support structure. In AA and Al-Anon, the process begins when you listen to other members share their stories. Angelo, a father of four whose wife has been sober for six years, remembers how powerful this experience was: "I had kept it all inside for so long. I was so afraid. Even after she put down the bottle, I was still terrified of the things I had done. It felt like my guilt would be a life sentence. When I heard other folks tell their stories, it was reassuring; I felt so much better knowing that people had gone through what I had gone through. Some had been through worse. Not only was I hearing that I wasn't alone, but I was seeing men and women who had the courage to get up and tell their stories. I didn't realize it at the time, but they were teaching me how to tell my story. When I spoke for the first time, I felt numb. I heard the memories come out, but I was waiting to be struck by lightning. When I finished, it struck me that it was the first time I had ever said the words aloud, and I had done it with others listening. The things I had squashed and hidden and was so ashamed of for all these years were suddenly out there in the world rather than haunting me on the inside. It was the hardest thing I've done and the most satisfying. Hearing others tell their story allowed me to tell mine. Telling mine probably helped others tell theirs. It's a great system."

The goal of the story is not to prove some objective truth about what happened, but to uncover the past as you experienced it. As you've seen in chapters 2 and 5 and will see again in chapters 8 and 11, different family members will have different points of view. The alcoholic may not remember things well due to the effects of drinking. The coalcoholic may have a clearer view, but a harder time admitting he was part of the problem. The children may have had such deep denial and been so frightened that remembering confuses them. Again, you need to focus on your self and your own past experiences, even if there are frustrating holes in your story (as there are for most people who live through active alcoholism).

Early recovery task: Maintain a focus on individual recovery.

When you face these past experiences, you will also be facing the guilt and shame you felt at the time. It's important that you recognize that these feelings are rooted in the past. When you're confronted with difficult memories, you're vulnerable to the emotional attitudes you had when the event occurred. This can be a source of real anxiety during this process, but it is a natural result of looking back. Your external supports and your recovery language will help you reconstruct the past without being withered by the shame, guilt, and denial that were the norm at that time.

The narrative is not something that you put away when you finish; it continues to grow as you do. Over time in recovery, your memory may grow clearer, you may learn new information, or you may make new connections that help you redefine a certain period of time.

Your stories can help you stay in recovery: they document the realities of the drinking stage. The moment you feel like the past is dead and no longer has meaning to you, you risk repeating it.

Maintaining Ongoing Surrender

As you gain confidence in your abstinence and your urges to drink begin to weaken, a new challenge arises. The loss of control, which was at the forefront of your mind in the early months of abstinence, can begin to seem less tangible. It's not uncommon for people to feel "back in control" as the crisis of transition ebbs. Curtis, who we'll hear more about in chapter 8, started to treat his recovery the same way he treated his drinking. "I was dealing with recovery as something I could master. When the desire quieted, I figured I was cured and couldn't understand why it took all these other folks so much time to get where I already was. I hadn't really surrendered after all. It was a conditional surrender: I surrender until I feel better. It's no surprise that I was back at square one before long."

A second challenge for folks with control issues is that, unlike transition, which is divided into two concrete phases (drinking and abstinence), early recovery does not have a clearly identifiable form. There is no central transformation, like there was in transition, and there is no definite line between transition and early recovery. The tasks that need to be accomplished do not follow a specific order, nor do they head toward a simple, definable goal. The tasks are all ongoing.

Early recovery is about becoming comfortable with the fact that your journey is uncertain and evolves of its own accord. In early recovery, you practice your new behaviors and language one piece at a time and let the process take care of itself. The experience teaches you that you can set a goal and work toward it, but that the ultimate outcome is out of your hands.

Such uncertainty is threatening to alcoholics and coalcoholics, because alcoholism is a disease of control. Those living through active alcoholism usually don't want to participate in a project unless they can control the outcome; not knowing what will happen makes them too anxious. As the abstinence stabilizes, the uncertainty that characterizes early recovery can push the alcoholic or coalcoholic back toward old habits of taking over control. Only a continued focus on her surrender can disarm the alcoholic's or coalcoholic's impulses toward control.

One way to stay focused on your ongoing surrender is to give up control to a higher power. This does not demand a religious conversion; the higher power is different for each individual. When you grasp the reality that your impulses, thoughts, and feelings are outside of your control, you merely need to ask yourself, "Who or what is controlling them?" or "Where do they come from?" Your answer will reveal your unique higher power. For some it is the god of their religion; for others it is the forces of nature; for still others it is the support group or program itself.

By focusing on the higher power, you make the process of surrender an active, concrete action ("I give the control to you"). Giving up control does not mean making yourself a slave to another; it merely means that the power that is "controlling" these emotions and impulses is outside yourself, and that you have no power to change these things.

Early recovery task: Stabilize individual identities: "I am an alcoholic and I cannot control my drinking" or "I am a coalcoholic and I cannot control the drinker."

At first, saying "It is out of my control" can be anxiety-provoking. To feel comfortable giving up control, you'll need to lean heavily on your external support and, possibly, your higher power. Over time, you'll discover that saying "I don't have control" actually strengthens your awareness of the things you *do* have the ability to change. This distinction—knowing you can influence your effort but not necessarily your outcome—frees you from your fear of being responsible for a negative outcome. The importance of understanding what you can and cannot change is the thrust of the serenity prayer, which is central to the AA philosophy: "God grant me the serenity to accept the things I cannot change, the courage to change the things I can, and the wisdom to know the difference."

Maintaining ongoing surrender allows you to let recovery take its course. You work on the small things and let the overall process unfold at its own pace. Although recovery begins with a deep experience of surrender, a deep belief in ongoing surrender doesn't come all at once. As with many other aspects of recovery, the belief starts out being superficial and awkward and slowly becomes internalized.

Bumps and Backsliding

In early recovery, it's normal to experience setbacks. With the move from transition to early recovery, abstinence feels more stable and anxiety becomes, in general, more tolerable. Slowly the chronic state of crisis dissipates; but this increased calm can actually produce its own anxiety.

Although traumatic events may become less common, they may feel more painful when compared to the new state of calm. When you are engaged in the continuous crisis of the transition period, your overall life may feel worse, but each particular crisis may seem less threatening since it is seen in the context of the greater ongoing crisis. If you are expecting a bumpy ride, you tend to drive more slowly and brace yourself for shocks. But when the road smooths out, you may expect fewer bumps, and you might push the accelerator and speed up. The next bump you hit will feel more jarring than would the same-size bump on a rough road.

The crisis can seem to be evidence that you have not made the progress you thought you had, or that you are doing something wrong. Carla remembers struggling with such worries just as she thought things were finally getting better: "It was hard. I felt like I was laying the foundation for recovery one day on top of another. So every bad day made me doubt the work I had put in the days before. I thought that if the foundation was set, I shouldn't be feeling bad. When something went wrong I would instantly think that I was back at the beginning of the process, somewhere I desperately didn't want to be." Eventually, she began to see them as a normal part of the process: "Once I had survived a few of these problems, I started to recognize the off day as just that: one bad day among many good ones. The knowledge that a few bad days didn't spell disaster made them much easier to endure."

When the tensions of the drinking and transition stages ease, it can trigger other problems. Children often keep problems inside for fear of upsetting the fragile abstinence, but as things start to stabilize, the child relaxes and the problems explode onto center stage. Just as Carla started to feel hopeful and confident in her abstinence, her daughter, who had always been an excellent student, started having problems at school. "I thought things were going well and she brings home this report card and she's failing everything. I immediately panicked. This was all my anxiety come true. My daughter was suffering for my selfish recovery; that's how I saw it." The family may organize around the new problem in the same way they did around the alcoholism before recovery began. "I started focusing on her homework and pestering her to keep at it. I saw the schoolwork as a sign that she needed my help. I put everything else aside and started to focus on her and her schoolwork. I bulled through until I realized that I was right back where I started. I was focused on fixing her problems to make me feel better. It took some time with my sponsor to get me back on track. We got her a tutor and I asked her to do the best she could. By the end of the semester she had joined a recovery program for teens." Again, you need to make sure your children's needs are met, but this doesn't mean you have to take on the responsibility alone. As we saw in chapter 6, reaching outside the family for help with your children not only takes the pressure off of you, allowing you to maintain your self-focus, but it also shows your children that it's okay to ask for help.

Early recovery task: Maintain parenting responsibilities.

As you make progress, your fears about backsliding can make steps forward more difficult. You may question whether new behavior seems to be a step backward, or whether it is appropriate. This is natural and necessary, but it can also be confusing and awkward. If you clean up after your children, are you acting under the old system? When is it okay to help your spouse if you are a coalcoholic? It's often a good idea to consult your sponsor or an old-timer if you are having a hard time gauging whether your behavior is appropriate for your individual focus. Sometimes it's enough to know that by paying attention to boundary questions in the first place, you are doing the work of recovery. No one is perfect. You may overstep a boundary now and again, or retreat when an advance would have been appropriate. Early recovery is a time for education, so as long as you are attentive to and learning from mistakes, you are still making progress.

Thumbnail Map of the Early Recovery Stage

- The family environment is becoming more stable and predictable, though some tension continues.

- The biggest change is still the absence of alcohol.

- Some members may be feeling hopeful.

- Individual recoveries are well underway, with detachment from the old family system strengthened and supported by separate recovery programs.

- The family system remains collapsed, and the individual family members need to rely on external supports.

- Individuals focus on education, recovery language, and starting work on the "drunkalogue."

- Basic family responsibilities, especially parenting, are attended to often with help from outside the family.

(Adapted from Brown and Lewis, 1999)

The Environment in Early Recovery

Although individual family members may begin to see signs of healthy growth in themselves during early recovery, the environment may still carry the tension and awkwardness that characterized life during transition. The family is still adjusting to the changes that came with the shift into recovery, and the alcoholic system is still collapsed with no new family structure yet in place. While the family members are getting the support they need from external sources, anxiety and confusion are often the norm at home. However, fixing family relationships is not a priority at this time, since the family members in recovery need to be committed to self-focus.

New and ongoing family friction is common in early recovery. If your children had a hard time during transition, their difficulties may continue in early recovery; and even if your children seemed fine during transition, problems can develop at this time. It's common for children's expressions of frustration to be delayed until the hope and relief inspired by the end of drinking begins to wear off and the difficult reality of recovery sinks in. A feeling of abandonment, which was tolerated when there was a promise of things getting better quickly, may now result in genuine resentment.

Another reason the onset of problems can be delayed is that children may not have felt comfortable expressing their problems during the acute crisis of transition. They may have felt that speaking out would threaten the fragile abstinence. But as things begin to settle and the pressure lifts a bit, they may relax and begin to vent anger about their situation. Just because children may seem fine at the start of recovery doesn't mean they have escaped the active alcoholism unharmed. The parents need to keep checking in with the children to make sure their needs are being met.

Another source of overt tension within the family can be the relationship between the spouses. With each parent needing to focus on him- or herself and neither knowing how to interact with the other, friction may arise. Some couples choose not to interact at all; others only discuss the recovery, practicing the recovery language as a means of checking in with each other. The children may read this detachment as evidence that the marriage is splitting up.

Still, abstinence is beginning to solidify and the individuals are growing stronger in their new identities. Over time, the strength and solidity of their individual foundations can exert a stabilizing effect on the household, slowly making the environment safer. Children will begin to trust their parents' recovery when they see signs that the parents' once unpredictable behavior is more stable. Positive change happens, but it doesn't happen overnight.

The Environment in Early Recovery

- Moving from unsafe to safe
- The "trauma of recovery" continues
- Moving toward stability
- Still can be chaotic
- Characterized by hope mixed with tension and anxiety

(Adapted from Brown and Lewis, 1999)

Exercise: Environment in Early Recovery

■ Sit in a chair and relax. Take a few deep breaths, and think back to a memory from the period when you began to feel more stable in your abstinence.

■ Recalling these traumatic times can be painful, and if you feel you aren't ready, by all means let it go and come back later. There is no rush; the book will be here when you are ready.

■ When you have a memory in mind, relax and let it come to you. Instead of focusing on the event, focus on the surroundings: the feelings, sights, sounds, and smells. Write your feelings about the atmosphere in your journal. Write as much or as little as you need to.

Many people reading this book for the first time will be in early recovery. If this is the case for you, you will be trying to perceive the atmosphere in your family as it exists today. This can be difficult.

Don't forget to date the entry for future reference. You may want to try this again.

The Family System in Early Recovery

During early recovery, the family system is still collapsed, so the internal structure that everyone once depended on is no longer there for support. Each individual must rely on external support to help with the shift from family focus to individual focus. Outside the home, the new behavior and attitudes learned in the recovery programs can bring a sense of hope and excitement. Meanwhile, at home, things can be more challenging.

As individuals begin to improve during recovery, they will become more aware that the family dynamics at home seem to be frozen in an unhealthy state. Since the home is often where most of the dramas of active alcoholism played out, being there may mean being bombarded with thoughts of the past and its present-day repercussions. Phil, who has been sober for almost seven years, remembers his struggles to feel comfortable at home: "When I finally started to feel hopeful and confident at meetings, it was like the clouds parting and the sun shining through for the first time. The possibilities seemed limitless. Then I'd arrive home, and it was like stepping into a time machine. All the bad feelings would wash over me: the joy would disintegrate." Phil was devastated to have his rare bubbles of hope punctured, and he began to dread coming home. "The house took on a personality to me during that time, like it was haunted by the drinking. I would feel free out in the world, but when I returned, I was back where I started. It was so frustrating."

Home is often the last place that healthy change feels comfortable. People usually expect their home to be the place they feel most comfortable, so they may see the discomfort at home as evidence that they are doing something wrong. Instead, it is to be expected as a natural by-product of some easily overlooked facts:

• In recovery, you work at changing your behavior. This means avoiding the familiar places that challenge sobriety and bring back bad memories and habits. Your home is probably the most familiar place of all and has links to some of your most troubling memories and habits.

- You have probably spent so much time in your home that every corner holds a difficult memory. This can mean having to overcome an almost constant barrage of anxiety.

- At one time, your home was a refuge; during early recovery it can be the one place you can't allow yourself to relax, for fear of falling into old behaviors. The contrast between the "happy" past and the trying present can make things seem even worse than they actually are.

- Bad habits are more easily triggered when you are someplace where you were once comfortable. Comfort can be a habit, and if home was where you relaxed, you may let your guard down.

- New growth and new behaviors, which seem convincing and real when you are trying them out in the world, can feel artificial at home, where everyone knows who you are and what you were like in the past. One of the great challenges of recovery is integrating your family into your new healthy growth. Individual recovery must be solidly in place before this hurdle can be tackled.

Even in an ideal situation, where everyone in the family is in recovery and all are respecting each other's self-focus, home can seem a cold place to be, as the family members maintain a safe distance in order to focus on their own recovery. This was how it was for Phil: "When I was out in the world, my new boundaries seemed normal, but at home, they often felt inappropriate. I felt like I wasn't giving enough, or I wasn't getting enough. I couldn't help but compare my new behavior to the way I used to behave. I ended up apologizing for everything, but the apology was just another way of being enmeshed. You can tell yourself logically that your new way of interacting is appropriate, but it still feels wrong. It took a long time to get over feeling like I was an imposter in my house."

On the positive side, these awkward interactions with your family shed light upon defenses and denial that could otherwise be overlooked if your recovery took place on a remote desert island. Since home is often the last place that recovery feels natural, it can be a valuable standard by which to judge your progress. Remaining aware of the anxiety and tension at home reminds you of the work you have yet to do.

The length of time it takes to construct a functioning family system depends on how well the family adapts to life in recovery. The fastest transformations occur when each individual family member commits to a recovery program. Traveling on a parallel journey is the most healthy way for the family to connect in early recovery. If they try to share their individual recovery by including others or needing to be included by others, this will only echo the unhealthy system that took so long to overthrow. If everyone is committed to recovery, communication may still seem awkward and artificial, but this fact will seem less threatening.

However, if some members are in recovery and some are not, the prospects for family recovery may become limited. Those in recovery will still be able to move forward, but they may feel blocked by other family members who resist the changes.

These latter individuals often feel anger or resentment at the unfairness they have experienced, as well as fear of abandonment, or of discovering their part in the family's problems. If there is active resistance, the family system may remain in a state of "dry drunk"—even if the alcoholic is the one in recovery. The resistant individuals will still be relying on their enmeshed dynamics and the demand of self-sacrifice in the service of the family system. The family members in recovery may be dismissed as selfish and disloyal, or may even be condescended to by the rest of the family, who take no responsibility for their part in the alcoholic system.

Jean, who has been sober for just over a decade now, kept her focus on individual recovery even while her husband constantly threatened to leave her. "He would say that the only reason he was staying was because I would fall apart without him. He said that weak people needed AA. The only positive thing he'd say was that I had guts to admit my weakness. At first I was grateful that he was sticking around. I had so much guilt at the time that I thought he was right, that I deserved his resentment. But I gradually came to realize who was the weak one between the two of us; I began to see who was dependent on whom." In the end, the person who left was Jean herself, taking their ten-year-old son with her. "Once I let down my own denial, it became impossible for me to stay in a relationship where my husband was so invested in his own denial." For her husband, this was his moment of hitting bottom. He has since entered Al-Anon.

At the beginning of early recovery, the family system is much the same as it was in transition. The rules and roles are still confusing, and communication and interaction are still awkward and tense. Over the course of early recovery, as individuals begin to solidify their identities, the family system will begin to be organized around recovery. During the drinking stage, the individual was defined by a focus on the system; now the system is defined by the individual's self-focus. Much of this "work" to create a new family system occurs naturally. For instance, as the individuals focus on themselves, they begin to have better boundaries; by respecting these boundaries, the family creates a system where boundaries are respected as a matter of course. There will still be troubles that need to be ironed out, and when each family member's individual identity is strong enough to withstand focusing on the family, these issues can be tackled. So even though the system may feel absent and awkward, the seeds of future growth are being planted.

The Vacuum Continues

During early recovery, the system is still collapsed and the individuals are getting support from external sources. The emerging family system will be built upon the foundation of the individual recoveries. If an interim structure is put in place to keep the family running more smoothly, the family members must remain mindful of the new system and make sure it doesn't interfere with the individual growth. It's better to endure the friction of life without a system than to impose a new structure that suppresses the individual growth in favor of family harmony.

Rules

With the old rules gone, it's common for family members to be unclear about what they should and shouldn't do around the house. Should the coalcoholic still make his or her spouse's doctor's appointments? Should the oldest child still clean the younger children's rooms? Should the alcoholic take a more parental role with the children? Home is where the habits are; and even though you may be seeing progress in individual recovery, you might feel stuck at home.

Some families establish rules to support recovery, such as keeping the house alcohol- or drug-free. While positive and important, the new rules may spark resistance and problems. If the rules were strict during the drinking stage, new rules, even if they are made with the best intentions, may feel oppressive to family members who had to sacrifice individual focus under the old rules.

Exercise: Rules in Early Recovery

The purpose of this and the following exercises is to take inventory of your family's life in early recovery.

- Go back to the journal entry from the "Rules in Transition" exercise in chapter 4.

- Are the rules that supported the alcoholic system still in place? Are you still following the rules though there is no longer a need?

- Now make a list of rules that come from your recovery program (for instance, no drinking, attend meetings, work the steps, and so on). Are you following these rules? Are you meeting resistance from some of the old rules?

Remember to date the exercise in your journal so you can refer back to your answers.

Roles

During early recovery, the family's old roles no longer work, and new ones have not yet been put in place. This can lead to great tension in the family. As the alcoholic begins to get stronger in abstinence, another family member may take over the role of crisis maker. This is not usually a conscious choice: if you are used to conflict, you may create it to feel comfortable. Carla's daughter had been using school as a refuge from the alcoholism at home. She had also gained great self-esteem as the poster child for the family. But as things got better, and her mother went into recovery, she lost her means for feeling important. She stopped trying at school, and soon a new crisis replaced the old one.

People who held privileged roles in the family—the coalcoholic as nurturer, the eldest child as confidant—can also feel supplanted by the importance of the recovery program, sponsor, or therapist. Losing an important source of self-esteem can be devastating, especially during a time when stability at home is at a premium.

Family members who are in programs have a vital support network to help counter these feelings of being left out, maintain self-focus, and respect other family members' self-focus. In time, new, healthier roles will emerge in the family. Remember, roles are neither good nor bad; but the context in which they are used can be healthy or unhealthy. Take a few moments to consider the changes you've made and how they reflect your progress in recovery.

Exercise: Roles in Early Transition

Look at your journal entry from the "Roles in Transition" exercise from chapter 4.

- Is your role that supported the alcoholic system still in place? Have you given up the role in order to focus on your own recovery?

- Have other family members suspended their old roles?

- What new roles has your recovery program supported? Are you a student in AA? A social person at meetings? Are you more solitary at home?

Rituals

In early recovery as in transition, the rituals that supported the alcoholic system have been suspended and new rituals based on recovery are being put in place. Individuals in recovery become dedicated to the rituals that are built around their recovery programs (going to meetings, calling a sponsor). These rituals help the individual connect to the support system and serve as a means for internalizing the external support.

Some families try to create a calmer family atmosphere by replacing chaotic old rituals with healthy new ones. The Davis family—mom, dad, and three older children—had strict rules about attending the usually chaotic and sometimes frightening family dinners every night during the drinking stage. They revamped their dinner schedule to allow both freedom and a time for interaction. Sunday night was family dinner night, where everyone ate together and shared stories from the past week or plans for the upcoming week. The rest of the week, dinner was served at a specific time, but there was flexibility and tolerance for different schedules. Setting up an appointed time to spend with the family made the time apart from the family easier, because each member knew they would be touching base, on Sunday nights, even if only superficially.

As individuals experience healthy growth, free time becomes less anxiety-provoking. At this time, you may want to try a family outing, especially if there are children in the family. It's important that all the family members have a voice in planning the trips and also a voice in appraising the success of the outing.

Exercise: Rituals in Early Recovery

In your journal, return to the "Rituals in Transition" exercise from chapter 4.

- Are any of the rituals that supported the alcoholic system still in place?

- Have new rituals been established? Are these rituals open to family input?

- What recovery rituals have you been practicing? Does your family take part in any recovery rituals, such as sobriety birthdays?

Boundaries

In early recovery, the family members will be open and vulnerable in their recovery programs, but the boundaries between family members can be quite impermeable. Life at home can be cold and tense, especially if no one takes the time to talk about the changes that are taking place. Children, especially, are living with a great deal of uncertainty. The recovering family may find comfort in the fact that they are traveling on parallel paths. And as time passes, and the parents' recoveries stay on track, the children will slowly begin to trust that the changes will remain in place. An atmosphere of mutual respect can blossom if all the members are aware that what feels like remoteness is a self-focus that is necessary at this time.

Exercise: Boundaries in Early Recovery

Consult your journal entry from the "Boundaries in Transition" exercise in chapter 4.

- Has there been any change in the boundaries since early abstinence? Are things still cold and awkward, or have the family members grown comfortable with the new dynamics?

- What boundaries have you learned from your external support?

Hierarchies

The individual family members are each held in place by the hierarchy of their recovery programs. These hierarchies are clear-cut and tangible; they're based on the length of time an individual has been in the program. As the individual relies on the attachment to the external support, he or she focuses on being a student of the program, learning from the sponsor and other members. This is the central grounding point for individuals at this time.

At home, the natural family hierarchy—parents on top, children below—should be in place. It may take some time for this new ranking to become comfortable if this hierarchy was abandoned for any length of time. George, a father of two who's been sober for eight years, remembers having trouble maintaining his place in the hierarchy while trying to focus on his recovery. "I was hung up thinking that surrender and running the household clashed. I had been a control freak before I hit bottom. So the idea of being the head of the family made me extremely anxious. But for the sake of the kids I played the part. Like they say at the meetings: 'Fake it till you make it.' It took a while, but I did end up making it."

Exercise: Hierarchies in Early Recovery

Consult your journal entry for "Hierarchies in Transition" in chapter 4.

- Has the family hierarchy remained in place since the changes of early abstinence?

- How does the recovery hierarchy suit you? Does it clash with your hierarchy at home? Is it hard to balance the surrender of individual recovery with the authority at home?

Communication

Communication can be awkward and tense at home during early recovery. Family members may be afraid to speak for fear of upsetting the abstinence. With everyone focused on their own individual recoveries and detaching from each other, communication can be at an all-time low. It's important for the family to remain in contact, however. The key tool during early recovery is the new recovery language. Not only does it provide the family a shared vocabulary for discussing the realities of recovery, it provides a refuge from the old language of shame and blame that supported the alcoholic system. Shared recovery language can help improve communication and lay the groundwork for healthy boundaries in future communication.

Exercise: Communication in Early Recovery

Consult the journal entry for "Communication in Transition" in chapter 4.

- How does the communication in your home now compare with communication in early abstinence? Have things improved? Have they stayed the same?

- How would you describe communication in your recovery program? Do you feel more comfortable being open? Are you becoming comfortable with the recovery language?

- Is recovery language being used in your home? Is it helping people respect each other's boundaries?

Interaction

As with communication, family interaction during early recovery can be awkward and cold. Each family member's main source of support will be coming from outside the family, so time spent at home can often feel like walking through a minefield. As individual recoveries progress and stabilize, life at home will also calm, though improvement can be incremental. At first everyone may be afraid that the slightest altercation will upset the abstinence. Gradually family members will trust recovery and begin to relax. Still, the main support is external; the hard work of improving the family's interactions should wait until the foundations for the individual recoveries have all been put in place. Some families can begin that work now and others must wait.

Exercise: Interaction in Early Recovery

Consult the journal entry for the "Interaction in Transition" exercise in chapter 4.

- How does the interaction in your home now compare with interaction in early abstinence? Have things improved? Have they stayed the same?

- How would you describe your interaction at your recovery program? Do you feel comfortable? Is the comfort translating to your home life?

Stability

In early recovery, individuals begin to stabilize in their recovery. Meanwhile, at home, the tensions slowly dissipate. Every family is unique: some seem to cohere all at once, while others need to experience crisis after crisis before finally settling into a stable environment. The main factor that determines the speed of this transformation is whether or not each family member has reached out for help. If one of the family members is resistant toward recovery, this can keep the atmosphere at home tense and cold for much longer than if everyone is moving on parallel paths.

Change

As the system begins to stabilize in its collapsed state, the changes begin to slow down to a more tolerable speed. Crisis becomes more rare as the individuals, and the family as a whole, begin to evolve more slowly and naturally. The slower speed of progress can be a relief after the roller-coaster ride of transition, but it can also be distressing. With the massive shift from drinking to abstinence left behind, the new pace of change can seem sluggish in comparison.

A Summary of the Family System in Early Recovery

1. The system is stabilizing and moving toward health.

2. Recovery organizes the system.

3. As individuals continue their self-focus, detachment and separation continue among the family members.

4. The family members live parallel lives, relying upon external support and attachment.

5. The foundation of a new system is being prepared:

   - **Rules** have collapsed along with the family system, and individuals are guided by the rules of recovery.

   - **Roles** from the drinking stage are suspended in the family system while new temporary roles keep the family functioning during the change. The individuals are building the foundation of healthy new roles through their attachment to the external support.

   - **Rituals** continue to be evaluated for their support of individual recovery or their importance as a family focus for the children.

   - **Boundaries** are still detached between family members and more open between individuals and their external support system.

   - **Hierarchies** are in place for practical purposes at home, while in the recovery program the individual is making peace with the experience of being a newcomer.

   - **Communication** is still awkward. Trust builds slowly as evidence of long-term stability begins to show. Individuals are learning new recovery language, which can aid self-focus and improve family communication.

   - **Interaction** between family members may remain distant and awkward at home, while each connects to the external support of the recovery program. Over time, as family members grow more comfortable with individual recovery, family interaction will warm.

   - **Stability** is greater than during the transition stage. The system is still collapsed, but slowly the home becomes more stable as the family members begin to trust the changes.

   - **Change** is slowing, both for the individual and for the family as a whole. With the revolutionary transformation of abstinence in place, healthy growth begins to evolve at a more gradual pace.

(Adapted from Brown and Lewis, 1999)

8

"Shouting Down the Well"

Points of View in Early Recovery

In chapter 7, we explored the complex landscape of the early recovery stage. Now we can examine the perspectives of the individuals who have to navigate its tricky terrain. Things are improving: the abstinence is becoming more firmly grounded, and life in general is stabilizing. But with improvement comes risk. As the urge to drink or to protect the drinker finally begins to subside, denial continues to fall away, revealing not only the aftereffects of the alcoholic system, but also the everyday challenges of the real world.

So, while settling into abstinence allows you the first taste of freedom since hitting bottom, the freedom exposes you to a great deal of uncertainty. During the drinking stage and the downward spiral, uncertainty was not allowed: it was too risky. It threatened the control that the alcoholic and the coalcoholic tried to exert over their surroundings. In earliest abstinence, uncertainty is a reality, but it is pushed to the side, as the focus is directed only on the substitutions necessary to stop the addictive behavior. But now that you're able to lift your head and look around, the uncertainty, which is a natural part of life, may seem threatening. Old habits commonly reassert themselves to counter the vulnerability that comes with facing the unknown. For this reason, it is very important that you maintain your reliance on external support, keep your surrender in place, focus on your self, and continue to internalize the language of recovery. It's hard work but it pays off in the long run.

In a household where all the family members have committed to a recovery program, an interesting dynamic develops. At the very moment that the family members detach and become more separate than ever, they also become more similar than ever. The recovery path is a strong bond that can afford mutual understanding and respect. But it's easy to lose sight of this as you focus on your individual recovery.

The more the atmosphere at home is centered on recovery and healthy growth, the smoother the process of recovery will be for everyone.

Still, obstacles and setbacks will occur; falling down is a natural result of learning to walk. Remember that every experience has a part in shaping who you are. This realization can help immensely when you face unpleasant moments in the past and present. When you are experiencing something negative, it can seem impossible that the moment could spawn anything constructive. But as you emerge from the other side of the experience, you can frequently see it as a crucial step in your growth.

The Individual in Early Recovery

- Focuses on abstinence and on individual recovery
- Undergoes a period of intense education
- Is less dominated by impulse
- Begins to solidify a new identity
- Still feels confusion
- May experience depression or anxiety
- Concentrates intensely on self-examination and self-development

(Adapted from Brown and Lewis, 1999)

"I Am an Alcoholic"—Curtis Remembers the Early Recovery Stage

"When I was flying home after treatment in a hospital, I felt very enthusiastic. Here I was on an airplane, where I would typically have a few drinks, and I was doing fine. I had worried about being outside the structure of rehab, but now that I was in the real world, I felt confident: the worst was behind me, and everything was going to be great at home. I felt so relieved, so hopeful.

"When I got off the airplane, I had to go down a couple of floors to get my bags. I remember there were two sets of escalators and I had to choose one. I spent a couple seconds trying to figure out which would get me down faster, then a couple more seconds. I was struck by the thought that a few months earlier, I would have gotten very frustrated by not being able to choose an escalator. But now, I felt good. So I patiently made my decision. It took me a couple of minutes to finally decide. And I was certain when I climbed on that I had chosen correctly. Sure enough, on the way down I watched a guy on the other escalator, and I was going to get to baggage claim before him. I remember this so clearly. I felt like this was proof that I was headed in the right direction. I was already reaping the rewards of recovery.

"Today, I see this moment as the first sign of trouble. I needed to dwell on that choice and make sure I wasn't mistaken. That was my need for control showing through, clear evidence that my alcoholic thinking was still in place. Although I focused on my 'patience,' I was still trying to control everything. If I had gotten on either escalator without needing to make the 'perfect' choice, I would have arrived at baggage claim minutes earlier. The irony completely escaped me at the time."

Relinquishing control and surrendering to the loss of control are central experiences in recovery. The lynchpin experience of hitting bottom is founded on the recognition that you've lost control. The experience of surrender that comes after hitting bottom is often earthshaking, but it's not necessarily permanent. When the urge to drink begins to disappear, people often think their work is done. They don't recognize the need for continuing surrender. Surrender starts as an experience, then becomes a conscious recognition, but it takes a lot of work to keep focused on it and internalize it as a deep and ongoing belief.

Of course everyone will have slipups and backsliding. Realizing that you have just fallen back into habitual alcoholic thinking is a common occurrence throughout transition and early recovery. But Curtis mistook the loss of the urges as the completion of the task of recovery, and let himself go back to his old ways of thinking. Curtis' surrender had been conditional on getting better. Once he made progress, he went back to his old mind-set. He had surrendered his perceived control over alcohol, but not over the need for control that wove like deep roots throughout his life.

The Downward Spiral

Curtis and his wife, Sylvia, met and married in college. They had their first boy, Wallace, while they were both working toward their PhDs. Their second son, Raymond, was born six years later, when Curtis had been teaching English at a community college for a year, and Sylvia was doing genetic research at a local university. Curtis remembers these times fondly: "I was so hopeful back then. Everything seemed on pace to get me where I needed to go, if I just kept at it."

Five years later, Curtis was still teaching at the junior college when his drinking got out of control. "I had always been a decent drinker, enjoying wine and beer. My parents were both teachers and regular drinkers; I always equated a good intellectual conversation with a couple bottles of wine. They certainly never seemed to have any problems with the drinking; but they did drink every night."

What started out for Curtis as a casual drinking habit slowly escalated as, year after year, the rejections came back from the larger universities. "I assumed I would land a job at a good university after a few years at the JC. But when I was still there after six years, I was really losing hope, and I started to drink more heavily. When my youngest son started school, I realized that a kindergartner's lifetime had passed and I hadn't made the slightest bit of progress."

The years of slow and steady drinking never caused Curtis any serious problems, but they prepared him for a fall when he was pushed by the right circumstances. "The drinking just got out of control. I was drinking between classes. I started showing up for classes drunk. Sometimes I didn't show up at all. I used all the classic excuses: the stress of my job, my need to unwind. When things go bad and you don't know why, I think there's a part of us that needs to have a reason. I wasn't getting hired anywhere, and I made that understandable by becoming a drunk."

Sylvia did her best to keep things in place. She covered for Curtis and made a plea to the dean of the English department not to fire her husband. Curtis remembers: "The dean was compassionate; he gave me a leave of absence. I was really fortunate there. So long as I wasn't fired for being a drunk, I still had a future. I saw the light and took time off to go get sober. A couple months later, I was standing at the airport escalators, full of hope and ready for action."

The Pros and Cons of Intelligence

Curtis was "riding on a pink cloud" when he returned home from his stay at the hospital. He was focused on abstinence and was gaining a great deal of energy and enthusiasm from his early success. "I leapt into AA like a man converted: I loved the meetings, the people, the lingo. I loved how tangible the process was: the more you did it, the better you got. Not many things in life reward effort in such a straightforward way. I was a real zealot."

Curtis took on the task of recovery as he did everything else in his life: as a scholar. "I set out to be the perfect member of Alcoholics Anonymous. I studied everything; I did research on the roots and origins of AA and explored the psychological foundations of the process. Over time I became a kind of expert on recovery." Curtis' enthusiasm was understandable, but while he was studying recovery, he wasn't truly participating in it.

He was trying to control it the same way he had controlled many other ideas in his life. "When I was a child, school was my main source of self-esteem. My parents' lives were entirely dedicated to teaching, so school became an extremely important way for me to connect with them. If I earned good grades, I was a member of the club and I got the respect I needed.

"But this focus also taught me some bad habits. To me, the intellect was the solution to every problem—at least every problem I thought was valuable. So when I came up against alcoholism, I thought it was simply a case of not knowing enough about it. Recognizing the problem is certainly an important step in recovery, but it doesn't end there. The recognition must lead to change. I was serious about learning, but it was more like education for education's sake."

The intellect can be a powerful tool when it is used appropriately, but when it takes the place of feelings and emotions, it can become a powerful defense and a great obstacle to recovery. "I captured bits of wisdom like butterflies, pinning them down before they could be translated into action. For instance, I studied the concept of the higher power, drew parallels to many different cultural beliefs about god, saw how giving up your control could lead to change, yet I never truly surrendered. I understood the process and I confused this with participating in it. I would have moments of profound understanding that I took as experiences of deep change, but really they were only satisfying observations. These moments are profound, but they're different from experiences of deep belief. If you write about Buddhism, that doesn't make you a Buddhist. I wasn't *in* recovery; I was *doing* recovery."

By intellectualizing the process of recovery, Curtis was clinging to his need for control. He had shifted his focus from drinking to recovery, but he had maintained his alcoholic thinking. He needed to be in control of the process. "By trying to intellectually master recovery, I was trying to assault it by coming from my strength. But the path to recovery is accepting your weakness—understanding that you don't know. I had spent a lifetime fighting to acquire knowledge, and this is what drove me on in my life. If I didn't know something, I needed to learn it immediately. When I surrendered to my loss of control, I thought I had surrendered as deeply as I could. But I didn't even recognize this deeper level of control, my need to understand everything. If it wasn't understandable, then it didn't exist for me. This belief was so deep, I just thought it was part of being human—that it was identical to who I was; and that to lose it would be to lose my identity. It turned out it was just the opposite. This belief was imprisoning me, keeping me from accepting the real helplessness I needed to face in order to begin real recovery."

A Culture of Control

We're now in the twenty-first century, and more than ever, control seems to be the coin of the realm. Self-sufficiency, obsession, drive, and a desire for power are the accepted cultural "ideals" of an age where Hollywood defines reality and corporations define personal needs. There is tremendous pressure to conform to these messages of society, which are omnipresent in entertainment, advertising, and government.

In our bandwagon culture, we are shown the desired norm and then expected to jump on board. We are taught to master ourselves: if we don't like something about ourselves, we can fix it with superficial changes, like hiding a mole with makeup.

Recovery flies in the face of these cultural "ideals." Asking for help, admitting your powerlessness, surrendering to a force greater than yourself, allowing yourself to be vulnerable, even just admitting you have a problem—all of these principles seem to be taboo in our modern age. Yet all of these same principles are central to recovery.

When you live in a system that demands that you take care of it, you will be afraid of stepping outside, because others may attack you—both for betraying them and for doing what they can't allow themselves to do. After a while, you become a servant of the system, and your own anxiety keeps you in check: you're held in place for fear of upsetting others. You become ashamed of the very impulse that could save you. This self-censorship is subtle and extremely powerful.

It takes a great deal of courage to confront the family system and your own participation in it by stepping outside and asking for help. In a more abstract sense, you are stepping out of your culture—at least the control-driven, "just do it" culture that pressures us to keep pushing forward no matter what the cost. Throwing in the towel and taking some time out is not culturally acceptable, even when it's personally necessary.

Imagine a small tribe who thinks bicycles should be pedaled with their hands. They can't go fast or see where they're going, but they love riding. Then someone decides to try using her feet. She is ridiculed: "That's not how it's supposed to be done!" At first, she goes much slower than she did when she used her hands. But as she practices, she catches up to the others. And soon she is riding the bike faster and more safely. Many in the culture don't want to give up the comfort of what they know, if it means having to step backward and practice to get to another, better stage. Most leaps forward begin with a few steps back. And then you need to get a running start to escape the outstretched hands of those who desperately want to pull you back.

It takes a great deal of courage to admit you need help and to go and get it. Many of the pressures and anxieties that make that step so difficult are deeply set cultural beliefs that you are bombarded with daily. Overcoming these fears and getting help is a powerful and life-affirming act.

A New Unhealthy System

By not fully surrendering, and maintaining his need for intellectual control of his recovery, Curtis kept the alcoholic system in place. Instead of truly focusing on himself, he desperately sought the approval of others, particularly his wife. Sylvia was more than happy to give her support, since she was intensely guilty about "letting the drinking get out of control." She thoroughly encouraged any evidence of his speedy recovery.

"I really lorded it over the house with the recovery. Instead of making changes that would positively affect the future, I was creating a new system that replaced my false control over drinking with my false control of recovery. The control became the thing that everyone needed to protect. I needed a lot of applause. Also, if I'd had a hard day, and my children were loud, I would tell them they should be quiet because I was in recovery. That particular brand of manipulation was what really alienated my oldest son." Curtis would use recovery to excuse his bad behavior, and in the next second he would demand appreciation for the fact that he was in recovery. The family fell in line, supporting what was, in effect, the same old system; but instead of alcohol, there was recovery.

"Outside the house, I had two different personalities, depending on who I was with. With strangers I was the poster child for recovery. It's all I wanted to talk about. I felt like I was confessing and proving my piety at every moment. On the other hand, when I was with old friends, I was embarrassed about the recovery. I downplayed it as something I was doing out of a pragmatic need to get 'worriers' off my back. I went to meetings, and I loved them, but I always considered myself a bit of an anthropologist; I was there to study the natives." Even though Curtis had worked to free himself of some of his urges to drink, much of his denial was still in place. Until he fully surrendered, he was frozen in place.

"My sponsor and others at AA weren't buying my overnight success; they knew better. But I was really full of myself. I felt that they lacked the objectivity to understand the underlying concepts in the same way I did. In reality, my objectivity was what was keeping me from participating. My sponsor pointed out this exact point, but it didn't phase me. It's amazing how your beliefs color what you see and hear. They were right on the money but I wasn't ready to hear them, so I went merrily on my way. It was only when I really surrendered that I understood what a shallow gesture my first surrender was." Often it is only after you have made progress that you realize that there was progress to be made. Curtis, on the other hand, logically charted out the progress he felt he needed, made that progress, and considered himself cured.

Relapse

"After my one-year sobriety birthday, I was certain I had solved my problem. When people from my meetings brought up the idea that recovery is a lifetime process, I'd nod and figure that I was just better at it than most people.

"At that point I still didn't believe in alcoholism. I thought I was weak, and when I got strong I'd be able to go back to casual drinking. I felt that I needed to drink to prove I was cured. Drinking and not having trouble was the ultimate test. So I went out to a bar and tested myself with a beer. I ordered a beer, drank half, and left the rest on the bar. As I walked out, I felt great. I hadn't left a beer half-full since I was twelve."

Curtis returned to the bar every day for a week, having half a beer and walking out. "I considered myself cured. I went to the store and bought a bottle of expensive champagne to celebrate. When I got home with the champagne and announced my cure, my wife just stared at me. Until that moment, we had all been tied together on this journey, but in that moment everything changed. I repeated my claim of a cure and she said, 'There is no cure, there's only recovery.' When I didn't get the applause I felt I deserved, I got enraged. I suddenly felt ashamed, like I had made a huge mistake, but I was hiding that with my anger. She wouldn't budge; she told me to call my sponsor and tell him what had happened, and I told her I didn't need him anymore. I felt like something had broken in our relationship; and something had—her willingness to participate in my self-destruction."

Sylvia told Curtis that if he didn't go back to the meetings, she would leave him. And the conversation ended. "At first I figured, to hell with her. I would not sacrifice the truth of my newfound health for her unfounded fears. So I celebrated without her. This started a month-long game of chicken where I drank to prove my sobriety and dared her to leave me. I thought she was bluffing, but she was making plans to do it the entire time. She's a careful person. What I took as reluctance was really care to make sure that our children weren't too upset by leaving their father behind. I didn't care about anything but showing her up. I was in serious decline, a month-long nervous breakdown."

At the end of the month, Sylvia packed up her and her sons' things and walked out with the boys. "I was in a really bad way. I felt I had control over the situation and now I was alone. I refused to cave in, but the more I refused, the more the ceiling crumbled. I finally confronted her under the pretense of telling her that I was fine without her. And she was impassive, saying that I didn't look fine and that I needed help. I was losing it. I needed some response from her or I would go under. I hit her. I had never hit anyone in my life. And I hit her. My oldest son ran in and screamed at me to leave. My wife stared at me. I had just hit bottom for real."

Starting from Scratch

"When I surrendered for real it was annihilating. I was a complete wreck for months. I understood why I had been so delighted the first time around. I hadn't really started over the first time. My deepest beliefs in my intellect and my control had remained in place. I didn't have to face the awkwardness of learning to walk all over again. If you're unwilling to start over, you're cut off from the ability to learn and grow. For me, a lot of early recovery was about learning that it's all right to be awkward."

A baby's almost limitless ability for growth is partly fueled by the fact that the child has no shame about awkwardness. If a baby fails at something, she will try over and over again. The child may be frustrated, desperately wanting to succeed, but she does not feel worthless for not succeeding. She feels no shame in failing, nor does she boast of success. Success usually means that the child moves immediately on to the next step.

In order to start from scratch you have to allow yourself to be awkward. During transition, the awkwardness can be easier to tolerate, since the relentless focus on the addiction allows little time for self-consciousness. But as the urges lessen, you become more aware of your surroundings and this can lead to your feeling self-conscious and uncomfortable about your awkwardness. In order to grow, you need to accept that awkwardness is a necessary step. You have to be bad at something before you are good at it. If you won't allow yourself to take that step backward, you can never unlearn the problematic behavior. Like the people pedaling the bicycles with their hands, you stay tied to the old ways for fear of looking out of place.

Curtis was extremely uncomfortable doing anything he wasn't very good at. "I have always been a perfectionist. Basically this makes everything new and challenging off-limits. You are stuck on your path and you keep working at it and working at it. You're getting better and better, but it gets more difficult to start anything else, because the early attempts seem so poor in comparison to the things you've mastered. I had friends who took up hobbies outside their studies and I'd always ask why. They could be spending that time getting better at what they already knew. Now I think of that relentless pursuit of expertise as an extremely limiting factor. To take chances, I needed to be willing to make mistakes; and until I really surrendered, I was not able to take those chances."

Surrender and the Higher Power

Rigidity and perfectionism don't allow growth because they don't allow the necessary freedom and experimentation to learn and change. "For me, being intellectual was a protection. It allowed me to predict and explain things and thus keep myself safe. I lived in a permanent state of anticipation. I was prepared for the worst, which kept me focused on the worst.

"But in recovery you learn to become comfortable not predicting. You allow yourself to say 'I don't know.' You learn to accept the unknown. Real understanding can only come after real not-knowing. Otherwise you are basing your perceptions on assumptions that are often left over from a past, unhealthy system. Until I really surrendered, I was still a slave to my old instincts; I kept my old assumptions until I ran smack into a relapse."

In order to learn, you have to open yourself up and be vulnerable. When Curtis finally let go of his false sense of control and truly participated in AA, he began to understand the individual focus of recovery. "Taking responsibility for myself and my situation was a very scary thing, but it was so important. For the first time I became aware of myself as separate from my anticipations and explanations. I became aware of my own voice beneath the control.

"It's like a little boy who fell down a well, and you're trying to rescue him. Your first instinct is to shout into the well and say, 'Where are you?' And when you don't hear anything you shout louder. The irony is that the only way to rescue the boy is for you to hear the boy's voice, but your shouting is drowning it out. It can be a difficult and anxious situation to realize the only way to help is to do nothing. You need to sit back and listen. It takes a while to hear that tiny voice after all that shouting. Listening means making yourself open to the outside world—being vulnerable. The little boy knows where he is; your job is to listen."

For Curtis, the clearest expression of his change came with his giving up control to the higher power. "I had been stuck on the concept of the higher power. I understood how it worked, I understood what was beneficial about it, and it appealed to me. But there's a big difference being moved by the truth of a concept and actually experiencing that truth in your life. After my wife left me, I saw that I had reached a dead end. I was drinking, unhappy, and alone. It didn't take a genius to realize that I was doing a subpar job in navigating my recovery. When I rejoined AA after my relapse, I surrendered myself to the organization, to the higher power. I knew a helplessness that reached to the bottom of my soul. I focused on the higher power as I felt it to be. This was the breakthrough for me. Instead of an intellectual recognition, I had a deep experience of freedom after giving myself over to the higher power. It had been so important for me to define it in the early days, but now I just wasn't interested in defining it."

This was crucial for Curtis. He was finally having more than a cognitive interaction with recovery. Instead of merely understanding the concept, he was experiencing it. "It was such a relief. For so long in my life I always felt responsible for explaining everything, and anything I couldn't explain needed to be pushed aside. But part of the joy of connecting with the higher power was the fact that the burden of explaining the situation was lifted off of my shoulders. I'd leave the explaining to someone else. It was a freedom I hadn't known. My place in the world shifted. I no longer felt like I was the center of the universe; I was just one of many folks perceiving the world."

The Developmental Model of Recovery: Early Recovery

During early recovery the alcoholic bears a resemblance to a toddler who is beginning to learn his first words. At this stage of development, the child understands that there is a difference between his impulses and his actions, and much of his day is spent trying to master the actions that would quench the impulses.

It is at this time that the child takes an important step and begins to acquire language. At first, forming words may seem to be a superficial activity; words are just sounds that are imitated in an almost random manner. But soon the child is discovering that the words have meanings and can be used to communicate with the outside world just as well as his hands and fingers. Over time, language will be internalized, giving the child his most powerful mediator between impulse and action: reflection.

This process parallels the alcoholic's acquisition of recovery language in early recovery. As the alcoholic learns the new vocabulary, at first the words may seem awkward and the language superficial. But soon the words and phrases become second nature, and the alcoholic's perception of the world is transformed by a new cognitive framework shaped by the recovery language.

As the alcoholic internalizes the language, she simultaneously internalizes the principles of recovery it expresses. This, too, mirrors the toddler's journey, wherein the child internalizes her culture's cognitive framework along with the new language. The assumptions and perspectives that come with language will be all but invisible to the toddler. The alcoholic, however, pays attention to keeping them conscious.

The Alcoholic in the Early Recovery Stage

The alcoholic's primary focus is the recovery program and the higher power; these are beginning to be internalized.

Behavior

- Less dominated by impulse
- Practicing new abstinent behaviors based on new recovery language and beliefs
- Possible return of old behavior, with a threat of relapse or a new addiction
- Continuing reliance on external support

Thinking

- Continuing to develop new identity as an alcoholic
- Deepening sense of the meaning of the new recovery language
- Continuing to challenge defenses that threaten relapse
- Beginning a process of self-exploration with the help of therapy or a twelve-step program
- Continuation of individual focus

Emotional Expression

- Beginning to experience feelings attached to drinking and the past
- Maybe exploring feelings about the present
- Depression, grief, and even mourning common prior to or as a result of self-exploration
- Feelings about past traumas may emerge

(Adapted from Brown and Lewis, 1999)

The Benefit of Mistakes

Facing your loss of control means facing the fact that you never actually had it. What you actually had was a false belief in your control, which protected you from the encroaching uncertainty of a chaotic world. And often the world was made even more chaotic by your efforts to control it. Giving up control can leave you feeling like you wasted a lot of time trying to change things that were outside your control. "I was depressed for a long time when I realized my mistake," recalls Curtis. "I felt like I had wasted my life. The period of time that I thought I was recovering was symbolic of my whole life: thinking I had power when I didn't.

"But as I began to really work at early recovery, and educate myself about my own life, I came to see my mistaken efforts as very important to my recovery. Instead of feeling foolish or awkward about my mistake, I recognized that, back then, I was not yet ready to let go of my deepest belief in control. It took those months of torture for me to recognize my deep need for control, which makes the experience a positive one in the long run."

In order for Curtis to learn what he needed to know—in order for him to really participate in the recovery process—he needed to learn about the depth of his control problems. These lessons come when you give up trying to control your world and let yourself be vulnerable to what actually happens. "I often thought of my newfound path as the second time around, but really it is still the first. Now I see that I am on the path, and even then I was on the path. I just wasn't as far along as I thought I was. I value those memories enormously. I learned a great deal about humility and my place in the universe by making those mistakes."

Things were much more difficult for Curtis when he faced recovery without the crutch of his intellectual distancing. "I was depressed but I felt like I was headed somewhere. I resumed my alcoholic education, but instead of thinking of it in an academic way, I treated it like learning to dance. Academics are allowed to make many of their mistakes in the privacy of their head. I used to think this was a positive thing, since no one saw your errors, but there was a negative side, too. Mistakes can live unchallenged if unseen by others who could point out a simple error you have overlooked. Dance, on the other hand, takes place on the outside. Mistakes occur for everyone to see; they're demonstrable. Though at first this can seem scary, over time it allows the mistakes to become less troubling. You realize that mistakes are part of the progress. Being willing to make a mistake in public means not having to hide my attempts; it means allowing myself to be vulnerable.

"When you stop needing to choose the right escalator, you can focus on more important things. Once you stop fearing mistakes, you allow yourself to take chances. If you always prepare so as not to make a mistake, you never learn that mistakes are not so bad, but that, in fact, they often point you in a whole new direction."

The recovery process makes use of a relapse the same way it makes use of the drinking stage: by understanding the past we better understand the present. There is nothing to hide from; there are only things to learn from. If you get back on the path of recovery after the relapse, then the relapse was part of the recovery. Though you thought you were in early recovery, it may just turn out that the transition stage took a bit longer than you thought. "I spent an entire year and a half thinking I was in recovery, gloating about my progress and basically making none. But this lack of progress became a central focus during my real progress. Instead of looking on it as a negative, I came to see it as a positive. It demonstrated the fiction of my control better than anything could."

Being able to see the positive in a mistake was another large step forward for Curtis. "I now see mistakes as valuable for learning. It's only a failure if you fail to learn from it. Nowadays, I can still get a bit pedantic about recovery. You don't change everything at once. But without the mistakes you can't judge the progress. Until there is a bump you can't really sense how long it's been since you've had one. If you are making mistakes, it means you are growing."

Exercise: "I Am an Alcoholic in the Early Recovery Stage . . ."

The purpose of this exercise is to gain some perspective on the alcoholic when he or she is in the early recovery stage. If you are the alcoholic, then it's purpose is to explore the thoughts and feelings you had about yourself during this time. (It's also possible that you are in early recovery presently. If so, just think about these questions as they relate to your current situation.)

- In your journal, describe how the alcoholic experienced the early recovery stage. How did the alcoholic adapt when abstinence began to settle into place? Was there more anxiety or less? How did the alcoholic respond to the education about recovery? How did the alcoholic seem around the house? If you are the alcoholic, imagine how someone else might have described your behavior during the time when recovery began to be internalized.

Write as much or as little as you like. If you feel like it, you can write it as a story. Don't worry about capturing the absolute truth as it happened or is happening. Just write it as you see it. Historical accuracy is not the goal; writing down your perceptions is.

- Now describe how you felt about the alcoholic when the above behavior occurred. Did you feel tense, angry, sad, or a combination of these emotions? Did you feel happy, safe, or committed to the alcoholic's progress? Did you rationalize the alcoholic's behavior? Did you feel relief? Were you disappointed by the slow progress? Again, if you are the alcoholic, think back on how you felt about yourself and your behavior during the early recovery stage.

- Now, instead of recalling the emotions you felt in the past, describe how you presently feel about the alcoholic's experience of early recovery. Do things make more sense when viewed from afar? If these events occurred recently, did the information from the last two chapters affect your perception of these situations?

Remember to date the entries; you may want to come back to this exercise and see how your perceptions have changed.

"I Am a Coalcoholic"—Sylvia Remembers the Early Recovery Stage

"I was struck dumb the night Curtis came home and declared himself cured," recalls Sylvia. "Until that moment I had such faith in his recovery; I was so invested in his doing well. And it suddenly hit me over the head that I was in denial about his happy recovery the same way I was in denial during the drinking. There he was with this really nice bottle of champagne, completely believing that he had left the trouble behind. In that moment my entire universe was transformed."

Keeping the Past in Place

Curtis and Sylvia were joined at the hip in college and remained very close afterwards. Even when Curtis' drinking got bad, Sylvia would stay up late with him, talking about any number of subjects, ignoring the fact that Curtis would repeat his main point a half-dozen times. "I felt I was supporting my husband through a tough time. Even when I made arrangements for his rehabilitation, I chose it as the lesser of two evils: if he were fired, everything he had worked so hard for would have been burned to the ground. I never really faced the fact that Curtis had a drinking problem. It wasn't until he actually got on the plane that I realized he was going to get help for his drinking."

When Curtis left for his thirty-day treatment, Sylvia was devastated. "When Curt went off to rehab, that left me alone with the boys for a month. I was so depressed. I tried to keep my chin up for the kids but I was crushed. I felt like the whole thing was my fault; if I had been more diligent, I wouldn't have let Curtis get so lost. I just tried to have faith that he would be able to get himself under control."

While he was gone, Sylvia started attending Al-Anon meetings. "The main message of detaching myself from my husband and focusing on myself was not sinking in. I basically felt that I had let my husband down, and I thought Al-Anon was about working on that guilt. The folks at the meeting tried to get me to talk about myself, but I couldn't; I had too much guilt. I could only talk about Curtis. But I kept going, because the recovery folks said I should, and it was nice to have a place to go and talk."

When Curtis came home feeling so confident and hopeful, Sylvia was elated. "It was like I had gotten a reprieve. I was getting a second chance to be supportive, to help my husband. I was determined not to let what had happened happen again. I was fully invested in being a coalcoholic to the degree that I took full responsibility for my part in creating a drinking system. I just could not grasp the fact that my enmeshment with my husband—the fact that I depended on his current happiness to relieve my depression—was where the deepest issues lay. I was so inspired by his quick recovery, that I just figured that my recovery was going well, too. His enthusiasm was the cure for my depression. I didn't need him healthy, I needed him happy; but at the time I thought they were one and the same thing. It wasn't until much later that I realized the road to health can pass through a great many hardships."

Sylvia was inspired by the way Curtis threw himself into twelve-step work. "He was very diligent about going to meetings and pointing out when he needed space to focus on his recovery. I was happy to give him space. His recovery became the central work of our household. Everyone needed to pitch in to keep Daddy on track. One important way I contributed to his recovery was by keeping his visit to the alcohol treatment place a secret. We both understood that part of the twelve-steps was living in the open as an alcoholic, but we needed to keep the truth from his colleagues or there could be trouble at school. Thinking back on it, I have a hard time believing I could have been that naïve; I just went right back to the same old alcoholic thinking we had shared before. But because my husband was smiling and going through the motions of recovery, I was happy to do my part."

But Sylvia was still worrying about her husband all the time. "I would tell myself to trust him; after all, he seemed to have everything under control. But still I was very anxious. I worked with Al-Anon to help me stop worrying. I had the twisted logic that I needed to stop worrying so I wouldn't hurt his recovery. I literally didn't form a single thought about taking care of myself. The way I took care of myself was to make sure he was okay. I think I was shell-shocked from his going to the hospital. I was terrified that it might happen again if I wasn't on my toes."

Curtis and Sylvia spoke often about their mutual recovery paths, saying many of the right words and congratulating each other on their hard work. They were moving forward in recovery, but they also had old beliefs and behavior patterns that were strongly set in place. They remained overly dependent on each other. "At times, Curt would need support for the good work he was doing, and I was right there to offer it. We figured this was the way it was supposed to work. It wasn't until his second crisis that I really got on board my own recovery."

Breaking the Pattern

When Curtis walked in the house and announced that he had the champagne to celebrate his cure, Sylvia suddenly saw the situation for what it was. "I finally saw the part I played in Curt's alcoholism. Until that moment, I thought his drinking was my fault, and it all ended there. But all of a sudden, with Curt standing there with that bottle, I realized that I had been as blind this time as I had been before. My part in his drinking was that I took full responsibility for it. I suddenly realized that the drinking wasn't about me. It was about my husband. I felt terrible, but I also felt that the only way to help this situation was to help myself. My efforts with Curt had led to my worst nightmare. It felt like I grew up in an instant."

That's when Sylvia gave her ultimatum: "I remember telling him I would leave him if he didn't get help, but the words seemed to come from somewhere else, like someone was speaking through me. Still, I knew the words were true. I think this was the first time I got in touch with my own needs. It was just a spontaneous moment. Everything was so clear. I can still see that expensive bottle of champagne swinging in his hand, his smile, his desperate need for me to affirm his belief. I realized his happiness did not add up to his health, or my happiness. I had to turn to my own health, come what may. Our problems went deeper than our false recovery, they went down to the core of our connection. It was very scary to admit this—that the same pathology that resulted in drinking was a major source of connection for us."

Sylvia left Curtis standing there and drove to an Al-Anon meeting. "I had the sense that I was going for the first time. I had probably been to close to a hundred meetings in the past year, but though I listened, I hadn't really heard. Even before I got to the meeting, the message of the other meetings started to sink in. The truth of my unhealthy connection to the drinking, my need for detachment, my need to discover my own needs, all these things swam in my head."

Over the year before her breakthrough, Sylvia had seesawed between enthusiasm and depression. As her denial melted away, the depression also seemed to dissipate. "It felt like my depression was tied to my resistance to seeing the reality of my life and my relationship with my husband. I've often thought of depression as a sadness where you can't face what it is that you are sad about. I wouldn't allow myself to see the sad truth, so I was depressed instead. Once I opened my eyes to it, my resistance fell away, and much of the depression with it. I had been so afraid to look behind the door that when I opened it, I felt relief. I suddenly found I had determination and strength, two things that had been missing for a year. Instead of looking for what I could do for him, I focused on what I could do for me."

Sylvia still had a hard time, and still fought with bouts of depression. "I lost my resolve many times, but I went to meetings instead of trying to find help in my husband. One thing that stuck with me after that day was that I knew saving my husband wouldn't solve my problems; neither would fixing our couple relationship. I had the deepest urges to do these things, but I was aware that these strategies would lead me back where I had been. The only way to solve my problems was to focus on myself."

Fake It Till You Make It

Sylvia had an important insight on the way to her "first" Al-Anon meeting. "The last thing I said to Curtis before I left him alone with his bottle of champagne was that I cared about him, but I couldn't worry about him anymore. And as I drove to the meeting it struck me that I had learned that at the Al-Anon meetings." The language she had been hearing for that year of meetings suddenly made sense, as though she had struggled to learn it and one day woke up fluent. She hadn't been wasting her time; she had been preparing herself for this moment, even though she was never aware of it.

"Going to the meetings had made me familiar with the words. I just didn't understand them until that night, and they were there when I needed them. I suddenly remembered where my ultimatum had come from. I remembered a man telling the story of his relationship with his alcoholic wife. In the end he told her he would leave her if she didn't get help." Those words that Sylvia had heard months earlier had percolated inside and had come to her rescue when she needed them. "I realized that the support of Al-Anon had been there even when I didn't know I was leaning on it. When I was ready to truly step away from my unhealthy relationship, my recovery was waiting for me."

Because of her time in Al-Anon, when Sylvia finally committed to her recovery, she found that she had already set her external support in place. "Al-Anon offered me a place to be someone else, someone new. It felt like it had been waiting for me all along. When I was ready to commit to new beliefs and behavior, I found that I was already deeply familiar with them. Even though I had been resistant to recovery, I had been studying the others who were really doing it. Their attitudes had been rubbing off on me without my even being aware. It was very important to me to have been going to those meetings, even though I thought I was getting nothing out of them but company.

"It was very hard to finally let go of my responsibility for Curtis. It took another two years to really cement the early work of recovery, but I had the benefit of the time I had put in before. I was able to hit the ground running, making sure that my children's needs were being met and keeping the household functioning in general. At the same time I investigated other living situations should Curt decide he wanted to be on his own. I tried to get the kids in recovery programs of their own, but with the flip-flopping that had taken place, Wallace would have none of it. I don't know how I would have handled all this if I hadn't been 'wasting my time' at those meetings."

Sylvia learned a valuable lesson that she has taken with her: you can learn even if you don't understand what you are studying. "I didn't get it for the longest time, but the information was still sinking in. When you're faced with something you don't understand, sometimes you have to just prepare yourself to learn. You do the work and trust that it's helping you. Then one day the crucial piece of the puzzle falls into place and the whole picture makes sense." This is the essence of recovery: doing the work one step at a time and letting the larger process unfold for you. "You've got to fake it till you make it. When you're learning something new, even if you don't know what you're doing or why you're doing it, keep at it. If you're practicing, then you're learning. Even if you can't demonstrate what it is you have learned, it doesn't mean that the pieces aren't slowly being put together. One day you discover that the preparation has paid off." It's like the mountain climbers stringing up the ropes; though the work can seem tedious and unfocused, one day they simply climb to the next plateau.

Accepting the Things You Cannot Change

In the early months, even when she was at her toughest, Sylvia couldn't break entirely with her old patterns. "If I looked deeply enough, somewhere in the back of my mind was the belief that my taking care of myself was the best thing for Curtis. There was a time when I took pride in that, and a time I was ashamed of it. But as I worked on my recovery I came to see my attachment to my husband for what it was: something I had no control over. It wasn't a choice; it was how I had learned to see things. My troubling habits were neither a virtue nor a vice; they were merely a part of me. As I began to see myself more objectively, I became very keen on finding the attitudes that had gone unchallenged. Facing these attitudes didn't mean that I would erase them, but it was a first step toward understanding them, and ultimately understanding myself and my own unique path of recovery."

It was extremely difficult for Sylvia to watch her husband come apart after she had taken the kids to stay at her uncle's house nearby. "When I finally walked out, I was terrified. I realized that this would never be undone. But I knew, deeply and with certainty, that this is what I needed, and I believed that this is what the boys needed, too. I also believed that it's what Curtis needed, but I tried to keep this from being my main motivation. At first he pretended he didn't care, but he went on a sharp decline in the months after we left. I just tried to keep my resolve. It got easier to be away from him over time, but when I'd have to see him, it felt like I had made no progress. I so wanted to take care of him. And he was getting worse and worse. I was going to one and sometimes two meetings a day during this period."

During this time, Sylvia began to see more clearly how to get healthy. "I needed to focus on something that I had some power to change, and that was myself. I had heard the serenity prayer again and again at meetings. But I never really got it. 'To accept the things I cannot change' always struck me as advice to be passive. But when I saw my relationship with my husband for what it was, I realized that the serenity prayer described the healthiest way a person can interact with the world. Some of the most painful things in life are realities you try to change because you can't face them. You hold on so tight that you never look up to see that you were hiding from the truth. When you surrender and take recovery into your life, you realize that trying to force things to be the way they are not is harder than accepting them the way they are."

The night Curtis struck Sylvia was the night she truly let go. "Hitting me was his last desperate attempt to bring me back to him. I was shocked, and I was very angry, but I was also compassionate. The fact that he would hit me said so much about how far he had sunk. I suddenly felt like I needed to help him, that he wouldn't make it without me, and that I had to dive back in to save him. But then Wallace ran in to protect me. He was screaming 'Get out of here! We don't want you here!' And that set my heart in stone. I might be able to sacrifice myself for this man, but I would not sacrifice my children. And that's what was at risk here. I told Curtis to go, and when I closed the door behind him, I was very aware it might be the last time I'd ever see him."

The Coalcoholic in the Early Recovery Stage

The coalcholic's primary focus is the recovery program and the higher power; these are beginning to be internalized.

Behavior

- Less dominated by impulse
- Practicing new, abstinent behaviors based on new recovery language and beliefs
- Possible return of old behavior, with a threat of relapse or a new addiction
- Continuing reliance on external support

Thinking

- Continuing to develop new identity as a coalcoholic
- Deepening the sense of meaning of the new recovery language
- Continuing to challenge defenses that threaten relapse

Continued on next page

- Beginning a process of self-exploration with the help of therapy or a twelve-step program
- Continuation of individual focus

Emotional Expression

- Beginning to experience feelings attached to drinking and the past
- May be exploring feelings about the present
- Depression, grief, and even mourning common prior to or as a result of self-exploration
- Feelings about past traumas may emerge

(Adapted from Brown and Lewis, 1999)

Surviving as a Couple

After Curt went back to his twelve-step work and recommitted himself to recovery, it was still a few months before the family was reunited. Sylvia was cautious: "I was determined not to go back until I felt it would be good for me. The children were ambivalent about it. When we moved back in, things were quite tense at first. I thought I was making huge progress, but when I returned home, I had more anxiety than ever. I was extremely protective of my recovery. It was much easier being strong from a distance. Now that I was back surrounded by all that history, I felt the pull of old habits and the tensions of our old relationship. I was constantly on guard against slipping backward. It got to the point that any time I had a positive thought about Curt, I worried that I was falling back into my old role. For the longest time, the only thing I could say to Curt was, 'I can't talk about that right now.'"

Over time, Sylvia learned that letting go of responsibility for her husband did not have to mean emotional abandonment. But at first she chose to err on the side of caution. "It was hard spending time together. We knew what didn't work, but we didn't know what did. This left us in a perpetual state of not knowing how to interact with one another. There was a lot of friction. Whenever we tried to have a conversation, we'd end up fighting." Sylvia and Curtis came to an understanding that helped them negotiate these difficult conversations. If either of them felt that they "needed" to talk to the other, this was a red flag. "If you *need* to have a conversation, then there is *something you need* from it, and this suggests blurred boundaries. In a healthy conversation you want to communicate what you have to say and hear what the other person has to say."

Alcoholics Anonymous and Al-Anon can offer crucial support during the earliest vulnerable times: instead of needing the acceptance from the partner, you get it from the group. This allows you to interact with your spouse without having demands and needs. It can take a long time to retool the relationship, but it is worth it in the long run.

Over time and with their individual focus on their recoveries, Sylvia and Curtis made progress, and their household became less tense. "The one constant topic of safe, productive conversation was our recoveries. This proved to be a major source of connection when we had little else going on between us. We shared the things we were learning and listened to each other recount experiences at meetings." Their shared interest in recovery became an important foundation for their shared experiences later, in ongoing recovery. Though they were not focusing on fixing the couple, the foundation for their future interaction was being built on the strengths of their individual recoveries. The future was being put into place even though they didn't know they were preparing for it.

Exercise: "I Am a Coalcholic in the Early Recovery Stage . . ."

This exercise will focus on the perspective of the coalcoholic during early recovery. If you are the coalcoholic, you will be exploring the thoughts and feelings you had about yourself when your urges to focus on your partner began to wane and recovery began to sink in.

■ In your journal, describe how the coalcoholic reacted as abstinence solidified. How did the coalcoholic adapt when abstinence began to settle into place? Was there more anxiety or less? How did the coalcoholic respond to education about recovery? How did the coalcoholic seem around the house? If you are the coalcoholic, imagine how someone else might have described your behavior during this period as your healthy growth began to evolve.

If you feel like it, you can write this as a story. Don't worry about capturing the absolute truth as it happened. Just write it as you recollect it.

■ Now describe how you felt about the coalcoholic when the above behavior occurred. Did you feel tense, angry, sad, or a combination of these emotions? When you saw progress from the coalcoholic, did you feel happy, safe, committed, or some combination of these feelings? Did you rationalize the coalcoholic's behavior? How did you feel when the coalcoholic started to see real progress? Did you feel relief or disappointment? Again, if you are the coalcoholic, think back on how you felt about yourself and your behavior during the early recovery stage.

■ Now, instead of recalling the emotions you felt in the past, describe how you presently feel about the coalcoholic's experience of early recovery. Do things make more sense when viewed from afar? If these experiences happened recently, do they make more sense after your having read about the context for these situations?

Remember to date the entries. As you work through recovery and gain more insight into the past, your perceptions will change.

"I Am a Child of an Alcoholic"—Wallace and Raymond Remember Early Recovery

"I remember hearing him screaming at her, then a slap, and then hearing her fall down," Wallace remembers almost ten years later. "I ran in as fast as I could. I was crying and I screamed at him to leave. I remember hating him for reducing me to tears. I felt like every ounce of dignity I had, every ounce the whole family had, just evaporated in that one second. I felt it was the final nail in the coffin of my relationship with my father."

For Wallace, the first nail was driven in when his father admitted his problem and went into recovery the first time. "I remember feeling pissed. The two years leading up to then had been pretty chaotic, but my parents never admitted anything. Now here was real proof that things were screwed up. It didn't seem fair." Sylvia had a talk with Wallace and explained recovery and pointed out that it was courageous for his father to take that step. "I accepted that he was trying to get help," says Wallace, "but I was skeptical."

Leaving the Nest

A teenager when his father first entered recovery, Wallace was at a difficult developmental period for an upset in his family. He was in the middle of adolescence and was taking his first steps toward breaking away from the family—the natural process of individuation. This is a period when teens begin to recognize that their parents are imperfect, and start to discover that there is a big world outside their family unit. But in order for children to make this transition smoothly, there needs to be stability in the family. Wallace's father had seriously fallen down on the job. Wallace's discovery of his father's imperfections was not so much a conquest of his father as a shameful realization. Instead of feeling proud to be growing up, he felt stupid for never seeing the "obvious" weakness before. "I just felt so disappointed. But I tried to keep an open mind."

When Curtis arrived home proclaiming his newfound health, Wallace was slow to trust the conversion. "Even though he claimed he had seen the light, it felt like nothing had changed. He'd try to prove what a great guy he was by taking Ray and me to the museum; and then he would spend the entire time telling us how difficult life was for him and how impressed we should be with his progress. We just wanted to see the dinosaur bones, and he'd be going on about his recovery. Everything was about him. I tried to be a good sport, but I felt like he was pretty pathetic. I'm sure it didn't help that I was fourteen, midpuberty, when I started finding out that my father was not only human, but, in my eyes, a complete loser. I was disgusted. We weren't allowed to be open about what was going on. It was still a big secret. Nothing had changed."

As angry and disappointed as Wallace was with his father's shortcomings, he kept it to himself. He worked under the oppressive belief, one that many children share, that he should not let his feelings and needs out for fear of rocking the boat. "I just gritted my teeth and hoped for the best. I wanted to say that I didn't think things had changed, but I was afraid I would disturb the peace. And anyway, there was a tiny part of me that really wanted to believe my father knew best and that it would turn out okay.

"Just as I began to believe that maybe he was going to get better, my father started drinking again. I felt like a complete fool. I should have known better. It was like I was a chump all over again. His relapse basically fulfilled all my worst beliefs. It's horrible to have your worst-case scenario come true. I think when you are a sensitive kid, and you begin to sense danger, you want to be proven wrong. You want your prediction skills to be proven false, 'cause then you won't have to predict anymore. But when you are proven right, it's like being put in a jail where you can't ignore your worst-case scenarios. It reinforces your need to guess the worst and then expect it."

A Family Divided

When Sylvia nervously broached the subject of leaving her husband, Wallace was enthusiastic. "I wanted to leave that night, but she said we needed to give him a chance to choose the high road. My little brother was really thrown off by the family problems. Until that time, he had been pretty well insulated, which seemed good for him until he just got blindsided by reality. The night we left, Ray was hysterical. He couldn't put two words together; it was pure anguish. And my father kept saying to my mother, 'See what you're doing to the children?' I was so angry at that, partly because he was blaming my mother for his problem, and partly because he was lumping me in with Ray, because I was happy to be getting out of there. For the longest time, I regretted that I didn't speak up right then, and let him know how happy I was to be getting away from him."

Wallace was stuck in the difficult in-between role of not yet being an adult but no longer feeling like a child. He wanted to help, but there was nothing he could really do. "When my father attacked my mother, I was so angry. I think that anger was all about being helpless. I couldn't rescue my mother, and I couldn't beat up my father. I wanted to run away and be alone, and I needed to take care of my brother. It was such a horrible period of my life; I couldn't wait to grow up and get out of there."

During the months that Sylvia and Curtis were split up, Wallace saw himself as the man of the house and did his best to take care of his brother. "My mom did her best, and she was always checking in with me to make sure everything was all right. I was happy taking care of Ray; I felt needed. He was really shaken by the whole thing. He had nightmares and often wanted to sleep in bed with me. My mother tried to be there, but she needed to go to meetings all the time. I had a hard time with that, since the meetings had obviously done nothing for my father. But that's what she did."

When Wallace found out that Sylvia was moving back in with Curtis, he was furious. "I refused to go back to that house. I wanted to stay with my uncle, but my mother wouldn't let me. I don't think I said a dozen words to my father over the first six months we were back. I was so angry. I couldn't take the hypocrisy: my father had already shown recovery to be a sham. It seemed to me to be a way to get sympathy and escape responsibility. They both tried to tell me what was really going on, how real recovery was about taking responsibility for their lives, but I just shut them out. I felt I had done enough listening. I wouldn't let them fool me again."

With both Curtis and Sylvia deeply committed to recovery, Wallace was now the odd man out. "Suddenly they were teammates in the whole thing. And Ray really wanted to be a part of the process, too. He joined a program for kids. It might have been easier to accept losing my parents to recovery if I still had my little brother to look out for, but he was so happy to be reunited with the family. After how sad he had been for the past months, I couldn't begrudge him his happiness in feeling connected to the family again, but for me, too much water had passed under the bridge."

Wallace used school as his main source of stability and self-respect. He poured himself into his studies and excelled. "Until that time, I was pretty blasé about school, but once I was set off by myself, I dove in as deep as they'd let me go. I was so ashamed of my father's alcoholism, I didn't want to be at home at all. I pretty much hid from them for my junior and senior years, and then I escaped to college."

Children need a place to express their feelings about the alcoholism and the recovery. If they don't get it, those feelings can get turned inward and end up being expressed through new and related problems, often a substance abuse problem of their own. Even if the children reject recovery, it is important to see to it that they have somewhere to talk about what they have experienced.

Wallace's resentment and hostility stayed buried inside for some years and was expressed mainly through his distance from his family. The words finally came out in a graduate English program where he was studying for his PhD. "I wrote about my experiences in a graduate creative writing seminar. I really let loose; I held nothing back. It was a tremendously purging experience. The coup de grace was that I sent the memoirs home to my father. I felt really angry and I wanted him to know how I felt. When my father called me, he was in tears, but not so much because I had hurt him. He said he was proud of how good a writer I was, and how truthful and thoughtful my descriptions were. I was floored. What I meant to be the death-blow had actually ended up reopening our relationship. He told me about creating a narrative of his alcoholism. It was the first time I felt connected to him in almost a decade.

"Since then, we have spent a great deal of time discussing recovery and my experience of those years. He was thankful to finally get the privilege of hearing my side of the memories. And I have had the benefit of seeing the changes in him, which helped me change my mind about recovery. I started attending Al-Anon a little over a year ago. It was scary at first, but it was so freeing. You don't know how much you are keeping in, until you start letting it out."

A Younger Point of View

Much of a child's experience of alcoholism is shaped by that child's age and the amount of direct experience he or she has with the drinking. Raymond was young enough to remain oblivious to most of the trauma until the problem became unavoidable. "I didn't know there was a problem until Mom left Pop," recalls Raymond, who recently finished his sophomore year of college. "I was pretty much protected from the whole thing. I was young, and most of my father's drinking was done outside the house. I could tell Wallace was not happy with him, but they always had friction. I think it's mainly because they're a lot alike."

When his parents split up, Raymond was traumatized. "I thought everything was going just great and then one day I didn't have a father anymore. It was terrifying. I actually remember very little from those months. I know I spent a lot of time with my brother, and I got really good at Nintendo. Mom was busy with her recovery at the time; she tried to get me out of the house but I was really scared. I figured if I could lose one parent that easily, who knew what could happen. I felt I needed to stay home and keep an eye on things. I didn't want to get surprised again."

When Curtis and Sylvia moved back in together, Raymond experienced a lot of anxiety; he became hypervigilant to ward off future calamities. "I believed that I hadn't been careful enough the first time and had let my parents down. I wasn't going to make that mistake again. I became sort of a spy: I was always sneaking around, trying to be invisible and not cause trouble while at the same time making sure everything was okay. This was when my brother and I started to drift apart: he snubbed my father all the time, and this wasn't acceptable to me. I was so afraid everything was going to fall apart again."

When his parents suggested he might profit from a program for the children of alcoholic families, Raymond jumped at the chance. "The recovery program was like a dream come true. I suddenly felt like I was being included in my parents' world. I could finally relax, because whatever was happening to my mother and father would be happening to me, too. That was a great relief. Unfortunately, I soon realized that I was moving further away from my brother. I was sad, but when you're ten, your parents are everything to you. And Wallace was itching to get out of the house at that time."

Raymond not only profited by joining his parents, but the program itself turned out to be of great help to him. "I learned that there were other kids who had been through what I had; I learned that it was okay to talk about my feelings; and most important, because of the anxiety I had felt since coming home, I learned that the alcoholism wasn't my fault. I often think how my life might have been different if I had continued believing that I had caused the breakup. That's a terrible burden to function under. When you take on that kind of responsibility, you really have to squeeze yourself into nothing to keep from 'harming' other people. I learned the alcoholism was not about me. I was just a kid. I tried to tell my brother about this stuff, but he was too angry to listen."

Raymond learned some valuable lessons by being exposed to recovery at such an early age. "I knew my parents weren't perfect, but I also saw them doing their best to improve. They set a great example for me. I don't know what they were like before, but with recovery, they were very courageous about trying new things. They were never afraid of sticking out or being embarrassed. I definitely picked this up from them. Meanwhile, my home was transforming into a safe place, and I began to have a real sense of security again."

Raymond cites his early experiences with his recovery program as setting a strong positive foundation for his growth. "Establishing a healthy relationship with my parents after recovery really helped me when it was time to go out on my own. I think of Wallace who carried around all that anger. His need for distance actually kept him glued to the past. We've talked about it quite a bit. You need to face those past traumas if you want to stop being a slave to them. I feel I was lucky to have worked on these things before I was old enough to really be ashamed of the whole process. I was just so happy to be included, and so happy to have my parents back, I never even noticed that my life was any different than anybody else's."

Children in the Early Recovery Stage

Much of the child's experience of this stage is dependent on his or her age and specific experiences during the drinking and transition stages.

Behavior

- The degree to which parents can successfully attend to their children's needs while taking care of their own recoveries will have a large effect on the children's behavior.

- If children have behavior problems, these can continue, and new problems can emerge.

- With increased stability at home and a place for the child to feel safe in expressing thoughts and feelings, the child may start showing improvement.

Thinking

- The quality of a child's adaptation to recovery depends on the degree of stability in the environment; whether or not a new, healthy system is being put in place; and the solidity of the parents' recovery.

Emotional Expression

- Children may still feel frightened and confused, or abandoned because of their parents' focus on recovery.

- They may also be settling into stronger and healthier relationships with their parents, with greater feelings of hope and trust.

(Adapted from Brown and Lewis, 1999)

Exercise: "I Am a Child in the Early Recovery Stage . . ."

This exercise will focus on the perspective of the children during the early recovery stage. If you were the child, it focuses on your perspective and those of your siblings.

- In your journal, describe the child's behavior during early recovery. How did he react to the changes that came with early recovery? How did he try to make things work? How did he experience the changes in the home environment? If there was more than one child, you can repeat the exercise for each.

  Just write it as you recollect it. Historical accuracy is not the goal.

- Now describe how the parents felt about the children's reaction to early recovery. Did they have problems with guilt? Were they hopeful for the children's future? Did they experience anxiety when their recovery clashed with their need to focus on the children?

■ How do the parents presently feel about the children's experience of early recovery? Have your feelings changed over time? Do they see their past anxieties as accurate or exaggerated now that they can see the events from a more objective perspective?

The important thing is to explore your own perceptions of the children's experiences, and of the parents' perceptions in relation to the children. These perceptions will change as your perspective changes over time, so remember to date the entries.

9

"Looking Forward to Looking Back"

Surviving the Early Recovery Stage

Now that we have mapped the early recovery stage and explored some individual perspectives on this period, we need to discuss the toolbox that will help you with your own unique journey. The central tool is education: the more you understand your experiences as a natural part of the recovery process, the more likely you will be to let recovery take its course rather than trying to fix things that are not broken.

As we saw in chapters 7 and 8, early recovery is a time of great progress and hope, but it is also a time of great challenges. The complex and interwoven experiences of growth and anxiety can leave you feeling cautious and uncertain. This chapter is meant to help you endure the painful and anxious situations that are common in early recovery.

Please remember that neither this chapter nor this book as a whole is meant as a substitute for an established recovery program. It's meant to complement your external support structure.

Setbacks

One day you notice that your cravings and impulses have lessened. The energy, concentration, and action required to manage these once overpowering urges can now be applied to a wealth of new learning. Early recovery can indeed be a time of mental, emotional, and social growth and expression. But it can also be a time of newfound anxiety and trauma.

As we've seen throughout this book, setbacks are an expected part of the recovery process. When you are changing life patterns that took many years to put in place, it's only natural to occasionally fall back into these old habits.

The process of change during recovery is often a slow upward trend, but the day-to-day experience of early recovery can swing frustratingly from high to low. One day may offer insight, inspiration, and clear evidence of progress, while the next makes you feel like you're right back where you started, or that things have even gotten worse.

It's not uncommon for people to experience almost rhythmic cycles of hope and despair as they settle into recovery. The painful shifts from high to low can disguise the fact that you are moving toward equilibrium, with the highs becoming less unrealistic and the lows less painful. "I sometimes felt that the lows were caused by the highs, and vice versa," says Pam, who remembers feeling like she was going insane, but thinks of her early recovery as a slowly stabilizing roller-coaster ride. "When your expectations get too high, you get struck down by the slightest imperfection. And when you start to despair and think you are worse off than ever, you can be brightened by the slightest glimmer of hope. When you get the perspective of a few years' distance, you can see that both sides were balancing each other, like a swinging pendulum that is slowing down."

As you begin to understand and accept the progress of recovery, you can relax and stop looking for constant proof that you are doing things right or wrong. You will trust that things are getting better, even on days when everything seems worse. Lawrence, a retired stockbroker who's been sober for almost twenty years, uses financial investment as an analogy for recovery. "I have described investing in the market by comparing it to a person walking up a flight of stairs playing with a yo-yo. The investment is the yo-yo, and despite its upward and downward fluctuations, there is a steady upward trend. This is just like recovery. When I began, for months I focused only on the daily shifts. Then one day I realized I wasn't fixating on the immediate mood swings anymore; I worked the program every day, and trusted the fact that things would get better." Lawrence points out that people new to recovery are much like people new to investing. "The new investors are always terrified, and check the papers every day. But the seasoned investor knows that in ten years the money will have increased significantly. I would tell my new clients, 'Ignore the yo-yo and focus on the progress up the staircase.' It takes a while to trust this process, but when you do, you can ride out the daily ups and downs and trust the slow but steady growth. Recovery is the same."

Causes

By understanding the different causes of setbacks, you can put them in perspective when they occur. Also, the more you recognize your behavior's natural causes, the more you will be able to forgive yourself for experiencing setbacks. Many people mistakenly look on backsliding as evidence they're doing something wrong in recovery. It makes sense—especially if past trauma has make you hypervigilant—to look inside yourself for cause of the problems, and it is wise to do so. But the causes may also be natural and uncontrollable realities of the recovery process. You can't control your emotional reaction to a situation, but by recognizing that a certain situation evokes that emotional reaction, you can learn to avoid that situation until you feel stronger and less threatened by it. Becoming aware of such triggers will also alert you to leftover defenses that you may want to challenge in the future.

There are a number of causes of setbacks during recovery. **Progress** itself can bring on backsliding, by the very fact that it opens you up to troubling memories and parts of reality that you had previously kept hidden from yourself. Backsliding can also be triggered by a familiar **context** related to drinking. An important and often overlooked cause of backsliding is your **physical circumstances**: early recovery can be an exhausting time, and you need to recognize when you are just plain worn out. Finally, the setbacks may be part of the **normal course of growth**: the unknown brings anxiety, which brings back old beliefs and behaviors to cope with it.

Progress

As we saw in chapter 7, each step upward brings with it an expanded view of reality: the higher you climb, the farther you are able to see. This expanded vision can be quite challenging when you confront information that you have long blocked out or hidden from view. Progress means experimenting and taking risks, so some anxiety will be a natural by-product of moving forward.

In the transition stage, it is common for you to feel you have nothing to lose: you're starting from scratch, so there's nowhere to go but up. In early recovery, however, important growth has taken place, and with this progress comes a sense of hope, and a pride in achievement. But along with these benefits comes some vulnerability: you now have something to lose, namely, the achievements you have worked so hard for. As you make the slow shift from anxiety to confidence, you may have twinges of fear that accompany the realization that you are doing well. Again, this is a natural result of healthy growth. Until you build trust in yourself and your recovery, anxiety about achievement will feel like a threat to your recovery as a whole.

When you think you have made substantial progress, you can become insensitive to the more subtle headway you have made. Barbara, who just celebrated her ninth year of sobriety, was often frustrated during early recovery when she experienced an urge to drink. "I remember an instance when I had been sober over a year and I went to a party where there was booze, and I suddenly felt uncomfortable. After the party I got mad at myself, thinking that I hadn't made the progress I thought I had, so I had therefore been fooling myself. But a few days later it hit me that the anxiety I felt at the party had been manageable. It was there, but it was not really threatening. I was frustrated by my lack of perfection, without seeing how much progress I had made. Six months earlier I would have been close to a nervous breakdown in that situation. Instead, I was able to say to myself, 'This situation is making me uncomfortable,' and move on. That was actually a huge stride from a year earlier."

Progress can also make you feel like you can do more than you really can, thus putting you in a position where you are doing too much and straining your new skills. When you begin to feel confident in your abstinence, you may think you are ready to solve the other family members' problems. It can be easy to fall into the trap of feeling strong enough to help everyone else out. Similarly, when you take the cast off a mended leg, you may feel strong, but you are not ready to carry someone else around. You must first learn to support your own weight. Even though you begin to feel comfortable, you need to remain focused on your own recovery.

Context

If you visit an old drinking buddy, your new skills and beliefs may conflict with your past behavior. It's natural for you to feel uncomfortable among the scenes of your drinking past when you are still building the foundation of your new alcoholic identity. Similarly, if you are a coalcoholic in a situation where people need your help, you may find that focusing on them interferes with your self-focus. When traumatic memories are triggered by the places where those memories took place, it can feel like you have been transported back in time.

Some contexts are less obvious. Your old watering hole or the family dinner table may be obvious sources of difficult memories, but other, more subtle situations may trigger the past. Sometimes a brand new set of circumstances can have elements that recall a troubling part of the past. Ellen, a mother of two who has been in Al-Anon for six years, was worried at her new job. For some reason, she found the coalcoholic impulses coming back, and old behaviors creeping into her daily life. She started to feel resentful and angry at her coworkers, but she couldn't see any source worthy of her fury. After some long conversations with her sponsor, she realized that the interactions at the office were very much like those among her family members during the active alcoholism. Her boss reminded her of her husband when he had been drinking, and when she was at work, she would fall back into the familiar and "comfortable" role of caretaker, while seething inside. The work situation also triggered problems at home. Even though her relationship with her husband was not a problem now, she found herself falling back into old behavior at home as well. Her work problems, though relatively new, tapped a deep vein of anger. In the long run, Ellen used this new information to help her work on this anger and practice recognizing situations that could spark it.

You can be at different stages of recovery in different contexts. Even a person in ongoing recovery can be shocked back to the anxiety of transition when faced with a threatening context. Often, a visit to the family you grew up with can bring such a flashback. Barbara, who we met above, rarely visits her parents anymore: "I always feel like I'm a kid again back there. It's like time has frozen, and when I enter that situation, I just become the person I was years ago. It is a disheartening feeling. Suddenly the cravings return. After a while I realized I couldn't go home anymore; not until I got stronger. Maybe never." Once they have started recovery, many folks have a hard time going back to their old home, particularly if it was alcoholic. "At first I thought going home was the ultimate test of my sobriety—like the song 'New York, New York': If I could make it there, I could make it anywhere," says Barbara. "But after a time I realized that unless my parents changed a lot, no amount of work could ensure my comfort."

An external event or crisis can also cause a setback and trigger old behaviors. A crisis will have a destabilizing effect in even the healthiest family, so when a crisis occurs in a family in early recovery, it makes sense that anxiety and old behavior may rise back to the surface. The very existence of a crisis can trigger memories of the drinking stage or of the difficult times in transition. It can also be hard to cope with a crisis when you are afraid it will derail recovery, throwing off the delicate balance you have in place as you loosen your guard and begin to trust recovery. When Judy's husband lost his job, she was devastated. She began to wonder what good her eighteen months in AA had done her if she could be undone so easily. "When the crisis first set in," Judy recalls, "the benefits of recovery were not that apparent, and I began to have some doubts. But as the initial waves of panic subsided, I discovered that my foundation was still in one piece; it hadn't been washed away." Crises will always be upsetting, but over time they will not feel quite so threatening.

Physical Circumstances

Health is multidimensional. Alcohol and stress can keep you in an unhealthy equilibrium that mutes the highs and lows and gives you a smooth (though negative) ride. It can take months and even years for your nervous system to come back to normal after years of alcohol abuse. The same is true for years of psychological neglect and stress. Sobriety offers a sharper view of reality and with it comes greater sensitivity to your surroundings. Hypersensitivity can cause you to overreact to problems, leading to emotional setbacks.

Being tired, like drinking too much coffee, can also leave you in a state of anxiety. It's natural to wonder what part of your life is causing the anxiety, but as we saw in chapter 6, sometimes your physical state alone can be the cause of the anxiety. If you are unaware that caffeine or exhaustion are stressing you out, you may worry about your recovery and even resort to old behavior.

Normal Course of Growth

In his book *Touchpoints* (1992), developmental expert T. Berry Brazelton describes children's natural developmental setbacks and uses them to gauge individual children's development. "Touchpoints . . . are those predictable times that occur just before a surge of rapid growth," when a "child's behavior falls apart." Children will revert back to older behavior just as they are about to make a breakthrough. Dr. Brazelton goes on to say that, in his experience, "no developmental line . . . proceeds in a continuous upward course. Motor development, cognitive development, and emotional development all seem to proceed in a jagged line, with peaks, valleys, and plateaus." As we've seen before, the developmental stages of recovery parallel the growth of a child; and like the growth of a child, growth spurts in recovery are often preceded by setbacks. Dr. Brazelton refers to these "touchpoints" as important windows into your child's behavior. When seen as normal and predictable parts of the growth process, "These periods of regressive behavior are opportunities to understand the child more deeply and to support his or her growth, rather than to become locked into a struggle. A child's particular strengths and vulnerabilities, as well as temperament and coping style, all come to the surface at such a time. What a chance for understanding the child as an individual!" By accepting your own setbacks as necessary obstacles on the path of recovery, you can use them as opportunities to learn about yourself.

Enduring the Setbacks

It is a major step to become aware that backsliding can have an external source that is triggering an internal response, rather than necessarily pointing out an internal flaw in your recovery. If you become aware of the causes of your setbacks, you can be prepared for or even avoid situations that threaten your confidence. Even a person in ongoing recovery will have periods of being "symptomatic." You never outgrow setbacks; you merely become better at coping with them, and they become less threatening.

Don't focus on the yo-yo. As Lawrence recommended to his clients, focus on the long-term ascent, not the daily ups and downs. The more you are invested in the day-to-day roller-coaster ride, the more you will cling to the ups and resist the downs; and both of these efforts can have negative effects. In order to take the long-term view, you need to trust your recovery. This trust will come over time, as you keep focusing on your loss of control. You have no power over the speed of recovery; you only have influence over one task at a time. But when you attend to one moment at a time, a process slowly unfolds. The sooner you realize that the daily swings are out of your control, the sooner you will be able to relax and allow the recovery to take place at its natural speed.

Look for subtle progress. As you become more solid in your recovery, you may take for granted the subtle but important steps you have made to get there. If you're feeling down, you may need to look more closely to realize you are doing better than you think. For instance, you may feel a little anxious one night and think to yourself, "This was the way I felt when I was drinking." This may seem bad until you realize that in the present you feel like you do *without the help of alcohol*. Suddenly, what looked like a regression may appear to be a major improvement: you now realize that you have feelings that are separate from the drinking.

Don't punish your mistakes; learn from them. During early recovery you may begin to feel empowered and think you can handle things you are not yet ready for. You may drive past the old bar and get hit by difficult memories. Instead of thinking of this as a failure or as proof that you are not as far along in recovery as you thought, look on it as a learning experience. Old feelings and mistakes are valuable: they teach you about your limits. As you grow stronger in recovery, you will learn strategies to deal with difficult feelings, recognizing them not as objects of shame or guilt, but as clues that there is more work to be done.

Check in with yourself. When you find your attention is on alcohol or your partner, ask yourself, "What do I need to do for myself at this moment?" or "What does this outside focus mean for me?" If you have a hard time answering this question, contact someone who can help you answer it, such as your sponsor or therapist.

Run a checklist for physical causes. If you are having a setback and you can't seem to find an external cause, you may want to run down a checklist of possible physical causes. Are you hungry, angry, lonely, tired, or sick? (You can use the abbreviation "HALTS" to help you remember these possible causes.) Curtis, from chapter 8, found that a surly bad temper—an anger he had mistaken for backsliding—was often caused by hunger. He found that a snack would cure him of the problem in the short term, and in the long term, he set out to maintain a schedule for his meals. This way he wouldn't discover himself irritable and sad and worried about recovery when all he needed was some carbohydrates.

Maintain your transition coping skills. Understanding the cause of your setbacks will help, but it won't necessarily make the impulses pass any faster. Remember that recovery is a developmental process; each stage builds on the last. Even after a year of recovery, you may have times when you feel just as unstable as you did in the earliest sobriety days. For this reason, you never entirely leave the coping strategies of one stage behind. The coping strategies for the transition stage are still valid when you feel the pressure of old impulses. Although these setbacks will become fewer and farther between, there will probably always be situations where they return. Just as the stages build one atop another, the coping strategies of early recovery essentially build on those of transition. You may want to check back on those strategies to refresh your memory.

Stay patient. Realize that foundations are built to withstand being shaken. You can no more control an earthquake than you can keep yourself from being shaken by it. But you can come to depend on the groundwork you have done to help you endure the disaster; a good foundation is built to last. It will probably take a few tremors before you begin to trust your new foundation. You could even say that these challenging experiences help build your trust in your recovery.

Reframing the Fear of Drinking

As you slowly begin to get comfortable with abstinence and feel like you are emerging from the single-mindedness of transition, you may suddenly start to fear the possibility of a relapse. Even if you are not having urges these fears can strike at you. As we saw earlier, one reason that the fear starts to emerge is that you are making progress, and you suddenly have something to lose. Also, as you come out of transition, you begin to see the world more clearly, and the larger ramifications of accepting your loss of control can seem quite intimidating.

Although it is important to learn to cope with your anxiety, these fears can actually have beneficial results. Just as we discussed the constructive side of anxiety in chapter 6, we can also look at the fear of drinking as an asset to your recovery:

- Initially, this fear is helpful in providing the motivation and energy to establish supports and to learn new behaviors.

- Fear keeps the focus on alcohol, which is necessary to create a safe, sober environment.

- Later in early recovery, when abstinence is strong, a fear of drinking can function as a danger signal that new awareness, conflicts, or memories of the past are emerging.

It's natural to think, that when you are anxious, you are doing something wrong. But it may be the case that your anxiety is announcing the arrival of new and challenging information that had been suppressed by the drinking. Anxiety may seem like backsliding, but it might point to progress. If this is the case, the real backsliding would occur if you succumbed to the anxiety and undid your positive growth in order to soothe your nerves. Sometimes a few steps backward are necessary to make a few steps forward, but try to be clear about the source of your anxiety.

Suppressed Disorders

As you grow stronger in your recovery and your self-focus, you'll begin to relax and feel more sensitive to the world around you. It is possible that with the unhealthy behavior lifting, other problems that were hidden by the drinking may start to emerge. Martina's transition went smoothly, but after about six months she began to experience severe mood swings. "At first I tried to gut it out; I thought the anxiety was a side effect of the denial lifting. But soon the ups and downs made it hard for me to function: I was missing work, and I couldn't take care of the kids." Her sponsor recommended she see a psychiatrist, who diagnosed Martina with bipolar disorder. Over the years, the cyclical mood swings had been suppressed by the alcoholism. Once she quit, not only did she have to wrestle with the normal hurdles of recovery, she had to face the emerging symptoms of manic depression and the mood swings that go along with it. If you suspect that your experience is too extreme or that your downs or ups are lasting too long or are interfering with your ability to maintain the necessary parts of your life, it is important that you get help.

Depression is very common among people in transition and early recovery. It can be a normal by-product of a difficult transition into abstinence—the equivalent of withdrawing into your shell for protection from harm. But when it lingers too long and begins to keep you from moving forward, it may be time to seek medical help. If you are having problems with deep depression, don't take it lightly, and don't try to "gut it out." See a professional. When searching for a therapist to treat your depression, try to find someone who specializes in substance abuse. It's important that the doctor know about addiction in order to make a reasoned judgment about whether yours is a depression that is a natural part of recovery, or a mood disorder that may need special treatment.

Metaphors for Objectivity

One of the most powerful tools for surviving the obstacles of recovery is being able to step back and see your problems in the context of your overall situation. When you're in the middle of a difficult period, the problem can seem life-consuming. But if you can find a way to view your problems in relation to the rest of your life, they can suddenly seem less threatening and more manageable. If you understand a thought or emotion, even if you can't control it, you will be less likely to fight something that is a natural part of the growth process. One of the main goals of this book is to provide you with an objective overview of the seemingly random events that can add up to life in recovery.

It can be hard to summon up all of your knowledge about recovery when you are faced with a crisis. To give yourself some instant perspective, focus on a simple metaphor that describes the process you are in; for example, "You are missing the forest for the trees." Recovery is a forest that you experience one tree at a time. Until you have explored and grown comfortable with your surroundings, it is easy to get lost.

We've already seen Lawrence's stock market metaphor for the daily ups and downs that add up to long-term improvement. The following pages contain some other metaphors that can help you endure the obstacles of early recovery.

Recovery as Narrative

Imagine yourself sitting by the fireplace with your children. The hardest parts of recovery are behind you: your foundation is set in place and your family is connected and healthy. Think how you might look back on your present hardships. You may laugh; you may cry: whatever your emotional reaction, you will see the present crisis as an event among other events that add up to the story of your recovery. You may even see it as a necessary building block of your healthy growth. You can't know the importance or unimportance the moment will play until you have some time with which to reflect upon it. It helps to "look forward to looking back."

The shared stories at twelve-step meetings and the stories of the mentor families in this book help demonstrate how specific events, both good and bad, add up to an overall experience and narrative of recovery. One of the benefits of the drunkalogue is that it teaches you that your past is meaningful to your present. This carries with it an important implication: your present is meaningful to your future. Therefore, a crisis you are suffering through is not the entire measure of your recovery; it is a moment tied to other moments, often in ways you are unaware of at the time. You may look back from the room with the fireplace and see that you were on track after all. Just as the mentor families have looked back over the obstacles they faced, you will get a sense that trauma you feel during growth is often normal, that accepting loss of control is courageous, and that perseverance builds your strength.

Recovery as Process

During a crisis we often think of the present as the end toward which all of our life has been headed. This view adds a lot of pressure to an already difficult situation. It may be more useful to consider the present as a thin connection between the past and the future. You move through your life one moment at a time; each moment is one among countless moments that make up a life. All you can do is take good care of each moment, and the life that these moments add up to will take care of itself. With this frame of mind, you may be able to relax a little and not make the crisis worse than it already is.

Recovery as Exercise

Working out is another instructive metaphor for recovery. If you wish to get in shape, one day of jogging will not do the trick. In fact, your first few times out running will probably make you feel worse, both while you experience the work of running and afterwards, when your newly exercised muscles cry out in pain. In order to get in shape, you need to maintain a steady and patient exercise regimen. Pushing too hard one day may make it harder the next. The trick is to focus on one day at a time, one step at a time; no one day is more important than any other. The early weeks and months may be difficult, but if you stick with it, the exercise will pay off. Soon you will be jogging with ease and enjoying the other parts of your life more fully because of your better overall health. Another similarity between recovery and exercise is that in order to stay in shape, you need to keep exercising: you never get "cured" of being out of shape.

Coping as Painting

A painting is created one brushstroke at a time: you may sketch out your intentions and expect certain results, but it's not until you put the final strokes of paint in place that you actually get to see the work come together. You can think of a crisis as a painting; you live through it one brushstroke at a time, and you can finally see it for what it was only when it's finished. At first you may remember many of the brushstrokes, but over time they meld into a single image, an integrated whole.

When another crisis comes along you start over again, the same way you start a new painting. Though you may feel like you're starting from scratch, you have your experience of the last painting to guide you. Each painting brings with it new experiences and education that you take with you to the next one. As long as you break down the process into a series of strokes, painted one at a time, you can keep it manageable.

Divided Families

We mentioned this in chapter 7, but it bears repeating: if your partner is still drinking, or refuses to cooperate with your recovery, it can limit family growth. When one partner is uninvolved in or resistant to the recovery process, the marital system may remain alcoholic. The individual in recovery may be progressing through the stages and focusing on him- or herself, but the family as a whole can be stuck in a dry drunk, with the old ways of relating, coping, problem-solving, and communicating still in place. The partner and other family members who are not in recovery may remain defensive, resistant to change, chronically tense, and, perhaps, violent.

If you are in recovery alone, it can feel at times like you are going crazy. This is no wonder, since you are living in a home with two diametrically opposed systems in place. If you are in this situation, your main coping strategy should be to focus on maintaining your sobriety. This is the number one priority. To do this, you'll want to remain steadfast in doing the following:

- Work toward stabilizing your alcoholic or coalcoholic identity.

- Maintain your focus on your loss of control.

- Attend recovery meetings.

- Work the steps.

- Develop a strong working relationship with your sponsor or therapist.

- Maintain relationships with a few "safe friends" whom you can relate to honestly.

In time, your spouse may become involved in recovery, therapy, or some other form of help. This does happen. Your partner may do nothing and your couple relationship may still be satisfying. But if, over time, your partner is unwilling to change and your relationship is unsatisfying, you may decide not to stay in the marriage because the price is too high. Be patient, though; recovery happens one step at a time and you do not need to make decisions immediately. Focus on your own recovery, and wait to see if the benefits of your own growth rub off on your partner and the rest of your family.

Parenting Work in Early Recovery

As you grow more comfortable with abstinence in early recovery, you will have more time and energy to focus on parental responsibilities and on slowly acquiring healthier parenting skills. In chapter 6, we discussed ways to cope with caring for your children when you don't have the time or energy to meet their needs personally. Those coping strategies are still important, and will continue to be necessary. But as you grow more stable in your recovery, you can begin to explore ways in which you can become a better parent.

Parenting is a not simply an innate ability; it is a skill that can be worked on and improved. And though your individual recovery must stay at the center of your focus, working to improve your parenting skills can be an excellent way to spend your time constructively. Like recovery, you never stop working at it. As you have more energy and awareness available, you can do more to connect with and help your children.

It's best to limit your focus to parenting responsibilities and skill building. Marital issues and more emotionally volatile family issues should probably either be set aside for later work or undertaken with a therapist's guidance. Unlocking your pain, resentment, and rage at this time can interrupt and interfere with responsible parenting. You may need to seek outside help at any time to navigate these unpredictable waters.

You may want to find an experienced family therapist who will focus on helping each parent build basic parenting skills. Make sure the therapist is familiar with the recovery process and understands that the focus of the therapy needs to be on clear, direct, practical help for each person. The following is a short list of skills to work on:

- Assigning parenting tasks

- Building routines for the children

- Finding safe friends and family members to serve as resources for the children

- Developing clear communication skills between the parents to facilitate parenting duties

You can also do other research on parenting. Read parenting books, or ask friends in your recovery group or twelve-step program about parenting ideas and suggestions they have found helpful. (Choose mentors who have more experience in recovery than you.)

When things get tough, pause and remember the importance of your children. Although recovery is built on self-focus, you are still responsible for your kids. Remember also that your healthy growth will benefit not only you and your spouse, but also your children. Take breaks, take care of yourself, and breathe. Cultivate patience, which, though sometimes in short supply, can be the greatest tool of all in parenting.

Listening for Rituals

In early recovery, as your abstinence stabilizes and you begin to have more time and energy for your children, you can begin to experiment with new family rituals. A ritual that everyone enjoys can be an excellent source of connection for the family, giving everyone a safe and nonchallenging environment in which to connect to one another. Even though the family is slowly building up healthy boundaries, it is important that the members maintain contact, especially the children with the adults.

You can plan regular trips to the park, weekly family dinners, or even a time spent sharing stories and music. You could even take up a family hobby, like bird watching or playing a sport. The important thing is that you make an effort to find a safe context within which to interact.

A good family ritual will respect each individual's wants and needs. When trying out new family rituals, try not to get too invested in the rituals you suggest, possibly feeling rejected when other family members have criticisms. However, giving up rigid control over potential rituals does not mean you should do nothing but wait for the ritual to magically appear. Instead, try out rituals and see what works.

Finding a family ritual takes time. The process can provide excellent exercise for new recovery skills and boundaries. You'll need to learn to be patient as the ritual is shaped and reshaped by the needs of the family as a whole and the children in particular. You need to listen for rituals. This means you listen to your children's feedback about what they like and don't like, and that you stay open to suggestions and are able to let the ritual unfold for all, rather than trying to control the outcome. The best rituals are built by trial and error: it takes experimentation and feedback to get it right. You may try out something you thought would be a good idea only to find others didn't enjoy it, and this may make you feel vulnerable. But you'll learn to give up an idea if it's not working, or remain open to suggestions about how to make it work better.

At first, the rituals may seem uncomfortable, but the input of the family can shape them into activities that everyone enjoys. Meanwhile, the family spends time together in a neutral and safe environment, and learns communication skills from the discussions that make these activities better. If this process doesn't work yet, give it time.

Planning vs Controlling

The process of finding a family ritual illustrates an important distinction: planning is not the same thing as controlling. A goal in recovery is to learn to plan events without needing to control their outcome. Some folks have a difficult time trying out new activites because they feel uncomfortable giving up control of what will happen—in other words, they are afraid something might go wrong. When a person is new to focusing on loss of control, she can make the mistake of thinking that this means she needs to become passive and let others make decisions. But these choices are two sides of the same coin: whether you try to control everything or you remain passive, you are insulating yourself from being vulnerable. In order to fully participate and discover new things about yourself, you need to try new things, allow yourself to trip and fall, and learn from your experiences.

This is where planning comes in. You can plan a picnic, but then you need to let yourself have the experience. You need to be open to things "going wrong." Instead of describing unexpected events as "things being ruined," you will learn to see that the unexpected creates new possibilities. Giving up control can seem scary, but this is where much of the magic of life comes from. Life is a rushing river, and you can't interact with it by standing on the bank; you need to be in the flow of the moment.

Human beings have two important, related tools to help them withstand the unexpected: the ability to change and the ability to adapt. By using these tools, you may discover that what "went wrong" actually led you to something "right." A mistake can be the key to success; you just have to keep listening and stop trying to control. Don't punish yourself when things don't go as you expected: this only turns your focus inward and obscures the opportunities that may be sitting right in front of you.

Letting go of control may be particularly difficult for families who struggled with loss of control. Learning to allow life to influence you may bring painful memories and trigger knee-jerk grabs at control. Time will help; just keep trying.

Pockets of Health

When you start to consider new rituals for your family, you may want to consider looking back to the past. Even in the most stressful alcoholic system, there can be positive rituals that represent the seeds of healthy growth: a monthly trip to the city with your daughter, Sunday mornings reading the newspaper with your son, or perhaps movie night with the whole family. The constructive rituals that successfully left the tensions of the alcoholic environment behind were pockets of health that allowed your children to endure the trauma of active alcoholism and foster some level of safety and hope. These activities may even contain the roots of your own recovery. And instead of being left behind, these rituals could be brought along and celebrated.

When the alcoholic system collapses during transition, it's normal to want to let go of it entirely. In an effort to clean house, these positive activities are often discarded with the unhealthy ones, since they are tainted by their connection to the drinking stage. Even if a ritual was steadfastly constructive, the fact that it was a port in the storm can mean it brings back memories of bad weather.

But in early recovery, when you are growing stronger and abstinence is finding a solid foundation, it may be worthwhile to look back at the rubble to see if any healthy activities were disposed of along with the fallen alcoholic system. As you stabilize in recovery, you slowly learn to see the world in all its many shades. You don't have to view all of your past as unhealthy. Much of the self-exploration done during early recovery focuses on making sense of the many dimensions of the alcoholic experience, rather than just viewing it in a black-and-white manner as all bad.

In this way, rituals can suffer a similar fate as the roles that one played during the drinking stage. As we saw back in chapter 3, a valuable skill can be seen as a trait you feel is shameful because of its relationship to the drinking stage. If you relied on your social skills in order to make friends and survive the pressures of active alcoholism, you may feel that being social is merely a means of escape, thus robbing yourself of a strength to be proud of.

In the beginning of early recovery it may be too painful to face old activities; you may need all of your energy to focus on your recovery. But as you grow stronger, these experiences can be inspiring and affirming. If trips to the zoo were a valuable "escape" from the alcoholic life, they may be a ritual that deserves to be celebrated.

The test is whether your individual focus is threatened by rekindling these pockets of health. If by reviving a lost ritual you discover that it brings with it past unhealthy behavior, then it is not something you want to incorporate into recovery. But if you discover that these lost activities can be brought back and enjoyed while you maintain a recovery focus, you will be taking major steps toward creating a life built on your strengths rather than ruled by your fears of the past. A familiar link between past and present can also be very helpful for a child whose world has changed so much over the course of recovery.

Integration and Growth

We live in an age of quick-fix "self-help" solutions that focus on distinguishing between "good" and "bad" qualities and then attempting to rid ourselves of the bad. A similar sentiment characterizes fad diets: if the food doesn't fit the narrow parameters of healthy nourishment (today it's protein, yesterday it was carbohydrates), then it needs to be cut from the diet altogether. This method of change is basically control-based—an attempt to create the identity you want for yourself by forcing out the parts of you that don't conform to this image. Since you can't truly delete a part of yourself, you do the next best thing: deny it. And with that denial comes the same unhealthy relationship to the world that fuels the alcoholic family system.

Much of your unhealthy behavior—the parts of you that might be seen as "bad"—was put in place for a reason, and as you explore your past you discover that your troubling behavior usually starts off as a solution to some other problem. Often the behavior is there as a misguided attempt to protect yourself; or sometimes it's a constructive attitude taken to an unhealthy extreme. To simply cut out these trouble-some behaviors by a force of will would be to surgically remove a part of yourself. Troubling behavior offers you a window into yourself, if you can get past your resis-tance to it. To deny this behavior would be to deny a part of yourself, which goes counter to the work of recovery.

Instead of isolating and discarding the troubling parts of yourself, you have to integrate them. This is a central theme in recovery. The basis of dealing with the alco-holic impulses is not to push them down, but to learn to plug in substitute behaviors. To cut out the impulses would be to cut out a part of yourself; conquering control with greater control.

As you move from early recovery to ongoing recovery, you learn how to let healthy growth take place. In some cases the best thing you can do is to stay out of the way and let yourself evolve. Recovery is not about separating out the good from the bad, but about seeing your entire spectrum of behavior as various aspects of yourself . . . and accepting it.

Healthy growth concerns discovering who you are, not who you want to be or think you should be. Recovery is not a matter of pruning the rosebush to make it look like you want; it's about getting the roses to grow fully and freely. As an AA old-timer put it, "Life does the pruning; the best we can do is keep blossoming."

Part 4

The Freedom of Balance

The Ongoing Recovery Stage

10

"The Goal Is the Process, and the Process Is the Goal"

Mapping Ongoing Recovery

The transition and early recovery stages can be thought of as the construction stages, when the framework of individual recovery is built from the ground up, one step at a time. First comes the foundation, then the outer and inner frames, and soon your structure is standing on its own. The external support functions as scaffolding, keeping the building standing until it can carry its own weight. As abstinence stabilizes and the alcoholic identity becomes a deep belief, the individual learns to trust recovery and healthy growth, in essence internalizing the external support. With recovery standing solidly on its own, the individual no longer needs to focus on construction as the primary work, and can move into a new phase: maintaining healthy recovery.

Recovery's fourth and final stage is called ongoing recovery. This is when the individual and the family build a deepening trust in the healthy changes brought on by recovery. For perhaps the first time ever, the family members live in a stable environment that offers safety, consistency, and predictability. All three are key to fostering healthy growth, allowing children a safe environment within which to experiment and grow, and giving adults a reliable center that allows them to take risks and meet the uncertainties of life with optimism and hope.

The key word is "ongoing." Recovery is a process that is never finished. A healthy family system is one that adapts to change, that is strong but flexible, and that offers safety so the individual and family can trust their surroundings and grow. An adaptable system remains forever new, as it adapts to the needs of the individuals and the family as a whole. Things may break or fall down or wear out, but these events become the exceptions to the rule; the stability and predictability of life in ongoing recovery allow family members to trust that things will work out. Individuals can therefore work on problems without having the problems threaten their overall sense of security. Fixing the little details no longer entails covering up larger problems.

The stability of the family system is based on the strength of the individual recoveries of its members. In ongoing recovery, abstinent behaviors have stabilized. The behavioral substitutions are internalized so that individuals can reflect on an impulse to drink or control the partner rather than having to deliberately substitute a concrete action. This freedom allows individuals to develop new interests or pursue old ones in a different and more meaningful way, pursuing new relationships and expanding the personal limits they once placed on their lives. Some individuals construct a social life and support system that includes nonrecovering individuals; they are able to bridge differences that exist in recovery and nonrecovery environments. For others, social life remains centered in their external support system; this is often the case when both partners have strong individual recovery programs.

Much of ongoing recovery involves finding the right balance between individual focus and couple and family focus. In ongoing recovery, each adult can stand on his or her own, each becoming an anchoring force for the household. With the individuals stabilized in recovery, more attention can be turned back to the couple and the family.

The stability and peace achieved during ongoing recovery allow the couple to nurture their relationship. They learn that "I" and "we" are not opposites. Since each "I" has been solidified by long-term self-focus, the individuals can explore the "we" without fearing they'll lose themselves in the couple. Not only does this allow the adults an expansion of trust and understanding, it provides the children with the increased security of more healthy and unified parents. The parents model an increasingly mature relationship, where the partners' separateness allows for greater connection, and vice versa. Strong individual recovery lays the foundation for a return to a couple and family focus on healthy, open communication, equality between adults, and possibly greater intimacy.

Ongoing recovery is commonly a period of deepening spiritual growth. This is because a deep acceptance of both alcoholic identity and loss of control is often accompanied by the development of a personal concept of and relationship to a higher power. Individuals in recovery vest control in a power greater than themselves. Their increased trust in the recovery process facilitates their emotional and spiritual growth. This spiritual foundation changes recovering individuals deeply, allowing them to feel a more solid connection with other people and with the universe as a whole.

For many readers, the more peaceful terrain of ongoing recovery still lies in the future. There are no clear signs or tests that let you know when you've arrived. Like most other evidence of recovery, progress is often detected only *after* it has been made. A good map will help you know the landscape of ongoing recovery when you see it. But also, and perhaps more importantly, if you have not yet reached the last stage of recovery, this map will offer you hope for the future and the healthy growth that is possible there. When you have the safety and security of a strong recovery behind you, you can open yourself up to the world with a confidence that no matter what the world has in store, you'll be able to handle it. Your vulnerability is no longer a predicament to be feared, but a reality to be celebrated.

The following are the developmental tasks that need to be performed during the ongoing recovery stage:

- Continue abstinent behavior.
- Continue and expand alcoholic and coalcoholic identities.
- Maintain contact with external supports (though it may lessen over time).
- Continue to work on and internalize your recovery program, such as the twelve-step principles.
- Work through the consequences of alcoholism and coalcoholism to yourself and your family
- Begin to focus on couple and family issues.
- Balance and integrate individual and family recoveries.
- Deepen spirituality.

(Adapted from Brown and Lewis, 1999)

The Meaning of Ongoing Recovery

"I spent a lifetime pushing toward goals, and then being disappointed when I arrived," remembers Gwen, who worked for ten years as a salesperson for a large software company. "I would take these disappointing successes as evidence that I hadn't aspired to a high enough goal, and I'd immediately dive into the next challenge. It was an oppressive cycle that led to and was aided by my drinking getting out of control. I analyzed the problem endlessly: Was I working too hard to attain my goals? Was I not working hard enough? It wasn't until I'd spent years in recovery that it struck me that I was asking the wrong questions; however I answered, I was still focused only on a momentary goal and was ignoring the long journey to get there." In recovery, you learn to focus on the small steps that lead to the big ones.

Ongoing recovery is a lifetime process, and that can seem very daunting if you focus on the goal. "The concept of never drinking again really intimidated me in the beginning," says Gwen. "Never is a long time, and just thinking about it made me really nervous. But you learn early on that you can't focus on the rest of your life; you can only focus on the present and take things 'one day at a time.' If you take care of today, tomorrow will take care of itself."

At first, the concept of focusing on small pieces and letting the bigger picture fall together can cause anxiety. However, the recovery experience itself shows how the process works: for instance, in the slow but steady internalization of recovery language and behavior, one piece at a time. As you begin to trust the recovery process, your patience slowly grows. "I used to be a very impatient person," Gwen recalls. "I always thought that patience required endurance; but what patience actually requires is the acceptance of your limits, and the trust that things will work out if you attend to the present. Endurance is only necessary when you suffer over your work; and the suffering more often than not comes from the weight of the goal sitting on your back. In ongoing recovery, the goal is the process, and the process is the goal."

The concept of an ongoing recovery may have seemed impossible at the start, but the small steps you have taken to get to this stage have prepared you for it. Just as you slowly learn to accept the uncertainties that characterize real life, you also become comfortable living out a process that has no end. "Nowadays, I take great enjoyment in the little things. I no longer measure myself by how far I've come, but by how the journey is going. I used to be afraid that if I stopped grinding, I wouldn't get anything done. But it was only when I slowed down and started living that I really started working efficiently. Life is a flow, and it takes so much less effort to flow with it than it does to fight against the current." Gwen still sets long-term goals, but she works toward them one piece at a time. "You can't enjoy the goal if you don't enjoy the journey."

Continuing Challenges

In ongoing recovery, the hard work of early recovery pays off, and life calms down and stabilizes. It's not a state where you have solved all your problems, but one where you have learned the skills to deal with problems as they arise. The person in ongoing recovery has developed the attitude that problems can exist without threatening the progress.

In fact, some of the hardest work can occur in the ongoing recovery stage. Individuals start to delve into childhood trauma and, for some, into their relationship to their own parents' drinking. Working on problems with intimacy and on emotional problems, such as anger, can be difficult. Couples work can also be very challenging. But in ongoing recovery, with the foundation of recovery firmly set, individuals can face these problems with the faith that they will be able to work through them.

There is no clear-cut line between early and ongoing recovery. But if there is a litmus test for being in the ongoing stage, it is that the appearance of a crisis will not automatically send a person back to the chaotic behavior that is the hallmark of the drinking mind-set. Ongoing recovery means that the individual has solidified her recovery enough to trust her progress and stay on course, even when faced with a major trauma.

Some folks mistakenly believe that ongoing recovery will be a time of rest, and that their progress will result in their exhibiting the calm radiance of the true believer. "I remember thinking that I must not have made it, since I still had so many things that needed doing. When I began, I envisioned the goal as my becoming this peaceful and serene woman, the envy of everyone else. Instead, I was a bundle of energy, non-stop. Instead of finding that everyone envied me, I found I was pretty much uninterested in what other people thought about how I looked. Occasionally I would wonder whether I was stepping on toes in my enthusiasm, but I wouldn't fixate on it. The anxiety would pass, and I would go back to running full speed ahead with no apologies. Recovery isn't the state of being fixed; it's the state of being strong enough to fix the things that can be fixed."

Another common belief is that the goal of recovery is to outgrow the need for support. But this is not the case. Some people do feel they want to try life without ongoing outside support, using their programs only for periodic maintenance, but many folks keep strong ties to their recovery programs for life. Health does not entail outgrowing your need for support!

When people look forward from early abstinence, they often view life in a black-and-white manner, expecting that the goal of recovery will be some simple truth or clear-cut solution to all their problems. But in ongoing recovery you learn to accept that life is more complex than that. John, who has been sober for eleven years, came to understand this complexity with respect to his relationship to his wife: "I always thought that only one of us could be right. So we'd fight, and unless she saw it my way, I was unsatisfied. Now we both recognize that there can be more than one perspective on an issue. The goal of a discussion is not getting the other to agree with your side, but helping him or her to understand your point of view. Nowadays we agree to disagree. We still lapse into our old argumentative style occasionally, but we catch ourselves. This is a major step forward that would have been impossible before recovery." The ability to accept the complexity of life enriches us, allowing us a greater appreciation of the variety of other opinions in the world.

Keeping Up the Good Work

Part of the work of ongoing recovery is simply a continuation of the work you have done in transition and early recovery. Once the foundation has been built, it still needs to be maintained.

The tasks from the earlier stages of recovery continue to foster further growth. Your alcoholic or coalcoholic identity and acceptance of your loss of control continue to deepen the more you work. In a twelve-step program, the steps are meant to be repeated indefinitely. With every new breakthrough come new perspectives, which inform another cycle of the steps, which then allows for additional insights. It's a never-ending process, and its goal is long-term healthy growth. The process is analogous to formal education: the more you study, the more you realize there is more to know. So you study more, then question more, and so on.

Ongoing recovery tasks:

- Continue abstinent behavior

- Continue and expand alcoholic and coalcoholic identities

- Maintain contact with external supports (though the contact may lessen over time)

- Continue to work on and internalize your recovery program, such as the twelve-step principles

(Adapted from Brown and Lewis, 1999)

The Healthy Individual Foundation

In recovery, individuals do not "recover" their former identity. Rather, they allow the emergence of a new and healthy identity. People are profoundly different after working through a long and focused recovery. The changes take place at the very core of their identities, altering even their most subtle assumptions about who they are and where they fit into the world. Paradoxically, the chief result of this powerful metamorphosis is that people become more themselves, and less who and what they thought they should be.

In ongoing recovery, the individual's focus shifts from his external behavior to more internal reflection. Mediation of impulse is becoming as automatic as the unhealthy behavior used to be. This shift points to a major distinction between "not drinking" and being in recovery. Abstinence alone does not lead to healthy growth; in fact, when abstinence is attempted without external support or a focus on recovery, the change to the individual is more likely to remain superficial. In order to change at a deep level and move beyond a focus on concrete behaviors, you need to be guided by the organizing principles of recovery. These include an increasingly profound understanding of your loss of control, a solid alcoholic or coalcoholic identity, and a focus on the next step.

Deepening Self-Exploration

In ongoing recovery, people are becoming ready to tackle issues concerning emotions, intimacy, and the deeper causes of the drinking and codependency problems. These issues may have felt too threatening to address during earlier stages; alternatively, a person may have had the urge to confront these problems earlier. But it can be risky to a still-unstable abstinence if deep exploration is attempted too early in recovery: the individual may resort back to chaotic action and alcoholic thinking in an attempt to cope with these complex issues. With a solid internalized foundation of abstinence and recovery in place, however, the individual can feel safer dealing with threatening questions and problems that might have derailed the recovery earlier on.

> **Ongoing recovery task: Work through the consequences of alcoholism and coalcoholism to yourself and your family.**

While many people can appreciate the growth they have had, the arrival of more work can be discouraging. Often, people in the ongoing stage experience what they describe as a "second recovery," which emerges after their alcoholic or coalcoholic identity is firmly in place. Some wonder what they have done wrong to cause their new anxiety, depression, or other symptoms. But these new feelings result from these individuals' growth: they are now strong enough to open themselves up to older problems. Thus, ongoing recovery is often a time when people pursue individual therapy to work on deeper issues (if they haven't already sought out a therapist during the course of recovery).

In recovery, individuals work to make distinctions between situations where they have personal responsibility and those where events are out of their control. For some, this work is most difficult in ongoing recovery. Adult children of alcoholics (ACOAs), for instance, have to sort through their family histories and look, sometimes for the first time, at the alcoholism that spawned their own problems.

For the ACOA, the question "What am I responsible for?" becomes harder to answer. Their own alcoholism or coalcoholism had an impact on others, just as their parents' drinking and codependency had an impact on them. When so much of the environment you were brought up in affects the way you perceive your own world, it's hard to see where your responsibility ends and your parents' begins. The ACOA can have a hard time with the ambiguity of the answer, "You were responsible and you were not responsible." The ACOA issues we discussed in chapter 3 can call for the deepest and most long-term work a person can do in therapy, going on long after the issues of his or her own family and children have been resolved.

Reconnecting the Couple

In ongoing recovery, the family is functioning well enough to allow the couple to work on relationship issues such as intimacy, communication, and emotions. This can be a wonderful and exciting period, when each partner is discovering the other as an individual for the first time. After the time spent focusing on separation, it can feel new and exciting to connect again.

After working through the earlier stages of recovery, the partners now have an increased ability to communicate and problem-solve and are able to be more flexible and adaptable. Couples may feel free to explore differing levels of intimacy, as old habits that were based on need and control have been left behind. One couple who used to feel uncomfortable showing affection in public became more open about it. Another couple, who had always needed to stay close whenever they were home, found it more comfortable to spend time apart. Now when they were together it was because they wanted to be.

Often, uneven roles have been leveled by the time of ongoing recovery. In many alcoholic systems the alcoholic is dominant, controlling the coalcoholic and the rest of the family. In the ongoing stage, the two partners have usually taken on more equal roles in running the house. One recovering alcoholic reported his new ability to listen to his wife and adult children. He was also able to take a more equal role with others in the family instead of automatically becoming "The General," as his children called him.

Ongoing recovery task: Begin to focus on couple and family issues.

Couples in ongoing recovery are learning to be a "we" without feeling their individual "I"s are threatened or about to be swallowed up. Their stronger individual foundations allow the partners to develop a deeper level of trust and intimacy between them, which allows them both separateness and togetherness in their relationship. The partners are learning to be honest and direct with each other, perhaps for the first time. Because this level of vulnerability is so new, it can be scary. Many couples will avoid conflict, thinking they are protecting their new closeness. But there comes a time when difficult issues must be faced, and working through them together deepens a couple's intimacy.

If the partners have no experience with healthy intimacy, it can be very confusing to try to negotiate a proper balance between individual focuses and their couple focus. It's common for partners to see a couples therapist who can help them learn the skills to create an intimate bond.

Separate and Together

After years spent working on a healthy individual focus, your first steps toward reconnecting with your partner can feel like backsliding, since you have been monitoring your distance for so long. The experience of connection can bring back difficult memories of the enmeshed relationship that existed before recovery. Also, people sometimes fear they will lose control when they start to become intimate. Often couples will try to maintain their distance, putting off building the relationship for fear they will discover their individual recoveries are not strong enough to survive within the relationship. When two people try to unite while keeping their individual focuses intact, it can be a slow and careful process.

Kelly and Brian lived through the awkward, cautious period of reconnecting. Kelly remembers: "We thought we were going crazy. Both of us had spent almost seven years in AA, and we were very committed to our individual programs. The first step in reconnecting was strictly verbal. We began sharing our recovery stories. This was very awkward at first, since, except for discussions about the kids, we had mostly spoken about neutral topics for the past few years. Each of us was opening up to the person who used to be too close, and sometimes the pressure would get too great. Often one of us would have to go out to a meeting so we could check in with our support and make sure our boundaries weren't being violated. It had been a long time since we had made emergency runs to AA, but they were helpful. It was like having a safety net: it allowed us to go deeper the next time."

Brian recalls that coming back together felt different because both of them were fine on their own. "For the first time we were coming together because we wanted to, not because we needed to; it was a choice. We would have been fine going on being separate, but we both thought there could be something more if we could start sharing again. It was like having the best of both worlds: our recovery was in place, and we could reach out and touch someone else. Still, it was a slow process and it took a lot of work. We had to check in with our programs and each other and keep reminding ourselves we were not the same people who were enmeshed years ago. But when you start to get close again, and those feelings of love and desire come up, it can look like need, and that was terrifying. In the end, we just had to be patient with each other. The key was that we kept communicating and kept in touch with our programs. When we felt unsafe, we could always reach out and make contact with our recovery support systems."

Kelly and Brian's experience shows that in order for a couple to connect in a healthy and fulfilling way, they need to be able to stand alone. If two people have no support but each other, their situation will be highly unstable. If either partner moves, both will fall. This unhealthy mutual support creates a bond that keeps them stuck in place. The earlier stages of recovery are about detaching from the couple relationship; this detachment makes a deeper and more mature relationship possible in the long run. After each individual has gained the ability to stand alone, the two can reestablish a connection wherein they can offer each other real support: giving that does not demand receiving.

Focusing on the Family

A healthy family is built of healthy individuals: the best way to construct a healthy family system is to let it fall into place around the family members' solid individual recoveries. In the alcoholic system, upholding family denial was the central demand placed on the family members, and any self-focus was mediated by the need to keep the denial in place. But in recovery, self-focus is put first. The new family system is constructed in a slow and careful manner, respecting the individual focus of its members. Meanwhile, the family is also creating a new way of communicating based on healthy boundaries.

> **Ongoing recovery task: Balance and integrate
> combined individual and family recoveries.**

In a family where all of the members have recovery programs in place, the environment and system are becoming healthy right along with the individuals. As the family members feel confident in their self-focuses, and as they recognize the others' commitment to recovery, they begin to trust their surroundings and feel safer taking chances.

The first step in reconnecting the family is for someone to take a chance and reach out. This reaching out will often be followed by the need to pull back, as each family member begins slowly and carefully expanding his or her realm of trust to include the other people in the house. It's easy to "trust" someone who is safely outside your defenses; but when you let someone in, you make yourself vulnerable to that person. When someone reaches out to make contact, other family members should be aware of the vulnerability that person is showing.

Communication is central to reconnecting a family, and everyone needs to share their feelings about connecting. As both children and adults begin to encounter the anxieties of letting their family members back in, it is easy for them to feel they are backsliding. But even if there are real setbacks, the process can continue as long as the problems are discussed. It is when people begin to withhold their feelings, fearing that their words may be harmful or that they must guard against the needs of others, that the emerging, healthy system starts to break down and revert back to old habits.

Kids may not want to talk about their hopes and fears, or may think that their feelings could have a destructive impact on the rest of the family. Parents need to take responsibility for their children, including them in the process of reconnection but not forcing them. This can be a tricky balance. Kids need to know their parents are responsible, but kids also need plenty of space.

Each member will slowly learn to balance his or her own individual recovery with the family recovery. It can sometimes seem easy to sacrifice a bit of self-focus to help others. But the goal is to realize that self-focus and other-focus are not mutually exclusive; both can be done at the same time. If you feel you need to sacrifice your own recovery to connect to your family members, the connection will be an unhealthy one for you and the whole family. Self-sacrifice is no longer an acceptable coping strategy; the adults need to keep the lines of communication open and guard against this kind of unhealthy bonding.

As it was in the couple relationship, the key to negotiating family reconnection, is reliance on external support systems when things get problematic. As individuals reconnect with the family, they need to check in with their own recovery programs and make sure their self-focus has not been compromised by the focus on the family. So while family members make themselves vulnerable to each other and navigate the complex terrain that makes up their new interactions, it's normal that they check in with their recovery programs a bit more frequently. This doesn't mean things are slipping backward, but rather that the individuals are doing a good job maintaining recovery. The number of meetings may increase again for a time, but this will be beneficial to the individuals and the family in the long term.

Writing the Family Story

Until ongoing recovery, the story or drunkalogue is mostly a solo creation. The goal in early recovery is for individuals to clarify their own stories, weighing the history of their drinking lives to gain a better perspective on their alcoholism or coalcoholism. The individual may hear about other family members' experiences—particularly when adults listen to their children. However, in most cases this listening is meant to validate the other person's experience without letting the other person's emotions interfere with the listener's self-focus.

But in ongoing recovery, these stories can truly be shared for the first time. In fact, the creation of the family narration is an excellent metaphor for the reconnection of the family. Just as the family story is a collection of unique and valid points of view, so the family is a group of individuals each able to stand on his or her own. The goal of the family story is not to come up with one composite, "objectively true" point of view, but to appreciate the uniqueness of each member's experience. The family story is not one story; it is many stories. It is not an argument; it's a true discussion.

The connection fostered by shared stories is possible when the individual family members have stabilized their abstinence and their recoveries. Then, each person is strong enough to commiserate with the other members without having to control the situation by asking for forgiveness or trying to solve the others' problems. When a person can hear a painful memory and sympathize with the teller, but not feel the need to make the pain go away, then recovery is solid. It's natural for people in ongoing recovery to feel bad when hearing about pain that they caused or failed to avert, but they don't focus on trying to undo the past. They focus on accepting responsibility for their part in the event, learning from it, and moving on.

Sharing stories can be a hard process; it can be very painful to hear about the pain others have inflicted and received. This is especially true for parents who hear about the suffering that they caused their children. During the ongoing stage, individuals have enough recovery behind them that they can hear about the pain of others without feeling threatened and needing to flee. The most helpful thing a person can do is to try to understand what the other person experienced. As each family member embraces the others' stories, the family reconnects in a healthy and constructive manner. In this way, the members validate and inspire each other, and the new connection fuels the family's healthy growth.

Building Trust

As the family begins to reconnect, members may encounter difficult memories of blurred boundaries or past hostility. One man, who had endured years of his spouse's yelling, found he was thrown back to these memories whenever his wife got excited. "Her voice would get loud, and even though I'd know it was out of enthusiasm, it would throw me off just the same. All those memories would flood back and I'd feel the armor hardening in my defense." Family members can't control the memories that strike them or how they feel, but they can talk about their feelings and memories, and the family members can learn about the triggers that still exist for one another. As long as communication stays open and healthy, and boundaries remain clear and flexible, the family will find its way.

Healthy adaptation is the hallmark of healthy family interaction. In a safe environment, the family members are able to experiment; it is through experimentation that a person finds out what works and what doesn't. This leads to constructive adaptation: people become aware of behaviors that trouble others and work at either avoiding them or limiting them to private time.

A safe and consistent family atmosphere also allows emergency thinking to dissipate. Individuals can then take their time choosing what to do or how to solve a problem. When people are no longer afraid that a misstep will cause the house to fall down, they have the time to weigh their feelings, listen to their intuition, and act out of desire rather than panic. This was impossible during active alcoholism, when everyone was intertwined and enmeshed. Back then, each member carried the weight of the alcoholic system on his or her shoulders, so that if anyone stopped to rest, the family would come crashing to the ground.

As life stays stable and consistent, the family begins to trust that things will not become chaotic in the house. Trust is an ever-expanding thing: it starts with trusting the recovery program. This slowly translates into learning to trust yourself; then after some time you begin to trust your partner and the others in your home. In this way, the home becomes a steady and dependable environment, fostering health and growth.

With deepening trust comes deepening patience. In early recovery, you act *as if* you were patient; in the ongoing stage, the patience becomes a real part of your life. It then becomes almost automatic to take things one step at a time. You learn to think to the next step, but no further. If something is too much to handle right now, you have the patience to set it aside, knowing you can come back to it later. When you have trust and patience, you accept that you can do only what you are ready to do, and that where you are is where you need to be.

Spirituality

For many, the existential crisis of life is rooted in the absence of something to believe in. Evelyn, who has been sober for six years, suffered from this particular emptiness for most of her adult life. "Everything had to be proven to me. The only way I could trust anything was if I had proof that it couldn't hurt me. For me, hope and optimism were impossible. They seemed like superstitions, founded on nothing. To hope for something was just to set myself up to be made a chump. Instead, I was extremely pessimistic. But recovery changed the way I viewed everything." The need for a rational proof of safety is a symptom of control-based thinking: unless you control a situation, it is a threat. Evelyn projected her feelings of vulnerability onto the world, and everything became a threat she needed to defend herself against.

But as Evelyn settled into the security of her recovery and, later, the security of her family's recovery, she found she could let down her guard. When she did, she had a stunning realization: "I suddenly saw that trust does not rest on a foundation of proof, it rests on a foundation of security. When you have a stable foundation, you can hope for good things without fearing a catastrophe. Nowadays I believe in myself: I know I'm strong enough to bounce back from anything, and that gives me the courage to put myself out there and take a few risks."

Ongoing recovery task: Deepen spirituality.

As the safe family environment endures, trust deepens, and individuals begin to believe in the security of the household. The support that was provided by the external program can begin to shift over to the reliable home life. Soon individuals have faith in their family members, a faith that comes from newfound feelings of optimism and hope. Growing trust allows individuals to be fully themselves, a state that is the opposite of self-vigilance. Trust is not built by keeping danger out and denying the unsafe, but by knowing that you and your family are strong enough to withstand anything that comes your way.

Help from the Higher Power

In ongoing recovery, healthy dependence becomes less concrete and external and more abstract and internal. Instead of being conscious and based on substitutes for impulsive behavior, dependence becomes part of the individual's deepest core beliefs and experiences.

The act of vesting control in something greater than the self is an important catalyst for internalizing recovery. It starts out as a matter of conscious thought and concrete behavioral practice. As impulses slowly diminish over time, the meaning of the higher power slowly changes. Ongoing recovery can be a time of deep spiritual transformation. As abstinence becomes deeply rooted, individuals experience the security of trusting themselves, and can expand their sense of loss of control to more than just the alcoholism. Loss of control and giving control over to the higher power become the foundations of a new way of perceiving the world and how the individual fits into it.

Evelyn's recovery awakened feelings of connection to her family and to the world around her: "I think of spirituality as a deep understanding of my own healthy boundaries—experiences flow in, and experience flows out. The mistakes and problems that used to really trouble me now roll off with greater ease since I no longer see myself as a dead end. I'm part of a larger process; I'm neither the most important nor the least important person. I'm just one among many; and we're all alike in being unique."

As long as ongoing recovery is maintained, spiritual growth can continue. Each step upward offers new perspectives that need to be processed before the next step is taken. In twelve-step programs, the final steps are meant to be repeated indefinitely, with ongoing recovery consisting of a continuous cycle of growth, new challenges, new perspectives, and further growth. In essence, the knowledge and behavior that help individuals free themselves from addiction ultimately color their perception of the universe. The process that begins as an attempt to shape a life without alcohol slowly becomes the foundation of a worldview connecting individuals both to themselves and to humanity.

From Spirituality to Hope

The sense of hope and optimism provided by the deepening spiritual foundation can have major positive influences in a person's life. Safety means you can take chances. Stability comes with the feeling that there is nothing you can't handle. For people who need control, the desire to change things over which they have no control intrudes on their ability to perform to their capacity. But the person who has internalized a deep belief in the recovery principles will accept those things that are outside his or her realm of influence. The serenity prayer is not so much a request as an aspiration.

When a person lets up on the need for control in life, a remarkable transformation can take place. Maxwell saw his improvement on the basketball court: "I had always been so hard on myself playing ball. I worried so much about missing my shots that these negative thoughts actually interfered with my shooting. Basketball just became one huge frustration. One day, after a few years of recovery, I suddenly noticed that I was no longer thinking about the outcome of my shots; I realized I had no control over them. I discovered I was comfortable playing in the moment. I had always talked about 'letting go, and letting god,' but I was finally doing it, finally living it. My game improved just because I was not sabotaging myself. I finally accepted that when I shot the ball and it left my fingers, the outcome was literally out of my hands. I was no longer my own worst enemy on the basketball court."

When individuals let go of control, they make room for hope. When Maxwell was drinking, he thought that hope and expectation were the same thing and therefore resisted both. Since then he has seen the distinction: "Expectation is when you need something to happen, demand that it happen. Expectation is tied to control. Hope simply means wanting something to happen, but accepting that the results are ultimately out of your hands. Hope makes room for optimism, which inspires constructive thinking and hard work. If things don't work out, the entire experience can still be looked on as a positive one."

Thumbnail Map of the Ongoing Recovery Stage

- The family environment is characterized by a feeling of safety, consistency, and predictability, with minimal anxiety or tension.

- Crises and normal problems of living can be addressed without threatening the stable environment or causing a return to the unhealthy alcoholic system.

- Individual recoveries are strong and growing, which facilitates the inclusion of couple and family focuses. The individuals' sense of an independent self need not be sacrificed to the needs of the couple or family, but can coexist with improving communication and growing intimacy.

- The world doesn't change, just the individual's attitude toward the world.

(Adapted from Brown and Lewis, 1999)

The Environment in Ongoing Recovery

In ongoing recovery, the family environment becomes mostly stable and predictable. The atmosphere is usually friendly, secure, and open, rather than anxious or hostile. Parents can now be counted on to provide continuous safety, so children can relax and feel secure enough to explore and grow. With a safe environment in place, trust builds slowly and steadily. The environment of a family in ongoing recovery values, supports, and reflects both abstinence and recovery.

The new, safe environment will suffer fewer crises, and the family will be less dominated by the problems that do occur. There is less, if any, trauma left over from the drinking stage, and less of the anxiety that was common during transition and early recovery. Setbacks or external crises may occur, but these events are understood to be temporary variations from the norm, and do not typically overwhelm or radically alter the stable foundation.

If a family has experienced a lot of chaos and turmoil in the previous three stages, they may still be dealing with traumas, such as illness, children who continue to act out, employment difficulties, and financial instability. The important difference is that these traumas, whether chronic or acute, do not threaten abstinence or the basic health of the family system. The couple may have a lot to deal with, but they generally feel more relaxed, stable, and solid as they work through their problems.

In essence, as the family grows in ongoing recovery, its environment reflects the stability and health of its individuals. In order to reach ongoing recovery, the family has learned about and come to depend on a variety of skills, such as openness and communication. They have learned to trust these tools to help them cope with hard times. Although life during ongoing recovery is not all sunshine and light, it can be extremely rewarding, and characterized by feelings of confidence and hope. Surviving difficult experiences strengthens the individuals and the family, and teaches them how to survive and grow strong for future obstacles.

The Family Environment in the Ongoing Recovery Stage

- Safe
- Stable, predictable, consistent
- Comfortable, secure
- Not organized and dominated by crisis or trauma
- Supports abstinence

(Adapted from Brown and Lewis, 1999)

Exercise: Environment in Ongoing Recovery

For many readers, ongoing recovery is still in the future. This exercise therefore concerns visualizing the environment that will exist when you reach ongoing recovery.

- Sit in a chair and relax. Take a few deep breaths and clear your mind of your present concerns. Try to imagine a peaceful setting, with your family gathered together: perhaps you're sitting around the fireplace, or at the dining room table, or at a picnic. The important thing is to visualize all the members together, and imagine an atmosphere of safety and openness.

This can be difficult. Until you reach a place where being vulnerable and being safe can coincide, this image may be anxiety-producing. If it is, just try to concentrate on a calm and stable environment.

- When you have an image in mind, relax and explore the details. Focus on the surroundings, sights, sounds, and smells. Write your feelings about the atmosphere in your journal. Only write as much as you feel necessary, whether a few descriptive words or a few pages.

- If you are in ongoing recovery, just relax and try to experience what is different about your environment now. Perhaps your house is a quiet place, or maybe it's a bustling den of activity. Whatever the reality, draw it to mind and think about the atmosphere that you live in. If you have trouble envisioning your current environment, think of a recent event and retreat to take in its atmosphere.

The Family System in Ongoing Recovery

During ongoing recovery, a new family system is being built upon the foundation of the members' individual recoveries. The new system supports the individuals and helps the family function. This is the opposite of the way things worked during the drinking stage, when the system was built to smother the individual in order to keep the family denial thriving.

The healthy system usually bears little resemblance to the old one. Parents, who may have had unequal power in the home, become more equal as they learn to share parenting duties and decision making. As the adults learn to take responsibility for their positions, the family roles become more clear and appropriate, with parents acting as parents and children allowed to be children. The boundaries between family members and between the family and the outside world are now clear, but also flexible. Interaction and communication are characterized by openness and comfortable boundaries; this leads to the parents' cooperation and shared responsibility for the house and the children. These changes do not happen overnight, and they do not remain perfectly consistent, but the further the family goes into recovery, the more reliable the system will become. In general, things make sense, and over time the family members begin to trust the new healthy system.

If both parents are united in recovery, they offer a sense of safety to their children and each other. When both adults are working toward reconnecting and improving their relationship, the children see their parents modeling healthy growth. This will help the children trust their parents enough to reconnect with them as well. But if only one parent is actively pursuing healthy change, there may be limits to family growth. A household that is divided between a recovery system and an alcoholic system may yet be stable and safe. Or, children may receive mixed messages that can leave them confused and anxious. In this tense environment there will be little safety and therefore little trust and growth. Sometimes a parent can bypass their different points of view, finding a unifying common ground that allows for positive relationships and growth. If not, and parents are hostile, they should seek help to protect their children.

Most individuals in ongoing recovery have learned how to problem-solve in a thoughtful manner, taking their time when necessary instead of feeling forced to fix problems all at once. In this way, parents learn to balance their family focus with their self-focus. As is the case in reconnecting the couple relationship, the goal in reconnecting the family is to be able to maintain the "I" while focusing on the "we." Again, improvement comes a little bit at a time, and it's not uncommon for parents to seek therapy to help them work through sensitive situations. Some parents choose to bring the entire family to counseling to help improve family interactions.

Since the parents are more stable in ongoing recovery and their work has been largely internalized, they often discover that they now have more time to spend with their children. Parents may want to resume some of the responsibilities that had been shifted to external sources of support. Children may want to maintain their outside connections and the security they afford. Not only does ongoing outside support provide children with a safety net, but it offers them help in establishing their independence from the family, which is often a real issue with teenagers. Again, parents will need to balance what they want to do with what their children want them to do. Parents need to listen to their children and respect the importance of the children's outside support.

A strong foundation in the present does not guarantee protection from a troubling past, and children may still have long-term issues that they need to work out. When children grow up in an insecure environment, it can be a long time before they learn to trust. Young children may have a hard time adjusting to safety if it has been unknown to them. Meanwhile, older children who may have distanced themselves from the family during the tensions of transition and early recovery may want to reconnect and share in the recovery.

As we've seen in earlier chapters, children can build up a lot of animosity during their parents' recovery, especially those kids who are old enough to understand what they were missing. Teenagers often face two contrary urges: one pushing them to set their own course in life and start moving away, and the other pushing them to settle past accounts and vent their frustrations and anger. It's possible for teens to balance these two impulses, given a secure environment and a place to talk about these issues. Some kids need time before they are able to understand what they have experienced and what they feel about it. Until then, it's usually best for parents to give kids the space they need, while maintaining contact by modeling good recovery behavior and offering support without demanding it in return.

The family recovery is only as strong as the recoveries of its individuals. If one person has a particularly hard time, it will be reflected in the family system. If, as is common, an adult enters a "second recovery" as a result of self-exploration, this will affect the entire family. Deep ACOA issues can take a long time to sort out. In these situations, the family needs to make sure that communication remains open; otherwise, the atmosphere of denial and isolation can creep back into the system.

If someone is having difficulty, it not only affects the family's growth but it can slow down the other members' individual growth as well. Peter, who has been sober for fifteen years, had a hard time when he began facing his ACOA issues five years ago. As he struggled with his memories, he became tense and depressed, which led to his wife's falling back into her coalcoholic behavior. But with more than a decade of recovery, Peter and his wife recognized what was happening before real damage could be done. Peter reached out for help by finding a therapist, and worked on his childhood issues outside the family. This was still a painful process for Peter, but he kept these problems from rubbing off on his family members. In fact he took the opportunity to share the insights he gained with his family and, ultimately, he was able to open a constructive dialogue with his own children about what they had suffered and what they might hope for with their own children. As Peter's case demonstrates, you don't outgrow the need to reach out for help.

Among healthy family systems, there is no one right way for things to work. There are as many different family systems as there are families, and not all experience ongoing recovery as a joyous celebration. Even when both parents are committed to recovery, many families have to work through years of stored-up anger and resentment during the ongoing stage. The difference is that during ongoing recovery, this work is done in a healthy manner. The family members take things one step at a time while remaining confident that difficult feelings and challenging memories will not threaten their healthy foundations.

Individuals need to stay conscious of the growth of the new, healthy system and keep checking in with their individual recovery supports and with each other. The family system is continually living and growing, and as long as it remains flexible, it will adapt to the needs of the individuals who comprise it. In the end, the ongoing stage can be a period of expansive growth for the family.

Rules

After a long period of uncertainty about family rules, in ongoing recovery the rules are clear and out in the open. The days are over when rules meant to hide a painful reality were tacitly acknowledged. The new rules are structured around respecting individual recoveries, and the new family system is built to support abstinence and recovery.

As with much of the family system, the rules often spring naturally from the foundation of the family members' individual recoveries. When the individuals maintain their own healthy boundaries, the rules will support and reflect these boundaries. Rules may need tinkering with and adapting, and new rules may have to be introduced to solve a family problem, but the test will always be whether or not the rules support the individual and family recoveries. As the family members grow and change, the rules will grow and change right along with them.

The parents are responsible for enforcing the rules, but there is an emphasis on fairness. Open communication allows children and adults to discuss the different sides of an infraction, letting everyone participate in the rule-making process. Unlike during active alcoholism, when rules were unbending and meant to keep individuals in check so the unhealthy system could thrive, the new rules are built to support the individual and to assist the way the family functions.

Exercise: Rules in Ongoing Recovery

The purpose of this and the other exercises in this chapter is to take inventory of the changes you have lived through in your recovery. Instead of looking ahead to ongoing recovery, you will look back at the distance you have traveled.

- Reread the journal entries from the "Rules" exercises in chapters 1, 4, and 7.

- After reading each entry, write down any additional information you might have, including new memories that may have emerged since then, or further insights about that stage.

- When you are finished reviewing all three entries, think about the progress you have made since the drinking stage as far as rules are concerned.

- Write down your thoughts in your journal. Your comments can be brief or expansive, emotional or objective. The important thing is to spend some time reflecting on the part of the path you have already walked. This will provide insight into the journey yet to come.

  Remember to date this exercise in your journal so you can refer back to it at a later date.

Roles

In ongoing recovery, parents will usually share their power more equally than they did during active alcoholism. This shared responsibility creates stability at the top of the hierarchy. With the parents reclaiming their responsibilities, the children are allowed to return to being children. This can be a difficult transition for children who have held roles that went beyond the scope of a child's responsibility; such children may resist being "demoted." However, it's best for their long-term development that they are permitted to relax and experience the more carefree life of a child.

Some roles will change as a result of the individual's growth in recovery. The tyrant who ruled the house and listened to no opinion but his own will be learning how to listen to other family members. This new two-way communication allows other family members to participate in decisions and responsibilities that affect the family, so it may change their roles as well as the former tyrant's.

Since the household is becoming more consistent and predictable, the family members are given the opportunity to be a bit less consistent, exploring new roles and perspectives. This kind of experimentation is central to creativity and healthy growth.

It's common for individuals to eliminate familiar roles in transition and early recovery, but in ongoing recovery, they may rediscover the healthy part of their rejected roles. Coalcoholics may feel very uncomfortable nurturing others during early recovery, but as they grow more stable in their identity, they are able to distinguish healthy nurturing from unhealthy enmeshment. It may take a while before people are able to sort out the various facets of their roles.

Exercise: Roles in Ongoing Recovery

■ Repeat the rules exercise in this chapter, but focus on roles.

Rituals

By the time they reach ongoing recovery, many families have solid rituals in place that support their newfound connection. As recovery becomes strong and reliable, the parents may have more time to spend with their children, and therefore more time for these rituals. The rituals don't have to be complex or expensive, just repetitive and consistent: something family members can count on and look forward to. The predictable and consistent family environment becomes reflected in the family's activities.

Often, rituals are the main source of bonding during the difficult early stages of recovery. Even superficial activities allow the family to connect. But as the ongoing stage advances, a ritual can become an area where the family can make deeper connections—a sort of microcosm of the healthy recovery environment. One mother and son made time after school to discuss the son's feelings and for the mother to answer questions.

The rituals, like the rest of the system, become stable while remaining open to change. Rituals evolve and change; new ones come, old ones go. Some old rituals that were pockets of health will be rediscovered and included again in the family's life. Like the rest of the recovery landscape, rituals become reliable and consistent, but the family keeps checking in with the rituals, making sure that the activities are rewarding and enjoyable for all.

Exercise: Rituals in Ongoing Recovery

■ Repeat the rules exercise in this chapter, but focus on rituals.

Boundaries

Healthy individual boundaries, which are set in place by the individual focus of recovery, result in healthy family boundaries for communication and interaction. These new boundaries are semipermeable, which means they let things in and out. Unlike during active alcoholism, when the boundaries were controlled by impulses and based on defending against pain and trauma, each family member now has a solid individual foundation and can manage the boundaries without feeling a need to control or take care of the other people.

Healthy boundaries are clear but flexible. No longer the products of defensiveness, they are tools for taking in a variety of experiences. The healthy, assured self-focus of ongoing recovery allows the individuals to feel safe reaching out for contact. This leads to more warmth and comfort in the household, which then leads to more feelings of safety: a constructive circle is formed.

The boundary between the family and the outside world also becomes more healthy in the ongoing stage. Family members will feel more comfortable bringing people home or reaching out to new friends. Whereas in the past stages the family members may only have wanted to have friends who came from the recovery background, the family may now be able to include nonrecovery friends in their life.

Exercise: Boundaries in Ongoing Recovery

■ Repeat the rules exercise in this chapter, but focus on boundaries.

Hierarchies

Just as the rest of the structure stabilizes in ongoing recovery, the hierarchy settles into place. The pecking order is stable and clear, but the household rulership is no longer autocratic and severe. The parents may occupy the top tier of the family government, but they exercise their authority with an ear open to feedback. Executive decisions are only the last resort for difficult problems. For the most part, individuals will be allowed to hear the reasoning for decisions. Because the rulers are listening, the rules and choices are more fair. As the children come to trust the parents' fairness, they may resist their decisions less.

Parents are learning how to balance their individual loss of control with their family responsibility. It's hard to comprehend in the early stages of abstinence, but in ongoing recovery the two can be balanced. The parents take responsibility for their families while respecting the rights and individuality of their children, and therefore not trying to control them. In a healthy system, rules are meant to guide, and punishment is meant to teach and reinforce accountability.

Exercise: Hierarchies in Ongoing Recovery

■ Repeat the rules exercise in this chapter, but focus on hierarchies.

Communication

The openness and flexibility of the individuals in the family will result in improved communication, which in turn leads to greater openness and flexibility. The strength of individual recovery gives family members a better idea about what part of an interaction is their responsibility and what part is not. Good communication is based on healthy boundaries and non-defensive interactions. Though it is difficult to maintain at first, your family members' healthy vulnerability will become a matter of course as you build trust with each other.

Since people are listening to one another rather than trying to force their own points across, they hear what each others' perspectives are. Openness to other perspectives not only lets in alternative opinions, which can be helpful, but also draws the family together, since each member can celebrate the other family members' distinctive and varied points of view.

Improving communication is a job that is never done. Triggers for past feelings and pain may still be in place. Family members need to talk about these problems with one another as they arise, keeping the pain and discomfort from going back underground where they dwelt for so long.

Exercise: Communication in Ongoing Recovery

■ Repeat the rules exercise in this chapter, but focus on communication.

Interaction

As with communication, more safety means more open interactions. A predictable environment allows individuals to relax and let themselves open up to other family members. This can take time, and if the past environment was very stressful, individuals may never fully open up, at least not within their family. But they can become less defensive and more willing to share opinions and talk things over.

Many people discover that their family dynamics have been reorganized by recovery. Families that thrived on isolation and distance often find that they wish to explore being more affectionate. Showing affection can make them feel vulnerable, but this may be just the thing the individuals need. And the stronger the individual's foundations, the more vulnerability they can tolerate.

The awkwardness of early recovery slowly goes away, and the family starts to interact more smoothly and naturally. Although every family is different, ongoing recovery tends to be a time of warmth and friendliness among the family members. They may share a connective feeling of having survived something together.

Exercise: Interaction in Ongoing Recovery

■ Repeat the rules exercise in this chapter, but focus on interaction.

Stability

After a long period of unpredictability and tension, the family structure stabilizes in ongoing recovery, as the family dynamics become predictable and consistent. This stability allows the family members to pay attention to other things. There is no longer a need for hypervigilance, as the family grows to believe it can withstand whatever obstacles may come. In ongoing recovery, the firm foundation acts as a shock absorber, allowing the family members to feel secure even when they are struck by a crisis. When the family environment is stable and safe, everyone can enjoy the freedom to grow and evolve.

Change

Major crises are easier to deal with because the family is balanced and sturdy. The sturdiness is a product of flexibility—the ability to evolve and adapt to new situations. During active alcoholism, families often mistake inflexibility for stability. But an unchanging and resistant system cracks before it bends. The alcoholic system is like a brick house, cemented into place, and inflexible. It may look stable because it's unmoving, but when an earthquake comes along, the brick house falls to the ground. But the new family system, like a quake-proof building, is built to flex and bend in a quake, holding together through the tremor. By being able to change, the family is able to remain stable, and because it's stable, it can change.

Summary of the Family System in the Ongoing Recovery Stage

1. The healthy new system has stabilized.

2. The system is organized according to recovery principles.

3. Individuals have a capacity for focusing on both self and system ("I" and "we") without sacrificing either.

4. It's possible to start creating the family story.

5. The family structure and processes are stable and predictable, and support individual recovery.

   - **Rules** are clear and consistent and open to discussion.

   - **Roles** are becoming more appropriate, and the safety of the environment allows family members to experiment with new and varied roles.

   - **Rituals** are becoming more consistent, but remain open to evaluation and reassessment.

   - **Boundaries** are based on the strength of the individual recoveries, which allows family members to reconnect with one another.

   - **Hierarchies** are clear and allow parents and children to return to their appropriate roles.

   - **Communication** is more open and trusting due to improved boundaries and a safe environment.

   - **Interaction** warms up, since strong individual foundations allow for more intimacy and openness.

   - **Stability** is improved in the new system, which is founded on the strengths of the individual recoveries and offers safety and support to the family.

   - **Change** does not pose a grave threat, since the system is flexible and allows the family members to adapt and evolve. This increases their ability to withstand obstacles and problems.

(Adapted in part from Brown and Lewis, 1999)

11

"A Group of Healthy Individuals"

Points of View in Ongoing Recovery

Now that you have a map of life during the ongoing recovery stage, you can explore the different points of view typical of this stage. Ongoing recovery means that your individual recovery is securely in place and your core identity now centers on being alcoholic or coalcoholic. The beliefs attached to your new identity are now mostly internalized. When you have an impulse, instead of rapidly substituting a behavior, you are both aware enough to recognize the impulse and secure enough to consider different coping options before choosing what you need to do.

If all of your family members have recovery programs in place or are at least open to positive change, your family can become steadily more stable and supportive. As each family member learns to trust the healthy improvements of the others, a newfound sense of safety will settle over your home. Your recovery and your partner's are reliable, which means there is less need for focus on the basics of recovery. There is extra time for both self-examination and a broadening of focus, which can include working on family relationships.

This safe atmosphere can also result in your feeling less threatened by the process of self-examination. Over time, you may gain an aptitude for honest self-appraisal and realistic self-portrayal. Combined with the ability to honestly experience the world around you, this aptitude ultimately allows you to maintain good boundaries while taking steps toward reconnecting with your partner and your family.

As we saw in chapter 10, this healthy progress is a cycle: growth leads to more openness, which makes room for further growth. A deeper sense of your recovery identity not only helps you keep your life on course, but may also lead to feelings of intense gratitude and hope. Safety and trust are internalized, resulting in a deep sense of security that you carry around with you always, as if your higher power has taken up residence inside you.

You may experience significant challenges during ongoing recovery as you begin to face the deeper issues of your own psychology, your past, or the more difficult problems that existed in your family or your marriage. Just as recovery brings you to face these issues, it can also give you the confidence to work through them. As in earlier stages of recovery, hardships can feel like mistakes; but they are more often symptoms of solidity and courage—hallmarks of a strong recovery. In times of need you can fall back on the tools of recovery to help you live a healthy and satisfying life.

The Individual in Ongoing Recovery

- Stable, secure individual recovery behavior and identity
- Capacity for interpersonal focus demonstrated by the ability to combine "I" and "we" without threatening either
- Increased spiritual development
- Shift from external to internal support (higher power)
- Intense self-examination

(Adapted from Brown and Lewis, 1999)

"I Am an Alcoholic"—Emily Describes the Ongoing Recovery Stage

"I was down at the real estate office looking through the new listings and I had one of those moments when I was suddenly aware of myself standing there, as if I were my own cinematographer. Here is this middle-aged woman in her own office, lost in the details of a job she enjoys; she has a husband and four grown children whom she loves: not a bad picture.

"As I watched myself, I had a simple thought: 'Emily is sober.' Just like that, a simple statement of fact. Sobriety was a goal that had seemed an impossible distance away when I began recovery, and now it was in my grasp; it had been in my grasp for some time. This middle-aged woman had worked very hard to be where she was, and she would go on working hard to make sure she remained there.

"I had thought of my sobriety many times before: I celebrated it at sober birthdays, described it to my friends and family, and taught it to a young woman I sponsored. But this was the first time that this thought did not come with a feeling of surprise that I had achieved my goal. It was the first time I had this thought without some anxiety creeping in, reminding me not to gloat, but to keep working at it. It was the first time that this thought didn't come with some enthusiasm—patting myself on the back and thinking about keeping up the good work. This time, inside that statement was a deep knowledge that I am an alcoholic, and that I would keep working at recovery for the rest of my life. It was no longer something I wanted to be, it was who I was. I had become a person who worked at recovery. I had become a sober person.

It wasn't connected to the future or the past; it was just true, and I knew I had the ability to keep it true. I trusted myself to keep it true.

"I've never been a religious person, but I suddenly felt I understood the concept of faith. I had faith in my abstinence. There was no question about it: I was certain of myself, and I didn't need proof. I was sober. I'd still need to check in with it at times—that's part of the process—but I wouldn't have to keep an eye on it all the time. It had become something I could rely upon."

For Emily, abstinence had become so deeply internalized that it was now written into her beliefs. After years of building, her recovery was now thoroughly in place. Abstinent behavior, which had once been so challenging, was now routine; recovery language and beliefs were strong and solid. She felt the sense of comfort and deep satisfaction that is only possible when you have spent long hours exploring your needs and facing your fears. She was grateful for her sobriety and hopeful about the future. "It was a moving experience. I recognized just how far I had come. And anytime I face a new challenge, I draw strength from that moment and know that everything is going to be okay."

Hitting Bottom

Emily and Will met at a first-grade parent-teacher night. Both were single parents of six-year-old girls; Emily had recently divorced, and Will had been abandoned by his alcoholic wife a year earlier. "Will was attracted to my negativity. We 'completed each other's tragedies': that's how I described it. It was true: we were stepping right back into the roles we had left in our failed marriages. The courtship was short and tumultuous; Will and I got along great, but our kids despised each other."

They were married six months later. "I don't remember our wedding, but I got a DUI that night. I hung a copy of the citation next to our wedding picture. Though I hadn't lost my sense of humor, we were not off to a very good start. I was angry during the day and drunk at night. Will drank with me, but not a lot. He could make a single beer last all night. For me, quantity was quality. And every night, at some point, things would get 'interesting.' That was our word for things getting out of control. Will would get upset, I'd embarrass myself, and the evening would end. Somehow this cycle satisfied both of our needs. Things stayed like this for the next two years; some days were better, some worse. The kids gradually started to tolerate each other, but there was no closeness there. Then things started to really go downhill. I think I couldn't face the fact that Will was hanging in there with me. Whatever level of happiness I had, I didn't think I deserved it; I needed to spoil it. So the drinking got worse, and I had an affair, and then I hit bottom."

For Emily, bottom was her third DUI, which was issued after an accident with both children in the car. The citation came with a mandatory sentence of six months in jail. "At first I played it off as a big joke, but when the jail door clanged shut on me, I honestly thought I might die on the spot. I was terrified. Part of me was saying that I was finally getting what I deserved, but another part chimed in, I think for the first time. The second voice was telling me I needed to get help. I went to my first AA meetings while I was still in jail. The only positive feeling about drying out in jail is that the agony takes your mind off of your guilt. I thought about the accident and how I put my kids' lives at risk. I thought about how I had turned out just like my parents—I had visited my father in jail on more than one occasion. When my kids came and visited me, it made my commitment to change even greater. Because of jail overcrowding they let me out after only six weeks, but that was plenty."

Watching My Reactions

In her thirteen years of recovery, Emily has changed a lot. "The most important difference between myself as I am today and myself as I was before I entered recovery is that now I can see the world as it actually is. I don't have perfect vision, but it's far better than it has ever been in the past. Back then, everything I experienced was screened through my defenses. I had developed a strategy where I assumed everything was a threat until proven otherwise: if my husband said, 'You look good today,' I'd hear that I didn't look good the day before. If you expect the worst, you can't be surprised. Before I started recovery, my negativity was so much my second nature that I didn't even know it was there."

Emily had become a prisoner of her defenses. "Since I expected the worst from everything, everything made me feel bad. It even went a step further: I basically believed that everything *was* bad. The best compliment I could come up with was that something 'wasn't too bad.' I blamed the outside world for my misery."

Emily certainly had good reason to be unhappy. She had grown up in an abusive home, with alcoholic parents who constantly fought and intimidated her and her brother. Emily's negative coping goes back as far as she can remember. Growing up in a threatening household, she needed to have a shield up to protect herself, and her shield was built of anger and distrust. As she remembers it, the drinking was the one thing that allowed her to let her defenses down. "That's how I unwound. That's how I made peace with the world. But then out would come all this recklessness. It's like I was paroled every night, and I'd drink and party like I was afraid tomorrow would come and I'd have to go back to the cell. At no time during the day was I seeing the world clearly: it was either an evil prison or a chaotic funhouse."

To Emily, the outside world was a threatening place, and at every moment she was either hiding from it, fighting against it, or escaping from it. "But as I worked in recovery, I began to see that the outside world wasn't where the problem lay. The world is neutral, but it was triggering a fearful reaction in me. Because I was set up to protect myself, I assumed the world was attacking. This was a crucial distinction for me. Instead of focusing on the world, which I had little power to change, I focused on myself, watching my reactions and trying to learn from them." This is an example of the self-focus that is the essence of recovery.

This process evolved slowly but steadily for Emily. "The first big step was to be aware of my reactions. Then it was a question of keeping an eye on them. In the beginning I drove myself nuts because I noticed every little thing. You begin to see so many places where your defensive instincts are forcing your hand that it starts to feel like you're getting worse. The truth is, you're just becoming more aware of the defenses."

Over time, Emily learned to accept the things she had no control over. "The key for me was the concept of a higher power. This allowed me to discover that my defenses were just as much a part of the world as the things I was defending myself from. The defenses were out of my control. You don't fight them or get rid of them.

You become aware of them again and again, and soon the awareness becomes second nature, and the defense is no longer steering the car.

"After many years of recovery, I am solid in my self-awareness. The defenses still bristle now and again, but I've learned to spot them and to let them pass. I see the world as it actually is now, including my defenses."

Acceptance and Accountability

When a clearer vision of the world first unfolded for her, Emily faced a number of difficult challenges. "I had a lot of painful memories: things that were done to me and things I had done to others. For a long time I just kept them all at arm's length. I was afraid to look at these things because I would feel guilty and start to punish myself. I tried during early recovery to face some of these issues, but I never had enough security to withstand the nervousness they caused me."

Emily's newfound spirituality allowed her to begin to accept the things that she had once desperately tried to deny. "In ongoing recovery, I found the first step was giving these memories over to the higher power and seeing that the events in my past were now outside of my control. I had been reacting to these memories like they were still occurring: I would start to feel responsible for some past event, and I would instantly start making excuses, trying to divert the blame away from myself. I was afraid that if I took responsibility the floodgates would open and I'd be drowned beneath all the mistakes I had ever made."

As Emily's recovery grew stronger, she found she could look on these past events without shame and blame fogging her view. Instead of being overcome by the memories and the guilt and fear that came with them, she was becoming aware of the complexity of these events. "I crashed the family car when I was fifteen, and that had stuck with me as maybe the biggest mistake of my childhood. It hung over me like a black cloud. But one day I suddenly realized how young fifteen is. I remembered that I had been driving to get milk for dinner, because my parents were too drunk to do it. I realized that when my father beat me up for it, his action was completely inappropriate. Instead of one cloudy ball of shame and guilt, I could see this messed-up family, and this poor little kid making a mistake, and her alcoholic father completely losing control. That realization had me in tears for almost a week. I had blocked out so much for fear of seeing my own mistakes, that I had never really assessed these situations." In order to see the past with clarity, you need to let go of your control over it. You have to be willing to see what is there. "It was scary, but by letting go of my control, I actually got a sense of objectivity. Until that time, I had seen these events through the eyes of a terrified kid, or in later cases, through the eyes of a depressed drunk."

By gaining some objectivity on past events, especially those that occurred during the drinking stage, Emily was able to assess her own accountability for these situations. Not only did this new perspective allow her to let go of the shame she had carried with her, she was able to begin to empathize with the person she had been: a person who made mistakes and who was enslaved by her impulses to drink and protect the drinking. She also began to learn where others were accountable for their part in past problems. This didn't entail blaming them, punishing them, or teaching them right from wrong; it merely meant being aware that they bore some of the responsibility. "This was an enormous breakthrough for me. By allowing myself to see how I was responsible, I saw how others were responsible. What I thought would be a flood was actually a cleansing shower. For my whole life I believed that everything was my responsibility. Suddenly I was able to see the real limits of my own powers, and the limits of other people's powers. It was as though the weight of the world started to lift from my shoulders. It was freeing, but it was also scary, because although the weight of responsibility was off my shoulders, a new weight replaced it: uncertainty. I'm still learning to carry that load."

It takes guts to say, "I'm accountable," but it also takes guts to say "I'm not accountable." Being honest is hard work. It gets easier; it even becomes habit, but it is hard work that builds the habit. This is the work that you do in individual recovery. You learn healthy boundaries and solidify your individual foundation. Emily depended on her acceptance and accountability in order to begin the challenging process of reconnecting to her husband.

The Road to Reconnection

"During most of recovery, Will and I kept our distance. We even slept in separate beds. There were times when we would try to get closer, but we would just dive in with no preparation and it always ended up with both of us feeling like we were right back where we started. These attempts usually occurred during anxious times: when a crisis would come, our first impulse was often to look for familiar comforts, and we did. In a way, I think we wanted to prove that our recoveries were strong enough for connection. But I have since come to realize that little good comes out of trying to prove something to yourself. By needing to prove it, you're basically admitting that you don't trust it."

Emily and Will continued on parallel recovery paths, but with little interaction. "We appreciated each other's recovery from afar. We checked in about the kids and had weekly house meetings to settle the practical stuff, but warmth and bonding were nowhere in sight. That's how we wanted it. And then one day, we realized that our trust had grown when we weren't looking, and that we liked each other a great deal. So we had a talk about getting closer. As comfortable as we had grown with each other, this conversation was quite awkward. We had both gotten strong, but we were both nervous. We had learned enough in recovery to know that this was anxiety about potential growth. We both knew we were ready; we had discussed it in our meetings. We didn't *need* to reconnect, we *wanted* to."

But reconnecting was a slow and sometimes difficult process. "We both had so little training in appropriate intimacy that every bit of contact seemed like too much. We tried to stay focused on just talking with one another. This was more difficult than it sounds. I had well-defined boundaries by then, but I had yet to try them out in a situation as complex as the one I had with Will. After all, he was the person I had shared my drinking years with. Being close brought back a lot of old issues."

Their attempts at connection made them both aware of new places where they were vulnerable, and old defenses would often emerge to protect them. "At that point in my recovery, I had become aware of many of my buttons, so I was shocked when a whole new set of buttons appeared. It felt like I was back at the starting line. I kept monitoring my reactions, but at times I couldn't keep up with the number of new anxieties. I started seeing a therapist. I needed to talk about some of my own issues, which ultimately helped me clarify my boundaries with Will."

Emily and Will found themselves in a crisis, experiencing the types of anxiety they had not felt in years. But since they were both in ongoing recovery, they were able to do what they couldn't in the past. They stuck with the problem, and worked at solving it. "We moved a little bit at a time, and we were thankful for each little step forward. We trusted that if we did the work, we would get better. So we just kept up the communication, and kept progressing. We agreed that as long as our individual recoveries were intact, we could continue pursuing intimacy. We actually discovered that reconnecting strengthened our individual recoveries. It was another frontier to pass. It was empowering to realize that I could be an individual at the same time that I was in a couple. Getting clear about myself allowed me to connect with others. This is one of the greatest gifts of recovery."

Lessons from Recovery

Emily and Will's optimism and the progress that they made with their relationship were direct outcomes of skills they learned in recovery. "Back when I began recovery, if I had a problem or made a mistake, it meant I was a bad person. So I either had to solve the problem immediately, or I had to hide from the blame. This was an extremely anxious experience for me: there was no time for insight or exploration—it was solve or die. And with that kind of pressure on, very few problems ever got solved, and if they did it was only for the short term."

Emily therefore only believed that she was doing things correctly when she encountered no obstacles. "I was extremely superstitious. If something went wrong, it meant that I was doing the wrong thing. If I was driving and I made a wrong turn, then the journey was ill-advised. If I tried to learn to type and I made mistakes, then I wasn't meant to be a typist. Anything less than magical perfection meant that the activity I was pursuing was off-limits for me. Ultimately, the only place I could find that perfection was through the cloud of alcohol."

But recovery taught Emily that goals aren't governed by magic, they are governed by work. "When I hit bottom, it was a profoundly dark experience, one that I will never forget. But as powerful as it was, it didn't stay with me every minute of every day. There were moments when I felt fine, and I would think that if I could be distracted from my surrender, it must not have been the real thing. The magic spell had been broken, so I wasn't entitled to sobriety." But instead of giving up, she called her sponsor and talked about her feelings. Over time, she came to understand that these "feeling fine" moments were normal. "One particular thing my sponsor said really stuck with me: she told me to think of surrender as a door that I had thrown open, but that without tending, it would slowly swing closed again. The door doesn't keep itself open, I have to do it. I may not be able to keep it open all the time, but as time passed I have learned to keep it open more and more."

This lesson also applied to Emily's focus on her relationship. "When Will and I were working on our relationship, I thought of it as a door we were opening between us. I knew it would stay open a bit at a time, and I knew that there would be times when it would close up again. When we encountered problems, we didn't give up; we kept trying. There was a time when I would have assumed that since we weren't having an easy time getting back together, that it wasn't meant to be. But the immediate successes or failures no longer led my way. I knew what I wanted, and I was willing to work at it to get it. I no longer expected magical perfection as proof that I was on the right track."

Recovery also provided an important strategy for approaching obstacles when they arose. "The first step in recovery is to accept the problem; you have to admit that you are an alcoholic and that you have lost control of your drinking. In my opinion, admitting that you have a problem is the key to solving problems in general. When Will and I were starting to work on our relationship, the first thing we did was agree to be open about any discomfort we had. We didn't have to solve the discomfort together, but we would admit when we were feeling uncomfortable. This allowed both of us to become aware of situations that caused discomfort and to explore what was going on at these times. Our openness prevented resentment and helped us maintain our boundaries. We would take a time out if one of us was anxious, and we'd talk about it later, when the discomfort had passed. This created a real sense of safety between us. We slowly learned how to talk and deal honestly with each other. We became very open to one another and came to understand each other's point of view." The ability to speak and be understood is a very powerful bond in a relationship. "There have been times when we couldn't sort it out alone. In these cases, we didn't beat ourselves up; we got help. When my father died, I went through a deep depression. During this time we needed more practical, hands-on work, and we found an excellent couples counselor."

When you accept your problems, you can stop feeling ashamed about having them. You can hold your head high, keeping a lookout for new paths that this learning opportunity has provided. "In most cases, it's not the problem itself that causes the most strife, it's being ashamed of the problem. By talking about it, you let go of the shame and reveal the problem as just a set of circumstances that need to be changed or let go. For us, talking about our discomfort slowly led us to talking about other things. As we started to find we could have a dialogue about our pain and both be accountable for our own part in these feelings, it allowed us to start to really talk about the past. It was there that we hit on some of the really difficult stuff."

Six years after they first moved closer, Emily and Will are still learning about each other. "We've learned how to be open and honest with one another. We look forward to our conversations. We've learned how to be together well, and we can also be apart well. Our security at home helps us go out into the world, and our security in the world means we bring home large chunks of the world to talk about. It's a great system."

The Developmental Model of Recovery: Ongoing Stage

As a child learns to use language to interact with the world, this language slowly becomes internalized, moving from the realm of behavior to the realm of thought. This gives her a new and important foundation for negotiating between her impulses and the world around her: conscious reflection. When an impulse hits her, instead of automatically acting on it, she can think about the best way to bring about the desired ends. The child has a logical framework that helps her understand the world. Experimenting can now be done inside her head, not just outside in the world.

The alcoholic or coalcoholic in ongoing recovery has internalized the new recovery language; this language is now a healthy lens through which she views the world. For the first time, she has the freedom and space to reflect upon her instincts and the problems that affect her. Now when she recognizes an impulse, she can negotiate a healthy solution by first making sense of the desire and then exploring possible options.

For both the alcoholic or coalcoholic and the toddler, a foundation now exists that supports lifelong learning and growth. The ability to reflect is not an end in itself but a tool for living. This tool helps a person navigate the uncertainties of life, and the resulting new life experiences contribute to sharpening and strengthening this tool.

The security of the healthy new mind needs to be maintained, however. With a child, it is the parent's responsibility to create this security, checking in on the child's feelings and perceptions to make sure she is growing strong. But for an adult, the responsibility for upkeep is her own.

The Alcoholic in the Ongoing Recovery Stage

The alcoholic's primary focus is on the recovery program and the higher power; these have been internalized.

Behavior

- Abstinent behaviors have been internalized and are now secure.

- Old behaviors may return as a result of a past or present trauma.

- The return of old behaviors is taken as a cue that self-exploration is needed.

Thinking

- The new identity as an alcoholic is now securely in place.

- Defenses and unhealthy traits continue to be challenged.

- The ability is developing to hold an "I" focus while also having a "we" focus.

Emotional Expression

- There is an ongoing exploration of feelings attached to drinking and the past.

- There may be ongoing problems facing present or past traumas.

- The relationship with a higher power is maturing.

(Adapted from Brown and Lewis 1999)

Ongoing Challenges

After thirteen years in recovery, Emily feels stronger and more stable than ever. But she is the first to admit that there are still challenges, and that there is still work to do. Just as there is no magic at the beginning, there is no magic at the end. "I often remind newcomers, 'Your goal is not perfection, your goal is health.' Good health allows you to live a good life; but health isn't a place where you simply arrive. It's a process; it needs to be maintained. I still go to meetings. I like to feel that connection, and I feel like I'm giving back when I'm working with new members."

No matter how much you take care of yourself, there will always be challenges. When you make yourself open to life, you are also open to pain along the way. When Emily's father died, it really shook her up. "I hadn't seen him or my mother in over six years at that point; it was just too hard being around them when they wouldn't face their own drinking. His death brought back a lot of memories and a lot of pain. I had a hard time accepting that I had gotten better and that he ended up drinking himself to death. I realize that there are still issues there that I haven't dealt with. When I'm ready, I will focus on my relationship with my parents; but I am well aware that I may never be ready. I have made my peace with that as much as I can. I still hope that my mother will get sober, but I no longer worry about it."

More than anything, Emily feels ready for whatever comes. "Life is still unfolding. At times it all seems like a miracle, at times it seems like it's been a long hard road. Lately it just feels good. The ability to trust yourself is a very powerful thing."

Exercise: "I Am an Alcoholic In Recovery . . ."

The purpose of this and the following exercises is to take inventory of the changes you have lived through in your recovery and to look back at the distance the alcoholic has traveled (or the distance you've traveled if you're the alcoholic).

- Reread your journal entries from the "I Am an Alcoholic" exercises in chapters 2, 5, and 8.

- After reading each of your entries, write down any additional information you might have to add; perhaps some new memories have emerged since then, or maybe further insights about that stage have been sparked by your reading.

- When you are finished reviewing and updating all three entries, consider the progress the alcoholic has made since the drinking stage. Also consider how far you've come in learning to understand the alcoholic. If you are the alcoholic, think about the distance you have come, and how much more you know about yourself since you began recovery.

- Write down your thoughts in your journal. The comments can be brief or lengthy, emotional or objective. The important thing is to spend some time reflecting on the part of the path you have already walked. This will provide insight into the journey yet to come.

Remember to date the exercise in your journal so you can refer back to it at a later date.

"I Am a Coalcoholic"—Will Describes Ongoing Recovery

"When Emily and I met, we were perfect opposites. She avoided responsibility like the plague, and I couldn't live without it. This was the perfect combination for having absolutely no boundaries. She'd throw off blame and I'd catch it willingly. At the time, I thought I was selflessly compensating for her problems, but the truth was that the only way a situation was comfortable for me was if I was shouldering her burden. I needed to be shouldering the burden, because if I wasn't, my own troubles would start to spill out."

This was shown most clearly when Emily arrived home from jail. "She was in the earliest period of abstinence, but she was doing well, all things considered. I immediately leaped in to take care of her. It made me uncomfortable to see her struggle. I talked about how she needed my help, how she didn't need to make it on her own. In fact, I needed her to need me. So I went on 'taking care of things' and basically getting in the way. I had a very hard time when she started to get better, because she seemed more animated, and this reminded me of when she was drunk. So I would swoop in and rain down my worries upon her.

"One day Emily told me flat out that I needed to stop hovering over her; she had to get strong on her own, and I needed to deal with my own issues. I was flabbergasted; after everything I had done, she was turning on me. So my overbearing behavior turned to spite: if she wanted space, then that's what she was going to get. I decided to stop paying attention to her. I thought it was that easy. Now, instead of worrying, I started resenting her." Although Will thought he was stopping his focus on Emily, he merely switched it from a positive to a negative focus. "She just needed her space, but to me it was all or nothing. Since I couldn't lead her recovery, I wouldn't participate at all."

Things stayed like this for a few months: Emily slowly improved, but it was despite Will's antagonism. "The thing that finally opened my eyes was when my daughter asked me whether it was a good thing that her stepmom didn't drink anymore. I told her that of course it was. Then, with the innocence of an eight-year-old, she asked, 'Then why are you so mad at her?' Although I couldn't answer her, I suddenly knew what the answer was: I was afraid I was going to lose her if she got better. I needed her to be weak to hold on to her. It made me sick to my stomach to admit that to myself."

Searching for the Self

Will's need to focus on others was written deep in his beliefs. "At one of my first Al-Anon meetings, a woman spoke about her husband getting hurt in a car accident. Her main focus was on how *she* was affected and how *she* felt about it. I was outraged by her self-centered attitude; if this was what was being taught at these meetings, I wanted no part of it. My morality swooped in with the passion of religious dogma: people have to look out for each other; you need to sacrifice yourself to make others happy. I have since learned that dogmatic thoughts often mask defenses. In this case they covered up my fear of ignoring other people's needs and focusing on myself." If Will thought someone was upset, he instinctively sacrificed himself to make the other person feel better. He felt this need with a moral urgency.

In recovery, Will slowly learned to free himself from the control of these instincts. The fear still rose in him, but he was able to recognize it. The impulses no longer forced him to act. It wasn't until ongoing recovery that he had the courage to seek out the source of these fears. "My parents had very strong opinions about things. They never discussed, they only argued. A topic couldn't be left until everyone agreed or the odd opinion had been ridiculed into oblivion. I used to envy my parents' certainty, and figured I lacked the intelligence to compete with them. After going over these memories for many years, I understood that the real reason for their certainty was that they were afraid of being wrong. They couldn't see anyone else's opinion because it threatened their own. Because I was afraid of them, I thought they were strong. But the truth of the matter was that I learned to take care of them. I learned how not to threaten their self-esteem. If I had a thought that went contrary to theirs, I bent it to fit their point of view. In the end I lost access to what I really thought. I worked very hard to protect my parents from being wrong, but all this work had a cost."

When Will began to settle into recovery, he couldn't believe the freedom it gave him. "Once I started to trust my program, I saw that I didn't have to take care of everyone else. I allowed other people to carry some of the burden. I started to see my old attitude less as a selfless act of rescue and more as an attempt to control interactions, and I began to let go of that control. Instead of thinking that everyone was so vulnerable that I needed to hold up their end of the relationship as well as mine, I held up my end and trusted them to do the same. Instead of protecting everyone else, I trusted them to protect themselves. The liberation I felt was mind-blowing."

Resistance to Reconnection

Because of Will's hard-fought success constructing his boundaries, he found he had some reluctance to rebuilding his relationship with Emily. "I remember the day we sat at the kitchen table and agreed to start working on the relationship. It was a thoughtful conversation: we both wanted to make it work, and we both felt that a healthy new path lay in that direction. We shook hands on it and went our separate ways. And the second I was alone, I was terrified. I knew I was ready for the transition, but I was suddenly very concerned about my freedom. The only relationships I had ever known were possible because of my self-denial. After all the work I had done to free myself, I was scared of being sucked back into that familiar jail."

Will decided to go to a meeting, and when he was there he had an important realization. "It struck me that if I was afraid to lose my freedom, then I wasn't really free. I knew that my recovery was strong enough that I would be able to take care of myself no matter what the future held. I think this was the point where I let go. I was in touch with my fears and impulses, but I also knew I could make healthy choices and decisions."

Getting back together was sometimes hard work. "Since all we had ever experienced was unhealthy relationships, it was hard to tell when we were headed in the right direction. Was it okay to help each other with work, or should we be separate? Was it okay to comfort each other? We were both nervous, but for opposite reasons. Emily was afraid she wouldn't be able to connect, and I was afraid I wouldn't be able to stop once I started. I was worried I might start trying to control things again. We were basically scared of falling back into our old roles. But we had powerful tools at our disposal in our individual recoveries. I knew that as long as I checked in on my own health, I was safe to push at the frontiers of our relationship."

Both Emily and Will had solid recoveries by then, so they were able to gradually become a "we" while checking to make sure that each "I" was intact. "We would both go to meetings when we encountered problems—our attendance often rises during times of growth. It's a great feeling of security to know you have that support system out there if you need it. It's helpful to go and talk to folks who have been through what you are going through. And when you are having doubts, it's rewarding to meet the newcomers. Not only do I feel like I am helping others start their journey, but I also see how far I have come. It helps me get focused by reminding me where I'd be if I stopped working on my recovery."

At first, Will found he had trouble speaking of his feelings with Emily. "I have never felt comfortable letting my feelings out; I always thought that if someone else heard them, I would be forced to act on them. Sharing my emotions felt like I was leaving a piece of myself unprotected. But I discovered that when I let my feelings into the world, my shame about them evaporated, and instead of needing to act on a feeling, I was able to experience it."

As Will and Emily began to make progress, Will was surprised to find that he was entering new territory. "I had always assumed that I gave too much of myself in relationships. But as Emily and I started opening up to one another, I saw that I had never really been open in the past. I had never shared myself. I took care of others to protect myself from them. By making sure the other person was happy, I wasn't connecting; I was keeping that person at arm's length. I discovered that intimacy was as new for me as it was for Emily."

Even as things went well, Will occasionally had to battle his worries. "I still sometimes find myself trying to predict where we're headed. I have to remind myself to let things unfold as they unfold; all we can do is put in the effort. We each maintain our individual recoveries and leave the rest in the hands of the higher power. We put in the work and allow the results to arrive on their own." This is the same way recovery works. When you trust it, you allow it to evolve naturally. Take care of today, and tomorrow takes care of itself.

"Over time, we have come to depend on one another. But now it's a constructive dependence, one that makes each of us stronger, rather than shrinking each of us down." The difference between a healthy relationship and an unhealthy one is the difference between healthy dependence and unhealthy dependence.

The Coalcoholic in the Ongoing Recovery Stage

The coalcoholic's primary focus is on the recovery program and the higher power; these have been internalized.

Behavior

- Abstinent behaviors have been internalized and are now secure.
- Old behaviors may return as a result of a past or present trauma.
- The return of old behaviors is taken as a cue that self-exploration is needed.

Thinking

- The new identity as a coalcoholic is now securely in place.
- Defenses and unhealthy traits continue to be challenged.
- The ability is developing to hold an "I" focus while also having a "we" focus.

Emotional Expression

- There is an ongoing exploration of feelings attached to drinking and the past.
- There may be ongoing problems facing present or past traumas.
- The relationship with a higher power is maturing.

(Adapted from Brown and Lewis, 1999)

Becoming a Family

Will and Emily's reconnection as a couple was the key to integrating their family. "Our children had never really known a stable home until the recovery started to settle. The girls were from different marriages, so they never really felt like sisters. When there was stress between Emily and me, the kids felt they had to take sides.

"The first few months of recovery were very difficult for both Emily and me. We tried to be available for the girls, but we were in such upheaval that it was hard. I was particularly distracted. It was too easy for me to start overmonitoring how they were doing; I would start feeling guilty and lose my own recovery focus. Emily did better; for her, the kids were a safety valve. She had spent little time with them during the drinking, and the time she spent with them now represented evidence that she was making progress. But she still had lots of meetings to go to. So at times it felt like we were neglecting them."

Will and Emily reacted to the problem by reaching out for help. "We were blessed to have a recovering family who lived in our neighborhood. They were further along, and they were able to provide a safe house for the girls when we needed someone to look after them. It's a wonderful thing to have contact with people who understand. They were available in emergencies, at all hours of the day and night. There were some weeks when that was the girls' primary residence. Our neighbors had been where we were, and they were more than happy to help us out."

During early recovery, much of the crisis had passed, and the girls spent more of their time at home. "Both girls wanted to join recovery programs. They were young, but quite social. They learned a lot about self-esteem and became strong little kids through the process. While Emily and I were respectfully keeping our distance, they struck up a mighty friendship. In some ways, they modeled a good relationship for us. They were both very definite about their boundaries, but loved to share with one another."

Will and Emily started a weekly ritual that they called "family time." "Even though Emily and I were nowhere near ready to get closer, we tried to set up gatherings where we did stuff as a family. Each Saturday morning we would get together and we would do an activity that one of us had chosen; the person who chose changed each week. The only rule was that it had to be something that the whole family could participate in. The girls really loved it. Ten-year-olds can come up with some elaborate plans: we saw llama farms, hunted for hermit crabs, and picnicked in the middle of a vacant lot across the street."

The outings were helpful, but it wasn't until Will and Emily came together as a couple that the whole family finally congealed. The girls already had safety and consistency, but not the added foundation of parents who were united. "We were fortunate to reconnect while our daughters were still young enough to appreciate it. We had three years till they started college, and though they were teens, they were very open to hanging out with the folks. Our girls are away at college now, but even over a distance we are close. We have become a strong family, a group of healthy individuals."

Exercise: "I Am a Coalcoholic in Recovery . . ."

- Reread the journal entries from the "I Am a Coalcoholic" exercises in chapters 2, 5, and 8.

- After reading each of your entries, write down any additional information you might have to add; perhaps some new memories have emerged since then, or maybe further insights about that stage have been inspired by your reading.

- When you are finished reviewing and updating all three entries, consider the progress the coalcoholic has made since the drinking stage. Also consider the distance you have come in learning to understand the coalcoholic. If you are the coalcoholic, think about the distance you have come, and how much more you know about yourself since you began recovery.

- Write down your thoughts in your journal. The comments can be brief or lengthy, emotional or objective. The important thing is to spend some time reflecting on the part of the path you have already walked. This will provide insight into the journey yet to come.

Date the exercise in your journal so you can refer back to it later.

"I Am a Child of an Alcoholic"—Kayla and Ruby Describe Ongoing Recovery

"It was definitely weird for us when Mom and Dad started to get close again," remembers Kayla, who is Emily's daughter. "We grew up with them being good friends, but they were never very affectionate. So when they suddenly started walking around arm in arm, we were pretty shocked. At first I was kind of grossed out, but deep down I was happy for them."

When Emily and Will told Kayla and her stepsister, Ruby, that they were going to be working on their relationship, the two girls were supportive, but didn't really know what to expect. Kayla had come to understand how transitions worked: "Our parents have always been clear about when they were trying to make changes; but transitions are always awkward times." To maintain a secure family system, the family needs to be made aware of changes that are planned; this way no one is caught off guard when things are suddenly different.

Emily and Will informed their daughters about their plans from the very beginning. When the girls were eight, Emily and Will told them about recovery and advised them that things would be changing. Kayla and Ruby were encouraged to ask questions, and were told that if their parents couldn't answer, they would be honest about it. Kayla appreciated being let in on the process: "It made me feel respected to know that they were telling me what was going on. It was scary, but I was excited. They made it very clear that things might be strange but that it was for the best."

Will's daughter Ruby recalls that the transition into recovery was difficult. "It scared me to see them both change. I had these funny, outgoing parents and suddenly they were replaced by these worried, distracted people. My father used to have a lot of time for me, and suddenly he was nowhere to be seen. For the first few months we pretty much moved in with the Muellers down the street."

Joining Recovery

Kayla and Ruby were not very close when recovery began. Kayla remembers being very competitive with her new sibling, and this only intensified with recovery: "There just wasn't enough of our parents to go around; we had to battle for attention." But things started to change when Kayla and Ruby entered their own recovery-based children's program when they were nine. "Both Ruby and I really profited from our involvement with Ala-Kid. I feel like I learned some important lessons when I was very young, lessons that most people don't learn until they're much older, if at all. In Ala-Kid I learned that I wasn't responsible for my parents' problems. I also developed good boundaries and a strong sense of who I am."

Ruby points out that having a stepsister to share the experience with was a bonus. "We were sometimes teased in school for being 'alcoholics,' but we presented a united front. We really bonded over recovery. We knew that we were the ones with experience, and that these other kids were just acting out about their own problems. We were in touch with ours." Ruby felt that she and her stepsister were more mature than their peers. "It wasn't so much that we grew up fast; it's more that we learned to appreciate the things we had. We had both lived in unstable homes, so we saw recovery as a second chance. We didn't take things for granted. We watched our parents get well and we were proud of them for it."

Ruby admits that things weren't always perfect. "We weren't little angels. We got into our share of trouble, especially early on when we had less supervision. But we were happy when the structure was provided. I know kids who have had structure all their lives and never appreciated it. Gradually our family came together and we really felt like we belonged. Our parents made themselves available, but they respected our space. By watching their experience, we learned a lot about the importance of honesty and patience."

Kayla remembers that when their parents first set up the family outings, both she and Ruby spent the whole week looking forward to them: "It was like Christmas once a week. We were starved for a family. Looking back, I think we got one just in time. We had it long enough that when it was time to go off on our own, we could take that sense of security with us."

The Same but Different

As much as Kayla and Ruby shared their recoveries together, they remained individuals. One important way their difference was manifested was in their curiosity about the past. Ruby wanted to know everything: "I needed to talk and talk and talk; I wanted to go over things that had happened. I had an unending fascination with the events during drinking and early recovery. I had my own memories, but I wanted to hear it from my parents' side. My parents were always very good about telling me what I wanted to know. But they were also careful to ask if I really needed to know the details. I think they were worried that I might be bothered by the things I heard, but I never was. I don't know where the fascination comes from; I think it's just who I am. I am fascinated with that stuff and Kayla is just the opposite. She has no interest. I would sometimes talk to her about what I had discovered. She would be surprised by the information, but she never seemed to need more of it."

Kayla has no explanation for her lack of curiosity: "It's just not what I'm interested in. I enjoy Ruby's fascination with it, but I have other things I'd rather spend my time on. For a while, Ruby and I wondered which one of us had a problem, but we couldn't figure it out. Did she want to know too much? Did I want to know too little? Maybe I'll get curious in the future, but for now, it's just not that interesting to me. Ruby wants to be a writer and I want to be engineer. That may say it all right there."

Ruby says that for all their similar experiences, she and her stepsister are still very different people. "She is studying computer science and I am studying comparative literature. She wanted to go to a state school and I wanted to go to a small liberal arts college. We've never needed to be the same person. We learned early that it was okay to be different. We each like who we are and we each appreciate the other person. It's our differences that make our relationship so interesting."

Saying Good-bye

When it came time for Ruby and Kayla to leave for college four years ago, it was a profound moment that the entire family could appreciate. Ruby remembers it clearly: "We had a family dinner and talked about all the changes that had taken place and about all of life that was still to come. We spent the evening considering the family we had become. It had not always been there, and now it was. I feel like I have brought a piece of that family with me into my new life. I know who I am, and the type of person I want to be. My parents are now alone at home. My sister and I are on our own in the world, but we carry our family inside us. A safe and supportive family, a loving warmth: we carry it all inside us. I think of that warmth as a gift our parents gave us."

Children in the Ongoing Recovery Stage

Much of a child's experience of this stage is dependent on his or her age and the specific experiences he or she had during the drinking, transition, and early recovery stages.

Behavior

- The degree to which parents have successfully been able to attend to their children's needs while taking care of their own recoveries will have a large effect on the children's behavior.

- With increased stability at home and a place for the children to feel safe in expressing thoughts and feelings, the children can focus on themselves and begin to heal any damage that may have been done in the drinking or earlier recovery stages.

Thinking

- The reconnected family can offer children new experiences and ways of thinking of themselves and the other family members.

Emotional Expression

- Children may need help dealing with past traumas.

- Children may still be settling into stronger and healthier relationships with their parents, with greater feelings of hope and trust.

(Adapted from Brown and Lewis, 1999)

Exercise: "I Am a Child of an Alcoholic In Recovery . . ."

■ Reread the journal entries from the "I Am a Child" exercises in chapters 2, 5, and 8.

■ After reading each of your entries, write down any additional information you might have to add; perhaps some new memories have emerged since then, or maybe further insights about that stage have emerged from your reading.

■ When you are finished reviewing and updating the entries, consider the progress your children (or you and your siblings) have made since the drinking stage. Also consider the distance the parents have come in learning to understand the children.

■ Write down your thoughts in your journal. The comments can be brief or lengthy, emotional or objective. The important thing is to spend some time reflecting on the part of the path you have already walked. This will provide insight into the journey yet to come.

■ Remember to date the exercise in your journal so you can refer back to it later.

12

"Keeping Up the Good Work"

Maintaining Ongoing Recovery

Recovery does not have a finish line. You don't wake up one day to discover that you have arrived and that there is no more work to be done. It doesn't end when abstinence is strong. Instead, recovery is an ongoing process of developing the skills and attitudes that make your journey through life more rewarding and inspiring. Your strong foundation offers you the self-confidence and hope to open yourself up to the world and live a rich and satisfying life.

Alcoholism or coalcoholism will always be present; they are not illnesses that are cured, but conditions that you learn to live with. When you have internalized your alcoholic or coalcoholic identity and the loss of control that goes with it, you become able to open yourself up to new experiences that unfold outside of your control. This gives you the freedom to discover life as it occurs and to prepare for events without having to control their outcome. This openness and acceptance, in turn, make room for further growth, a process that can continue for the rest of your life. The final stage of recovery is open-ended: the "goal" of recovery is a lifelong process of growth.

Ongoing recovery is a time for fine-tuning your recovery skills as well as maintaining them. The recovery process is analogous to how an athlete trains: part of the program is dedicated to building strength and endurance, and part of it is focused on building skills. There may come a time when the athlete's body reaches maximum efficiency; at this point, the strength and endurance training are meant to maintain this optimum condition. Skills can always be improved, however. The same is true for recovery. When you have the healthy foundation in place, you work to maintain it, but you also work to improve the living skills, such as communication and self-exploration, that improve the quality of your life in recovery.

This chapter offers coping strategies for some common challenges in ongoing recovery. These tools can help you negotiate these obstacles when you encounter them.

The Recovery Engine

The process of recovery is like fixing an engine. During active alcoholism, the engine of family life runs poorly and is highly unpredictable. Whenever the engine light blinks on, it means something terrible might happen—and the light blinks on often. To compensate for this poor performance, the family members try to will the engine to run, hoping to predict and avoid breakdown. But a faulty engine only improves if you repair it, and the family in active alcoholism is afraid to look under the hood.

In order for an engine to run well, it must be in good repair: the process of recovery repairs the family engine. Further, the engine must be allowed to run on its own. This means that you have to trust it to run without your constant supervision of every cog and wire. In the early stages of recovery, this trust can come slowly and with more than a little anxiety. But over time you begin to recognize that the engine in recovery is predictable and dependable. You also discover that the more you trust the engine, the better it performs; and the better it performs, the more you trust it. By trusting the engine to do its job, you free your mind to plan the trip and steer the car.

This engine needs periodic repairs just as a real engine does. But in ongoing recovery, when the engine light comes on, it's no longer viewed as an emergency, but as a warning that some work needs to be done. Since you have learned to trust the engine, you have time to think over a solution patiently; there is no need to revert back to the chaotic and out-of-control thinking that used to demand immediate and therefore uninsightful action.

Perhaps the most ingenious characteristic of the family engine in recovery is that it is largely self-maintaining. The skills that are needed to maintain recovery are the skills that are taught *by* recovery. Recovery teaches you to listen to yourself, which ultimately allows you to listen to others. The oil that greases the healthy family system is openness and honesty: the more honesty there is, the more openness, and vice versa. By being open and honest, you become sensitive to your surroundings; this sensitivity is no longer the protective vigilance of active alcoholism, but a relaxed and confident awareness of and trust in how the engine of a healthy family works.

Coping

Whether you have been in recovery for six years or for twenty-six, you will run across roadblocks every now and again. The traumas of drinking are now in the past, but crises may still arise related to the drinking or connected to life stresses that occur independent of the drinking past. You have already been acquainted with a variety of coping skills from chapters 6 and 9. Old memories can trigger old responses, so it's important to keep in touch with the coping strategies that you found helpful in the earlier stages of recovery. Your familiarity with facing these problems is part of what allows you to face new problems in ongoing recovery without their threatening your sobriety.

Now that you are in ongoing recovery, you have access to a very powerful coping skill: experience. As your foundation stabilizes, you are able to look back over the process of recovery and see its specific events in context. The context of a past trauma, which was elusive at the time, may be much clearer today. Now, when you face a new problem, you will have an easier time letting go of your desire to know why it is happening. Thus, you can surrender to the moment and trust that the context will be revealed.

When you meet a challenge in ongoing recovery, try to remember the context of the problem within your life. Here are a few tips to help put setbacks in perspective:

- Remind yourself of the distance you have come and the problems you've worked through. Your recovery is a success story; the fact that you made it to ongoing recovery is evidence that you can work through even the deepest problems in your life.

- If you feel down and stuck in place, remember that progress can go unnoticed at times. Remember the mountain climbers stringing up their ropes day after day? After a week at one plateau they suddenly found they could climb to the next. Often you don't know you are making progress until after you have made it.

- Remember the patience you have learned in recovery. Although your optimism can wane in times of crisis, if you are in ongoing recovery, you are very familiar with the power of hope.

If you feel you don't have the skills to deal with this problem when it comes time to act on it, it may be that you are simply forgetting the subtle lessons that recovery taught you. Not only does your recovery offer a model of healthy long-term problem solving, but it offers a treasure trove of skills and strategies for facing problems. The following are just a few examples:

- In order to solve a problem, first accept that the problem exists.

- Once you accept the problem, set out to see it clearly.

- To see the problem clearly, challenge your preconceptions—both the defenses you have built up and the mistaken beliefs you have brought with you from earlier days. In other words, start with a self-focus and work your way outward.

- Break the problem into smaller parts and work on the parts one at a time.

- Explore the degree to which you are accountable for the problem. Determine what is in your power and what isn't.

- Be willing to reach out for help; otherwise you are not looking for a solution, you are looking for control over the problem. These are very different things.

- You can't force the solution, so relax and let it come. Working on the problem using these skills makes access to your intuition that much more open.

By accepting your own accountability, being able to evaluate yourself, and being willing and able to struggle through difficult times, you have built up a strong arsenal of coping strategies. Recovery not only teaches you *how* to endure, it teaches that you *can* endure.

Self-Assessment

In order to reach the ongoing recovery stage, you have had to develop abilities for self-assessment and sensitivity. You can rely on these skills when you are faced with difficult thoughts and emotions. Often when you have an unpleasant emotion, you have other feelings that are a reaction to the original emotion. For instance, you may feel angry at your son and then suddenly feel ashamed of feeling angry, thinking that you shouldn't be getting angry now that you are "all better." So instead of encountering just the anger or the shame, you get a confusing mixture that you don't know how to resolve.

When this happens, try to separate the feelings you are experiencing. What starts as a cloud of emotion can often be picked apart if you just ask yourself one simple question at a time. When you see the different parts of your emotions, you begin to see your situation more clearly and the emotions become more manageable. An intense feeling that needed to be acted on right away may suddenly become one that you can deal with how and when you choose. So rather than being driven by unconscious impulses, you can now make conscious decisions about what you want and don't want.

Clarifying Your Feelings

If you are experiencing unpleasant emotions, the first step is to try to identify the feelings. Ask yourself the following questions:

- Can I describe the emotion?

- Can I locate its source?

- Do I need to act upon it immediately or can I wait?

- Does the feeling need just acknowledgment rather than action?

Once you have isolated an emotion, you may be unclear about the degree of your own **accountability**. It's helpful to recognize whether an issue relates to you personally, your couple relationship, or your family as a whole. You can ask yourself the following questions to explore your own accountability:

- What is my part in the problem?

- What do I want from this situation?

- How can I go about achieving my goal?

- When would be a good time to act on this, and do I need to act at all?

Difficulty with **anger** is common during the early part of ongoing recovery. This can come from unleashing difficult memories or from confusion brought on by lingering feelings of shame and blame. Adults in recovery commonly feel wary about expressing their anger around their children. It's hard for them to know what an acceptable, healthy expression of anger is, and which feelings of anger are tied to blame and enmeshment. When anger occurs, it can feel like an emotional relapse. Here are some questions to help occurs, it can feel like an emotional relapse. Here are some questions to help you break down the emotion and evaluate your present state:

- What am I angry about?

- Is it a present trigger or one from the past?

- How do I want to handle the anger?

There are a number of ways anger can be expressed constructively: through journal writing, talking to someone impartial, or talking to the person who angered you. No matter what course of action you choose, you must acknowledge your anger to yourself. Even if the anger is founded on an outmoded defensive response, you need to acknowledge it in order to let it go. If you smother it, it will most likely emerge where it doesn't belong. If you discover that your anger at someone else is really rooted in a personal issue or misperception, you might consider letting the anger go—but only if you can. By all means don't dismiss it unless you can truly let it go; otherwise it may turn into resentment, even if you know the person who angered you is not accountable.

Issues with **intimacy** can arise when reconnection triggers memories of the former, unhealthy dependence. When you are feeling close, you may fear you're relapsing into that dependence and losing yourself in the connection. It takes time and practice to find the right balance between "I" and "we." Even when you find the right balance most of the time, you can still experience anxiety when memories are triggered. Remember that you have time to come to the right balance and find a way to be comfortable in close relationships. Here are some questions you can ask yourself to clarify your feelings:

- Is our new closeness at my expense?

- Is the closeness causing problems for me?

- Do I feel clingy or trapped when we're together?

- Do I feel abandoned or guilty when we're apart?

- Do both of us feel enriched by our intimacy?

- Is our closeness based on a problematic need or a healthy desire?

Neediness often conceals unconscious desires, and this can cause some slippery problems. In the case of intimate relationships, feelings of need may be compensating for another desire that you are afraid to face. For example, "I need you" may really be a simplification of "I need you, because I'm afraid to be alone." Desires often involve more conscious awareness, though these too can be colored and conflicted. When intimacy problems arise in your couple relationship, give each other room and check in on your self-focus. Later, you can reflect on what happened. If the feelings and emotions you are experiencing are too overwhelming or are becoming a serious barrier to your healthy growth, you might consider seeking help from a psychotherapist (see the discussion in the following pages).

Because you have had to face difficult personal issues, both in the past and in the present, both individual and relating to your family and couple relationship, you have explored your life more deeply than many people ever do. Often folks with more subtle problems never have to face them, so the minor obstacles that impede their progress are never challenged; not so for anyone in recovery. Deep, challenging exploration must accompany the work of recovery. It is the only path to building a new healthy identity. One woman in recovery for fifteen years says she's actually learned to appreciate her darkest drinking days. She says, "If I hadn't been so messed up, I might never have gotten better."

Reconnection

By giving up your attempts to control the world around you, you become a part of it. By letting the process of recovery unfold, you unfold with it. You let the outside world in and your inside world out. You are able to connect more deeply to the world because you are more comfortable with your own boundaries.

Transition and early recovery took you through separation and individuation, and in ongoing recovery you are able to reconnect with others. This ability to make contact depends on your ability to make yourself vulnerable. At first, opening up can be very anxiety-provoking, but (as with many things) it gets easier over time.

The more stable your individual foundation is, the more you can let yourself be vulnerable. The mistakes you make or the misperceptions of other people are both only superficial intrusions on a solid identity; they don't challenge your deep belief in yourself. Emily, whom we met in the last chapter, said that she always thought strength was about toughness and invulnerability: "That's how my father did it. But that's not how it works. A person with real strength allows herself to be vulnerable. Toughness is a way of hiding from the outside world. It's a defense, a shield built to hide fear. If you want to find out what you're truly capable of, you've got to let it all hang out."

Couples

According to Ellyn Bader and Peter T. Pearson, in their book *In Quest of the Mythical Mate* (1988), couples' development occurs in stages that can loosely be described as enmeshment, separation, individuation, and reconnection. These stages of relationship line up with the stages of recovery. During drinking, the couple relationship is usually in a state of enmeshment, where the individuals sacrifice themselves to protect each other and the system. When one or both members of the couple hit bottom, the intense focus on the self and the addiction forces a separation. The couple relationship is then no longer based on the need to keep the system in place. Separation is scary, but it's the only way possible to get to a point of individuation, which allows connection and recommitment. In early recovery, both the alcoholic and the coalcoholic go through the slow but steady process of individuation, learning to become strong and independent as they stabilize their individual recoveries.

When both individual recoveries are internalized, the couple can begin the process of reconnection. The transition from individuation to reconnection is also a slow and careful one. Some couples start the process by sharing their parallel recovery experiences. Some couples go to joint meetings to foster this connection, others make a point of discussing new information they've learned. Couples also bond through recovery language, creating from their recovery experiences a shared framework for understanding.

Only if two people are separate can they truly share themselves. A healthy relationship is one of connection, not enmeshment. Enmeshment means that there are no clear boundaries between the two people, so you can't tell where one ends and the other begins. This may sound romantic, but it means that each partner has no knowledge of his or her own personal boundary; this is an unhealthy state. Connection, on the other hand, suggests a relationship between two separate entities. In geometry, a straight line is a "connection" between two points. The separation between the points is obvious, and this separation also clarifies the connection between them.

In essence, over the course of recovery, the couple shifts from an unhealthy relationship to a healthy one. A healthy relationship is one of mutual interdependence. Both partners can give because neither demands. They accept each other, both the good and the bad. They grow individually and are sustained by one another. Closeness today may be followed by distance tomorrow, but neither partner interprets distance as negative. No longer is progress by the other seen as a threat.

When the two partners have very strong individual recoveries, they can bridge their two perspectives. This means they can both hold their own point of view and appreciate the other person's point of view. There can also be a shared point of view, a compromise position that doesn't undermine the beliefs of either individual. Instead of the sharing being built on dependency, the dependency is built on the sharing.

Families

In active alcoholism, family members often believe that the system must be maintained at all costs, even if that includes sacrificing themselves. Since each member likely feels responsible for the system as a whole, each shoulders the full weight of the system. In the healthy family, however, since the system is built upon the foundation of the individual recoveries, the weight of the family system is evenly distributed among each of its members. Each tends to the health of the system by tending to his or her own individual health.

The path from unhealthy family to healthy family is much the same as that for the couples. The family members start out enmeshed, separate after hitting bottom, individuate, and later reconnect. The main difference is that, in a family, it is the parents' responsibility to see that their children are given the opportunity to separate and individuate. We discussed how this is done in chapters 6 and 9. In ongoing recovery, with the family connecting in a deep way, parents need to continue to check in with their children and make sure that they feel able to communicate and express their feelings.

During ongoing recovery, parents have more time to spend with their children than they had in the past stages. Now that the parent's individual recoveries are stable, they can be even more open to the children, listening to fears and stories that may have been too challenging for them to tolerate hearing in the past. Parents can also set up new rituals to keep the children in touch with the rest of the family. They will also have more time to work on their parenting skills, so they can continue to improve as parents.

Many of the parenting suggestions described in chapter 6 are still relevant in ongoing recovery. The main difference is that now the parents have more time to help their children themselves rather than reaching outside the family for help. The importance of fostering healthy communication skills and encouraging children to voice their thoughts cannot be overstated. Children may tend to keep their feelings to themselves, and it is up to the adults to approach them and make it clear that it is safe to either speak or not speak as the children choose. It's important that kids learn it is appropriate to have uncomfortable emotions and thoughts. If this fact is not made clear, children can box their feelings up, even in a healthy household. When their feelings go underground, they'll come out somewhere, sometimes years later. When they do they will be thoroughly confusing since they are so far removed from the source. But don't force kids to talk about their feelings. If the home is safe and parents are modeling healthy communication, the children will join in in their own way.

The Family Story

Creating the family story can be a ritual that bonds the entire family. Sharing stories is equivalent to sharing points of view, and as the children learn the family's stories they also learn that the family can accommodate different perspectives. During active alcoholism it is common for there to be a single story that the family must stick to; but in ongoing recovery, this is no longer the case. Over the course of recovery, family members have explored their own individual stories. Now, by sharing these stories, the family takes part in a symbolic act of connecting while at the same time respecting individuality. This is a key to healthy family relationships.

The goal is not to construct a single "true" story from bits and pieces of individual stories. Instead, the family is working to discover and share the multiple points of view within their family. In this way the children are given a lesson in balancing their "I" perspectives with a "we" perspective. This is a powerful model for family unity: each individual carries his share, holding his own part of the story and hearing the other stories. Each family member ends up possessing a piece of the whole.

It is important, however, that children hear only age-appropriate information. Also, some children may not want to participate, and their level of interest needs to be respected. If one of your children does not want to be included, don't call story-telling meetings a family event, since one of the family members is not part of it. Remember that although your child may not want information, she may want to know that it is there if she should need it. Check in with your child every once in a while to see if things have changed.

Therapy

In ongoing recovery, couples learn to share their emotions and work out problems together. But not every problem needs to be worked out immediately. You can put some things away to deal with when you are better prepared, or you can decide to accept imperfections and move on. Whatever your decision, make sure you don't bury or deny your emotions. It's all right not to deal with certain issues, but if you have to close yourself off to certain parts of reality in order to do this, these issues may become a serious barrier to healthy growth.

Some people experience a natural second "hump" in recovery that occurs in the ongoing stage. When you embark on deep self-exploration, you may encounter troubling memories and dark emotions; memories that carry intense feelings can be hard to get a perspective on. As you begin to have a clearer view of past events, you may also need help distinguishing between those you had a choice about and those you didn't. Under each of these circumstances, a therapist, as an outsider offering expertise and objectivity, can be a helpful guide. There are a number of different styles of therapy that can be helpful, depending on the source of the problem.

Individual Therapy

One-on-one therapy can be good at any time during recovery, even early on. A coalcoholic in transition might explore with a therapist what it would be like if she stopped focusing on her partner. This clarity can lead to a greater commitment to recovery. In the transition and early recovery stages, however, it is particularly important that the therapist understands the shape of recovery, because if a therapist focuses only on short-term "repairs," the therapy could undermine recovery. For example, if a person has hit bottom and is having a great deal of anxiety over the new experience of surrender, a therapist unfamiliar with recovery might seek to build the alcoholic's self-esteem and thus lessen the anxiety. This could inhibit the process of foundation-building, which is based on the acceptance of powerlessness. At this stage, the alcoholic and coalcoholic need to embrace their helplessness and begin the hard work of undoing the deep-seated beliefs that are causing their anxiety. To support the immediate tasks of transition and early recovery, the alcoholic and coalcoholic must learn to endure their anxiety and maintain a focus on surrender. Maintaining abstinence must be tantamount.

During ongoing recovery abstinence is stable and the individual foundation is solid. At this point you can begin to deal with more difficult issues, such as intimacy, finances, sexuality, compromise, and responsibility. Individual therapy can be particularly helpful for family-of-origin issues and ACOA work, both of which can be highly traumatic. The emotional roller coaster that goes along with a person facing these issues can throw the whole family out of balance. This work can often be done best with the help of a professional.

Group Therapy

This can be helpful for the individual, especially if the groups are organized by recovery stage. This way the meetings can help with the tasks of each stage: people in early recovery can have more of a focus on the nuts and bolts of recovery, whereas those in ongoing recovery can focus on reconnection issues and emotional work.

Couples Therapy

Some couples fear making the move to the "we" focus, because the "I" focus is safer. Others go to the "we" but retreat back to the "I" whenever they face difficult emotions. These are understandable reactions early in the process of reconnecting, but if this behavior lasts too long, it can create a very real barrier to reconnection. This would be a good situation in which to seek outside help with your relationship. Couples often profit from having a third party to moderate conversations and point out subtle and hidden defenses that make communication difficult. In couples therapy you can explore your relationship dynamics and perhaps discover where the blockage is coming from. When you feel a confusing combination of emotions, it is often difficult to break them up into smaller parts. It can be harder still when the emotions are sparked in a relationship: you may have less of a chance to call a time-out and consider what is going on. A good therapist can be very helpful in these situations.

Family Therapy

If your family seems to have barriers against reconnecting, it can be helpful to see a family counselor. If there are problems with communication, a family therapist can offer practical advice on interaction and intimacy. Family therapy can also be helpful in the earlier stages of recovery, but the therapist needs to be sensitive to recovery dynamics. If this is the case, the therapist can help the family find ways of communicating during the tensions of transition and early recovery. If the therapist isn't familiar with the tasks of recovery, the therapist might push for the family to reconnect before it is ready. By doing this, the family anxiety may be lessened, but individual focus is threatened and so are the hopes for family recovery. In this way, long-term growth is sacrificed for short-term contentment. This quick-fix mentality can also make it harder for the individuals to maintain their self-focus later on, since they now have an outside authority telling them, in essence, that the family comes first. If you are going to use family therapy during the early stages, you need to make sure the therapist is familiar with recovery. When this is the case, therapy can help the family appreciate the need for individual focus and learn that though the circumstances at home may seem strange, they are in fact normal.

The Freedom of Balance

After years of work, you will find in ongoing recovery that there is now more time for appreciation of both the present and the past. Curtis, who we met in chapter 8, is often moved when he reflects on the path he has traveled. He can recall the intense trauma of hitting bottom and appreciate the peace and serenity of his present life: "When I finally hit bottom for real, it was a gut-wrenching shift. I went from being isolated and completely dependent on the bottle and enslaved by my alcoholic thinking to being completely immersed in recovery and dependent on the support of AA.

"In recovery, I slowly let AA inside of me, one piece at a time, until the support became internal. But as I internalized my dependence, a funny thing happened: I became more independent. The internal support allowed me to be by myself without feeling alone; and at the same time, my independence allowed me to connect with others without being swallowed. This has made a wonderful change in my relationships, especially with my family. There's an ease with which I love my wife and kids now. I no longer feel the need to *prove* my love; I just love, which is so much simpler and at the same time so much more profound.

"What I feel most of all in my present life is a sense of inner balance, an equilibrium that is a combination of solidity and motion. A few weeks back, I came across the word 'equilibrium' in a textbook. 'Equilibrium' literally means 'balanced weight'; but as I saw the word this time, it seemed to be a combination of 'equality' and 'liberty,' as though it meant 'liberated by balance.' To me, this is what the ongoing process of recovery is. It's a freedom that comes from balance: a balance of individuality and connection, of acceptance and preparation, of vulnerability and strength. By achieving this balance, you no longer need to level the world to make up for your own imbalance; you no longer need to change your bearings to compensate for your own misperceptions; and you no longer need to control your surroundings to protect yourself from falling down. This balance allows you to move through life, free to see the world as it is and let it evolve as it evolves.

"Today I just focus on keeping up the good work and taking things one day at a time. When I think of where I am today and where I was ten years ago, I am so grateful for my recovery. Only a person who was once enslaved can truly appreciate freedom."

Resources

Alcoholics Anonymous
P.O. Box 459
Grand Central Station
New York, NY 10163-1100
212-870-3400

Al-Anon/Alateen Family Group Headquarters, Inc.
1600 Corporate Landing Parkway
Virginia Beach, VA 23454-5671
1-800-356-9996

National Association for Children of Alcoholics
11426 Rockville Pike, #100
Rockville, MD 20852
301-468-0985

National Clearinghouse for Alcohol and Drug Information
P.O. Box 2345
Rockville, MD 20852
301-468-2600

Save Our Selves
P.O. Box 15781
North Hollywood, CA 91615-5781

Women for Sobriety, Inc.
P.O. Box 618
Quakertown, PA 18951-061
215-536-8026

References

Al-Anon Faces Alcoholism. 1984. New York: Al-Anon Family Groups.

Alcoholics Anonymous. 1955. New York: AA World Services.

Bader, Ellyn, and Peter T. Pearson. 1988. *In Quest of the Mythical Mate: A Developmental Approach to Diagnosis and Treatment in Couples Therapy.* Philadelphia, Pa.: Brunner/Mazel.

———. 2000. *Tell Me No Lies.* New York: St. Martin's Press.

Black, Claudia. 1981. *It Will Never Happen to Me.* Denver, Colo.: MAC.

Brazelton, T. Berry. 1992. *Touchpoints.* Reading, Mass.: Perseus Books.

Brown, Stephanie. 1985. *Treating the Alcoholic: A Developmental Model of Recovery.* New York: John Wiley and Sons.

———. 1988. *Treating Adult Children of Alcoholics: A Developmental Perspective.* New York: John Wiley and Sons.

———. 1993. Therapeutic Processes in Alcoholics Anonymous. In *Research on Alcoholics Anonymous,* edited by B. McCrady and W. Miller. New Brunswick, N.J.: Rutgers Center of Alcohol Studies.

Brown, Stephanie, editor. 1995. *Treating Alcoholism.* San Francisco: Jossey-Bass.

Brown, Stephanie, and Virginia Lewis. 1993. *Maintaining Abstinence Program (MAPS): A Curriculum for Families in Recovery.* Palo Alto, Calif.: Mental Research Institute, Family Recovery Project.

———1999. *The Alcoholic Family in Recovery: A Developmental Model.* New York: The Guilford Press.

Jacob, Theodore, editor. 1987. *Family Interaction and Psychotherapy: Theories, Methods, and Findings*. New York: Plenum.

Kagan, Jerome. 1984. *The Nature of the Child*. New York: Basic Books.

Moe, Jerry, and Don Pohlman. 1989. *Kids' Power*. Tucson, Ariz.: ImaginWorks.

Moe, Jerry. 1995. Small steps becoming large: Effective strategies to assist children of alcoholics in the healing process. In *Children of Alcoholics: Selected Readings*, edited by S. Abbott. Rockville, Md.: National Association for Children of Alcoholics.

Moe, Jerry, and R. Zeigler. 1998. *The Children's Place ... At the Heart of Recovery*. Redwood City, Calif.: The Legacy Foundation and The Children's Place. Petaluma: Acid Test Productions.

Reiss, David. 1981. *The Family's Construction of Reality*. Cambrdige, Mass.: Harvard University Press.

Sapolsky, Robert M. 1998. *Why Zebras Don't Get Ulcers*. New York: W. H. Freeman and Company.

Schmid, Joyce. 1995. Alcoholism and the Family. In *Treating Alcoholism*, editied by S. Brown. San Francisco: Jossey-Bass.

Steinglass, Peter, Linda Bennett, Steven Wolin, and David Reiss. 1987. *The Alcoholic Family*. New York: Basic Books.

Van Bree, Gloria. 1995. Treating the Alcoholic Couple. In *Treating Alcoholism*, edited by S. Brown. San Francisco: Jossey-Bass.

Watzlawick, Paul, John Weakland, and Richard Fisch. 1974. *Change*. Palo Alto, Calif.: Science and Behavior Books.

Wegsheider, Sharon. 1981. *Another Chance: Hope and Health for the Alcoholic Family*. Palo Alto, Calif.: Science and Behavior Books.

Wolin, Steven, and Linda Bennett. 1984. Family Rituals. *Family Process* 23:401–420.

More New Harbinger Titles for Personal Growth and Change

THE ADDICTION WORKBOOK

This comprehensive workbook offers simple, step-by-step directions for working through the stages of the quitting process.
Item AWB $17.95

YOU CAN FREE YOURSELF FROM ALCOHOL & DRUGS

A balanced, ten-goal recovery program helps readers make needed lifestyle changes without forcing them to embrace unwelcome religious concepts or beliefs.
Item YFDA Paperback, $13.95

DON'T LEAVE IT TO CHANCE

This step-by-step program gives the families of problem gamblers new strategies to manage the problem, repair relationships, and develop a road map for the future.
Item GMBL $13.95

FROM SABOTAGE TO SUCCESS

Real-life examples, exercises, and action plans help you identify self-defeating behaviors and learn skills that can help you reach your life's true potential.
Item SBTG $14.95

VIRTUAL ADDICTION

Explores the warning signs of Internet abuse and suggests a variety of steps that netheads can take, including help for those who can't seem to stop shopping or find themselves compulsively trading stock.
Item VRTL $12.95

THE SELF-FORGIVENESS HANDBOOK

Guided exercises take you on an empowering journey from self-criticism to self-compassion and inner strength.
Item FORG $12.95

Call toll-free 1-800-748-6273 to order. Have your Visa or Mastercard number ready. Or send a check for the titles you want to New Harbinger Publications, 5674 Shattuck Avenue, Oakland, CA 94609. Include $4.50 for the first book and 75¢ for each additional book to cover shipping and handling. (California residents please include appropriate sales tax.) Allow four to six weeks for delivery.

Prices subject to change without notice.

Some Other New Harbinger Self-Help Titles

Family Guide to Emotional Wellness, $24.95
Undefended Love, $13.95
The Great Big Book of Hope, $15.95
Don't Leave it to Chance, $13.95
Emotional Claustrophobia, $12.95
The Relaxation & Stress Reduction Workbook, Fifth Edition, $19.95
The Loneliness Workbook, $14.95
Thriving with Your Autoimmune Disorder, $16.95
Illness and the Art of Creative Self-Expression, $13.95
The Interstitial Cystitis Survival Guide, $14.95
Outbreak Alert, $15.95
Don't Let Your Mind Stunt Your Growth, $10.95
Energy Tapping, $14.95
Under Her Wing, $13.95
Self-Esteem, Third Edition, $15.95
Women's Sexualitites, $15.95
Knee Pain, $14.95
Helping Your Anxious Child, $12.95
Breaking the Bonds of Irritable Bowel Syndrome, $14.95
Multiple Chemical Sensitivity: A Survival Guide, $16.95
Dancing Naked, $14.95
Why Are We Still Fighting, $15.95
From Sabotage to Success, $14.95
Parkinson's Disease and the Art of Moving, $15.95
A Survivor's Guide to Breast Cancer, $13.95
Men, Women, and Prostate Cancer, $15.95
Make Every Session Count: Getting the Most Out of Your Brief Therapy, $10.95
Virtual Addiction, $12.95
After the Breakup, $13.95
Why Can't I Be the Parent I Want to Be?, $12.95
The Secret Message of Shame, $13.95
The OCD Workbook, $18.95
Tapping Your Inner Strength, $13.95
Binge No More, $14.95
When to Forgive, $12.95
Practical Dreaming, $12.95
Healthy Baby, Toxic World, $15.95
Making Hope Happen, $14.95
I'll Take Care of You, $12.95
Survivor Guilt, $14.95
Children Changed by Trauma, $13.95
Understanding Your Child's Sexual Behavior, $12.95
The Self-Esteem Companion, $10.95
The Gay and Lesbian Self-Esteem Book, $13.95
Making the Big Move, $13.95
How to Survive and Thrive in an Empty Nest, $13.95
Living Well with a Hidden Disability, $15.95
Overcoming Repetitive Motion Injuries the Rossiter Way, $15.95
What to Tell the Kids About Your Divorce, $13.95
The Divorce Book, Second Edition, $15.95
Claiming Your Creative Self: True Stories from the Everyday Lives of Women, $15.95
Taking Control of TMJ, $13.95
What You Need to Know About Alzheimer's, $15.95
Winning Against Relapse: A Workbook of Action Plans for Recurring Health and Emotional Problems, $14.95
Facing 30: Women Talk About Constructing a Real Life and Other Scary Rites of Passage, $12.95
The Worry Control Workbook, $15.95
Wanting What You Have: A Self-Discovery Workbook, $18.95
When Perfect Isn't Good Enough: Strategies for Coping with Perfectionism, $13.95
Earning Your Own Respect: A Handbook of Personal Responsibility, $12.95
High on Stress: A Woman's Guide to Optimizing the Stress in Her Life, $13.95
Infidelity: A Survival Guide, $13.95
Stop Walking on Eggshells, $14.95
Consumer's Guide to Psychiatric Drugs, $16.95
The Fibromyalgia Advocate: Getting the Support You Need to Cope with Fibromyalgia and Myofascial Pain, $18.95
Working Anger: Preventing and Resolving Conflict on the Job, $12.95
Healthy Living with Diabetes, $13.95
Better Boundaries: Owning and Treasuring Your Life, $13.95
Goodbye Good Girl, $12.95
Fibromyalgia & Chronic Myofascial Pain Syndrome, $19.95
The Depression Workbook: Living With Depression and Manic Depression, $17.95
Angry All the Time: An Emergency Guide to Anger Control, $12.95